Environmental Politics
and the Creation of a Dream

WISCONSIN LAND AND LIFE

Arnold Alanen
Series Editor

Spirits of Earth: The Effigy Mound Landscape of Madison and the Four Lakes
Robert A. Birmingham

A Thousand Pieces of Paradise: Landscape and Property in the Kickapoo Valley
Lynne Heasley

Environmental Politics and the Creation of a Dream:
Establishing the Apostle Islands National Lakeshore
Harold C. Jordahl Jr., with Annie L. Booth

A Mind of Her Own: Helen Connor Laird and Family, 1888–1982
Helen L. Laird

When Horses Pulled the Plow: Life of a Wisconsin Farm Boy, 1910–1929
Olaf F. Larson

North Woods River: The St. Croix River in Upper Midwest History
Eileen M. McMahon and Theodore J. Karamanski

Buried Indians: Digging Up the Past in a Midwestern Town
Laurie Hovell McMillin

Wisconsin Land and Life: A Portrait of the State
Edited by Robert C. Ostergren and Thomas R. Vale

Door County's Emerald Treasure: A History of Peninsula State Park
William H. Tishler

Environmental Politics
and the Creation of a Dream

∿

Establishing the Apostle Islands
National Lakeshore

Harold C. Jordahl Jr.
with Annie L. Booth

THE UNIVERSITY OF WISCONSIN PRESS

The University of Wisconsin Press
1930 Monroe Street, 3rd Floor
Madison, Wisconsin 53711-2059
uwpress.wisc.edu

3 Henrietta Street
London WCE 8LU, England
eurospanbookstore.com

5   4   3   2   1

Printed in the United States of America

Library of Congress Cataloging-in-Publication Data
Jordahl, Harold C., 1926–
Environmental politics and the creation of a dream : establishing the Apostle Islands
National Lakeshore / Harold C. Jordahl Jr. with Annie L. Booth.
p. cm. — (Wisconsin land and life)
Includes bibliographical references and index.
ISBN 978-0-299-28194-6 (pbk. : alk. paper)
ISBN 978-0-299-28193-9 (e-book)
1. Apostle Islands National Lakeshore (Wis.)—History. 2. Apostle Islands (Wis.)—
History. I. Booth, Annie. II. Title. III. Series: Wisconsin land and life.
F587.A8J66   2011
977.521—dc22   2010044624

Keep the faith!

This is a unique collection of islands. . . . There is not another collection of islands of this significance within the continental boundaries of the United States. I think it is tremendously important that this collection of islands be preserved.

—GAYLORD A. NELSON

Contents

Preface

I first experienced the Apostle Islands region in the late 1940s while on a vacation traveling through the northern Great Lakes region. While there, I took the excursion boat around the islands. The boat made frequent stops at fishing camps to collect fish for the commercial markets. We docked at Rocky Island for a splendid fish lunch. I fell in love with the beauty of the archipelago. Some years later I was employed by the Wisconsin Conservation Department at Spooner as the wildlife biologist for the northern Wisconsin region and became more intimately acquainted with the islands.

One of my responsibilities was to monitor a burgeoning deer population on the islands. Each winter the area wildlife manager and I would charter a ski-equipped plane and have it land us on safe ice adjacent to an island. On snowshoes, we crisscrossed the islands, recording our observations on deer habitat and use; then we were picked up and flown to the next island. During the 1953 summer season I hiked and camped on Stockton Island to judge its suitability as a site at which to reintroduce pine marten, which had been extirpated throughout the state. In cooperation with the Wildlife Ecology Department at the University of Minnesota, I released twelve adult marten that had been trapped in northern Minnesota. For several years I snowshoed with university researchers predetermined transects across Stockton Island searching for marten tracks. They showed modest reproduction for a few years and then vanished. A transfer to the Madison, Wisconsin, headquarters a few years later made my visits to the Apostle Islands less frequent. In 1960 I joined the staff of a newly formed state agency spearheaded by Governor Gaylord A. Nelson, who would go on to found Earth Day a decade later. From a midlevel bureaucrat in the large Conservation Department I suddenly became a staff person to the director of a new department, the Wisconsin Department of

Resource Development, as well as an advisor to the governor. I worked closely
with Gaylord Nelson on his new and exciting initiatives in conservation in the
1960s, including work toward the protection of the Apostle Islands. During
the year 1963, and over several years to follow, I witnessed significant changes
in the political and bureaucratic landscape that would have a direct influence
on the creation of the Apostle Islands National Lakeshore. That year, Nelson
was sworn in as Wisconsin's junior U.S. senator. Charles Stoddard, a personal
friend and impassioned colleague, and then director of the Resource Policy
Staff Office in the U.S. Secretary of the Interior, invited me to join his staff. I
became the regional coordinator for the Upper Mississippi River and Western
Great Lakes area and was attached to his policy staff.

This position was affirmed in September 1963 by President John F. Kennedy in his speech to the Land and People Conference in Duluth, Minnesota,
after an aerial inspection of the Apostle Islands and a public speech at the
Ashland airport. After being mentioned in a presidential speech, and with the
imprimatur of the secretary of the Interior's office, I suddenly had significant
influence in working with or enlisting the assistance and support of various
bureaucrats during the creation of the Apostle Islands National Lakeshore.

In 1967 I joined the faculty of the University of Wisconsin–Madison
but, with the encouragement of Senator Walter Mondale of Minnesota and
Senator Nelson, I also accepted a presidential appointment as the alternate
federal co-chair of the Upper Great Lakes Regional Commission (while still
teaching part-time). This commission was composed of the governors of Minnesota, Michigan, and Wisconsin, as well as the federal co-chair and alternate
co-chair. I returned to the university full-time in 1969, but in the 1970s I also
served as Governor Patrick Lucey's alternate for the Upper Great Lakes Commission. Lucey also appointed me to the Natural Resources Board, the policy
body for the Wisconsin Department of Natural Resources (the successor to
the Conservation Department), where I served for five years.

In 1962, while Gaylord Nelson was governor of Wisconsin (1959–1963), he
proposed to Interior Secretary Stewart Udall that the Apostle Islands be named
a national lakeshore. It took almost a decade to accomplish this goal (plus an
additional sixteen years to add the last island to the lakeshore). I was in the
fortunate position, given the different positions I had held, of being able to
use my knowledge and influence to aid Senator Nelson throughout the long-
term and often controversial planning-policy political process. Only after the
election of Richard Nixon to the presidency did Nelson and I lose our direct
influence with the secretary of the Department of the Interior and his staff.
Nonetheless Nelson held power in the U.S. Senate (where the Democrats held
a majority), and I had influence as a university faculty member. Along with

my close association with members of Congress, we still had considerable pull with the myriad federal bureaucracies and federal committees and subcommittees whose members were working on a national lakeshore. My relationship with Governor Lucey also eased the way with the state of Wisconsin in completing the lakeshore. Although success was achieved, there were several points when the effort was in serious danger of being aborted. Nelson's persistence, and the persistence of the numerous individuals and groups who sustained their vigorous support over many years, accounted for our eventual success. The protection of the twenty-one islands and an adjacent twelve miles of mainland shoreline, the largest archipelago in the U.S. region of the Great Lakes, was a significant achievement for this period and well worth the effort.

Although the book in your hands touches upon the history of the Apostle Islands and the human interaction with the region, it is not intended to offer a true historical perspective within the traditional approach of a historian. Rather, the book describes and analyzes the myriad forces (both government and private interests) which shaped, influenced, and directed a series of events that resulted in the creation of the Apostle Islands National Lakeshore in 1970.

I have drawn extensively on my personal files and experience in documenting events. Thus there is a personal perspective on what transpired. It is important to note, however, that the achievement of the lakeshore reflects the collective action of numerous citizens, politicians, bureaucratic leaders and their staff, and various private organizations. I was privileged to be a participant, by being there at the right time, and privileged to work with an incredibly dedicated group of people who turned the lakeshore from dream to reality.

I hope this book will be of interest for, and useful to, those who visit the lakeshore today. As well, I hope it might enable future generations to understand the incredible effort and kind of political negotiation that achieved the lakeshore they enjoy. Last, I hope this case study might help to illuminate some of the challenges that are common to most efforts aimed at protecting land and water bodies. I have been involved with many such efforts during my career as a bureaucrat, academic, and just plain citizen. My experiences suggest that these challenges are endemic, and I trust that this study offers lessons from which all of us might learn. Citizens who are prepared to take action to protect neighborhood and regional parks, wild areas, wilderness, and the few remaining great places in this country may find this account of use. I suggest you try to think broadly, with a vision that extends into an invisible future, tighten your belts, and go at it! The rewards can be enormous.

Harold C. Jordahl Jr.
December 2009

Acknowledgments

Bud Jordahl died on May 11, 2010, just a few weeks after submitting final revisions to this manuscript. Immediately prior to taking ill, Bud celebrated the fortieth Earth Day by giving a speech that recalled the politics and history of the first Earth Day. Then he drove up to his beloved Richland County farm to enjoy spring turkey hunting. He left behind a tremendous legacy for his family and friends, and for generations yet to come.

Like the creation of the Apostle Islands National Lakeshore, this book is the result of collaborations, support, and assistance from many people over quite a few years. We would like to specially acknowledge and thank Dr. Annie Booth, who was Bud's last PhD student and now is associate professor in the Ecosystem Science and Management Program at the University of Northern British Columbia. She contributed to the 1994 National Park Service report that this book draws upon, and her involvement has been essential for the successful completion of this book.

Kathleen Lidfors and Carl Liller were also contributors to the 1994 NPS report; they also deserve recognition for their earlier work with Bud that metamorphosed into this book. There were many others who played a role in producing the earlier report, and Bud appreciated and acknowledged their assistance at that time; they include Steven Pomplun, Patricia Cantrell, Blake R. Kellogg, Pat H. Miller, Alford J. Banta, Edwin Bearss, Ron Cockrell, Martin Hanson, Barry Mackintosh, and David Weizenicker. Supporters included the University of Wisconsin Department of Urban and Regional Planning, University of Wisconsin Extension, and the National Park Service. We would like to once again acknowledge everyone who helped with that earlier project (and we hope we haven't omitted anyone).

Bud also wrote in the 1994 report, "My wife Marilyn provided enormous support to me during the entire period the lakeshore was under consideration. Her love for and knowledge of the area equals mine."

Bud retired from the University of Wisconsin in 1988; he stayed involved in environmental and conservation efforts throughout his retirement. He regularly continued to go to his office on campus to work on many projects, including the initial 1994 National Park Service report.

Everyone—and most importantly Marilyn—encouraged Bud to transform that initial report and write this book because of his unique ability to write a first-person history. We are glad that he and Annie finished this manuscript and left us with this wonderful account of the creation of the Apostle Islands National Lakeshore. Bud recognized that it was an important project to complete. He also knew that it would be his last project; so this was a historic and perhaps bittersweet labor of love for him, as he revisited his history, of a place that held such deep personal meaning for him, and also for his family.

Bud shared his love of the Islands and the north with his children, their spouses, and with his grandchildren. We all were fortunate to have experienced trips with him in and around the Apostles, Lake Superior, and the north country he loved so much. Road trips with Bud were rolling discussions and seminars of history, geology, forestry, sociology, wildlife ecology, and political science. And they were fun because we always had coffee and chocolate (licorice too, when Marilyn was alive).

We found the book's cover photograph of Bud on Chequamegon Point in his desk after his death. None of us had seen the photo before. Although there's no photo credit, we believe it's from a trip Bud and Marilyn took in 1964, and that the photo was taken by Marilyn, who was Bud's adventure companion. He told the story of a boat trip the two of them took out from Ashland when the wind shifted and the lake turned rough. Unable to motor back to Ashland, they thought they would end up spending the night on the Point with only a thermos of coffee. Fortunately, a fisherman came in from the lake and picked them up and delivered them to the landing on the Bad River Reservation where they were able to get back to Ashland. Maybe the photo is from another trip—we can't say for sure—but we remember stories of their life adventures when we see this photo.

This book would not be possible without the final push and assistance from coauthor Annie Booth and the staff of the University of Wisconsin Press, including Gwen Walker, Adam Mehring, and Carla Marolt. We are also grateful for the wonderful photos provided by Bud's colleague and friend Arnold

Alanen, Professor Emeritus of Landscape Architecture and the UW Press series editor for this book. Bob Mackreth, former AINL ranger and historian, offered additional information for several of the photo captions. Thanks to everyone for your tremendous efforts, patience, and support.

As Bud would say, "Keep the faith!"

Kristine Jordahl, Manawa, Wisconsin
Harald "Jordy" Jordahl, Madison, Wisconsin
Kari Jordahl, Waunakee, Wisconsin
January 2011

List of Abbreviations

BIA	Bureau of Indian Affairs (United States)
BOR	Bureau of Outdoor Recreation (United States)
CCAINL	Citizens Committee for the Apostle Islands National Lakeshore
DNR	Department of Natural Resources (Wisconsin)
DRD	Department of Resource Development (Wisconsin)
LAWCON	Land and Water Conservation Fund (United States)
LCCC	Legislative Council Conservation Committee (Wisconsin)
MCCA	Milwaukee County Conservation Alliance
NCAI	National Congress of American Indians
NCFC	North Central Field Committee (United States)
NPS	National Park Service
NRB	Natural Resources Board (Wisconsin)
NRCSA	Natural Resources Committee of State Agencies
NWWRPC	Northwest Wisconsin Regional Planning Commission
ORAP	Outdoor Recreation Act Program (Wisconsin)
ORRRC	Outdoor Recreation Resources Review Commission (United States)
UGLRC	Upper Great Lakes Regional Commission (United States)
USDI	United State Department of the Interior
WCC	Wisconsin Conservation Commission
WCD	Wisconsin Conservation Department

*Environmental Politics
and the Creation of a Dream*

Map 1. Location of the Apostle Islands National Lakeshore

Introduction

The Apostle Islands are located in Lake Superior off the tip of the Bayfield Peninsula in northern Wisconsin. Historians generally believe that the French explorers named the islands the Apostles, given their initial belief that there were only twelve islands, and following their custom of giving names of religious significance (the indigenous peoples, of course, had their own names, which the newcomers simply ignored). Twenty-two islands form the archipelago. Twenty-one islands (excluding Madeline Island) plus a twelve-mile stretch of shoreline on the Bayfield Peninsula make up the Apostle Islands National Lakeshore. Together, the islands and peninsula form a compelling, beautiful, and unique ecosystem.

The twenty-one islands making up the lakeshore are Basswood, Bear, Cat, Devils, Eagle, Gull, Hermit, Ironwood, Long, Manitou, Michigan, North Twin, Oak, Otter, Outer, Raspberry, Rocky, Sand, South Twin, Stockton, and York. Islands range in size from tiny 3-acre Gull Island to the 10,054-acre Stockton Island. Shorelines are characterized by cliffs, coves, caves, pristine sand spits, and beaches. The largest collection of lighthouses in the U.S. National Park System is found here, as are remnants of the old-growth forests, now gone from much of the Midwest. People have used these islands from the time of the earliest Paleo-Indian immigrants to more recent farmers, fishers, miners, and loggers. The entire archipelago was designated as the Gaylord A. Nelson National Wilderness by the U.S. Congress in 2004. This designation might startle the early exploiters and the descendants of mainland settlers. It would perhaps have been even more startling to the 1930s National Park Service planners, who had dismissed the possibility of the area having any potential as part of the National Park System!

This book examines the story behind the creation of the Apostle Islands

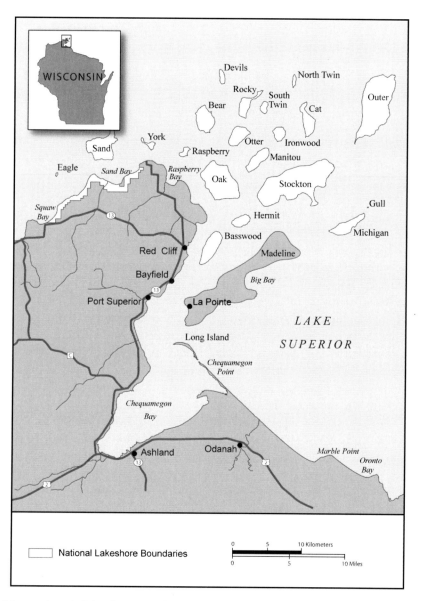

Map 2. Apostle Islands National Lakeshore

National Lakeshore by Congress in 1970, which in turn set the stage for an official public policy declaration several decades later that most of the islands would henceforth be permanently designated wilderness.[1] The book also documents the effort to include state lands and a previously excluded island within the lakeshore after the 1970s congressional action. We examine a number of themes, both implicitly and explicitly, within the narrative that have meaning and significance beyond the lakeshore for policy questions debated by our national and state governments on appropriate uses for the lands and waters.

We argue that the serendipitous conjunction of key individuals invested in the creation of the lakeshore was vital to its eventual success. The election of John F. Kennedy to the presidency and the election of Gaylord Nelson to the Wisconsin governor's office during the same period resulted in a heightened enthusiasm on the part of conservationists that placed natural resource management and protection back on the public agenda both in the state and nationally. The creation of the Apostle Islands National Lakeshore was a part of a national dialogue on the use of land and water. Under less favorable political circumstances there would have been a significantly smaller chance of a public park type of proposal succeeding.

We examine the complex system of public and private institutional frameworks through which the proposal was forced to navigate. In this case, everyone from federal and state politicians and bureaucrats to local governing boards and the two Native American tribal councils in the area had a significant stake, and say, in the outcome.

We also pay substantial attention to the political process itself. The proposal underwent a ten-year odyssey before eventual congressional approval. A 1970s political compromise to exclude Long Island resulted in a second process to add that state-owned island to the lakeshore sixteen years later. At several points the politics within the legislative and executive branches, as well as within and between local, state, federal, and tribal governments, came close to killing the proposal. It was only the fortuitous continuity on the part of key public officials and private citizens committed to the proposal that resulted in a successful outcome. The key roles of the secretary of the Interior, a U.S. senator, supportive citizen organizations, influential local citizens, and sympathetic local and state newspaper reporters suggest the importance of individuals in any political process. Similarly, the loss of continuity in the political process (through the election of Republican president Richard M. Nixon and the associated change in the secretary of the Interior) threatened the proposal, although the ongoing influence of supportive members of key Senate and House committees kept it alive.

We examine the significant role that planning institutions played in the creation of the lakeshore. Planners had various recommendations for the archipelago. Some favored national involvement, whereas others were critical of the idea of a national park or recommended state action. Some argued for extensive economic development, others advocated preserving the wilderness. Regardless of their conclusions, the very fact that time, energy, and planning resources were being devoted to the Apostle Islands region helped sensitize peoples' perceptions to the fact that there was an archipelago out there in Lake Superior and that it was important. The planning documents developed within the U.S. Department of the Interior during the 1960s became highly significant for the eventual passage of lakeshore legislation.

We also examine the role of a key constituency, the Native American tribes, in the creation of the lakeshore. The spark that ignited the entire drive for the lakeshore was a 1962 resolution by the Bad River Band of Lake Superior Chippewa Tribal Council at Odanah requesting that the Wisconsin governor and the secretary of the Interior explore the possibilities of a national lakeshore on the Kakagon–Bad River Sloughs, adjacent to the southern shore of Lake Superior. Native Americans then became deeply involved in the creation of the lakeshore. In addition to the local Bad River and Red Cliff Tribes, national activists became involved in the politics of the lakeshore. We give substantial attention to the role of Native Americans, their interests in the land, their rights, and their attitudes regarding the lakeshore proposal as it evolved and changed. Eventually both tribal councils and their lands were excluded from the bill enacted by Congress, but they were essential participants in the development of the lakeshore.

We also look at the role of the media in the creation of the lakeshore. In any public park proposal, the media play a significant role through influencing both public and political perceptions. On the whole, local and state newspapers were in favor of the lakeshore. It was significant that a few key reporters consistently followed the story from inception to conclusion and became intimately aware of the issues and were fully informed on the complexities of the proposal. The key media were the newspapers. Radio and television generally followed newspaper reports. Major proponents were skilled at working with and exploiting the media, ensuring that while citizen protests and controversies with the tribal councils were covered, in general the focus remained on the beauty of the region and the potential of a park.

Last, the inherent integrity of the lakeshore cannot be overlooked. The land, water, skyscapes, miles of gorgeous shoreline with fascinating sandspits and caves, and lush forests created an entity of great beauty and rich diversity. To argue that such a magnificent place needed to be protected for the public was an easy and delightful task.

In part 1 we start by offering a short description and history of the Apostle Islands region. We examine the broader federal and state policy context around parks and conservation that established the groundwork for a lakeshore proposal. Part 2 tells the story of the drive to develop and establish a park in the Apostle Islands. Part 3 discusses key issues around the lakeshore's establishment, including the role and function of planning, the role and impacts of professional (and personal) politics in the debate, a discussion of the key role that the media played, the critical, and often challenging, involvement of the Native Americans, the conflict between state and federal governments, and the influence that local government and residents brought to bear. In part 4 we offer some reflections on the process and the lessons learned.

This book is drawn from a much larger report written for the National Park Service, entitled *A Unique Collection of Islands: The Influence of History, Politics, and Planning on the Establishment of the Apostle Islands National Lakeshore*, which was submitted to the National Park Service in 1994. Those seeking an expanded history can find this report on the Apostle Islands National Lakeshore website.[2]

As this work reflects much of the understanding of the first author, Harold C. Jordahl, who was a key figure in the establishment of the lakeshore, much of the book is written in first person from his perspective. The second author, Annie L. Booth, has contributed substantial research to this book, to the analysis chapters, and to the overall editing and organization of the book. Other contributors are identified in the notes.

❧

PART ONE

The National and State Context for the Apostle Islands National Lakeshore

CHAPTER I

The Apostle Islands in Historical Context

When the U.S. Congress passed the Apostle Islands National Lakeshore Act in 1970, it was done with an implicit recognition that the islands were largely undeveloped and as a consequence would have high public recreational values. These conditions were the result of generally benign human use from the postglacial era to the highly developed industrial society of the 1960s. Other than mining the sandstone for building blocks, most impacts from use were eventually reversible. There were some periods where use rendered the islands unsuitable for recreational use, as was the case during the 1930s, when the first interest in an islands-based park was proposed (see chapter 4 for a brief discussion). In this chapter, we look at the history of the region, and at the state and national political history that led to interest in a national park. The lakeshore was timely: the 1960s witnessed a massive growth in land and water exploitation for private recreation purposes by the wealthy. It is likely this growing demand would have reached the Apostle Islands, resulting in exclusive subdivisions and private ownership of many of the islands. It would have become a rich man's paradise only.

Today, it is of shorelines, trees, water, and beauty that people think when they remember the Apostle Islands.[1] And indeed, these are the dominant forces shaping the lakeshore. But the lakeshore is more than the trees and the lake. Millions of years of geologic history are written in the islands. The advance and retreat of glaciers during the Pleistocene Era carved the islands and the peninsula out of Precambrian sandstone, exposing beautiful white sand beaches, dramatic cliffs, sculpted shorelines, and water-worn caves. The sandstone deposits formed the basis of a short-lived brownstone quarrying operation at the beginning of the twentieth century.

Trees dominate the landscape. The region is one in which the southern temperate hardwood forests reach their most northern edge and the northern boreal forests begin. On most of the islands, the forests are mixed hardwoods with some hemlock–white pine complexes. On the mainland and on a few of the islands, boreal spruce-fir forests exist. All of the islands except for Devils, North Twin, Raspberry, Eagle, and Gull were logged once or more. Fires and an eruption of whitetail deer further changed the forest composition. The lakeshore is currently home to thirty-seven plant species that are rare, endangered, or threatened.[2]

Birds are plentiful. A large proportion of the herring gulls thought to nest in Wisconsin's share of the Superior shoreline nest here, and double-crested cormorants also raise broods within the lakeshore. The loon's eerie cry is frequently heard. After DDT was banned, and after a thirty-year absence, bald eagles reappeared as regular residents. The endangered piping plover nests occasionally on Long Island.

The largest mammals in the lakeshore are the black bear and the whitetail deer. Deer were common in the 1940s and became abundant in the 1950s, when the new forest growth that followed logging and fires provided ideal habitat. As the forests have matured, the deer have declined. On several islands deer are overabundant and impact forest regeneration. Bear are common. Beaver live on Outer and Stockton Islands, and snowshoe hare, red fox, and coyote are also common. The endangered timber wolf lives on the adjacent mainland.

Historically, Lake Superior was very important for Native American life and with the arrival of European settlers supported a healthy sports and commercial fishery. Overexploitation, pollution, and the invasion of the parasitic sea lamprey and other exotics devastated the fishery. Fisheries programs have restored a vigorous fishery; lake trout can be caught here, along with the introduced brown and rainbow trout and three species of salmon. The native lake herring has recovered from earlier depredations and now provides the basis of a modest commercial catch. The popular whitefish is also caught and served in local restaurants.

Wicked and deadly storms, especially in the spring and fall, are not uncommon, and careless boaters underestimate the lake at their own peril. Even in mid-August, the water temperature of the lake rarely exceeds fifty degrees Fahrenheit. On land, in the summer, the weather is pleasant, moderated by the lake. July temperatures are cool. Temperatures in winter are more moderate than farther inland. The heavy snowfall is ideal for skiers and for those who snowshoe.

A number of shipwrecks, including the *Noquebay* and *Lucerne*, lie within and adjacent to the lakeshore. Historical lighthouses can be found on several islands (Raspberry Island's lighthouse is the best known), and restored fishing camps are located at Little Sand Bay and Manitou Island. Old sandstone quarries dot the islands. Archeological sites are found on several islands, the remains of the oldest civilizations to reside in the region.

People congregate in a number of small towns around the rim of the peninsula. Bayfield is the major jumping-off point for the islands. The lakeshore headquarters are located here, and a ferry to Madeline Island runs out of the harbor, supporting a healthy tourist population. To the west along the coast are the towns of Red Cliff, Cornucopia, Herbster, and Port Wing. To the east and south lie Washburn and Ashland. The moderate temperatures on the Bayfield Peninsula support fruit and berry orchards, and farms still operate nearby. The lands surrounding the Apostle Islands remain an attractive and pleasant setting for the islands.

The Historical Islands

Accounts of the earliest European travelers to western Lake Superior describe the drama and beauty of the carved shorelines and magnificent forests of the Apostle Islands and mainland coast. The exposed red sandstone bedrock was sculpted by forces of wind and water, and the cliffs and caverns are formed of some of the oldest sedimentary rocks on earth.[3]

As the ice sheets withdrew, the spruce and firs of the boreal forest advanced northward in the cool air and moist soil. White pine, yellow birch, and hemlock followed. As the climate warmed, hardwood species gradually entered the Great Lakes region.[4] Although logging has altered the primeval nature of the Apostle Islands forest, its character as a transition zone is one of the scientific values protected through the establishment of the lakeshore.[5]

With the establishment of vegetation on the islands, birds and mammals migrated to the area. Paleo-Indians who speared mastodons with fluted points of chipped stone, ancient Indians who worked quartzite quarries for their tools, boreal hunters with woodworking tools made of ground stone, and the Archaic Indians who made tools and weapons of copper and hunted elk and caribou, all flourished for a time in the Great Lakes region. These were followed by "woodland" Indians who lived by hunting and fishing.[6]

It is possible that some of the earliest peoples fished and hunted on the Apostle Islands, but no artifacts have been positively identified on the islands from the earliest chapters of northern Wisconsin's human history.[7] Some thirty-seven island sites are associated with the peoples who occupied the Lake Superior region from approximately 100 BC until Europeans arrived in the eighteenth century. Their campsites are found on sandy ledges above the beaches of a number of islands. Here they made tools from quartz beach cobbles, fished with nets weighted by stone sinkers, and stored provisions in pots of fired Lake Superior clay. Their camps were seasonal, and their mark on the landscape was just a trace. But the archeological record, with its story of Native culture, is one of the scientific values protected under the lakeshore legislation.[8]

La Pointe: International Crossroads in the Fur Trade

In 1659, when the French fur traders and explorers Pierre Radisson and Sieur des Groseilliers built the first temporary European outpost on the shores of Chequamegon Bay, they found a band of "Ottawa" Native Americans occupying the area along with eighteen other groups within a few days' travel.[9] Under attack from the Iroquois Confederacy, the Huron and the "Ottawa" had migrated to the Lake Superior region and established large villages in the Chequamegon area by 1665. Potawatomi, Sauk, Fox, and Illinois also came to Chequamegon Bay to trade.

One hundred years of conflict between tribes resulted in the termination of missionary activity for a century.[10] Then, in 1678, Daniel Dulhut, an emissary of Quebec, and the party of Algonquians who accompanied him successfully negotiated a treaty with the Lakota, which opened the way for a thriving fur trade in the region. He established a post, possibly on Long Island and later a fort on the south tip of Madeline Island. This post was replaced in 1718 by a new Fort La Pointe on the west side of the island.[11]

For forty years, the Apostles were the scene of a flourishing French fur trade. The first ship on Lake Superior, a twenty-five-ton sailing vessel, was built by the French to carry freight between La Pointe and the Sault. It was under Commander LaRonde that "Apostle Islands" became the official name, although it had already appeared on some of the maps prepared by early French explorers.[12]

The "Saulteurs" had carved out a role as middlemen in the French fur trade, settling in various locations in the Apostle Islands vicinity. In all likelihood, they made extensive use of the archipelago for fishing, hunting, and other subsistence activities. As the fur trade became a determining factor in their lives, the loosely related Algonquian Bands coalesced into the Ojibwe Nation. From this time on, the Ojibwe, or Chippewa, were a resident people in the Chequamegon region.[13] For three decades Chequamegon Bay was host to a number of rival independent traders and companies.[14]

By 1790 the North West Company had gained an upper hand in the Lake Superior trade. As under the French regime, Britain's La Pointe was an important fur depot and trading center for the entire Lake Superior region. The War of 1812, however, ultimately accomplished on the lakes what the American Revolution had not. British control gradually, but inevitably, yielded to U.S. interests. For the North West Company, what began as a management contract with the American Fur Company ended in British loss of trade south of the U.S.-Canadian border,[15] but it was not until 1816 that the American flag was raised over the Apostle Islands.

Although an abundance of furs flowed through La Pointe, beavers were becoming scarce. As a hedge against diminishing furs, the American Fur Company in 1835 began an experimental commercial fishing operation at La Pointe. A receptive market was found for salted whitefish and lake trout.[16] Although the fishing enterprise flourished, success was short-lived. The company was struggling under a shift in fashion from beaver to silk hats while it also suffered from the effects of a nationwide economic recession. In 1839 the company went into receivership.[17]

The islands were strategic for defense, subsistence, and trade, and they were the locale for the earliest commercial fishing venture on Lake Superior. A few structural remains and rich archeological sites on Madeline Island give evidence of this important chapter in the history of the Old Northwest. The presence of trade beads and other artifacts of early European contact in sites within the Apostle Islands National Lakeshore suggest that more of the story will yet be told.

The Era of Capital in the Apostle Islands

The decade between the decline of the American Fur Company and the opening of the Sault Locks was a time of transition for the Apostle Islands. Old patterns were broken while new ones were dreamed up and financed, sometimes in cities far removed from the archipelago.

Mineral discoveries and development in the 1840s brought the eclipse of La Pointe as a center of trade and Ojibwe settlement. Following geologist Douglass Houghton's reports of copper in the Keweenaw Peninsula, the United States entered into a treaty with the Ojibwe to acquire mineral-rich lands and the right to remove the Native Americans from these lands at the government's discretion. President Zachary Taylor acted on this option in 1850, closing the

La Pointe sub-agency and ordering the Ojibwe to relocate to Minnesota. The La Pointe Ojibwe dragged their feet so another treaty was promulgated four years later, dividing the La Pointe group into two bands and assigning them lands by their religious affiliations: Catholics were to relocate to the mainland to the west of La Pointe (now the Red Cliff Tribe), while Protestants were assigned Chequamegon Point (the spit of land where the "Saulteurs" first arrived) and adjacent lowlands, including the Kakagon River, along the south shore of the lake (now the Bad River Tribe).[18]

The Michigan Keweenaw copper boom affected the white population of La Pointe as well. Many who had lived on the profits of the fur trade now left to pursue their fortunes in Michigan ores in the Iron Ranges. However, La Pointe was far from a ghost town. The archipelago's fishery provided the backbone for a small-scale, but viable, local economy. A boat builder's shop and at least two cooperages were in operation at La Pointe. A small sawmill turned out local lumber. New acres were added to provide an agricultural base for the local population.[19]

By 1854 several new settlements had resulted from the speculation fever that preceded the opening of the Sault Locks, including the two villages on Chequamegon Bay, soon to merge as the city of Ashland, and at the head of the lake, the twin ports of Superior and Duluth. The future roles of settlement and tourism in the Apostle Islands were forecast when publicity on the area began to appear in New York newspapers as early as 1854.[20]

The Apostle Islands now became familiar to Washington, DC, politicians and eastern investors. With the opening of the Sault Locks investors formed the Bayfield Land Company across from La Pointe. A town was platted in 1856, and lots were quickly sold to investors and developers that became the first mainland base for more than a century of Apostle Islands ventures.

In those few years between the demise of the American Fur Company and the opening of Lake Superior to intracontinental traffic, elements of competing interests for the resources of the Apostle Islands emerged in patterns that are still evident today. One persistent theme is the role of politically influential and well-financed investors based in urban centers of the Midwest and East. Although this element has included individuals with widely divergent concerns, ranging from railroads to lumber and stone to concern for the preservation of the area's aesthetic and natural qualities, what they had in common was political and economic power, which they exercised in the Chequamegon–Apostle Islands region.

A second theme is the local use and development of resources, which provided a frequently marginal, natural resource–based, Chequamegon-area economy. Fishers, loggers, fruit growers, resort owners, and entrepreneurs dependent on tourism have, for the most part, been without political influence or organization. They often found themselves denying economic realities to hold on to known livelihoods.[21] Boom-and-bust cycles, though never acute enough to leave ghost towns on the shores of Chequamegon Bay, left fewer options for the future with each repetition.

The third element in the pattern of modern resource use in the Apostle Islands is the Red Cliff and Bad River Bands of Lake Superior Ojibwe. The people who used Apostle Islands resources such as fish, animals, and plants in early historic times have played a less constant role since the 1854 treaties. However, wild rice, fish, and game are still important sources of food for resident tribes and hold substantial symbolic meaning.

The Die Is Cast

The natural beauty, easy access by water, and cool climate of the archipelago fostered visions of a vacation paradise for hay fever sufferers and those who could afford to flee urban summer contagions. Permanent settlers were sought as well. With virgin forests still towering over the shorelines, the region was touted as a "land of milk and honey," needing only the touch of the plow for crops and gardens to flourish. However, it was the quality and abundance of timber and sandstone that fired promoters' dreams and prospectuses. These resources had the potential to become a major source of supply for the eastern seaboard and the growing Midwest. With the railroad and access to the Great Lakes, Bayfield could become a transportation center for the midcontinent and could well have impacted use in the islands.

The 1870s were a critical decade for the Apostle Islands. After two hundred years as a source of peltry for the fur trade, the archipelago had entered the industrial age. Now it was stone, lumber, and fish that traveled from the Lake Superior rim. These three industries, supplemented by tourism and agriculture, would dominate the Chequamegon Bay economy until the resources were depleted (except for stone), leaving tourism and agriculture as alternatives for the future.

The lumber industry got an early start in the Apostles region when the American Fur Company operated a small sawmill in the 1840s. By the 1860s several small mills had been constructed in the Bayfield area. What was unique about the Apostle Islands' logging industry in this early period was the variety of operations and species it utilized. While their mainland counterparts "went from pine stump to pine tree," island operators were cutting cord wood for direct sale to steamships as fuel, cutting pine and hardwood in the winter to transport to the mills in the spring, and cutting hemlock each summer for the tanbark industry.[22]

In the spring of 1870 a new industry appeared in the Apostle Islands that extracted island resources almost exclusively for export: the quarrying of sandstone. The city of Milwaukee's search for quality brownstone to build a new courthouse ended at Basswood Island, where Strong, French & Company opened a quarry. Rough-cut stone was shipped by schooner to Milwaukee. The success of this venture led to expanded operations on the island, the stone being sold exclusively to Milwaukee and Chicago yards. Unfortunately, dreams of a regional industry were premature. Disputes over land title and the economic crash of 1873 closed operations for another decade.[23]

Brief as this first quarrying episode was, it set a benchmark in the economic development of the Apostle Islands region. It marked a transition from land speculation to resource extraction. Later, during the 1880s and 1890s, wholesalers in stone and lumber in Chicago, Milwaukee, St. Paul, and other Great Lakes shipping or rail centers acquired large tracts on the Apostle Islands and south shore mainland to provide new materials for their rapidly growing urban markets.

The year 1870 also marked the resurgence of the commercial fishing industry, which had had brief importance in the Apostle Islands thirty years earlier. In August of that year the N. & F. Boutin Company of Two Rivers, Wisconsin, relocated to Bayfield, bringing in some fifty to one hundred employees and a small fleet of boats.[24] The Apostle Islands archipelago offered several advantages to the industry, which was now growing rapidly throughout the Great Lakes. Reefs, especially those off of Devils Island, were spawning grounds for lake trout and whitefish, the primary commercial species of Lake Superior; thus, the fishing grounds were rich. The islands offered protection from the winds of the open lake. Sheltered island beaches were excellent sites for fishing stations that could serve as bases of operation for an entire season. A fishing operation newly established on Sand Island would grow to be the only permanent, year-round island settlement on the future national lakeshore lands.

All three of the major island industries depended on finite resources; fishing alone survived to become a mainstay in the local economy. However, the region paid for the boom; the exhaustion of prime timber species led to a near collapse of the area's economy by the late 1920s. Commercial fishing, on the other hand, was more than an industry; it was part of the fabric of community and family life. As summer fishing enclaves developed on the islands and packinghouses expanded operations, women and even children became part of the workforce. Men could fish for the major companies in the area or, with some equipment and perhaps a partner, fish independently and sell to the Boutin Company, A. Booth & Company (which opened an office in Bayfield in 1885), or one of the smaller local companies. Fishing also provided a local source of food, especially important when times were hard. Although overfishing of the commercial species eventually played a role in the depletion of Apostle Islands' fishing grounds, the industry was the "bread and butter" of the region throughout the 1950s.

Fishing left fewer visible signs on the Apostle Islands than either logging or quarrying. Yet all three extractive industries had a major impact on island resources and continue to play a role in the character of the Apostle Islands National Lakeshore. The lumber industry's decimation of the forests forestalled the establishment of a national park on the islands in the 1930s. Although island fisheries have begun to recover through intensive research and management, court decisions related to treaty rights, competition among user groups, and the impacts of exotic species on the commercial fishery ensure that management of this resource will remain an important issue for the future. The relict quarries alone have a passive role, providing an opportunity for visitors to explore and understand related chapters in the geology and economic history of the Apostle Islands.[25]

The Land as Resource

Commodities were not all that the Apostle Islands had to offer. By the 1870s, steamship lines and railroad promoters had begun boosting the Apostle Islands region. Travel brochures described the sculptured shorelines and rich, green forests. Images of emerald islands in a sparkling sapphire setting filled copywriters' prose. The delights of sailing, fishing, and picnicking in the Apostles were promised at the end of a cruise up the lake on a luxurious modern steamer. The air was said to invigorate and restore. The climate, moderated by the lake, was celebrated as never too hot in the summer but mild enough in the winter to assure the seasonal flourishing of gardens and orchards for anyone resourceful enough to clear timber from the land, build a house, and cultivate the rich glacial soils.

The steamship lines garnered fares for passage to the Apostle Islands. Great Lakes excursions were already fashionable among the wealthy social elite of Washington, DC, Mackinaw, Michigan, and Madison, Wisconsin, and had become summer gathering places for such "Southern society."[26] Since Bayfield had acquired some amenities, its docks became the point of departure for Apostle Islands outings. Boating was the primary form of recreation, although trout fishing in local streams was also popular. Highlights of a cruise would include a chance to observe the quarry in operation, perhaps a stop at an island fishing station, and most certainly a visit to the Raspberry or Michigan Island Lighthouse to picnic and play croquet on the lawns.[27] This mode of tourism was to prevail in the Apostle Islands until the twentieth century.

Early island residents, whether homesteaders, lighthouse keepers, squatters, or preemptors, had an important role in the history of land use in the archipelago and the adjacent peninsula. Before the locks opened, smoke had curled from chimneys and gardens grew at the island home sites of Benjamin Armstrong and William Wilson. Basswood Island, however, was the first to see a homestead claim filed and "proved up."[28] A number of settlers developed island home sites during the 1870s.[29] The most important of the early settlers was Francis Shaw, who claimed land on Sand Island following the Civil War. Arriving on the island in the early 1870s, Shaw fished and gardened, selling his produce in Bayfield and, later, to island summer residents. In 1910 his daughter and son-in-law, Burton Hill, joined Shaw on Sand Island. Over the years the buildings of the farm provided island residents with a post office, general store, community ice and smoke houses, and a social center.[30] The Shaw Farm was the focal point of interaction between the government settlement that developed on the island by the turn of the century and the summer community of wealthy St. Paul businessmen and their families, who were initially attracted to the island by Camp Stella, the first resort in the Apostle Islands. (The Shaw Farm is now listed in the National Register of Historic Places.)

The Chequamegon Boom

Bayfield, which possessed a superior harbor, had been the focus of commercial activity and development in the region. With the railroad, Ashland came alive. Sawmills sprang up on its waterfront followed by ore and coal piers and charcoal furnaces.[31] As the railroad worked its way north, the town of Washburn was established to serve the lumber industry, followed in a few years by the extension of the rail line to Bayfield.

Within a few short years some thirty lumber companies operated on Chequamegon Bay, with mills stretching from Odanah to Red Cliff. Their crews worked the forests from the Bad River Reservation in the east, through the vast pineries south of Ashland, up the peninsula, out on the islands, and west to Squaw Bay. Logs were fed from spur roads to the main lines and rafted from the shorelines until Chequamegon Bay resembled a gigantic millpond.[32]

To the quarries and lumber camps springing up on the shorelines were added other less dramatic signs of late-century development in the Apostle Islands. When the Booth Company, the largest of the Great Lakes commercial fisheries, opened a branch in Bayfield, the area fishing industry doubled in size. Summer fishing camps accommodating several families grew up on Rocky and South Twin Islands, complete with gardens and milk cows. The 1880s influx of Swedish immigrants to Chicago and St. Paul spread ripples as far as Michigan and Bear Islands, where pieces of the New World were claimed and cultivated.[33] New lighthouse stations, bringing a total of six to the archipelago, testified to the increase of boat traffic around and among the islands.

To attract passengers to their new routes and to enhance the destinations, the railroad companies built luxurious resort hotels in Bayfield and Ashland. Tourists now arrived from all over the Midwest as well as from the East and South. The nature of tourism in the area had changed little from the 1870s, however. There were simply more tourists, more excursion boats, and more attractions in the bayside towns.

Two developments occurred on the islands, however, that foreshadowed recreation patterns of the years to come. On Madeline Island, the first summer residences had begun to appear. One row of cottages housed descendants of Dillon O'Brien, a teacher in the old La Pointe parochial school, while a more imposing row belonged to the family and friends of Colonel Frederick Woods of Lincoln, Nebraska.[34] Thus, in a familiar pattern of ownership on the islands, one group had roots in the fur trade era, the other in the post–railroad boom. Woods's "Nebraska Row" was augmented by Hunter L. Gary, founder of General Telephone, and other affluent friends and associates.[35] The social and political influence exercised by these families shaped the development of Madeline Island throughout the twentieth century and ultimately influenced the design of the Apostle Islands National Lakeshore.

A second development offered a new approach to recreation in the islands. In 1894, Sam Fifield, an Ashland newspaperman and politician, opened a summer resort on Sand Island that provided an experience in outdoor living. Guests slept in wall tents and cooked over an open fire. Their days were filled with hiking, boating, fishing, picnicking, and observing natural history.[36] The traveling Chautauqua show provided education and entertainment. Although genteel by modern standards, Camp Stella was the first tourist venture in the Apostle Islands to invite visitors to shed some of the accouterments of civilization and live more closely with nature and in an island environment.

In terms of social and economic structure, the Sand Island and Madeline Island communities had many similarities. Both had permanent populations who made a living from farming and fishing, with some involvement in logging and tourism. Both included affluent and politically influential summer residents whose families retained and used their island property into the third generation. On both islands the summer and local residents intermingled socially and developed shared traditions. In both communities the summer residents provided direction, leadership, and capital when land use and development issues arose.

The Collapse

The new century brought qualitative changes to Chequamegon Bay. The national economic shocks of 1893 and 1903 were felt on Lake Superior. The brownstone industry folded, the smaller operators were forced out of the lumber business, and only a few guests occupied the spacious rooms of the waterfront hotels. Building slowed in the towns, and fewer trains came through. The era of big capital and luxury tourism was ending.

Although a few big lumber companies were still active, distances were becoming greater between the timber and the mills. Pine was playing out, and the depletion of all marketable species was imminent. The Schroeder Company of Milwaukee was gearing up for a massive harvest of Apostle Islands hardwoods and remaining pine, but within a few years it would be towing rafts of logs across the lake from Minnesota's north shore to keep up production at its Ashland mill. Soon J. S. Stearns would leave Odanah, the Chequamegon mills would be shut down, and Schroeder would leave its locomotives and logging gear to rust on Outer Island.

As the cutover stretched for miles from Chequamegon Bay, settlers dug in to clear the stumps and make a living from the soil. What the island experiments had shown to be possible gradually came to pass on the mainland. Strawberry fields, apple orchards, hayfields, and vegetable gardens appeared where the forest had stood.

Most of the early homesteads on the islands had disappeared, with a few significant exceptions. McCloud's old farm on Basswood Island continued to flourish. A neighboring farm on Hermit Island continued into the twentieth century as well. Over on Sand Island, however, a new group of homesteaders was beginning to put down roots and establish a community. Several descendants of the original homesteaders still owned and made seasonal use of their property on Sand Island at the time that the national lakeshore was established.

Although the fishing industry had undergone some changes since the boom of the 1880s, it helped carry the region through the Depression and remained a major factor in the local economy until the fisheries collapsed late in the 1950s. During the 1880s, the Booth Company had introduced herring fishing to the Apostle Islands. This late fall fishery became increasingly important, especially as whitefish began to decline in the 1890s. Although whitefish populations increased again in the 1930s, in 1945 the herring fishery comprised 4.2 million pounds of harvest out of a total of 5.3 million pounds of fish caught.[37]

By the 1920s, visitors to the Apostle Islands came by car rather than steamship or railroad coach. They tended to live closer to the areas where they vacationed; they had less time and less money than the affluent "hay fever season" crowd of an earlier era. They rented cabins by the week and came to fish and see the sights. They did not own the large boats needed to get out on the lake. To serve this clientele, commercial fishers often took anglers out on their boats, charging by the day or the hour, giving the angler the first hundred pounds of the catch and selling the rest at market.[38]

From this initial diversification by commercial fishers grew a separate trolling industry. By the 1950s, boat captains specialized in outfitting and packaging recreational fishing trips on the lake. Some provided rustic lodgings and meals at resorts (often refurbished fish camps) on Madeline, Rocky, and South Twin Islands and at Little Sand Bay on the mainland. Some operators extended their services into the fall for island hunting trips. Deer, unknown before logging, now populated the emerging second-growth forests and provided a new source of subsistence and recreation.

As trollers and commercial fishermen vied for their share of a diminishing fishery, conflicts were inevitable. By the 1960s, however, these conflicts were moot. The Apostle Islands fishery was all but dead. Overfishing, pollution, introduction and invasion of competing exotic species, and sea lamprey depredation had reduced populations of market fish to levels that could not support commercial harvests. However, the visible scars of logging had begun to heal around the bay, as had the raw marks of industry in Ashland, Washburn, and Bayfield. The scenic beauty of the region once more recalled early travelers' lyrical descriptions. Although the Chequamegon area was suffering economic hardship, most of the nation was entering into a period of increased personal incomes and more leisure time. Developers at La Pointe were acting on their expectations of an increase in tourism, while Chequamegon Bay area chambers of commerce looked for new ways to promote their best hope for the future. Into this setting the concept of Apostle Islands National Lakeshore was born.[39]

❧

CHAPTER 2

The Apostle Islands National Lakeshore in Political Context

STATE AND FEDERAL INITIATIVES

The 1960s was an excellent time for the proposal for the Apostle Islands National Lakeshore to appear. It fit within a series of incrementally changing, occasionally inconsistent policies that had been enacted to create a national system of parks, monuments, seashores, lakeshores, trails, and wild, scenic, and recreational rivers. These areas would be administered primarily by the National Park Service (NPS). The building blocks for a vastly expanded national parks and recreation system were put into place during the 1950s using a number of special studies, plans, commissions, and reports. These reports and programs would give lakeshore and seashore proposals—including the Apostle Islands proposal—powerful arguments to use in persuading the public, the U.S. Congress, and federal and state bureaucrats that shorelands were legitimate, worthy, and necessary additions to the National Park System. This chapter examines the policy processes that, over a century, created a truly national system of parks as well as state conservation initiatives in Wisconsin, both of which created a foundation upon which U.S. Senator Gaylord Nelson could build when he introduced the bill to create the Apostle Islands National Lakeshore.[1]

The National Park Service

The first national park was Yellowstone, established in 1872. Yosemite, Sequoia, and General Grant National Parks followed in 1890. Precedents were established for setting aside large amounts of land in the magnificent mountain regions of the West, largely through a withdrawal of land from the public domain. Significantly, these lands, for the most part, were not yet degraded by human activity. By 1916, when Congress established the National Park Service, an odd assortment of lands were considered to be "national parks" or special preserves. This collection, according to historian Ronald Foresta, had come about as a result of "pork barrel politics, the need for a catch-all category for miscellaneous withdrawals of public lands and purely idiosyncratic circumstances."[2] A confusing mix of six different agencies and bureaus was responsible for the administration of these lands.

After the establishment of Yellowstone, and after several decades of bureaucratic wrangling and politicking, Gifford Pinchot, head of the U.S. Forest Service between 1905 and 1910 and close advisor to President Theodore Roosevelt, moved to place parks within his bureaucratic domain in the Department of Agriculture. Pinchot held a very utilitarian philosophy regarding the appropriate management of natural resources, in contrast with those, such as naturalist John Muir, who urged strict preservation. These differing philosophies clashed spectacularly and publicly during the turn of the century debate over a dam at the Hetch Hetchy Valley in California, which would supply a steady water supply for the city of San Francisco. Pitting John Muir and a newly fledged Sierra Club against government bureaucrat Pinchot, the public debate was won by the forces of development (helped by the 1906 San Francisco earthquake and devastating fires). Hetch Hetchy was dammed in 1913. Subsequent to this success, the Department of Agriculture fought hard to move parks into its purview. With the aid of the Sierra Club, preservationists waged a successful battle to establish a separate National Park Service.[3] In 1916 the NPS was established within the U.S. Department of the Interior, and Stephen T. Mather was appointed its first director.[4] Preservation was now an explicit public policy.

Unfortunately, while Congress was willing to create the NPS, it did little to ensure agency survival or financial support. The early survival of the National Park Service and its ability to acquire lands for parks was due primarily to Mather's willingness to use his own money and his ability to cultivate the support of rich and influential men to lend political influence and financial contributions, and, on occasion, even donate lands for national parks. For decades the NPS struggled; it would not be until 1961 that Congress would actually authorize funds for land acquisition for a recreational park when it established Cape Cod National Seashore, and it was a significant precedent for a future national lakeshore in the Apostle Islands.[5]

The 1930s and the Growth of Outdoor Recreation

In the 1930s, President Franklin Roosevelt established a National Resource Planning Board, and its Land Planning Committee commissioned the NPS to study outdoor recreation. This resulted in a 1935 report, *Recreation Uses of Land in the United States.*[6] The report proposed strengthening the role of the NPS as *the* national recreation planning agency not only at the federal level but at the state and local levels as well. One important recommendation included the purchase of ocean-beach areas for recreational use, a recommendation that would later be broadened to include lakeshores.[7]

The NPS took on other responsibilities for Depression-era programs including the Civilian Conservation Corps, which undertook park development projects across the country.[8] The NPS also developed regional parks for long-term operation by state or local governments; six were established in the eastern United States.

These new areas in the eastern United States, along with the four existing national parks, were slowly establishing the NPS as something substantially more than just an agency with responsibilities for the unspoiled wilderness parks of the western United States. Moreover, the recreational demonstration projects and the parkways had substantially different management criteria from those established for national parks. Mather and Horace Albright (who in 1929 succeeded Mather as director of the NPS) were indeed broadening their geographical base, as well as their management philosophy and, coincidentally, their political base.[9]

Another major public works project, the construction of Hoover Dam (begun in the 1930s) and the associated creation of mammoth Lake Mead, eventually resulted in NPS administration of five "reservoir-related recreation areas." During the 1930s the NPS also initiated a new concept—national seashores—which more than three decades later would have significant implications for the Apostle Islands.[10]

State Recreation Plans Begin

To counter growing concerns, and based upon the recommendations of the Recreational Division of the National Resources Planning Board, Congress passed the Park, Parkway, and Recreational Area Study Act of 1936. The object of the 1936 act was to establish a basis for coordinated planning among agencies responsible for park and recreation developments at all levels of government. It eventually would have an important role in expanding and broadening the National Park Service. Moreover, the act would establish the NPS as the dominant recreation planning agency at the national level and as a major leader and participant in planning at both the state and local levels.[11]

Under the authority of the 1936 Park Act, the NPS initiated collaborative planning programs with many of the states, including Wisconsin, which resulted in the first truly comprehensive recreation plan for the state. Recommendations were made for a state historic site on Madeline Island and the investigation of a state park on one or more of the islands.[12] Further, the recommendations called for the public acquisition of at least 10 percent of the nation's shorelines, including the shorelines of the Great Lakes, without identifying which level of government should accomplish this task.[13]

The NPS plan was careful to point out that the role of the federal government should be limited to areas of truly national significance. It recommended the creation of a state monument at Sleeping Bear Dunes in Michigan (which later became a national lakeshore) and reiterated the earlier recommendation for a state park in the Apostle Islands. Existing and proposed federal, state, and local recreational areas were identified for each state.[14] At this point in Wisconsin, there was no interest in suggesting the Apostles as a federal project. The Wisconsin Conservation Department's budget was too thin for new additions. World War II intervened in the process.

As the United States moved toward involvement in World War II, a final NPS report was released in 1942, under the authority of the 1936 Park Act.[15] When President Richard M. Nixon ultimately signed the Apostle Islands National Lakeshore Bill in 1970, the 1936 Park Act provided the basis for the recreation area concept as a part of the National Park System, which was explicitly acknowledged.[16] Ronald F. Lee, an NPS historian, has highlighted the significance of this 1936 act by noting that it initiated four new types of federal park areas—national parkways, national recreation areas, national seashores, and recreation demonstration areas. The 1936 plans developed under this act and Harold Ickes's supplemental 1942 report were significant planning benchmarks in the history of the NPS. Between 1933 and 1964 four national parkways, two recreation demonstration areas, five reservoir-related recreation areas, and four national seashores were added to the park system.[17] Lakeshores were not noted, but the framework for their inclusion was there as Congress began to authorize them. Fifteen years later, the NPS would again initiate comprehensive surveys for a new version of a national outdoor recreation plan.

Developing National Seashores and Lakeshores

All of the national recreation areas established in the 1930s were a marriage of conservation, economic, and public recreation interests. In most cases conservation meant the protection and enhancement of the existing environment for recreational and aesthetic purposes, rather than the protection of natural areas in a pristine condition. (The idea of restoring degraded areas, which could then fit into a National Park System, would come later.) However, the NPS interest in national seashores did shift the focus. Although public recreation was the rubric under which shorelines were considered for national designation, the motivating factor in the 1930s was a desire to protect large coastal expanses.

Shoreline property development was big business in Florida and along the Gulf Coast during the 1920s. Although the boom slowed during the Great Depression, the razed dunes along these coasts presaged the eventual loss of most of the nation's pristine shorelines.[18] Interior Secretary Ickes expressed the feeling of urgency behind NPS action: "When we have reached the point that a nation of 125,000,000 people cannot set foot upon the thousands of miles of beaches that border the Atlantic and Pacific Oceans, except by permission of those who monopolize the ocean front, then I say it is the prerogative and the duty of the federal and state governments to step in and acquire, not a swimming beach here and there, but solid blocks of ocean front hundreds of miles in length."[19]

With public works planning and development funds available, the NPS initiated surveys of the nation's shorelines, including the Great Lakes. These surveys identified both exceptional areas that might be added to the National Park System and other outstanding areas that would meet state recreational needs. The final report recommended that twelve segments of Atlantic and Gulf shorelines, totaling 4,327 miles of beaches, be considered as seashore units of the National Park System and that another thirty areas be preserved as state parks. Unfortunately, a lack of funds and desire precluded any detailed recommendations regarding the Great Lakes.[20] Out of this effort, however, came the genesis of national lakeshores along the Great Lakes, including the Apostle Islands. In 1937, as its first exercise of these new recommendations, Congress authorized legislation for Cape Hatteras National Seashore in North Carolina. This created a new type of area within the NPS. Although this legislation had a strong preservation emphasis, local commercial fishermen retained the right to fish. A 1941 amendment redesignated Cape Hatteras as a "national seashore recreational area," permitting limited hunting under carefully prescribed limits.[21] Commercial hunting and fishing, prohibited in national parks, were authorized in all subsequent legislation for national seashores and lakeshores, including the Apostle Islands. Had it not been for the hunting and fishing (both sports and commercial) precedent, the Apostle Islands proposal would have faced serious difficulty if not outright failure.

National Park Service planners had a difficult time delineating boundaries for Cape Hatteras. Seven small communities on the outer banks in Pamlico

Sound were eventually excluded to avoid a political uproar. The area was divided into "seven or eight" sections for planning purposes. The local newspaper printed detailed maps and, with the exception of vociferous opposition from employees of waterfowl hunting clubs, gained community approval.[22]

Other provisions for the use and development of Cape Hatteras were spelled out in a policy statement formulated by the NPS to guide planning for Cape Hatteras and other shoreline areas. The main policies stated that

- a seashore was primarily a recreation area and should include ample shoreline for all types of beach recreation;
- boundaries should "reach back into the hinterlands" to include adjacent lands important for scientific, historical, or scenic purposes;
- lands needed for both administration and protection of the recreational or other primary values of the area should be included in the unit; and
- seashores should be developed and operated in accord with "normal national park standards with the understanding that recreational pursuits shall be emphasized to provide activities in as broad a field as is consistent with the preservation of the area." Recreational fishing, boating, and aircraft landings would be permitted in designated areas when such activities did not "conflict with other factors of greater importance" and were consistent with "the interests of wildlife or proper development and use of the area."[23]

This policy statement went beyond the more pragmatic philosophy underlying the "emergency conservation" Depression-era projects. Seashores would preserve scientific and historical values by acquiring adjacent lands with important natural and cultural features; they would even include "buffer zones" of land or water as necessary to protect wildlife, scenic qualities, or recreational potential. Although seashore development would emphasize recreation and allow some uses prohibited in national parks, these uses had to be compatible with the preservation of the area. Had the Apostle Island planners been more fully aware of these sweeping national policies, the lakeshore boundaries might well have been much more inclusive, especially along the magnificent shoreline and hinterlands of the Bayfield Peninsula.

The tensions between preservation and public use implied in the National Park Service Organic Act of 1916 were written large in the Cape Hatteras *Prospectus* and would influence in a significant way subsequent policy decisions regarding national recreation areas, such as seashores and lakeshores. Although Cape Hatteras was the only seashore authorized by Congress before

World War II interrupted the program, the NPS would not lose sight of its goal to place significant portions of shoreline into the public domain.

The 1937 Cape Hatteras Act did, however, contain an almost fatal flaw. The language stated that the land had to be given to the NPS without cost before the area could be established. Sixteen years would pass before money would be directly appropriated for new additions to the National Park System, and ultimately at Cape Hatteras encroachments within the original boundary necessitated some land deletions. A combination of state and foundation money for land purchases finally allowed formal establishment on January 12, 1953.[24]

Cape Cod National Seashore

Almost a quarter of a century would pass before Congress again considered national seashores. It created the Cape Cod National Seashore in 1961 and established significant precedents for future national lakeshores and seashores. NPS director Conrad Wirth summed it up: "The legislation proved to be a milestone in the history of the National Park System, because Congress created a precedent by authorizing federal funding to buy the necessary land and all such bills passed by the Congress since then have authorized appropriations for land purchases. Until then legislation . . . had required that the lands be either federally owned or given to the government. It was what we often called the beg, borrow, or steal system."[25]

In contrast to Cape Hatteras, where villages were excluded from the boundary, Cape Cod used an innovative new approach. It included the settlements on Cape Cod within seashore boundaries, but prevented the Interior secretary from acquiring land as long as a local zoning ordinance was in effect that met the secretary's standards. Historian Ronald F. Lee declared, "The provision resolved serious problems of conflict between long-settled private owners, the historic towns and the federal government and helped stabilize the landscape without the forced resettlement of numerous families."[26] Owners of improved property outside of towns had several options. They could sell their property immediately; sell the property and retain a right of use and occupancy for twenty-five years with a right of assignment; or sell the land but retain the use of the property for life. Cape Cod thus created an important precedent for parallel provisions for other seashores and lakeshores.[27] The options provided to landowners on Cape Cod were also incorporated into the Apostle Islands National Lakeshore Act. The zoning provision, known as the "Cape Cod Formula," was considered during the debates on the Apostle Islands National Lakeshore but ultimately was not used, due to lack of local interest. The provision would have fit nicely with a broader lakeshore boundary that could have included many magnificent bays, Sand Bay, Bark Point, and the villages of Herbster and Cornucopia, and adjacent hinterlands.

Mission 66

By the late 1950s the NPS had turned its energies from expansion to remedying the critical need for facilities and visitor services in existing national parks.[28] Under Conrad Wirth's direction, "Mission 66" was launched to meet these needs with the same vigor that once fueled the Civilian Conservation Corps program. Local assistance and new authorizations were put on a back burner.[29] However, as a part of the Mission 66 effort, the NPS resumed its seashore studies. Because many of the areas proposed as national seashores in the 1930s were now lost to private development, comprehensive surveys were undertaken for a second time, initially through private funding and later with Mission 66 funds.[30]

Four studies were subsequently published: *Our Vanishing Shoreline* (1955); *A Report on the Seashore Recreation Survey of the Atlantic and Gulf Coasts* (1955); *Our Fourth Shore: Great Lakes Shoreline Recreation Area Survey* (1959);[31] *Pacific Coast Recreation Area Survey* (1959). Wirth was justly proud, stating, "Admittedly I take pride in pointing out that the shoreline preservation program sprouted from the NPS-CCC [Civilian Conservation Corps] program of the 1930s and came into full bloom in the Mission 66 period in the late fifties and early sixties. Perhaps more importantly is the fact that the shoreline program set the policy for the Park Service to assume its full responsibilities as defined by Congress, which backed the program by providing legislative assurance of proper funding."[32]

He gave great credit to supporters in Congress, especially Wayne N. Aspinall, a Colorado Democrat who chaired the House Interior Committee, and Pennsylvania Republican John P. Saylor. Both would subsequently become key decision makers on the Apostle Islands and other Great Lakes projects.

The NPS reports dramatized the lack of significant public access to the shorelines and waters of the Great Lakes system. Of the approximately 4,000 miles of mainland shoreline, only 497 miles (1.2 percent) were in some type of public ownership. The *Our Fourth Shore* study identified some 426 additional miles that possessed important opportunities for outdoor recreation, which would bring the total amount of lands in public ownership to a minuscule 2.3 percent.[33] In Wisconsin, areas identified as needing protection through public acquisition included several small units on the Bayfield Peninsula, Stockton Island, the Brule River, and the Lake Superior shoreline west of the mouth of the Brule. The potential national significance of the "Bad

River Marshes" was recognized by a recommendation for further study. The planners were obviously not thinking within a larger regional scale and looked only at small specific sites along Lake Superior's shoreline.

The U.S. Senate Select Committee on National Water Resources was to push the idea of seashores and lakeshores even further. In the report to the committee the NPS had urged legislation to effect a program of seashore and lakeshore preservation and use. The committee chair, Senator Robert S. Kerr, an Oklahoma Democrat, highlighted the need in his transmittal letter to the committee's report: "These [NPS recommendations] suggest that we should consider taking steps for the acquiring of 15 percent of our general ocean and major inland water shoreline; about 6 ½ percent are presently in Federal and State ownership for public recreation purposes along our Atlantic and Gulf coasts."[34] These were powerful arguments for an Apostle Islands lakeshore.

The Hartzog Era

To bring order into an increasingly complex and undifferentiated NPS, the new director, George B. Hartzog Jr., drafted a 1964 memorandum for Secretary of the Interior Stewart L. Udall's signature, instituting a new organizational framework. It was a major step in the evolution of the NPS. Hartzog's memorandum stated: "It is clear that Congress had included within the growing system, three different categories of areas—natural, historical and recreational. . . . A single board management concept encompassing these three categories of areas within the system is inadequate either for their proper preservation or for realization of their full potential for public use as embodied in the expressions of Congressional policy. Each of these categories requires a separate management concept and a separate set of management principles coordinated to form one organic management plan for the entire system."[35]

Lee noted the significance of this innovation: "The reorganization of 1964 prepared the way for Congress to replace the 1953 definition of the National Park System [which had related recreation areas to a category called "miscellaneous areas"] with a revised concept. For the first time it clearly and unequivocally established recreation areas as one of the three segments of the National Park System. Furthermore, it had the tremendous merit of differentiating recreation areas from natural areas. By this means, some of the earlier concern that identical policies might govern both natural and recreation areas was dissipated."[36]

Hartzog, in a 1985 interview with historian Kathleen Lidfors, reflected on how these changes were made:

Secretary Udall and Hartzog were forced into developing new policies for recreational areas because traditional NPS policies of no hunting and of the demand to acquire land in fee were great obstacles in establishing Ozarks, the first breakthrough in these kinds of areas. Ozarks residents responded to fee "taking" as originally proposed and the no-hunting policy by mobilizing the [International Association of Fish and Game Commissioners] against the NPS. There had been some previous skirmishes in Yosemite and Yellowstone, but they "bombed us on Ozarks." Ultimately a deal was worked out to allow hunting . . . and scenic easements were purchased in lieu of fee. The NPS had experimented with easements in Natchez Trace Parkway, but that approach was really worked out with Ozarks . . .

In response to "pressures" from the Bureau of [Outdoor] Recreation and the lessons of Ozarks, Hartzog looked for a workable management approach: "policies should recognize what each area was set up for, whether for natural, historical or recreational purposes. . . ." Hartzog liked the idea immediately. . . . He set up a task force to implement the new concepts but they dragged their feet and didn't come up with the results. One weekend Hartzog went home and drafted three sets of policies. . . . He got his division chiefs to review them, and the result was the Red Book, Green Book and Blue Book of NPS management policies.[37]

These three publications dealt with administration policies for natural, historical, and recreation areas.[38] The Apostle Islands and all the other national seashores and lakeshores then proposed would now become distinct elements in the National Park System. Between 1964 and 1972, twenty new recreation areas of four different types were added to the system: seashores, lakeshores (including the Apostle Islands National Lakeshore), reservoirs, and wild and scenic trails and scenic river ways (including the St. Croix–Namekagon and Wolf Rivers in Wisconsin).[39]

Outdoor Recreation Resources Review Commission

While Wirth and the NPS addressed seashores and Mission 66, at the expense of maintaining formerly strong relationships with states and local units of government, outdoor recreation problems were being felt across the nation. Federal recreation areas and state and municipal parks, many with facilities developed in the 1930s, were unable to handle the postwar increase in visitors. Additional recreational lands were needed to serve the nation's increasingly mobile and middle-class population. At the same time, cities were expanding without adequate land-use planning, and open spaces were rapidly disappearing.[40]

The Kerr Committee on National Water Resources highlighted a number of concerns regarding these circumstances, which it called a crisis in outdoor recreation, given a dramatic increase in visitors. In lieu of turning to the NPS for advice on burgeoning increases, Congress in 1958 established the Outdoor Recreation Resources Review Commission (ORRRC), chaired by Lawrence Rockefeller, to study this perceived national crisis.[41] Early in 1962 ORRRC reported to the president and Congress, supporting their recommendations with a 246-page summary report and twenty-seven study reports.[42]

One report, "Federal Agencies and Outdoor Recreation," reported that ten federal land- and water-managing agencies had major involvement with outdoor recreation, and that another eight had a "peripheral interest." As many as 450 million visitors came to federally managed, operated, or licensed facilities for recreational purposes; yet no federal agency had recreation as its primary mandate. As one official put it, "This thing is rolling over us."[43]

The ORRRC summary report constituted the most massive study of outdoor recreation ever conducted by the federal government. The recommendations were of significance to the Apostle Islands. First, and most importantly, the report called for a vastly expanded public outdoor recreation effort at all governmental levels. Second, it recognized water as a focal point of outdoor recreation. Third, it noted the economic benefits of outdoor recreation. Fourth, the report recommended immediate action on the part of federal, state, and local governments toward the acquisition of shoreline areas. Fifth, a new agency, the Bureau of Outdoor Recreation, was to be established by Congress to coordinate planning and to administer a new grants-in-aid program known as LAWCON (Land and Water Conservation Fund). The report also highlighted the need for access to the Great Lakes shoreline, where demand was great but public access scarce.[44] Shoreline needs, problems, and programs were discussed in a detailed appendix, which summarized each state's program. For Wisconsin, the report noted the unique biotic diversity of the Bad River Marshes but ignored the Apostle Islands completely.[45] The lack of state interest was obvious.

Although the appendixes were not formally approved by the Federal Outdoor Recreation Commission, they would influence public opinion and public policy. One appendix gave even greater credence to Great Lakes recreational needs. "Not one of the Great Lakes states ranks above the national average in federal recreation lands (relative to the total state area) and purchases by the federal government would have the advantageous result of spreading national facilities throughout the nation."[46] In its summary report, ORRRC recommended the establishment of a separate agency to coordinate federal agency recreation programs and to take the lead in national outdoor recreation planning. Although the NPS continued to argue that it should be the dominant recreation coordination and planning agency, three powerful individuals stood in its way: Secretary of the Interior Stewart Udall, Secretary of Agriculture Orville Freeman, and John Carver Jr., who had been appointed assistant secretary for public land management. Historians Fitch and Shanklin noted that "the odds against the Park Service had become prohibitive and . . . there could be no alternative to their somewhat grudging surrender."[47] A few months after the ORRRC report had been submitted, Udall established the Bureau of Outdoor Recreation (BOR) within the Department of the Interior and transferred the longstanding NPS responsibilities for the formulation of national outdoor recreation and coordination with the states to the new bureau.

The Bureau of Outdoor Recreation

Challenged by exciting new presidential and Interior secretarial leadership, the establishment of BOR, and proposals for a massive infusion of new funds through LAWCON, Congress began to respond. National seashores were authorized at Cape Cod, Massachusetts, in 1961, and at Point Reyes, California, and Padre Island, Texas, in 1962. Sleeping Bear Dunes, Indiana Dunes, Pictured Rocks, and the Ice Age National Scientific Reserve were also considered by Congress in 1962.[48] In no small measure, Udall was the motivating force behind this exciting new era in national parks development. Early in his administration he met nightly with his advisors to consider two items, the national parks and seashores and Native American affairs. His objective was to "double the acreage of the NPS in eight years."[49] He was well on his way to meeting that goal.

In May 1963, Congress passed legislation confirming the responsibilities of BOR. Although the act did not identify the bureau, the recreation authorities and functions enumerated were made the responsibility of the secretary of the Interior, who in turn delegated them to BOR.[50] Udall did permit the NPS to publish in 1964 a report titled *Parks for America*, which was in draft form at the time BOR was created. In the foreword he made it clear that the report represented only the views of NPS and did not necessarily reflect the views of BOR.[51] Nonetheless, the views and recommendations of the NPS would continue to carry weight and would be useful to proponents of a "national system" in the upper Great Lakes. In Wisconsin, the report urged the establishment of an Ice Age National Scientific Reserve as well as state action to protect Oak Island in the Apostles and the Bad River Marshes (reflecting a still limited planning vision for the Apostle Islands archipelago). Protection by the state of Wisconsin for recreational purposes was also urged for the Brule, Flambeau, Namekagon, St. Croix, and Wolf Rivers. The Namekagon, St. Croix, and Wolf Rivers would all later become part of a national river system.

Tucked away in the large Department of the Interior bureaucracy, with the responsibility of coordinating federal agencies, a new bureau could have been in a relatively weak position to meet its responsibilities. To deal with the potential weakness, President Kennedy formed a Recreation Advisory Council, composed of the secretaries of the Interior, Agriculture, Defense, Commerce, and Health, Education and Welfare and the administrator of the Housing and Home Finance Agency. The council was charged with coordinating federal outdoor recreation activities. The BOR would, in effect, serve as staff to the council.[52] Moreover, the director of BOR was appointed chairman of the staff of the Recreation Advisory Council, which in effect permitted him to act independently of the Interior secretary and increased his powers to influence coordination and planning functions.[53] The strong political base established by the NPS in the 1930s had eroded so badly that ORRRC and Udall easily set this new agency in place. Congress concurred. Instead of staffing BOR with NPS people, Udall selected a high-ranking official from the U.S. Forest Service, Edward P. Crafts, as director.[54] Crafts, in turn, did not go to the NPS when filling his top positions.[55]

The first policy decision of the Recreation Advisory Council was the adoption in 1963 of *Policy Circular No. 1*, which established criteria for new national recreation areas (including seashores and lakeshores).[56] In line with ORRRC recommendations, the circular envisioned a limited role for the federal government in the establishment of new recreation areas. States and local units of government were expected to meet most of the needs of the American people for outdoor recreation. National recreation areas were to be spacious, with a high recreation carrying capacity and with natural endowments greater than those normally associated with state projects, but less significant than the unique scenic and historic elements represented by the National Park System.[57] *Policy Circular No. 1* would later play a significant role as a major obstacle in obtaining Department of the Interior approval for the Apostle Islands National Lakeshore and other lakeshores on the Great Lakes.

These steps—the establishment of BOR, the Recreation Advisory Council, and LAWCON; the appointment of Edward Crafts; and the adoption of *Policy Circular No. 1*—would make an Apostle Islands National Lakeshore a real possibility. On the other hand, a new set of hurdles that would substantially slow lakeshore planning would now have to be cleared. Four years would pass after the adoption of *Policy Circular No. 1* before the Department of the Interior would formally endorse the lakeshore.

The Evolution of Conservation Programs in Wisconsin

The history of resource use in Wisconsin is similar to its history in other states and regions in the United States. The emphasis was on getting lands out of federal ownership and into private ownership and on seeing the wilderness tamed and replaced with farms, communities, villages, and cities. Utilitarianism and the exploitation of natural resources were the overarching themes of the settlement era of the 1850s through the turn of the century. In less than a century, the newcomers to the region accomplished just that. In the Apostle Islands region, the pace was somewhat slower due to a lack of good roads and the higher cost of transporting logs from the islands, but the devastation would eventually arrive.

The vast, rich forest regions of the state were attacked and subdued over a few short decades. Forest fires raged uncontrolled throughout the cutover (or logged) regions. Vast fortunes were made by a few timber barons. Immense heartache was felt by the settlers who followed the loggers under the public policy of "the plow follows the ax." Poorly informed, land-hungry early settlers found out the hard way that most of the soils of the cutover region were better suited for trees than farm crops. Farms failed. Millions of acres became tax delinquent and eventually reverted to county, state, and federal ownership.

Exploiting the Forests

In Wisconsin, concerns were expressed early on over the short-term exploitation and destruction of the forests, leading to a concern for conservation. As early as 1844 civil engineer Increase Lapham completed the first geographical overview of Wisconsin and called for a forestry program founded on scientific principles. A few years later Lapham began speaking publicly on the importance of protecting the forests while urging extensive reforestation efforts. In 1867 the Wisconsin Legislature created the Forestry Commission and requested Lapham further study the state of Wisconsin forestry.[58] The report detailed the terrible consequences of the uncontrolled destruction of Wisconsin's forests, particularly for the soils and waters. His report also noted that much of the northern part of the state, including the Apostle Islands region with its struggling farmers, was covered with soils unsuitable for any activity other than forestry.[59]

Lapham's report was the first of its kind in the nation. It had little effect on Wisconsin's forest policies, as the Wisconsin Legislature failed to heed Lapham's concerns. Progress continued to be defined in terms of economic growth; legislators saw more virtue in encouraging settlement and the development of agriculture in the northern region than in promoting forestry.[60] Amazingly, even an event as devastating as the Peshtigo Fire of 1871, which killed 1,500 people and burned more than a million acres in central Wisconsin, failed to raise serious questions about the "best" use of the cutover lands.[61]

Twenty years later, attitudes were beginning to change as Wisconsin historian Frederick Jackson Turner published his landmark essay on the closing of the American Frontier.[62] A new era of "rational" scientific resource management was developing in the nation, spurred in part by the recognition of the closing frontier. President Theodore Roosevelt and his chief forester, Gifford Pinchot, were beginning the fight to transform America's use of natural resources from exploitation to conservation. Preservation for intrinsic values such as scenic beauty or wilderness values was not a part of this management philosophy.[63] Pinchot brought this philosophy to Wisconsin and, in a significant speech to the Wisconsin Legislature, declared: "The heart of the conservation idea [is] that the resources which the earth affords for the use of man must be handled so as to secure the greatest good to the greatest number for the longest time; that needless destruction, waste or monopoly are both wrong, and foolish; and that the planned and orderly development of natural resources for the general welfare is the very essence of national common sense."[64] For over fifty years, Pinchot's theory of resource utilitarianism exerted a strong influence over Wisconsin's conservation policies and was still apparent in the debates of the 1950s and 1960s over the "best use" of the lands in the north and in the Apostle Islands region.

Conservation and the People

Out of early conservation concerns, the "rod and gun clubs" developed, stressing the use of fish and game for recreation and ensuring their prudent management. They successfully persuaded the Wisconsin Legislature to establish hunting and fishing licenses, seasons, and bag limits.[65]

John Muir, whose boyhood and youth had been spent on a Wisconsin farm and at the University of Wisconsin, left a deep imprint on the state's conservation history. In contrast to the practical, scientific approach of Lapham, Pinchot, and Edward Griffith (Wisconsin's first state forester), Muir wrote about the spiritual and ecological values of natural resources, in addition to an ideology of nature. He believed such an ideology would attract more people to enjoy natural environments, which, in turn, would lend support to park programs.[66]

Another important organization, the Wisconsin Federation of Women's Clubs, had a Standing Committee on Forestry Issues as early as 1904, which became the permanent Committee on Conservation in 1911. One historian notes that women's organizations, including the Wisconsin Federation, "stressed the feminine and spiritual qualities of nature and its importance for children and the intrinsic beauty and worth of wilderness forests, streams and wild animals."[67] Decades later the Wisconsin Federation became a formidable force in support of the Apostle Islands National Lakeshore.

The Izaak Walton League, established in 1922 at the national level, glorified both the frontier tradition and the wonders and virtues of nature. It became a leader in state fights for the protection of wildlife, forests, and public rights in navigable waters. The Wisconsin chapter of the league was a driving force behind the 1927 Wisconsin Conservation Act and would later provide valuable support for the lakeshore.[68]

Local conservation clubs developed rapidly in Wisconsin during the 1930s and 1940s, and in 1948 the Wisconsin Federation of Conservation Clubs formed. It attracted representatives from thirty clubs and claimed more than twenty-five thousand members. This federation later became another important voice in the drive for the protection of the Apostle Islands.[69]

The 1940s also gave birth to another highly influential conservation organization in Wisconsin, the Milwaukee County Conservation Alliance (MCCA). The MCCA formed from forty different county clubs representing interests ranging from butterfly collecting to bow hunting. It held a significant statewide influence.[70] In 1950, the MCCA was responsible for initiating discussion of an Apostle Islands "park," centering debate on the land's long-term public potential. Evolving as they did from the rod and gun clubs, these organizations largely focused on hunting and fishing issues without addressing broader conservation issues.

Finally, it is important to recognize the growing influence of newspapers in forming public opinion after the turn of the century. In Wisconsin, the *Milwaukee Journal* in particular took on the role of conservation advocate during the 1930s and continued this position for decades. Editorials often served to mediate environmental disputes. State officials were careful to both acknowledge the paper's position on an issue and to attempt to win an editor's favor. One writer, Gordon MacQuarrie, was particularly influential throughout his career as outdoor editor from 1936 until his death in 1956. His columns were noted as much for their interest in "ecological" issues as in the more traditional hunting and fishing stories.[71]

Wisconsin's Response to Conservation Problems

By the turn of the century, pressure was building for prudent resource management, which led to legislative interest in institutionalizing programs within state agencies. This resulted in a consolidation of all conservation activities and policy decisions involving fish, game, parks, forests, and law enforcement into one full-time, civil service agency. In 1915 a three-person Conservation Commission was appointed to direct the agency, but funding was minimal and the commission was plagued with political influence.[72]

To provide conservation programs with some insulation from politics and to achieve agency stability, the 1927 Wisconsin Conservation Act established a new Wisconsin Conservation Commission (WCC), made up of citizens who served part-time (and on an unsalaried basis). A full-time director ran the Wisconsin Conservation Department (WCD). By 1933, most natural resource decision making was removed from the Legislature and was delegated to the WCC and the WCD, which would become an agency staffed by professional resource managers.[73] The commission and its department were to remain the dominant force in state natural resource policies until 1958, when a new governor, Gaylord A. Nelson, challenged that monopoly.[74] To permit public involvement, the WCC in 1928 established a Citizen Advisory Council and in 1934 formalized it as the Wisconsin Conservation Congress.[75]

The early years of the Wisconsin Conservation Congress were turbulent. County representatives fought among themselves over resource issues. One participant commented years later, "Many Congress members were arbitrary and dogmatic in their views."[76] It would become fiercely protective of how hunting and fishing license dollars were used, raising a formidable challenge to the diversion of these funds for parks and strongly influenced the debate over a park in the Apostle Islands in the 1950s.

Forestry Programs Develop

In 1903 legislation was enacted that authorized the establishment of state forests. Under this law, counties were precluded from taking title to tax-delinquent lands.[77] In 1904, the State Forest Commission took a major step forward by hiring its first professional state forester, Edward Griffith. He organized and improved forestry operations, including tree nurseries, replanting, and fire protection. At this time, forestry was funded by legislative appropriations from hunting and fishing license fees. The limits of this source of funds proved to be a serious problem in later efforts to fund parks, including one in the Apostle Islands.[78]

Unfortunately, Griffith's efforts were cut short in 1915 when powerful interests, concerned about the loss of "agricultural" lands to reforestation efforts and Griffith's expansive state forestry programs, brought suit against the state over its forestry program. The Wisconsin Supreme Court agreed that the forestry program was unconstitutional. Wisconsin's budding forestry program was essentially dead, and Griffith resigned his position shortly thereafter.[79] Wisconsin lost the foresight Griffith had brought to the task.

Problems increased. By 1928 more than 4.5 million acres in twelve northern counties were tax delinquent, including lands in the Apostle Islands. The human suffering was enormous.[80] It was at this point that the problems of the cutover region and a renewed interest in forestry intersected. In 1927 voters ratified an amendment to the Wisconsin Constitution allowing the state to engage in forestry. The amendment also provided for a state property tax to permanently fund the program.

The private Forest Crop Law passed later in 1927.[81] This legislation was based on the concept that private investors would be willing to acquire tax delinquent lands and practice forestry. This law did not work, and there was a deepening crisis in the cutover region. State law was then changed to allow counties to add their tax delinquent lands into a public forest system with the counties as managers. To participate, the counties had to develop plans and zoning ordinances. The state provided technical assistance and financial aid. Today this 2.4 million-acre system is the largest public land base in the state.[82] In the Apostle Islands region, Ashland County eventually placed 32,000 acres into county forests; Bayfield County did the same with 167,000 acres. Some of these lands on the Bayfield Peninsula were, in fact, included in the initial discussions and boundaries for the lakeshore.

The Forest Crop Law and the Forestry Mill Tax Law were tightly worded. One of the legislative authors, William Aberg (a Madison attorney and conservationist), drafted a provision that stated that the mill tax could be used for no other purpose but forestry, and the terms were narrowly defined.[83] The clause would become a constant source of frustration to those looking for monies for the state's growing parks program and for state acquisition of the Apostle Islands.

The Ashland County Board and the town of La Pointe adopted zoning ordinances in 1934 and, with the exception of the unrestricted Madeline Island, zoned the balance of the Apostle Islands in Ashland County for private forestry and recreation. Buildings were limited to private summer cottages, service buildings, campgrounds, resorts, and structures associated with forestry, hunting, fishing, trapping, and mining. Harvest of wild crops such as berries and marsh hay was permitted. Permanent dwellings were prohibited. Bayfield County enacted a comparable ordinance for the four islands in that county.[84] There was no state or local interest in either a public forest or park in the region.

The 1920s also saw the establishment of the first national forests within Wisconsin. In 1924, in response to a state request, the Congress authorized the establishment of the Nicolet and Chequamegon National Forests in north central Wisconsin, which encompassed almost one and a half million acres.[85] Lastly, the 1920s witnessed the start of organized and comprehensive forest fire protection and suppression programs for Wisconsin's forests, which would demand increasing funding.[86]

While the 1950s proved unfortunate for Wisconsin's state parks, the state's forests benefited from a quiet but significant expansion in budgets as a result of property tax increases. A strong lobby on the part of forest product users helped ensure that forestry programs remained at the forefront of Conservation Department activities.[87]

In contrast, during the 1950s and into the 1960s, the parks system lost almost a third of its tiny budget.[88] While the WCC was contemplating shutting down some parks for lack of maintenance funds, it also added approximately 12,000 acres to the state's forest reserves.[89] It was a telling comment on the relative worth of forests and parks in the state of Wisconsin.

Forestry's Stepchild: Wisconsin's State Parks Programs

The concept of natural state parks was at least as old as the concept of forests. The first American state park was created in California in 1864 when Yosemite Valley was so designated (the land around it became a national park in 1890). In Wisconsin, the first state park was established in 1878 when a 50,000-acre parcel of land was acquired in Lincoln County for what one researcher described as a "northern state park." It met an ignoble fate two years later when the area was sold and promptly logged. Nevertheless, the idea of state parks persisted, and in 1900 land was acquired near St. Croix Falls for Wisconsin's first permanent park, Interstate State Park.[90]

In 1907, only a few years after the State Forest Commission came into being, the first State Park Board was established by an act of the Wisconsin Legislature. It immediately commissioned a study on parks, and in 1909 the well-known landscape architect John Nolen presented his report, *State Parks for Wisconsin*, to the board.[91] The Nolen Report noted that parks, in common with forest reserves, could serve an important function by preserving and protecting woodlands and stream flows (a conclusion similar to Lapham's on forest reserves some fifty years earlier). Nolen also argued that parks were the best form in which to preserve places of historical and scientific interest; as well as places of "uncommon and characteristic beauty," a function that forest reserves could not fulfill as most were destined for eventual logging. Parks would contribute economic benefits to the state by attracting tourists and tourist spending (an issue that resurfaced in the debate over the Apostle Islands in the 1950s and 1960s) and would also contribute a "necessity of modern life," physical and mental health, and a saner and happier life for Wisconsin's citizens.[92] The State Park Board took Nolen's suggestions to heart and established three of the four new parks recommended. The Wisconsin park system was supported by the Legislature in principle, but from the beginning it was severely underfunded.[93]

While forests and parks were seen as essentially complementary, it was easier to justify and fund state forests. The forest product industries were a powerful political force in Wisconsin and dominated the political process, affecting parks versus forest debates. Further, state forests would help pay for themselves. For example, a 1950s proposal to acquire Stockton Island in the Apostles as a state forest was to be funded through the sale of the island's timber. The state park system would remain dependent on irregular and inadequate legislative appropriations until the 1960s when Governor Gaylord Nelson approved a state park entrance fee and a tax on cigarettes, which earmarked substantial funds for parks. The records of the WCC during the 1940s and 1950s are a litany of constant and chronic pleading for regular park funding. The WCC and the Legislature, however, favored forestry, not parks.

In 1938 the WCC reached the end of its financial rope regarding parks. Its 1937–38 *Biennial Report* declared quietly but firmly:

> Monies for the support of the state parks have already been primarily provided from the conservation fund [derived from hunting and fishing license fees]. . . . It is timely to point out in this report, without going into too much detail, that one of the important concerns of the Department at the present time is to work out a more satisfactory and adequate method to finance the growing demands on the parks. . . . These conclusions are inescapable. More adequate funds are needed for . . . the state parks. . . . It is unfair and illogical for the state parks to be financed principally from the license fees of hunters and fishermen. . . . *The Conservation Department has been forced to the conclusion . . . that no new parks*

be established until a plan of more adequate financing may be worked out for the existing areas.[94]

Between 1938 and 1947 no new parks were established.[95] In no small measure this can be attributed to the fact that the WCD, dominated by forestry interests, did not help in organizing a parks lobby. Those concerned with parks, nature conservation, and aesthetics failed to organize themselves, leaving forest interests free to dominate the political process.

Almost three decades would pass from the time of the 1909 Nolen Plan before the Wisconsin State Planning Board, in conjunction with the WCD and the NPS, released its *Bulletin* number 8, "A Park, Parkway and Recreational Area Plan for Wisconsin," which outlined procedures for the development, maintenance, and operation of a proposed state recreational system. It suggested coordinating the use of state parks and forests, along with a system of county parks, roadside parks, and scenic parkways, to meet the state's recreational needs.[96] Significantly, it recommended that nine areas be investigated for addition to the parks system, including the Apostle Islands. The bulletin noted: "The Apostle Islands . . . possess extraordinary recreational aspects, which have been denied to many people desirous of visiting and enjoying them. Their physical separation from the Bayfield Peninsula may prove to be an insurmountable obstacle to their use by the public. However, the possibility of a state park on *one or more* of the islands should be thoroughly investigated."[97] The bulletin also recommended establishing a state historical site on Madeline Island (the site of Cadotte and Warren's trading post and the first Protestant mission in Wisconsin). Nothing came out of these recommendations. Although the report advised funding, there would be no fiscal relief until the 1960s.

In 1947 the State Parks Organic Act passed the Wisconsin Legislature. The law placed responsibility for park administration, protection, and maintenance squarely on the shoulders of the WCC, although "in each case the Commission would be guided by the professional or scientific groups which had the best knowledge of the intrinsic values of a particular site."[98] The new act and its policies established rigorous criteria for state parks.[99] The push during the 1950s for a state park in the Apostle Islands (as opposed to a forest or public hunting grounds) had considerable legal justification under this act. Many proponents argued that the Apostle Islands possessed considerable scenic, recreational, and historical values.

The establishment of clear lines of authority over Wisconsin's parks was helpful, but the 1947 act's most important contribution was to authorize regular and permanent (if modest) funding for the parks program. It really was no more than a patronizing pat on the back. The lion's share of this money still went to forestry, fish and game programs, and law enforcement.

Organizing constituent groups to support fish, game, and forestry programs had been relatively easy. Resource users had a direct stake in agency programs, and they were willing to either tax themselves through hunting and fishing licenses or to battle vigorously in the Legislature for state appropriations. The bureaus grew in size, staffing, budgets, and power. Parks, on the other hand, remained a stepchild for several reasons. First, park users were amorphous; they resided all over the state and many were nonresidents. They did not organize, as did the fish and game interests, through the statewide Conservation Congress. Further, the WCD made no effort to establish a similar organization to back a parks program. Second, visitors came to parks to see and to recreate; their use was nonconsumptive, in marked contrast to hunters and fishers, and especially to the direct and significant economic impacts of forest management. Although park proponents argued that tourists spend money, they could not make as persuasive a case as the other bureaus. It would not be until the 1960s that sophisticated studies on the favorable economic impacts of national parks would begin to influence legislative bodies.

A Decade of Struggle

The 1947 State Parks Organic Act had in a minuscule way increased parks funding. However, the budget was woefully inadequate to operate thirty-two state parks, which in 1950 totaled 18,043 acres and had received 3.3 million visitors. The 1950 annual budget to support this usage was $270,000, with a little additional income from park concessions, camping fees, and golf fees. As the Forest and Parks Division staff commented publicly, "This is still inadequate to meet public demands, and just how much should come from hunting and fishing license money is certainly debatable among the sportsmen of the state. . . . The public's desire for recreational opportunities has urged the establishment of new and expanded park areas. These, however, cannot be developed or maintained for full capacity use without adequate funds."[100]

In 1951 the Legislature reconsidered park funding. Some legislators felt that a proposal to use funding from the state general fund should be terminated. That would have posed a grave threat to the parks program. Fortunately, the majority voted in favor of retaining the dual funding system (using monies from both the conservation fund and the general fund). It even increased yearly appropriations from the general fund to $150,000, while the conservation fund appropriation increased to $220,000.[101]

Other sources of funding were explored, but with little success. In 1954 the Legislative Council Conservation Committee discussed the idea of using a new mill tax to support parks, as had been done with the forests in the 1930s. A mill tax, however, had failed to pass the Legislature during the previous session, largely due to opposition from the County Boards Association and the League of Municipalities. Committee members were not optimistic about another attempt. Senator Harvey Abraham commented at a public meeting, "Many people do not use the parks so therefore do not feel they should maintain them."[102]

In 1954 the Legislature considered a property tax to increase funding. Other options included park entry fees, modest sums from the highway fund, and a tax on soft drinks. They all failed to receive support.[103]

Attendance at state parks had increased by 250 percent since 1927 without a corresponding increase in funding.[104] The Conservation Commission in 1956, at the request of the Legislative Council Conservation Committee, released an insightful little brochure entitled *Wisconsin State Parks Going Downhill: WHY?* It concluded:

> However, the blunt and unvarnished truth is that our state parks have been steadily deteriorating. . . . In more than one state park today it has not been possible to provide minimum standards of sanitation, safety and police protection. Indeed a strong case can be made for the closing of some of the parks. . . . The Conservation Commission sincerely feels it is duty bound to report the state park situation as one of the most urgent conservation matters to face the Legislature in many years. Our state park program is at a decisive crossroad today; we must face up to the problem and the time is—NOW!!![105]

The brochure also contained rather dramatic figures: attendance from 1944 through 1956 had grown from 750,000 to more than five million, a 61 percent increase. Funding had grown only 3 percent. Wisconsin was spending a minuscule nine cents per state park visitor in contrast to substantially higher funding in other states. The Legislature still failed to act.

By 1957 the Wisconsin Conservation Commission was hearing increasingly from rod and gun clubs that they would be willing to support an increase in hunting and fishing license fees, but only if the funds were used for hunting and fishing programs. Funding for parks would not be tolerated.[106] Accordingly, the commission submitted a bill to increase license fees to the Legislature. It also decided to submit a bill to establish a one dollar park entrance car sticker. Although the Legislature's Joint Finance Committee was sympathetic with the Wisconsin Conservation Department's tiny parks budget, it held up the park sticker bill, fearful that it would turn tourists away.

Finally, in July, the State Assembly and the Senate voted on both the license fee increase and the park sticker proposal. The hunting and fishing fee increase passed both houses with two-thirds majorities. The park entrance sticker died.[107] State park programs had literally ended up with nothing. Although the Conservation Commission instructed Conservation Department Director Lester Voigt to inform the governor and the Legislature that parks were in desperate need of additional money, no action was taken to deal with the problem.[108] The department had managed to pick up a minuscule forty-five acres of land at a cost of $5,500 that year, eighteen of which had been donated. The attendance record for the state parks in 1958 was 5,491,874.[109]

In 1958 the WCC decided to take a different, if less direct, approach to the problem of financing parks. It approved funds for a travel-and-use study of the state's parks and forests to "pinpoint" areas needing improvement. The results would help shape future financing proposals for state parks.[110] It also decided to postpone any proposals for park financing until the following year. The WCC chair, Charles "Frosty" Smith, declared that an "aggressive program" had to be carried out to prevent the parks from deteriorating further. A lack of publicity on the parks situation, it was agreed, was partly to blame.[111]

In 1959 in the WCD's *Wisconsin Conservation Bulletin* summed up the problem by describing Wisconsin parks as slums, with inadequate thirty-year-old facilities.[112] Newly elected governor Gaylord Nelson decided to take matters in hand. He proposed a 1959–61 conservation budget increase from $25 million to $30.6 million. It failed to pass. Likewise a second attempt at a park sticker bill failed to pass; it would have provided almost half a million dollars for state parks. In spite of these budget woes, a special one-year appropriation of $80,000 was earmarked from the general fund for the acquisition of Blue Mounds State Park in southern Wisconsin.[113] The new governor had elected to throw his support behind the parks program; the results were slow in coming.

In the meantime, the WCC faced another fiscal crisis. Decreased revenue sources and increasing costs forced a $2 million budget cut. The WCD was suddenly in danger of going into the red.[114] The parks program was least able to stand a reduction in budget. However, encouraged by the governor's promise that the park sticker bill would be reintroduced and vigorously supported, the WCC reduced parks funding from the Conservation Fund by one-third.[115] Its optimism was unwarranted. In May the Legislature again failed to pass a parks sticker bill, which resulted in a severe crisis for the parks system.[116]

The WCC continued to favor a general park sticker admission fee rather than continued reliance on fish and game funds. Given the earlier lack of legislative support, Nelson was now less enthusiastic, feeling that a nonresident sticker might have a better chance of passing.[117] In 1961 it was agreed that the practice of funding parks from fish and game licenses would probably weather public opinion for another year.[118]

Because revenues were down, the Legislature adopted a significantly reduced WCD budget for 1961–63 and cut $1.4 million from the previous biennium.[119] Under the circumstances, it was clear that any attempt to improve budgets for parks would need to be postponed once again. As the decade ended, it was also clear that it had not been kind to the state parks and their supporters.

Charles Smith, the chair of the WCC, with a lofty statement late in 1949, had set the stage for the decade of the 1950s and 1960s: "One thing we must combat . . . is the conflict between different forces, commercial and selfish as well as unselfish. . . . We should preserve and conserve those natural resources God gave us for our children and grandchildren."[120] The statement was noble, but the decisions to be made regarding Wisconsin's natural resources were very much subject to economic and political forces and clashes of interests, and would be for some time to come.

CHAPTER 3

A New Era in Wisconsin

GAYLORD A. NELSON AND CONSERVATION

The 1958 election of Gaylord Nelson to the governorship marked a turning point in Wisconsin conservation and would be crucial for the fate of the Apostle Islands. Nelson was born in Polk County in northwestern Wisconsin. His parents were active in Progressive politics, and he would follow in their footsteps. After World War II, in which he served, and the demise of the Progressive Party, Nelson became active in Democratic Party politics. He was elected from Dane County to the state Senate in 1948, an office he held for ten years. Historian Thomas Huffman described Nelson as a person "considered both an intellectual liberal and a charming small town boy raconteur [who] personified the sophistication and subtlety of the new-style Wisconsin Democrat and developed these characteristics into an appearance that transcended partisan boundaries."[1]

Nelson, the first Democrat in the governor's office in more than a quarter of a century, brought to his new job a deep personal interest in conservation issues and natural resources management and a willingness to shake up entrenched bureaucratic complacency. It was Nelson and his staff who would take the debate over the protection and management of the Apostle Islands archipelago out of the state arena, advocating instead federal acquisition and designation. This was to be a dramatic shift not only in terms of the participants but also in the vision of what the islands could become. Nelson's fight for the Apostle Islands between 1960 and 1970 resulted in the protection of all but two of the twenty-two islands in the archipelago (Long Island was added in 1986). This was a significant departure from the five islands considered by the state in the 1950s for a state forest or the islands studied by the National Park Service in the 1930s. The preservation of an ecologically, culturally, and scenically unique area in the middle United States remains a significant Nelson legacy today.

Gaylord Nelson solidified Democratic power in 1958 by winning the governorship with 88,000 votes (54 percent) over Republican Vernon Thompson. In that same election, William Proxmire secured a seat in the U.S. Senate, taking 57 percent of the vote for the remaining one-year term of the late Senator Joe McCarthy. The majority in the State Assembly were now Democrats, the first time they had controlled either house since 1935. The Democrats also won two more congressional races while holding five of the state's ten seats, a major Democratic breakthrough.[2] The success in rebuilding the Democratic Party in large measure can be attributed to the efforts of Gaylord Nelson, John Reynolds,[3] William Proxmire, Patrick Lucey,[4] and Philleo Nash.[5] All would become lakeshore proponents.

Nelson Conservation Initiatives: 1958–1962

In the 1958 race for the governorship, conservation issues played a major role. Incumbent Republican governor Vernon Thompson paid scant heed to conservation matters during his two-year term, feeling comfortable that they were under the control of the party, and indeed they were. By exploiting this complacency, Nelson was able to develop a number of themes and charges in his critique of existing natural resource management policies. Part of his charges, according to Huffman,[6] included sharply partisan attacks that attracted media attention:

- "Twenty straight years of dry-rot Republican administration [had] left Wisconsin's fish, game and public parks programs helplessly behind the time."[7]
- "Wisconsin's conservation policy [was] largely dictated as if the state were running nothing more than a rich man's rod and gun club. . . . [The conservation commissioners] were wealthy men who have layman's interest in hunting and fishing, but a big businessman's interest in Republican politics."[8]
- The Wisconsin Conservation Commission should be abolished and a cabinet level governance system put in place.
- No long-range resources planning had been done. (The initial ideas for a Wisconsin Department of Resource Development, so important to the future Apostle Islands National Lakeshore, were being planted.)
- "Republican conservation was turning Wisconsin into a have-not-state,

forcing it to lag far behind its neighbors Michigan and Minnesota in parks and outdoor policy."[9]

These changes developed the base from which Nelson was later able to move toward establishing the lakeshore.

Although these charges were vigorously denied by the Wisconsin Conservation Commission and the Wisconsin Conservation Department, as well as by the incumbent governor, the charges held a broad appeal for Wisconsin voters, especially the large numbers of hunters and anglers.

Nelson offered new conservation programs with broad appeal. As Huffman explains, "This new theme was state-sponsored natural resources planning, strengthened environmental emphasis in the field of regional planning, in land and water zoning and recreation management in response to population growth." Nelson was appealing not only to the traditional rural Wisconsin conservationist but to voters in the sprawling urban areas of the state as well.[10]

Once in the governor's seat, Nelson and his young and energetic staff, called the "Crew Cuts" by the press because of the way they wore their hair, embarked on an ambitious conservation program based on the rhetoric of the campaign.[11] With new energy and no historical bureaucratic ties or loyalties, they had the opportunity to create significant change. They faced a Conservation Commission that was strongly Republican and a Conservation Department that would resist most of Nelson's initiatives.

To bring Wisconsin into the "modern age" Nelson proposed a massive reorganization of the seventy-nine uncoordinated agencies then in existence, including the WCC, over which governors had little or no direct control. The proposal failed because the political and bureaucratic forces behind this agency morass were simply too powerful.[12]

A second major reorganization proposal would give the governor more influence over the WCC. In addition, Nelson proposed some 250 amendments to the 50 Wisconsin statutes relating to conservation. These proposals caused intense public and legislative debate. The conservation institutions in Wisconsin (the WCC and the WCD, the pulp and paper industry, and the press, especially the *Milwaukee Journal*) came out in vigorous opposition. Although the Democratic-controlled State Assembly passed the bill, it lost on a party vote in the Republican-controlled Senate.[13]

Nelson had planted the seeds for what became the Wisconsin Department of Resource Development (DRD) in his 1957 campaign. A policy paper, written by University of Wisconsin law professor Jacob Beuscher and Nelson campaign advisor David Carley, called for a new department to integrate planning for economic development, natural resources, regional land-use planning, and urbanization. Beuscher said, "This horizontal agency, operating on a broad functional front could integrate these things."[14]

The proposals again stimulated vigorous debate. Predictably, the WCC and the WCD vigorously opposed the DRD as a major infringement into their areas of responsibility. After a fractious debate in the state Senate dealing more with the power of existing agencies than with substantive resource issues, the bill passed.

David Carley, then a thirty-one-year-old PhD candidate in political science at the University of Wisconsin–Madison (and vigorous campaigner for Nelson), was picked to head the Wisconsin Department of Resource Development and was the author and catalytic agent behind many of Nelson's planning programs.

The DRD brought together the Division of Industrial Development from the governor's office and the almost-defunct Division of State Planning (that several decades earlier had completed plans for public acquisition of some of the Apostle Islands). Major new functions were added to the agency's charge to undertake comprehensive planning, including recreation, resource, land use, and transportation planning. The authorizing act also provided for the appointment of a "recreation specialist" for resources planning and assistance to the tourism industry.[15] No wonder the WCD was worried. To assist these efforts, and after an extensive career with the WCD, I joined the DRD in 1960 as a field biologist and federal aid coordinator (I also had a crew cut). I eventually served as the director for eight months during the 1962 campaign year and finally as deputy director of the DRD. I became a key player in developing a lakeshore proposal.

Using state dollars and federal funds available under Section 701 of Title VII of the 1954 Housing Act, Carley and Nelson began to build an agency and to sell the idea of state and substate multicounty regional planning to the people of Wisconsin. Planners placed a strong emphasis on natural resources planning, which had significant influence on the Apostle Islands. With a strengthened and revised state law on regional planning, these efforts paid off. When Nelson left for the U.S. Senate in 1963, regional planning commissions were in place in the economically depressed resource region of northwestern Wisconsin, the urbanizing metropolitan region surrounding Milwaukee, Brown County (Green Bay), and the Wolf River Basin in the northeast portion of the state. The seeds of "regionalism," planted by Nelson and the DRD, would eventually result in most of Wisconsin being blanketed by planning commissions. Regional planning commissions also broadened the DRD sphere of influence statewide as the agency had influence over federal and state funding to support them.[16]

In spite of the resistance to Nelson's initiatives, in his first term he included substantial increases for the WCD budget. Also, under the direction of the DRD, the first systematic studies of the Wisconsin tourism industry were initiated at the University of Wisconsin–Madison School of Commerce by Professor I. V. Fine.[17]

In his first two years as governor, Nelson created an environment that stimulated and encouraged a new generation of ideas and approaches to issues in need of immediate attention, as well as those on the horizon. Nelson had an open-door policy, and influential citizens were called upon for advice. His interest in and love for conservation was contagious. Moreover, he was willing to take political risks.[18]

During his 1960 gubernatorial campaign, Nelson emphasized his record in conservation and promised more if re-elected—more parks, a massive new outdoor recreation program, strengthened lake classification and lake access programs, and more investments benefiting the tourism industry. He again indicated that he would reorganize the WCC and take it out of the control of rich Republicans.

In October of 1960 Nelson released the preliminary results of Professor Fine's studies (known as the Fine Study) on tourism. They documented the importance of recreation and tourism to the state's economy and the importance of maintaining the state's natural resources and scenic quality as a means of enhancing that economic importance.[19]

Although the WCC used its allies to counter Nelson's changes by appealing to its traditional political base (the hunters and anglers and the forest products industry), Nelson was appealing to a much broader bipartisan group of Wisconsin citizens. In the 1960 election, the conservative Republican candidate for governor lost to Nelson by approximately 50,000 votes, but the Democrats lost control of the Assembly. In spite of a lower margin of victory, the election was a considerable triumph for Nelson: "conservation was critical to his re-election; . . . [it formed] a non-partisan conservation coalition which would serve him as an electoral power base for years to come."[20] The victory ensured that Nelson's conservation initiatives would accelerate during the next two years. Many of these initiatives would strongly influence the Apostle Islands.

Not all of Nelson's initiatives succeeded. He would fail again to reorganize the Wisconsin Conservation Commission, and despite the fact that he had several appointees on the WCC, real control would continue to rest with the two savvy carry-over Republicans, Charles "Frosty" Smith and Guido Rahr, as well as Conservation Department Director Lester Voigt, who had now for eight years adroitly managed the department and had strong support from the commission.

In spite of the broad charges given the DRD, another statutory body, the Natural Resources Committee of State Agencies (NRCSA), had the potential to give Nelson problems. The NRCSA consisted of the WCD and five other agencies. Governors statutorily chaired the NRCSA, but they seldom attended meetings. The vice chair, elected by the NRCSA members, normally set the agenda and ran the meetings. The NRCSA had neither staff nor a budget. It published excellent reports on the state's natural resources, dealt with obvious needs for coordination, and each biennium recommended new laws to the Legislature. The NRSCA seldom tackled controversial conservation issues or tough inter-agency coordination questions. In spite of the NRSCA's inherent weaknesses, the WCD used the NRCSA effectively to support and advance its programs and to thwart the DRD initiatives. Nelson was determined during his second term to make the NRCSA more responsive to his policy goals.

As chairman, Nelson requested that the NRCSA appoint me as secretary. NRCSA members agreed, and I was placed in the single most important NRCSA post, where I could influence its direction. Nelson could now influence conservation policy through the NRCSA and the DRD. However, influencing the WCC was another matter. In spite of the fact that Nelson and I met with his appointees to the commission to outline Nelson's need for their support, they would support only those issues that would not directly challenge their agency's powers.

The establishment of an entrance sticker for state parks (priced at two dollars annually or fifty cents per day) to fund the malnourished state parks program and a statutory requirement that the WCD develop long-range plans were two significant bills passed under Nelson's leadership, in spite of opposition.

In February 1962 the first phase of the state's comprehensive plan, developed by the DRD, was unveiled in a day-long conference on the University of Wisconsin–Madison campus. This was widely attended by press, faculty, state government agency heads, and environmentalists. A key element was placing outdoor recreation in a much broader context than that of the traditional approach of the WCD. The purposes, in brief, were "to maximize social values which included those intangibles which we associate with outdoor recreation, and to maximize the economic value of recreation."[21] I had directed these studies.

As a result of these planning activities, and because a recreation plan was in hand, Wisconsin was the first state in the nation to receive a matching grant from the federal government for urban open space. The Federal Housing and Home Finance Agency followed this with another large grant to the DRD for state planning purposes, including recreation planning. Federal officials said Wisconsin had "the broadest planning and development program ever undertaken by any state. . . . Wisconsin, always a leader in social and economic movements, is now leading the way toward new concepts in shaping the future of cities, metropolitan areas, and entire regions."[22]

Nelson took yet another step to broaden and increase his influence statewide. He appointed an advisory committee to the DRD and called the first meeting. Consisting of three university professors, the director of the Wisconsin Geological and Natural History Survey, influential conservationists, and leaders from the business and tourism community, this advisory committee would help counter some of the strength of the WCC. Moreover, Nelson had in this committee a sounding board for his new initiatives and a source for new ideas and fresh approaches to old conservation issues.[23]

By far the most dramatic Nelson initiative during his second term was contained in his special "Resource Development Message" to the Joint Session of the Legislature on March 15, 1961. The program, later known as the Outdoor Recreation Act Program (ORAP), called for a one-cent-per-package tax on cigarettes to fund a $50 million expenditure over a ten-year period. This expenditure would pay for tourist information centers, the construction of new lakes in southwestern Wisconsin as a part of the Federal Small Watersheds Program, conservation youth camps, new parks, fish and wildlife projects, a greatly expanded program of conservation easements to protect beauty along the state's scenic highways, and open-space grants-in-aid to the largest metropolitan areas. Of this sum, $33 million was earmarked for parks, including a ring of new parks around the metropolitan Milwaukee region. Other parks were planned around the new interstate highway system to make significant outdoor resources available to the public and to meet the overnight camping needs of the traveling tourist.[24] Funds also went toward the Lake Superior South Shore Studies. Nelson barnstormed the state selling his proposals. The plan attracted national attention.

ORAP passed easily in the Assembly on a vote of eighty-seven to six. The Senate, however, stalled the measure for months. The Republicans were reluctant to pass a program for which a Democratic governor would take credit and that might influence his anticipated race for the U.S. Senate. When the state Senate finally acted, and much to the surprise of the Republicans, four former Progressives (now Republicans) voted for ORAP, giving it a one-vote majority.[25]

Much to the chagrin of the WCC and the WCD, and in spite of heated opposition on the floor of the Senate, Nelson successfully established a Recreation Committee to guide the ORAP. The Recreation Committee consisted of the chairs of the departments responsible for program implementation: the Highway Commission, the Soil and Water Conservation Committee, the Conservation Department, the Welfare Department, and myself as the recreational specialist in the DRD. The committee, the majority of whose members were Nelson appointees, was chaired by the governor and was responsible for guiding the program through outdoor recreation planning, managing program expenditures, preparing biennial budgets, controlling appointments of additional staff, and reallocating unexpended funds.[26] The Recreation Committee assigned the planning responsibility to the DRD. Through these moves and through his earlier actions, Nelson broke the almost complete monopoly of the WCC, the WCD, and the conservatives in the state Senate over state conservation policy. Moreover, a new flow of funds to DRD permitted staff increases. Slowly the Resource Development Department increased its capacity vis-à-vis the Conservation Department.

ORAP drew upon existing plans of the WCD and provided for the acquisition of 20,000 acres of fish, game, and forest lands. Also included were several public access points to lakes, including a site at Little Sand Bay on Lake Superior within the Red Cliff Reservation near the Apostle Islands. As a state forest had already been established on three of the Apostle Islands, there were no new plans for the acquisition of other islands. The concept of a national lakeshore would develop independently of ORAP. ORAP also appropriated funds to study the proposal for a South Shore Scenic Drive. The road had substantial support from Democrats in the north, especially from the city of Superior. The twenty-two-mile scenic highway along the lake from Superior to the wild and remote Brule River in Douglas County would tie in with the "Great Circle" Route around Lake Superior. Tourism impacts would be substantial. There were, however, major problems with the proposal. The proposed right-of-way traversed highly "erodible" red clay soils; streams and deep ravines would need bridging; and the scenic mouth of the Brule River, where it empties into Lake Superior, would be dramatically altered. Nelson now needed a study that would temporarily appease road supporters and would identify alternatives for capitalizing on the scenic qualities of the region in lieu of a new road.

A $50,000 appropriation for this study was to include a regional analysis of outdoor recreation, open space, scenic beauty, and harbors of refuge. It would also include an analysis of necessary improvements to existing State Highway 13 to capitalize on the area's scenic beauty, especially in Bayfield County (even though it traversed an area south of Lake Superior). Nelson also emphasized that the study would provide direction for the long-term economic development of the region through outdoor recreation and tourism. The funds were allocated by the Recreation Committee to the DRD, permitting the hire of a veteran employee from the Conservation Department, Ralph B. Hovind, to handle the analysis of public outdoor recreation demand, and Philip H. Lewis, a regional landscape architect, to study the recreation resources. Hovind and Lewis hired staff to develop their plans. Faculty from the University of Wisconsin were also engaged to initiate the South Shore Studies.

The momentum continued into 1962, although the Conservation Commission, upset with DRD's incursions into their turf, attempted to slow it by lobbying a bill through the Legislature weakening the Recreation Committee. Nelson vetoed it; his veto was sustained.[27]

With a sympathetic Democratic administration in Washington, Nelson and Carley were able to keep federal dollars coming to the DRD.[28] Nelson also turned around what could have been serious political problems for himself in northern and central Wisconsin. In brief, the WCC and the WCD, after two years of fractious debate with the twenty-seven counties owning county forest crop lands, had successfully lobbied a bill through the Legislature that would have effectively terminated the state-county partnership. At stake were 2.3 million acres of public forests. Nelson vetoed the bill, and the veto was sustained by one vote in the Assembly.

Nelson immediately appointed a bipartisan advisory committee (the Forest Crop Advisory Committee) to develop a new program. In an election year, deadlines were tight. Nelson wanted to be in a proactive position on the issue in the upcoming election. This advisory committee, which I cochaired, completed its work in August 1962 and published its report. The recommendations called for substantially increased state financial aid to county forests and a new method of sharing income from forest products sales. All told the counties benefited substantially, yet the forests would remain state-county partnerships and in public ownership.[29] Nelson immediately endorsed the proposals (which did become law) and used them effectively in the campaign, especially in the north.[30] One of Nelson's most significant conservation achievements as governor was in making this state-county partnership permanent.

In May 1962, as a capstone to his conservation programs, Nelson proposed to Stewart Udall (secretary of the U.S. Department of the Interior) a "national shoreline recreation area" in the Kakagon–Bad River Sloughs within the Bad River Indian Reservation, adjacent to the Apostle Islands. The initial steps were being taken toward an Apostle Islands National Lakeshore.

Conservation and the 1962 Political Campaign

When, on May 28, 1962, Nelson announced his intention to run for the U.S. Senate against the eighty-year-old, three-term incumbent senator Alexander Wiley, he was able to list fourteen major studies in the conservation field initiated under his administration, a host of new conservation laws, and the implementation of ORAP, which he viewed as his most significant achievement. He skillfully hammered on these substantial accomplishments during the 1962 campaign.

To lend support to the campaign Nelson used the DRD's preliminary south shore report entitled *The Recreation Potential of the Lake Superior South Shore Area*.[31] The report skillfully tied the protection of natural resources and scenic beauty to the existing and potential economic impact of commercial tourism for the region. It stressed the beauty of the Apostle Islands and noted Nelson's proposed national recreation area. Twenty-two recommendations were made for developing the recreation potential of the south shore area, including utilizing the cultural and ethnic values of the Red Cliff and Bad River Tribes' reservations. In lieu of a scenic road access from rural roads, scenic drives were proposed from the city of Superior to the mouth of the Brule River. Overall, Nelson found the report useful in his campaign travels into northern Wisconsin.

To highlight his accomplishments and to point to the future, Nelson called a conference entitled "The Unfinished Task," to be held in Madison only days before the election. My staff combed over every mailing list in our possession. All major conservation organizations in the state were invited; more than 139 people attended. Secretary Udall was the keynote speaker. DRD was able to once again bring to the attention of the attendees and indeed the entire state (media coverage was extensive) the Nelson conservation accomplishments of the past four years and to address future opportunities, including in the Lake Superior and Apostle Islands region. Out of the conference came the Wisconsin Council for Resource Development and Conservation, or more popularly, the People's Lobby, to serve the cause of conservation.[32] Martin Hanson, a notable northern conservationist and Nelson supporter, was elected secretary.[33] The People's Lobby would become a significant force for the lakeshore in the years ahead.

The 1962 elections would prove significant for the lakeshore. Attorney General John Reynolds, a Democrat, campaigned for the governorship on a broad conservation plank that included the Nelson initiatives. Reynolds squeaked by Phillip Kuehn by a mere 12,000 votes. Carley, who was one of Nelson's most prominent advisors and who campaigned on the Nelson and DRD programs, lost the race for lieutenant governor to Jack Olson, also by 12,000 votes. In the northern congressional district that included the Apostle Islands, J. Louis Hanson of Mellen, a personal friend of Nelson and Martin Hanson's brother, lost in his race against long-term incumbent congressman Alvin E. O'Konski.[34] In contrast, in his Senate race Nelson won over Wiley handily, garnering 53 percent of the vote. The importance of the "conservation vote" is clear: in the twenty-seven northern and central Wisconsin counties, Nelson outpolled all the other major candidates in total votes. The election broadened and strengthened Nelson's bipartisan conservation coalition that would stand him in good stead in the years ahead as he worked toward establishing a lakeshore.[35]

Gaylord Nelson was leaving for Washington, but he was leaving behind a marvelous set of agencies, organizations, and conservation leadership that would serve his political needs and that would maintain and enlarge his conservation initiatives as governor.

South Twin Island fisherman Charlie Benson presenting President Calvin Coolidge with a box of lake trout, Devils Island in 1928. (National Park Service, APIS neg. 1477-4)

Several of Sand Island's pioneers engaged in subsistence agriculture during
the first four decades of the early twentieth century. Here, in a photograph
from the 1910s, a group of men stack hay on either the Louis Moe or Bertrand
Noreng farm; the two women are probably bringing lunch or coffee to the men.
(National Park Service, APIS neg. 1207-20)

Thirteen students and their teacher pose in front of the Sand Island schoolhouse, circa 1910. The permanent population of Sand Island was sufficiently large to support the school, which served grades one through eight, from 1910 to 1928. (photograph by Emmanuel Luick, Pioneer Gallery, Iron River, Wisconsin, courtesy of Apostle Islands National Lakeshore)

Magnus and Anna Palm and their five children stand in front of their two-room log cabin in 1913, one year after the family established a homestead on Sand Island. Poor health and difficult agricultural conditions forced the family to depart the island during the 1920s. (photograph by Emmanuel Luick, Pioneer Gallery, Iron River, Wisconsin, courtesy of Apostle Islands National Lakeshore)

Wharf, Outer Island, circa 1930. (National Park Service, APIS neg. 1142)

Logs ready for rafting to Ashland, Wisconsin, circa 1930. (National Park Service, APIS neg. 1144)

Four adults and a child pose at an unknown Apostle Islands location. A gasoline-powered boat that transported passengers, supplies, and fish is in the background, while several Mackinaw fishing boats with sails are moored in the foreground. A net reel is at the far left. (courtesy of Apostle Islands National Lakeshore)

Moe's Dock at East Bay on Sand Island, sometime before 1940. To the left is the *Bobbie*, a fish tug owned by William Noreng; immediately behind the *Bobbie* is Carl Dahl's fishing boat, the *Freddie D*. (courtesy of Apostle Islands National Lakeshore)

A group of workers stand in the quarry operated by the Excelsior Brownstone Company on Hermit Island between 1891 and 1897. All quarrying ended on the island in 1897 when the company declared bankruptcy. (National Park Service, APIS neg. D6a [5])

PART TWO

Establishing the Apostle Islands National Lakeshore

CHAPTER 4

The 1960s Road to a Lakeshore

THE DECADE OF PLANNING, BUREAUCRATIC OBFUSCATION, AND POLITICS

Both federal and state governments flirted with the idea of creating some form of park in the Apostle Islands for some time before truly coming to grips with the concept in the 1960s. The debates of the previous decades, however, set the stage for renewed interest during the 1960s in preserving the Apostle Islands. This interest focused both through the era's emerging federal and state leadership in the conservation arena and the election in 1958 of a Wisconsin governor, Gaylord Nelson, with an explicit conservation-based agenda for the state. These serendipitous circumstances set the stage for a renewed, and ultimately successful, push to establish a distinctly 1960s version of an Apostle Islands National Lakeshore.

Early Interest in a Park

As early as 1891, the *Ashland Daily Press* proposed a national park for the Apostle Islands.[1] However, it was not until the late 1920s that local groups, pressed by economic need, organized to promote the establishment of a park. The economic picture was grim throughout the Apostle Islands region. The last sawmill had shut down in 1924, as had the Ashland blast furnace. The luxury railroad hotels in Bayfield and Ashland were being torn down, and few tourists in automobiles made their way as far north as the peninsula. This local economic decline would only be intensified by the onset of the Great Depression in the 1930s.

Given the region's relatively long history of tourism, it was logical that the business community would turn to the recreational potential of the islands and peninsula for future economic development. Little or no consideration was given to aesthetics, the potential for outdoor recreation, or the preservation of the islands' resources. During 1927 and 1928, a series of local organizations formed to promote the Chequamegon Bay and south shore area. A bill "[t]o authorize investigation and report on proposed Apostle Islands National Park" was introduced in the House of Representatives on January 17, 1930. The bill was signed into law on May 9, 1930, and Harlan P. Kelsey, a Boston landscape architect whose abilities were apparently known and trusted by the National Park Service, was appointed to review the area.[2] Although Kelsey remarked on the sandstone formations and the scenic qualities of the islands, the tone of his report is dominated by horror at the effects of logging: "What must have been once a far more striking and characteristic landscape of dark coniferous original forest growth has been obliterated by the axe followed by fire. The ecological conditions have been so violently disturbed that probably never could they be more than remotely reproduced."[3] This ended the first investigation.

In August of 1931 Arno Cammerer, the associate director of the NPS, traveled to Bayfield to personally investigate the Apostle Islands. At the banquet concluding his two-day tour, Cammerer explained to the group of park promoters that "the cutover character of the land was an insurmountable obstacle to its being considered for a national park."[4] Genuinely impressed with the scenic qualities and recreational potential of the region, however, Cammerer urged the local committee to work toward establishing a state park "which would be second to none in the country."

Before Cammerer closed the files on the Apostle Islands project, he contacted Herbert Evison, secretary of the National Conference on State Parks, to point out the area's potential as a state park. His words were prophetic: "This area holds marvelous recreational possibilities for the future, and in time will come into its own."[5] It is almost certain, given the urging of the NPS to proceed, that had the Legislature authorized a state park at Apostle Islands, full support would have been forthcoming from the NPS Midwest Region (Region Five) of the Branch of Planning and State Cooperation. Again the record indicates that there was little sustained local support for the idea, and no bill came forward.

It is not clear why in 1935 the NPS Region Five of the Branch of Planning and State Cooperation again investigated the Apostle Islands for a national park. Perhaps, as a courtesy to the state of Wisconsin, the Department of the Interior forwarded a report to the NPS for action, despite a stated opinion by Secretary Ickes that the matter was closed. Or the Apostle Islands may have been re-examined in the context of the mid-1930s national seashore studies, which were conducted through the state offices. Ickes's emphasis on recreation and ocean shorelines would suggest that this is the case.

The perceptions of G. M. Lamb, an NPS official who inspected the area in 1936, differed from those of Kelsey and Acting Interior Director Cammerer. Lamb found the surfaces of the Apostle Islands generally uninteresting because of their low topography and lack of streams. Although his descriptions suggested that the forest cover was inferior, he did not treat the effects of logging as a major factor in his recommendations except to say that if a national park were established, logging must stop. Lamb was primarily concerned with the recreational potential of the area. For him the chief attraction was the shoreline: "From the water [the islands] are intensely scenic and a boat trip among [them] is delightful as well as instructive." Lamb acknowledged that the islands "might be suitable for recommendation as a national park" and even claimed that "probably no similar area may be found in the United States."[6] Despite this finding, in 1936 NPS Director Conrad Wirth placed a memo in the files that put the Apostle Islands National Park issue to rest for another twenty-five years.[7] Local promoters had turned their attention to other projects. Local discouragement with park projects was reflected in the final entries of Lamb's report to the NPS: "Local attitude: Passive. Persons interested: Don't know."[8] In spite of this negative conclusion, the state continued to study the islands, and in 1939 a statewide recreation study recommended that a state park be established in the Apostles. As this was only a recommendation, no action was taken by the Wisconsin Conservation Department, and the matter was dropped for more than decade when state planners would once again examine the area for potential as a park.[9] Again the issue went nowhere and essentially went dormant until its revival in the early 1960s under Governor Gaylord Nelson.

New Beginnings in the 1960s

In spite of the fact that President John F. Kennedy would visit the Apostle Islands in 1962 and give a splendid speech to an assembly of 10,000 northern Wisconsin residents, implying his approval for a national lakeshore, it would not be until 1967 that a new president, Lyndon Baines Johnson, actually approved the proposal. As the following discussion demonstrates, the wheels of politics and bureaucracy grind slowly. The following pages trace the struggle to achieve consensus within the U.S. Department of the Interior and its many bureaus on a bill that would integrate both the national need to preserve outdoor recreational resources and the hopes and needs of the northern Wisconsin Native Americans, the Red Cliff and Bad River Tribes. In that struggle it was critical to minimize or avoid any conflict with the WCD (which had repeatedly asserted their interests in the region), while at the same time exploiting every possible source of support for a national lakeshore in the Apostles. This included using newspapers, television, and radio to create a favorable public support structure for an eventual proposal.

We turn first to the arguments Gaylord Nelson used to legitimize his interests and goals within the minds of the public as well as within the cultures of the various federal and state bureaucracies that would concern themselves with an Apostle Islands National Lakeshore. At stake was the need to convince all parties that the Apostles were worthy of a national-level proposal and deserving of thoughtful support. At several points in the debate the proposal could have easily been derailed, but an underlying belief, an almost intuitive feeling, infused the minds and emotions of key participants that the intrinsic values of this unique archipelago and the surrounding mainland were worthy of protection for future generations.

Nelson's Island Efforts

Governor Nelson had appointed the Department of Resource Development (DRD), in lieu of the Wisconsin Conservation Department, as liaison with the Federal Outdoor Recreation Resources Review Commission (thereby creating some consternation with the WCD!). Since I was the deputy director of the DRD, I was poised to become acquainted with major outdoor recreation policy makers at the federal level who were developing new national initiatives. Of special interest were the proposed new national seashores at Cape Cod (Massachusetts), Fire Island (New York), Point Reyes (California), and Sleeping Bear Dunes and Picture Rocks National Lakeshores (Michigan). Bills then under consideration in Congress were carefully analyzed to determine if they would set a precedent for Wisconsin, and especially for the Lake Superior region.

In the spring of 1961, on an Outdoor Recreation Act Program speaking tour in northern Wisconsin, Governor Nelson, David Carley (director of the DRD), and I met and stayed with brothers Martin and Louis Hanson at their forest lodge on Beaver Dam Lake near Mellen in Ashland County. We also visited the top of Mt. Whittlesey, one of the highest points in the state, which had possibilities as a state park and was potentially a site for a splendid ski hill. Both the Apostle Islands proposal and the state park proposal would have a significant economic impact on Mellen and the surrounding area. After a fa-vorable consultant's study was completed, the Hansons, along with represen-tatives of the Northern Five County Development Group, came to Madison to meet with the governor to secure state assistance on the development of Mt. Whittlesey.

As U.S. Steel, the company that owned Mt. Whittlesey, was unwilling to either sell or lease the land, this proposal was dropped. Instead, I made the sug-gestion that the group consider exploring, in conjunction with the Bad River Band of Lake Superior Chippewa Tribe, the potential economic implications of a national lakeshore in the Kakagon–Bad River Sloughs and the Chequa-megon Point portion of their reservation (adjacent to the Apostle Islands). The area had significant natural resources, scenic beauty, and fish and wildlife. A national lakeshore would not only protect these resources but would attract significant numbers of tourists and related economic benefits to the region. Native Americans on other reservations were beginning to see the positive benefits of developing their recreational resources. For example, the White Mountain Apaches in Arizona had successfully developed public recreation on their reservation, attracting 600,000 visitors annually.[10] The positive implica-tions for the Bad River Tribe were obvious. Colored, ten-foot-high maps pre-pared by Phil Lewis of the DRD were on display in the basement of the State Capitol Building and helped to make the point about the beauty of the region.

I also discussed the possibility of including some of the nearby Apostle Islands in the study but did not present the potential of the Bayfield Peninsula at this time. After discussion, the group dropped the idea of including the islands. Because of the lack of any kind of local public understanding and support, and with the certainty that the WCD would oppose any proposal in-volving "their" islands, initial discussions focused on the Kakagon–Bad River Sloughs and the sand spit.

Later, the Hanson brothers discussed the matter with Nelson while he was on another visit to Ashland and provided him with a copy of the Park Ser-vice's Great Lakes Studies, which identified the Kakagon–Bad River Sloughs as potentially of national significance. Nelson advised them to see what the Native Americans thought about it.

Martin Hanson and Bud Peters, as representatives of the Five County De-velopment Group, then met at Bad River.[11] Hanson described the meeting: "It was a Tribal Council Meeting. Donald Ames was Chairman and we met . . . at Muskrat Hall, which was built by the Mormons [in the old village of Oda-nah] and the chief people as far as I was concerned were George Ackley, Fred Connors, Albert Whitebird, and Donald Ames. . . . They passed a resolution in favor of making a recreation area out of the Bad River Sloughs . . . which were part of the ORRRC report where the report recommendations [indicating the sloughs] were a unique area."[12]

Louis Hanson also recalled the events:

> About the same time [as Nelson's first visit to the Hanson estate], the chairman of the Bad River Band of Chippewas [Don Ames] came to Martin and me, mainly to Martin, trying to see if we couldn't get some sort of federal recognition of that part of the reservation known as the Kakagon Sloughs in the Bad River. Back in the fifties the Rockefeller Commission [ORRRC] had identified the Kakagon Sloughs as of national significance. . . . We posed the question to Don Ames, "What would you think if we combined it with something to do with the islands so that it could be packaged and perhaps sold at the national level?" . . . We thought if we tied this bundle in with something Rockefeller called "nationally significant" people might look at it again. So we ran this by Gaylord and he had been born and raised in the same Congressional District . . . and had often come up to the Mellen and Ashland area with his father, who was a doctor in the area, to attend Progressive Party doings. His father and mother were very active Progressives in Wisconsin . . . so he was aware of the Apostle Islands and visited them as a young man, and as a teenager and he thought it was a great idea . . . What had happened is Don Ames had been looking at a *National Geographic* and had seen pictures of some bird sanctuary somewhere, where there were bridges and walkways built over the marshes and people could look at the various aquatic life and so forth. He wondered if something like that could be done in his area. We suggested to him that after he bought the idea of tying the thing together with the Apostle Islands, that he get the ball rolling by getting something from the tribal council. But we did not go to them. He came to us.[13]

The Bad River Tribal Council was interested and on May 10, 1962, unanimously passed a resolution requesting that the U.S. Department of the Interior (USDI) secretary and the governor of Wisconsin study the feasibility of establishing a "national shoreline recreational area on the Bad River Reservation." The islands themselves were not mentioned as they were not part of the tribal reservation. The resolution noted that President Kennedy had designated the area as chronically depressed and that future efforts should ensure that the ancient customs and culture of the Chippewa and the development of the area should contribute to the economic well-being of the Bad River Tribe. The tribal resolution stressed the scenic beauty and the important wildlife values of the sloughs and the shoreline to the people of the United States, as well as the need for prudent and sensitive development. The proposed study area consisted of 20,000 acres north of U.S. Highway 2.

Ames, as chairman of the Bad River Tribe and as secretary-treasurer of the Great Lakes Inter-Tribal Council, transmitted the statements to Secretary Udall, Governor Nelson, and Bureau of Indian Affairs Commissioner Philleo Nash. Ames stressed the economic potential of the project and urged early action.[14]

Thus the first step was taken in what would become an eight-year struggle to establish an Apostle Islands National Lakeshore. This effort involved the presidential administrations of John Kennedy, Lyndon Johnson, and Richard Nixon and resulted in twelve bills and bill drafts being written and rewritten before one was finally enacted. Every bill was considered by the U.S. Senate and House Committees on Interior and Insular Affairs and their subcommittees on many different occasions. This produced thousands of pages of congressional testimony and hearing records. The effort further involved countless numbers of citizens, elected and appointed officials, and numerous federal and state agencies. The final outcome of all this effort was to be substantially different from what had been envisioned by Nelson in 1962.

Nelson Meets with Udall

On several occasions, I met with Gaylord Nelson to discuss possible courses of action regarding the Bad River Tribal Council's resolution. Federal involvement seemed most appropriate for a number of reasons. First, although modest funds were available through his state Outdoor Recreation Act Program (ORAP) for the Lake Superior south shore area, no funds were targeted for the Kakagon–Bad River Sloughs. Second, the USDI secretary held trust responsibilities for the Native Americans and, therefore, could represent their interests more effectively than could the state. Third, federal involvement meant that a study of the sloughs could be extended to the larger region. Fourth, Nelson was already using ORAP dollars to emphasize a costly "ring of parks" around metropolitan areas in southeastern Wisconsin, which made the diversion of ORAP funds to the north difficult. Fifth, congressional initiatives were already underway on national seashores, making the possibility of federal involvement promising. Finally, Nelson had excellent relations with Secretary of the Interior Stewart Udall.

Later reflecting on the matter, Nelson said, "Well, I was satisfied, in any event, that it was a resource of national value. . . . By the time we really got

things going and studying it and so forth, I was in the [U.S.] Senate. I am not
going to be running something through state government from the Senate
position, but it would obviously involve a considerable amount of money. . . .
By the time we got around to designing the whole thing, in particular since it
involved the Indian reservations . . . and those lands were under the jurisdiction of the Interior Department . . . I decided the best way to finally push it
was to push for national recognition."[15]

While still governor, Nelson took the proposal to Washington. On May 22,
1962, he met with Udall, Bureau of Indian Affairs (BIA) Director Philleo
Nash, and Bureau of Outdoor Recreation (BOR) Director Edward Crafts. In
addition to the points raised in the Bad River proposal, Nelson noted that the
area under discussion should be designated as a recreation area rather than a
national park; this would permit continued Native American and non-Native
hunting, fishing, and harvesting of wild rice and would protect the area's wilderness character at the same time. Nelson also discussed the economic importance of the proposal and the relationship it had to his proposed $3 million
ORAP expenditure in the Lake Superior region. Intrigued, Udall instructed
Crafts to inspect the area. Media coverage was both favorable and substantial.[16] Although the meeting was upbeat, the Wisconsin Conservation Department, not unexpectedly, warned me that Nelson and the Department of Resource Development would be in for an arduous and long bureaucratic fight.

After more than three years of fighting with both the Wisconsin Conservation Commission and Wisconsin Conservation Department, Nelson was un-
fazed by the warning. In a news release he noted the upcoming meeting with
Crafts and the official inspection of the proposed recreation area. The inspection also included the Apostle Islands and the Bayfield Peninsula. Moreover,
discussions would center on federal participation in the recreational development of those areas.[17]

I arranged for the use of private boats for the inspection, to keep it from
appearing to be a WCD initiative. When, on June 11, 1962, Crafts, Nelson,
and staff from the state DRD and WCD inspected the sloughs by boat and
the islands and peninsula by air, Crafts was impressed. Most importantly, he
stated that "a more inviting package" would include the twenty-two islands
and the Bayfield Peninsula in addition to the sloughs. He did not, however,
commit the BOR to a federal study. Therefore, at a luncheon after the trip,
Nelson stated that the DRD would immediately initiate a study "of the feasibility of making the area more attractive while preserving its natural beauty."[18]
Craft's significant contribution had been to broaden the area for study, which
Nelson quickly embraced. In public, the WCD could hardly object.

Public momentum for the idea was pushed by the governor's office and the DRD. Enormous newspaper, radio, and television coverage resulted. Ahead, however, were bureaucratic, political, and institutional obstacles to overcome. Fortunately, control over recreation planning, and, therefore, planning for the lakeshore, was firmly in the hands of the DRD and myself. Further, Crafts had sanctioned the concept of a broader regional study. But the lack of direct federal involvement meant that the DRD would have to add the lakeshore proposal to a planning agenda that was already overloaded. I undertook two actions to deal with these problems. First, planners involved in the Lake Superior "South Shore Studies" were directed to work with local people and to begin to develop a constituency for a lakeshore. Second, I continued to study and analyze the federal bureaucratic and political thicket to determine how best to secure federal involvement.

In spite of the success of the inspection tour, warnings from the WCD increased. An editorial in the *Milwaukee Journal* cautioned that the recreational possibilities in the area "should be judged from the standpoint of total public needs and benefits, not what will especially help this group or that area or win local votes in some coming election,"[19] a pointed reference to Nelson's campaign at that time for the U.S. Senate. In spite of Nelson's substantial success as a "Conservation Governor" and his work with the WCD, the WCC and the WCD continued their challenges to his initiatives. In particular, they suspected that Nelson's efforts on the lakeshore would result in direct federal involvement. Thus they launched a counterattack. The Conservation Department, the Conservation Commission, and the press, including the *Milwaukee Journal*, inspected the area in July 1962. The governor's office and I knew nothing about the inspection and were not invited. Roman Koenings, the Wisconsin parks director (later appointed by Crafts to be regional director for BOR in Michigan), outlined an ambitious program for the islands.[20] Koenings said that the "state can't wait. . . . The National Park Service has rejected the islands twice. We will go ahead."[21]

The state parks' admission stickers and Nelson's ORAP had pumped millions of new dollars into the State Parks Program. In contrast to the 1950s, when the Parks' budget was minuscule, Koenings could now think and plan in an expansive manner largely with new money provided by Nelson. Again, Nelson did not directly challenge Koenings's plans. Rather, he kept the idea of federal involvement alive through his speeches and through press releases. These efforts were successful in broadening citizen understanding and support for a national area.[22] It was up to me, as Nelson's aide, to deal with the objections of the WCD.

Developing Support

Throughout 1962 and 1963 the Hansons and I worked to develop support for Nelson's proposal. There was a consensus that the area would include the Kakagon–Bad River Sloughs, the Apostle Islands, and the Bayfield Peninsula. An intense analysis of the Native American treaty complexities was initiated, including questions of land ownership and Native rights for hunting, fishing, trapping, and wild rice gathering. Subsequently, meetings were held with members of the Bad River and Red Cliff Tribes and the Bureau of Indian Affairs.[23]

At the federal level, a significant policy step was taken in early 1963 when Secretary of the Interior Udall and Secretary of Agriculture Orville Freeman announced that the president's Recreation Advisory Council had approved the creation of a new, limited system of national recreation areas to implement the Outdoor Recreation Program for the president's administration. Criteria for new national recreation areas were then being developed by the president's Recreation Advisory Council. These areas would be administered primarily for recreation but would permit the utilization of other resources if such use was compatible with, and did not interfere with, the basic recreation purpose. The secretaries also noted that national recreation areas would only be established by an act of Congress and could be administered by a number of federal agencies.[24] The Udall-Freeman announcement was a clear signal that Nelson's group could now develop lakeshore plans as an exclusive federal project. However, with the best of intentions, I prepared the first draft bill as a federal-state collaborative project (which was permitted under the criteria).

During the balance of 1963, the draft was discussed with officials in the WCD, the Attorney General's office, Governor John Reynolds (Nelson was now in the Senate), and with bureaus within the Department of Interior. Finally, late in 1963, I concluded that, given the complexities of Native American treaty rights, the pattern of land ownership, and the fact that the WCD was cool to the proposal, the establishment of a federal national recreation area was the route to take.[25]

In late March 1963, I resigned as deputy director of the Wisconsin DRD and joined the Resources Program Staff in the federal Office of the Secretary of the Interior. I eventually became the regional coordinator for the Upper Mississippi–Western Great Lakes Area. The substantial staff resources of the USDI would now be more readily available to me to help deal with the complexities of the Apostle Islands proposal.

The process of involving Interior bureaus began when I called a meeting in Ashland for July 9–11, 1964. Boat, car, and aerial inspections were made of the Apostles area. The meeting was attended by Andrew Feil of the NPS (who would play a critical role in lakeshore planning in later years), Emmett Riley of the BIA (a great supporter of Native American needs and concerns), Jack Eichstat of the Bureau of Recreation, Alan Nelson of the WCD, and Native American leaders Fred Connors (an early and consistent lakeshore supporter), Albert Whitebird from the Bad River Reservation, and Rose Duffy from the Red Cliff Reservation. Martin Hanson and Culver Prentice also attended, representing the recently formed Citizens' Committee for the Apostle Islands National Lakeshore. The Native American leaders were receptive to the broad outlines of the proposal. Most importantly, Feil was enthusiastic, and this was perhaps the most significant accomplishment of the meeting, as NPS support was necessary for any success.[26]

To develop further interest and support at the top levels of the NPS, I held another meeting to discuss the Apostle Islands and a system of national parks and lakeshores in the upper Great Lakes region with NPS Director Conrad Wirth and staff members George Hartzog, Theodore Swem, and Ronald F. Lee, the director of the Philadelphia Regional Office, which handled planning responsibilities for the Great Lakes region. In contrast to his opposition in the 1930s, Wirth personally told me that he liked my proposal for a national system of "star attractions" and was favorably disposed toward the Apostle Islands.[27]

The Philadelphia office of the NPS got busy. The first draft plan for the lakeshore, prepared by Feil, was completed in early September and marked "Not For Any Release." This plan proposed a national lakeshore of 294,000 acres (110,000 acres of land and 184,000 acres of water). The report was enthusiastic about the prospect.[28]

A Presidential Visit

After his 1962 election to the U.S. Senate, Nelson suggested to Attorney General Robert Kennedy that President John F. Kennedy should make a national conservation tour. As a selling point Nelson brought along a large scrapbook of press clippings reporting on Nelson's conservation initiatives. He noted that conservation initiatives were not only a substantively good idea, but were also good politics. President Kennedy made his tour and credited Nelson with the idea.[29] However a political flap between factions of the Wisconsin Democratic Party, Nelson, and the White House almost caused Wisconsin to be left off the tour agenda.

Nelson had had a disagreement with the White House, Governor Reynolds, and Democratic political leader Patrick Lucey over the appointment of
a federal judge to the seat in Wisconsin's Western District, left vacant by the
death of the incumbent.[30] While these events were transpiring, the White
House announced the details of the president's National Conservation Tour.
Wisconsin was excluded. Nelson was mad! William Bechtel, Nelson's press
secretary, recalls the dispute:

> Senator Nelson was called by the White House one afternoon . . . and was asked
> what he thought of John Gronouski. John Gronouski was a brilliant PhD from
> Michigan State . . . who[m] Nelson had recruited and eventually made Tax
> Commissioner. . . . When Nelson indicated that he was going to run for the
> Senate . . . John Reynolds indicated he was going to run for Governor [and] he
> recruited John Gronouski as his advisor. Reynolds and Gronouski immediately
> proposed to repeal Nelson's tax reform program [which in Bechtel's opinion was
> Nelson's greatest accomplishment as governor]. There is nothing more violent
> than political fights within political families, you know. This just enraged Nel-
> son, so he is down here a year or two later and the White House calls and says,
> "What do you think of John Gronouski?" Biting his tongue and digging his
> nails into his hands, he said, "Well, why do you want to know?" They said they
> were just building a talent bank . . . of people who might be considered, so Nel-
> son then relaxed and gave them a very positive description of John Gronouski,
> although he said he had this very sharp conflict with him but that he was an
> outstanding person, a very able person and would be great for anything they had
> in mind. Almost the next day . . . he picks up the paper and here [Gronouski]
> has been named Postmaster General and, furthermore, that Congressman Clem
> Zablocki from Wisconsin announced it in Milwaukee. Nelson went to a cocktail
> party that night . . . and he started talking . . . and said, "By God, those Irish-
> men in the White House didn't know what they were getting into now." And
> that he was half Irish and he was going to give them a piece of his mind and if
> they thought they were ever going to get that guy confirmed they were crazy . . .
> We came into the office Monday morning and these stories were coming back to
> us. Reporters were calling saying, "Is Nelson going to fight the Gronouski nomi-
> nation?" Which would have been a dramatic story. At almost the same time, we
> got an invitation: Would Senator Nelson be willing to come over to the White
> House and talk to the President? I drove him over and sat out in the driveway,
> drumming on the steering wheel. He came out [and] . . . was very delighted that
> he had had a nice chat with the President and that the President had pointed
> out that he had no idea that this was happening—"You can't oversee everything

your staff does. By the way, Senator," the President said, "I understand that you have requested that I come up to northern Wisconsin and that my staff had turned it down. I want you to know that I would *love* to come up there." And Nelson clapped me on the knee and said, "You are supposed to call Jerry Bruno at the White House and start making arrangements immediately." From the moment of this confrontation, everything fell into place. We worked with the White House, we arranged the tour.[31]

The Democrats had mended their fences, Gronouski was confirmed, and the president came to Ashland to see and talk about the Apostle Islands.[32]

The president's visit had another salutary impact within the bureaucracy. Responding to a request from the White House, I prepared a background statement on the proposal, which at this time included three units: the Apostle Islands (except Madeline Island), the Bayfield Peninsula, and the Kakagon–Bad River Sloughs, as well as the possibility of establishing a national monument on Madeline Island.[33] The statement was important in that it once again alerted top policy makers in the USDI to the fact that indeed there was a significant proposal out there and that the president was interested.

Bechtel, in summation of the trip, wrote:

Senator Gaylord Nelson's long campaign for conservation of natural resources was suddenly thrust on the national scene by the dramatic conservation tour by President Kennedy. For the first time since Theodore Roosevelt, a President is vigorously sounding the alarm to preserve outdoor resources. Joined by fifty of the nation's top reporters and cameramen, mobbed by throngs everywhere, the President marched across the northern and western United States carrying his conservation message.

For Wisconsinites, the climax, of course, came at Ashland, in the shadows of the Apostle Islands, where the President and his whirling retinue dropped out of the sky in a fleet of Army helicopters to find 10,000 cheering residents, fighting to break a cordon of snow fences held up by State Traffic Patrolmen.

For a time, it looked as if this might just be another day wasted. The Senate was scheduled to vote on the crucial Nuclear Test Ban Treaty at the very moment the Presidential jet was to take off. Nelson, a strong backer of the treaty, faced the prospect of missing out on the Presidential Tour.

But helped by some schedule juggling, Nelson and Senators [Hubert] Humphrey and Eugene McCarthy managed to vote for the treaty, then race to the White House lawn to catch the Presidential helicopter in time to link up with the big plane.

Then weather tried to waste the day. Northern Wisconsin, decked out in brilliant fall colors, was blanketed by a leaden sky. As the big plane neared Duluth, thunder, lightning and drenching rain lashed the Lake Superior shore which the President was to tour with Nelson. Secret Servicemen showed their concern and Nelson aides faced the possibility of months of work being washed out in a few minutes of grim luck. Actually, the breaks were all favorable. The jet got to Duluth before the storm broke and the helicopter armada promptly choppered off to the Apostle Islands and Ashland, which somehow had missed the downpour.

In the Presidential helicopter, Nelson . . . and Martin Hanson gave the President a solid briefing on the south shore area, the twenty-two islands and the marshes. Kennedy called the miles of sand beaches as "bountiful as any I've ever seen." Just as Hanson was telling him that this area was a nesting ground for the fast-disappearing national bird, the bald eagle, two of the big birds rose up from the marsh.[34]

Then on to Ashland.

There, two weeks of frantic work by Louis and Martin Hanson resulted in a smashing success. Five hundred civic leaders "sat in chairs while one of the biggest crowds Ashland has ever seen spread out across the meadows to view the first visiting President since Calvin Coolidge in 1928."[35]

Nelson also recalled the president's trip: "It is a remote area. Not many people are aware of the Apostle Islands—their uniqueness as an archipelago in the Great Lakes. So when Kennedy did his tour . . . I persuaded him to fly over to Ashland. . . . We landed; there was a big crowd. He gave a speech, including an endorsement of the idea of saving the Apostle Islands, so that kind of got it at the Presidential level and, of course, *it would be noticed by Park Service and everybody else*. Then the President was assassinated."[36]

Martin Hanson, in a 1989 interview, said, "I was the tour director. . . . I said, 'Well, let's take the short sweep around the islands. . . . ' I think he gained an appreciation; there were numerous sailboats out of Bayfield, out around Madeline Island, and of course he sailed Cape Cod, and then he started to understand better the recreational opportunities and the protection of the islands. . . . We actually [landed on] Long Island . . . saw a black bear running on the beach . . . and a pair of eagles flying over the mouth of the Bad River; so those kinds of things he hadn't been subjected to a lot . . . and [he] realized that there was a potential for not just sailing recreation, but for wild lands and for the appreciation of the beauty of the area."[37]

The president's speech emphasized the national need to preserve natural resources. He did not endorse the lakeshore per se, but he did say, "We, with you in this state and with your Governor, will work closely to develop the resources of northern Wisconsin so this area can rise and provide a life for its people and an attraction for people all over the middle west." He coupled the seeming incongruity of preservation and development by noting the economic hardships that the region faced, his efforts to deal with these issues through area redevelopment programs, conservation, rural development, and increased fisheries research, "all important parts of my program for rural America . . . and we have the brightest hopes in this section of Wisconsin for the development of outdoor recreation facilities. If promptly developed, recreational activities and now national park, forest and recreation areas can bolster your economy and provide pleasure for millions of people."

The President went on to say:

> The precise manner in which these resources are used, land and water, is of the greatest importance. There is a need for comprehensive local, state, regional, and national planning. . . . Lake Superior, the Apostle Islands, the Bad River area, are all unique. They are worth improving for the benefit of sportsmen and tourists. . . . Lake Superior has a beauty that millions can enjoy. These islands are part of our American heritage. In a very real sense they tell the story of the development of this country. The vast marshes of the Bad River are a rich resource providing a home for a tremendous number and varied number of wild animals. In fact, the entire northern Great Lakes area, with its vast inland sea, its 27,000 lakes, and thousands of streams, is a central and significant part of the fresh water assets of this country and we must act to preserve these assets.[38]

During the course of his visit, the president asked Nelson what the Apostle Islands would cost, and Nelson in turn asked me. I made a ball-bark estimate of $4 million to $5 million, which Nelson conveyed to the president, who indicated that this posed no problem. Nelson was quoted in an *Associated Press* story saying, "The President was astounded at the modest amount needed to purchase the islands, which the Senator said was the bargain price of $500,000."[39] The *Milwaukee Journal* reported the costs as $250,000 to $750,000. These estimates did not match the estimate given the president, but the point had been made, especially with the president, that the Apostle Islands project was not costly.

The benefits as a result of the president's visit were enormous. Interior Secretary Udall and Agriculture Secretary Freeman accompanied the president on his visit to the Apostles. Although Freeman was familiar with the area, it was Udall's first visit. The president's visit had given the idea of a "national park" in the Apostle Islands region a tremendous boost. Media coverage, in the region and nationally, was enormous. At his next stop, Duluth, Minnesota, the president made a significant recommendation. As the *Duluth News Tribune* reported, "He urged the Governors of Michigan, Minnesota and Wisconsin to develop a plan similar to that in operation by Appalachian States Governors working together across state borders to develop a regional program for action . . . 'and I would like nothing better than to sit down with the leaders of Michigan, Wisconsin and Minnesota to discuss a similar program for development in the upper lake states area.' The President also announced that 'to further improve federal participation I have directed the Department of the Interior to establish a North Central Field Committee with headquarters in Minneapolis and St. Paul.'"[40]

I was to chair the North Central Field Committee through the office of the secretary of the Interior. The fact that the Field Committee, as well as my appointment, was noted in the remarks of the president would be useful to me in later years in dealing with the numerous federal and state agencies involved in the lakeshore, some of which would prove to be obstinate.

The president's speech also noted that unemployment in the region was more than double the national average. "The economy of a region that should be prospering has reflected instead a series of economic setbacks as mines and mills shut down or curtailed their operations. . . . Our goal is the full employment of both the natural and human resources which this area still possess in abundance."[41] Advocates for the national lakeshore would use these statements in stressing the economic impacts of parks and lakeshores in the region. In spite of his successful tour, Kennedy stopped short of recommending the Apostle Islands as a national lakeshore. One can only speculate that it was either an oversight or possibly the influence of bureaucrats on Kennedy's speech.

In his speeches, the president had linked tourism, parks, and conservation with economic development. Regional approaches were stressed. Out of this came the Upper Great Lakes Regional Commission (UGLRC). Kennedy had set the stage for regional economic development in lagging regions in the United States. When Lyndon Johnson became president, he picked up on the idea and secured passage of the Public Works and Economic Development Act of 1965, which provided for regional commissions consisting of state governors and federal representatives, such as the UGLRC. This commission, consisting of the governors of Wisconsin, Minnesota, and Michigan and a federal cochair, would support the concept of a system of "star attractions" in the northern Great Lakes region. The system would include the Boundary Waters Canoe Area in Minnesota, six national forests in the three states, Isle

Royale National Park in Michigan, Grand Portage National Monument in Minnesota, the proposed national lakeshores at Sleeping Bear Dunes and Pictured Rocks in Michigan, the Apostle Islands in Wisconsin, a new Voyageurs National Park in Minnesota, and a National Wild and Scenic Riverway on the St. Croix–Namekagon and Wolf Rivers in Wisconsin. The "star attractions" were to be major inducements for increased tourism and tourist spending in the region. Economic development and new national parks were being tightly linked together. More importantly, a bipartisan political consensus was developing that would lead to UGLRC support for the new proposals, including the Apostle Islands, as they began to wend their way through Congress. The political significance of the concept is illustrated by Republican governor Harold LeVander's direction to put Minnesota's proposal for a Voyageurs National Park at the "top of their priorities" at an upcoming meeting of the UGLRC as an integral part of all three states' upper Great Lakes effort. LeVander had already endorsed Sleeping Bear Dunes in Michigan and the Apostle Islands in Wisconsin.[42] I was privileged to serve as the federal cochair for several years and had a major role in developing and securing support for the "star attractions" concept.

The Struggle to Control Planning for the Apostle Islands

During his visit to the Apostle Islands, President Kennedy had described the area as a tremendous and unique natural resource and had pledged the assistance of the federal government. But eight months would lapse before the Department of the Interior formalized a planning process for the area. The assassination of the president later that fall may have accounted for part of the confusion and bureaucratic delay in the department. In spite of my efforts, an ongoing struggle to control the planning task within the USDI accounted for most of the delay.

Shortly after the president's visit, I submitted a memorandum to Henry P. Caulfield, the director of the Resources Program Staff at the USDI, urging that a subcommittee of the North Central Field Committee be established by the secretary of the Interior to develop the plan. I argued that I knew the area intimately, had worked with Nelson on the initial proposal, and was under pressure from local citizens who wanted action. Neither the National Park Service nor the Bureau of Outdoor Recreation had personnel familiar with the area, nor were they acquainted with Governor John Reynolds and key state political leaders and legislators. At the time, it was assumed that state legislation had to be enacted and that such legislation had to come in the fall of 1964; otherwise, the Legislature would adjourn until 1965. I stressed that Nelson wanted a bill ready for introduction early in 1964. I believed that it was incumbent upon the Department of the Interior to act to prepare a plan and legislation for the end of the year.[43] By definition, giving a field commit- tee the responsibility for a national park or other reservation was a new ap- proach and moved responsibility from BOR.

The Bureau of Outdoor Recreation threw up roadblocks, and understand- ably so, as it had responsibilities assigned by the secretary for new area plan- ning. At a Washington, DC, meeting in October called by BOR, I agreed to prepare a preliminary analysis of the relationship of the area to the Recrea- tion Advisory Council's *Policy Circular No. 1*, which governed the selection of new federal recreation areas. We could not agree, however, on whether the Apostle Islands should be a state project or a national area. The BOR did, however, insist on reserving the right to make the final judgment as to whether or not it qualified for national status.[44] In spite of BOR's position, the NPS office in Philadelphia argued that the three-unit lakeshore had na- tional potential.[45] After the meeting, I prepared a detailed twenty-eight page single-spaced report, with twenty-four citations, reaching the conclusion that the area qualified. In it, the early authorization of the project by Congress was recommended. This report was probably the most detailed analysis of the relationship of an area to Recreation Advisory Council criteria that had been made to date.[46]

I presented the report to BOR representatives on December 6, 1964. John Shanklin, the assistant director of BOR, raised a series of questions and ob- jections. In spite of the fact that the report strongly recommended a national recreation area, including a national monument on Madeline Island, it was not clear to him if the area should be recreation area, national park, or a na- tional monument. Ignoring my analysis, he argued that BOR had not yet made a determination on whether the area met the criteria for national recrea- tion area status. He also had concerns regarding the Native American lands. In spite of the presence of Roderick Riley, a special assistant to BIA Com- missioner Philleo Nash, who indicated that the question of Native American lands could be worked out satisfactorily, Shanklin was not persuaded. He also felt that each island and the mainland area needed to be carefully analyzed to determine if preservation or recreational use was to be more significant. Shanklin grabbed the ball by indicating that the initiative was now with the BOR, and that he would call a meeting of BOR representatives in the near future.[47] I should have argued with more vigor that the criteria had been met in my analysis.

In the next meeting, Shanklin continued his objections and questioned further the priority that the area should have, particularly in view of administration efforts at the time to reduce federal spending. Shanklin ended the meeting by indicating that a memorandum authorizing additional study would be prepared for the secretary of the Interior.[48] I had lost the initiative, and BOR was now in control.

In January 1964, Crafts circulated to the bureaus a draft memorandum to the secretary of the Interior that was not encouraging.[49] Crafts, responding to the WCD's concerns, stressed the state's intense interest in the Apostle Islands area, as evidenced by state activities. This included the newly authorized Big Bay State Park on Madeline Island, dock construction on Stockton Island, comprehensive state recreation planning in the area and the state's interest in acquiring Oak, Outer, and Otter Islands. Moreover, the Federal Area Redevelopment Administration was financing studies of economic development opportunities on the Bad River and Red Cliff Reservations. The BOR contacts with the WCD had stimulated the department to expand its acquisition plans to include two additional islands within the existing state forest, which included Oak, Stockton, Basswood, Hermit, and Manitou Islands.

The memorandum was obviously designed to meet state concerns. Also, with the passage of the Land and Water Conservation Fund (LAWCON), state park agencies would be BOR's natural constituency, and Crafts wished to maintain good relations with the WCD.[50] I continued my politicking with Washington staff, especially with bureau chiefs, to try to secure the support of Secretary of the Interior Udall for a study of the Apostle Islands' potential. Sensitive to Udall's relationship and rapport with Nelson, and given my association with the region, on March 6, 1964, Crafts wrote Udall recommending that I chair a special subcommittee to undertake a "full-scale" study. He cautioned the secretary that the state had interests in the area, that there were Native American concerns, and that the analyses of the relationship to the criteria were inconclusive, so he had to substantiate the data.[51] Crafts also wrote Nelson informing him of the action.[52] I contacted the bureaus involved and wrote the draft memorandum, which Udall signed on April 4, 1964. It established the Subcommittee of the North Central Field Committee, which was to consist of representatives from BIA, NPS, BOR, the Bureau of Sport Fisheries and Wildlife, the Regional Office of the Solicitor, the state of Wisconsin, and the two tribal councils. I was appointed chair. A progress report was requested by July 1, 1964, followed by further reports every three months until the assignment was completed. The study was to accomplish the following:

- prepare a management and development plan;
- estimate costs;
- analyze economic impacts, including impacts on property taxes;
- analyze land ownership and tenure, and undertake a complete analysis of these factors as they related to Native American lands;
- document the relationship of the area to the Recreation Advisory Council's *Policy Circular No. 1*;
- study the relationship of the proposed area to other proposed federal recreation areas in the upper Great Lakes region;
- develop draft legislation to authorize the area as a unit of the National Park System; and provide for the equitable treatment of Native American interests.[53]

Letters were also sent to the Wisconsin governor and the two tribal chairs asking them to designate representatives to serve on the subcommittee. In addition to each tribal chair, one additional member of each tribe was to serve.[54]

Six months had passed since the presidential visit, and almost two years had gone by since the Bad River Tribal Council's resolution had been submitted. Finally the USDI was formally embarking on a study of the Apostle Islands region. The delay could be attributed to a number of things:

- the assassination of President Kennedy, which made agency and bureau chiefs uncertain of their tenure in office;
- uncertainty as to whether the Kennedy initiatives would be continued;
- the fact that, although the BOR had recreation area planning responsibilities, it was a new agency and was still working out its relationship with the NPS, which historically did new area planning;
- additional appropriations to federal recreation agencies and a new grant-in-aid program, LAWCON, were not yet authorized and funds were scarce;
- concern as to whether the area qualified for national status;
- the number of new seashores and lakeshores concurrently being proposed as additions to the National Park System, and the need for assurances that rigid criteria were being applied;
- the fact that field committees had not been involved in new recreation area planning, although they had substantial experience in river basin planning by bureaus of the Department of the Interior, particularly in the western states;
- the state's numerous interests in the area; and
- uncertainties regarding the incorporation of Native American lands into the proposal.

In spite of the long delays, the charge from Udall was clear and explicit: a complete study was to be done. The professional staff resources in the Department of the Interior's bureaus were now available for the effort, and the tribes and the state were to be full participants. Perhaps most important, Udall's charge implicitly recognized that the area had national status; he requested that draft legislation be prepared authorizing the area as a unit of the National Park System. Fortuitously, President Johnson had retained Udall as secretary of the Interior, which maintained the support for the Apostle Islands within the USDI.

Although not explicit in Udall's memorandum, a consensus had developed among the local communities, the Native Americans, and Nelson as well as within the USDI that the area to be studied consisted of the three areas, which included the islands, the sloughs, and the Bayfield Peninsula, as well as the potential for a national monument on Madeline Island. Specific boundaries were to be delineated when the detailed planning was complete.

The Subcommittee Report of the North Central Field Committee

Although the charge from Secretary of the Interior Stewart Udall to the Subcommittee of the North Central Field Committee in 1964 was clear and explicit, months would go by before the subcommittee approved its report for public release. The BOR insisted that it was merely a field-level document without Department of the Interior support. The report, entitled *Apostle Islands National Lakeshore: A Proposal*, was dated August 1965, but it would take six months for a response. Assistant Secretary of the Interior Harry Anderson, in a letter report to the chair of the Senate Committee of Interior and Insular Affairs, wrote, "S. 778 [Nelson's Bill on the Apostle Islands], if amended as recommended . . . would be in accord with the program of the President."[55] He made no reference to the Field Committee report. The long delays within Interior continued to be due to debates on substantive issues and bureaucratic political forces, to which we now turn.

The subcommittee was established because the full North Central Field Committee consisted of busy regional directors of bureaus having major responsibilities in the central and eastern United States. Their formal participation would have been at best sporadic. Thus, a subcommittee representative for each of their bureaus would keep the regional directors informed and allow them the right to approve the final report.

The state of Wisconsin was represented by Ralph B. Hovind of the Wisconsin Department of Resource Development, appointed by Governor Reynolds, and John Beale of the Wisconsin Conservation Department (who had obstructed the proposal from its inception). Department of the Interior bureau representatives were R. W. Sharp of the Bureau of Sport Fisheries and Wildlife, William R. Dryer of the Bureau of Commercial Fisheries, Carl E. Dutton of the U.S. Geological Survey, Paul Winsor of the BIA, Ronald F. Lee and Andrew G. Feil Jr. of the NPS, O. M. Bishop of the Bureau of Mines, Lawrence H. Mirkes of the BOR, and Daniel S. Boos of the Office of the Field Solicitor.

Martin Hanson of Mellen and Dr. B. Culver Prentice of Ashland, as members of the recently formed Citizens Committee for the Apostle Islands National Lakeshore, also participated informally. The subcommittee members brought substantial professional knowledge to bear on the many complex issues that needed to be addressed: minerals and mining potential; impacts of restricting logging; balancing recreational use with wilderness values; commercial and sports fishing; hunting and trapping; harvesting wild rice; water safety and navigation; complex legal and social issues affecting Native American rights and land ownership; and acquisition and development costs.

Udall had indicated that members of the Red Cliff and Bad River Tribes should participate in subcommittee deliberations and the preparation of the recommendations that would "provide the necessary equitable treatment of Indian interests." During the course of the study, Native American interests were represented by two former Bad River Council chairs, Albert Whitebird and Fred Connors; Gus Whitebird, the chair of the Bad River Resources Committee; Rose M. Duffy, a former member of the Red Cliff Tribal Council; and, Richard Gurnoe and Philip Gordon of the current Red Cliff Tribal Council.

The tribal representatives and subcommittee members agreed that formal action on their part regarding the report would be inappropriate. The legislation would be drafted in such a way that after enactment by Congress, each tribe would hold a referendum to determine their participation. This was a critical decision and was emphasized repeatedly as the process unfolded and Native American criticism was building. The two tribes fully participated in field trips, subcommittee meetings, and informal sessions, and they made many substantive suggestions that were incorporated into the final report. They supported the nineteen major recommendations regarding Native American matters and the principles embodied in the proposed legislation that reflected their needs, as they understood them.

To launch the studies a field trip and full meeting of the subcommittee was set for early summer 1964.[56] Unraveling the complex tribal issues took more time than anticipated. Thus, a progress report was submitted to Udall with a request that the deadline for the report be extended into 1965. Udall was pleased with the progress and hoped that the subcommittee would complete its work and submit a report to him by the first of the year so that any legislation could be presented to Congress at the beginning of the next session.[57] I took the drafts of the report prepared by the bureaus and developed a full draft copy that was then circulated to the subcommittee for comments in January 1965. The response was excellent.[58] BOR did not respond—a warning signal for future problems.

In terms of size, the final report was impressive; it was more than an inch thick with 112 pages of text; draft legislation was included. Appendix F contained an analysis of the relationship of the area to the Recreation Advisory Council's *Policy Circular No. 1*. The report was marked "Not For Release." To address economic implications of a national lakeshore, I hired Professor I. V. Fine of the University of Wisconsin–Madison's School of Business to develop estimates of the costs and benefits of the proposal; his study accompanied the report.[59]

The effort of the subcommittee had brought together the tribes and seven USDI bureaus to support the lakeshore proposal.[60] Only BOR remained aloof. On the state level Ralph Hovind was an enthusiastic and helpful participant in the planning process. The DRD's "South Shore Studies" and state recreation plans had consistently supported the lakeshore. Hovind also reflected the governor's favorable position. However, the Wisconsin Conservation Department would pose problems. Edward MacDonald, a tree nursery superintendent at Hayward, represented Beale and participated in all meetings and field inspections. I had hoped that all major issues of concern to the state would have been discussed, debated, and resolved. Failing consensus, my task vis-à-vis the WCD was to control adverse reaction and attempt to neutralize any opposition. Of course, a positive reaction from the WCD would have been highly desirable, but not likely attainable. In addition to MacDonald, I kept its top officials informed of every step in the process; they remained cool to the plan. An official Conservation Department position on the lakeshore would have to wait until congressional hearings. Thus, in the transmittal letter to the secretary of the Interior, I sidestepped the question of the Conservation Department and simply noted that both the DRD and the WCD had "assisted in report preparation and review."[61]

Although the WCD never publicly challenged the report, it criticized it internally, and the issues raised would repeatedly find their way into subsequent legislative debates and into the media. WCD officials questioned Fine's estimates of visits. They felt that a large swimming pool should have been recommended because the waters of Lake Superior were too cold for swim-ming. They feared that the high costs of boat trips would limit visits to the islands. They questioned Fine's assumption that state and county lands would be acquired at no cost. And they challenged the contention that the state would never have more than a modest program in the area, noting that the Conservation Department planned to spend more than a million dollars on lands and development and $30,000 in annual operating costs in the area. WCD officials *did* conclude that the state would benefit from a national lake-shore, provided the same goals could be achieved as under state management and that the state was reimbursed for its present equity in the lands involved.[62]

The state position eventually softened. Donald J. Mackie, the new super-intendent of State Parks and Forests, took a more favorable position toward the lakeshore, stating that he favored a national lakeshore that would comple-ment state programs.[63] Likewise, Wisconsin Conservation Commission Chair Charles "Frosty" Smith wrote Nelson indicating that the WCD planned to continue its programs in the area, but that it was possible that federal involve-ment would go a long way toward protecting the area.[64]

Securing Release of the Report

Gaining approval for the report at the field level had been relatively easy. Gaining approval from Washington for public release of the report would be much more difficult and would take another five months. Copies of the draft, which had been revised to reflect Department of the Interior's regional bureau comments, were sent to the Washington bureaus of the USDI. I ar-ranged meetings with Washington staff. At this point all the subcommittee was looking for was "informal approval" before the formal submission to Udall.[65] Scheduling a Washington meeting finally prompted a response from the regional office of the BOR. Its detailed comments on various sections of the report were of value, but they were couched in negative terms. Moreover, Roman Koenings, the new BOR regional director (and former WCD parks director), was concerned that the "rights" of Native Americans might conflict with other public usage and management of the area.[66] His views had not changed since his tenure at the state WCD.

A meeting with the Washington Department of the Interior bureaus was held on March 9, 1965. No major changes in the report were made except to delete the draft legislation from the formal report and to include it as a sepa-rate attachment. The Solicitor's Office insisted on a more careful review of the proposed legislation, especially as it related to Native American matters. The report was then transmitted by the subcommittee to Resources Program Staff Director Caulfield in the Office of the Secretary of the Interior on March 15, 1965.

The public release of a document of this size was obviously not realistic. Instead we developed a popular condensation of the report to be used in conjunction with the report by Professor Fine. No specific plan was yet available for public review, and people were becoming impatient.[67] Nelson was already publicly stating that he would have a bill ready for early introduction in Congress.[68]

The popular brochure would be funded by USDI bureaus; this in turn would reinforce bureau commitment to the report.[69] Caulfield advised the bureaus of the popular brochure with the understanding that it would not represent an official endorsement by the Department of the Interior. Moreover, no reference would be made to draft legislation "or the adaptability of the area to national recreation area criteria."[70] The Solicitor's Office indicated that it would proceed to improve the draft bill and prepare a transmittal letter for submission to Congress.[71] The Solicitor's Office was concerned, however, that Nelson would introduce legislation without waiting for a USDI draft and urged me to have him request one. Initiating his own bill "might put things 'out-of-joint' in the Department."[72] The BOR and the federal attorneys were still trying to control the process and were being successful in slowing it down.

By late July I still did not have the final Washington bureau's clearance for the brochure. Therefore, Frank Mentzer of the NPS (who worked with me on the popular draft), and I spent two days visiting bureau chiefs. All of the bureaus, except BOR, gave their approval. In spite of the fact that Mentzer and I met with BOR officials three times over two days, they could not be won over. They were still raising questions as to whether or not the area met *Policy Circular No. 1* criteria. I responded by noting that the subcommittee report, which included an analysis of the Recreation Advisory Council's criteria, had been thoroughly reviewed by Department of the Interior's regional bureau offices and at the Washington level. Moreover, the brochure had been reviewed three times at the field level and twice in Washington. Edward Crafts finally indicated that he would find it satisfactory if I were to include language to the effect that the subcommittee believed that the area met the criteria. Larry Stevens, his associate director, and others in BOR did not agree and continued to hold up the report.

Because BOR was not responding, I reminded them that the USDI secretary's charge to the subcommittee had been that it do a complete analysis of these factors as they relate to the Recreation Advisory Council's *Policy Circular*

No.1. Thus I stated that I was going to go ahead with the publication and that the BOR's comments should be in to Caulfield's office by July 26. The BOR's response was to insist that the brochure contain language indicating that BOR would judge whether or not the lakeshore met the criteria set forth in *Policy Circular No. 1*.[73] I was willing to compromise by including the following language: "In the opinion of the Subcommittee, the proposed Lakeshore meets the primary and secondary criteria for National Recreation Areas set forth in the Recreation Advisory Council's *Policy Circular No. 1*, [but] the finding is subject to review by the Bureau of Outdoor Recreation."[74]

Help finally came from James Smith, Caulfield's assistant, who decided to delete such language. Smith observed in a note to Caulfield that, "this is pure and simple bureaucratism. A report for public informational use should not be cluttered up with this sort of thing. . . . The lakeshore is still strictly a field level proposal and as such is subject to review of *all* of the bureaus at the Washington level. BOR will have a chance to take another crack at it if that is what they are after."[75]

While the arguments over the criteria raged, BOR launched another attack. Crafts, in a memorandum to Caulfield, raised a set of substantive issues. First, he reiterated the demand that BOR would make a final judgment on *Policy Circular No. 1* criteria. Second, reflecting Koenings's concerns, he said: "We have serious questions as to the wisdom of proposing the area described in this report as a national lakeshore. The management proposed for the area does not conform with the basic objective of a national lakeshore which is to provide outdoor recreation to large numbers of people. A large part of the area would be managed as a wilderness area and another large part pretty much as a wildlife refuge."[76] He then selectively quoted from the report those sections that emphasized that the islands would be managed as *wild natural areas*, and that most of the Kakagon–Bad River unit would be preserved as a *unique natural shore and marsh*. Crafts's most serious objection was that the provision of outdoor recreation was not listed as one of the three goals. He urged that the proposed management of the area, especially as applied to the islands, be reconsidered before the area was proposed as a national lakeshore. Some of his points were valid.

The subcommittee had erred in not placing greater emphasis on outdoor recreation in the primary goals developed for the lakeshore: "1) to preserve a splendid remnant of Great Lakes shoreline for public use; 2) improve the conditions of the Bad River and Red Cliff Bands of the Lake Superior Tribe of Chippewa Indians of Wisconsin; and, 3) to stimulate the local economy as a result of tourism expenditures and Federal investments."[77]

In spite of this bureaucratic error, the report did emphasize that the lake-shore, when fully established, would provide an estimated 920,000 visitor days (one person visiting for one day) of recreation annually. Visitors would spend $4.1 million, which when multiplied meant a total impact of $7.25 million annually. A multiplier of 1.75 was used; that is, every dollar spent by tourists results in spending of $1.75 in the area.[78] These estimates, which were repeatedly challenged by BOR and used against the lakeshore proponents, were realistic when compared to studies on the estimated number of visitor days for the proposed Pictured Rocks (750,000 annually) and Sleeping Bear Dunes National Lakeshores in Michigan and the Voyageurs National Park in Minnesota (480,000 annually).[79] The thirty-mile scenic road in the Bayfield Peninsula was a key element in the development plan because it would generate large numbers of visitors, thus meeting an important criterion of *Policy Circular No. 1*. Although Fine's analysis did not break down the estimated number of visitors who would be attracted to the lakeshore as a result of the proposed highway, he did emphasize that sightseeing was the single most important element in a vacation trip to Wisconsin.

Although they could not stop the report, some members of the subcommittee did have some reservations regarding the scenic road. It would be an intrusion into a spectacularly wild and remote Lake Superior shoreline, viewed perhaps more suitably from carefully designed hiking and skiing trails. Also, opponents of the lakeshore repeatedly raised the issue of the road and noted the potential adverse impacts on the peninsula, such as crossing deep river gorges and causing erosion, as well as costing too much. Numerous conservation organizations likewise objected. NPS Director George Hartzog would again address these issues when the enabling legislation was debated before the House Interior Committee.

Lakeshore proponents finally got a break: as the arguments went on over *Policy Circular No. 1* criteria, it came to the subcommittee's attention that BOR had completed an analysis for Pictured Rocks National Lakeshore. The BOR found that the "proposed area falls within the scope of the definition for national recreation areas."[80] The development plan for this lakeshore also envisioned a scenic road traversing the entire thirty-five mile lakeshore boundary. NPS estimated annual visitation at 700,000 to 1,380,000. If Pictured Rocks could meet the criteria, then the Apostle Islands, which were much more accessible to tourists than the remote northern portion of the Upper Peninsula of Michigan, also met the criteria.

In spite of BOR's continued objections to the Apostle Islands proposal, I received approval from the staff of the Resource Program director to print the report with a proviso that the subcommittee believed that the lakeshore met the criteria. I simply deleted any reference to BOR approval.[81] Program Director Caulfield advised the undersecretary and assistant secretaries of the Interior that the report, "in my opinion, . . . is an excellent product, representative of the best work of our bureaus in the field." James Smith transmitted the report to the Washington bureaus and thanked them for their help and cooperation in its preparation.[82] Secretary Udall was photographed in a public ceremony presenting the first copy of the report to a beaming Senator Gaylord Nelson (a photo widely used in later appearances throughout the state).[83]

Five years after Nelson's original proposal, the supporters of the lakeshore now had a specific plan to take to the public. Public meetings were held in Ashland to present the report. Private sessions were also held with the Bad River and Red Cliff Tribes. As expected, opposition came from private property owners on Little Sand Bay and from local hunters and fishers who used the sloughs. Overall, however, public response and media coverage were highly favorable. Members of the two Native American communities also viewed the report with favor. Momentum for the lakeshore was building.

Nelson received the draft legislation from the USDI at the end of August and, with Senator William Proxmire, introduced it in the Senate on September 7, 1965, as S. 2498. Congressman Alvin O'Konski also introduced into the House of Representatives on September 8, 1965, the companion bill, H.R. 10902. The NPS was totally supportive, and in response to Nelson's requests for comments on the bill, it recommended that it be enacted. It further noted that the Advisory Board of National Parks, Historic Sites, Buildings and Monuments had recommended national lakeshore status for the Apostle Islands and believed that the legislation met in full all Recreation Advisory Council criteria.[84]

Stanley Cain, the assistant secretary for Fish and Wildlife and Parks, also favored the proposal and noted that the report "should do much to speed the formation of a National Lakeshore at this site."[85] In spite of Cain's support, Nelson and I still needed two responses: a report from BOR Director Crafts on the *Policy Circular No. 1* criteria and a letter report on the legislation from the Department of the Interior to Congress. To speed the matter along, Nelson and his assistants Bill Spring and Bill Bechtel met with Crafts. Crafts then advised Udall, "I told Senator Nelson I thought this area qualified under the criteria for National Recreation Areas and that we would do our best to get a favorable report from the Department [of the Interior] as promptly as possible. It seems to me that the Apostle Islands might well qualify under the guidelines as something new and interesting, and also not costing too much money. I shall work with Max Edwards [of the Solicitor's Office] in trying to expedite this because I know you are for it."[86] Thus the BOR director finally overruled his staff. Another important bureaucratic hurdle had been cleared. It was obvious that Crafts paid more attention to Nelson's staff than he had to my efforts.

A few weeks later, Crafts's assistant director, Dan Ogden, formerly under Caulfield in the Resources Program staff and sympathetic to the lakeshore, ratified Crafts's decision and submitted a terse four-and-a-half-page statement finding that the lakeshore met all primary and secondary criteria.[87]

Another Bureaucratic Slowdown

Although the USDI now had a report and a plan before the public, fourteen more months would pass before they would transmit a favorable report on the lakeshore to Congress. Nelson and all of the staff who had worked so hard on the proposal were disappointed with President Johnson's 1966 *Special Message to the Congress Proposing Measures to Preserve America's Natural Heritage.* He urged the enactment of eight new national parks and recreation areas, including Sleeping Bear Dunes and Indiana Dunes National Lakeshores on the Great Lakes. But with regard to the Apostle Islands, Johnson proposed the "early completion of studies and planning."[88] The suggestion that studies on the lakeshore be completed was a signal to both the opponents within the USDI and the Bureau of the Budget, which had reservations, to delay the proposal. The situation was exacerbated by budget problems. As the war in Vietnam escalated, pressures on the federal budget had increased enormously and would affect federal agencies in many ways. In fact, the president and the secretary of the Interior had issued orders to federal employees to curtail travel. Any additional expenditures were being discouraged.

In addition to budget problems, and in spite of the fact that the report on the Apostle Islands had clearance from the USDI bureaus, one person in the Solicitor's Office, Lewis Sigler, a fiscal and ideological conservative, became a formidable obstacle.

The subcommittee report, the popular brochure, and the draft legislation all contained language that authorized the secretary of the Interior to acquire the substantial acreage of nonreservation land within the boundaries of the two reservations inside the lakeshore boundary. These lands were to be sold back to the tribal councils and then leased back to the secretary of the Interior for lakeshore purposes. Nelson's bill, S. 2498, contained this language. This provision had been reviewed numerous times with tribal councils and with field-level and Washington bureaus. Other than Sigler, no one opposed the plan. To change this provision at this stage in the planning process would have caused serious problems of trust with the two tribes.

I had held intensive discussions and meetings on Native American preferences within the Department of the Interior and with the Bureau of the Budget. I argued that the language in the secretary's memorandum establishing the subcommittee was intended to mean preferential treatment for the Native Americans. Sigler argued that the phrase "to provide the necessary *equitable* treatment of Indian interests" did not mean preferential treatment. The debate on this issue held up final clearance of the legislation within the USDI. Sigler's position finally prevailed. Because of this problem I tried, without success, to get the letter report out of the USDI. Bill Bechtel, in Nelson's office, also put pressure on the USDI and the Bureau of the Budget to no avail.[89] The year 1966 came to a close without formal clearances.

The impasse would be broken when White House staffers prepared the president's 1967 Environmental Message. President Johnson, in his message to Congress, *Protecting Our Natural Heritage*, said, "I recommend that the 90th Congress . . . establish the Apostle Islands National Lakeshore in Wisconsin, to add a superb string of islands to our National Seashore System."[90] A month later came those marvelous words, which were transmitted to Congress: "The Bureau of the Budget has advised that there would be no objection to the presentation of this report [the Department of the Interior's letter report to Congress], and that enactment of S. 778, if amended as recommended herein [by Sigler], would be in accord with the program of the President."[91] In spite of that support, the amendments, as drafted by Sigler, posed serious problems for the carefully negotiated language on purchases, sales, and leasebacks within the reservations. Sigler had successfully argued, and had included in the letter report, that lease costs would "exceed the amount it received from the sale of the land to the Indian bands."[92] Furthermore, the letter report indicated that the leasing of tribal land was not favored, and it was stricken from the bill. It instead provided for the outright purchase of such lands and payment by either a lump sum or in installments, which in the aggregate would equal the purchase price plus interest on unpaid balances. Sigler believed that payment in installments would, at least for a while, meet the subcommittee's objective of assuring the tribes of an annual income for a period of time. It did nothing, however, to assure them of long-term annual incomes.

In reflecting on these issues, I believe that I should have taken these issues to the secretary of the Interior and argued the question of the Native American position, as Sigler's amendments on leasing could have set a precedent that would impact many tribes. The letter report, however, was the last step in the Department of the Interior's bureaucratic process. Sigler's amendments were dealt with by Nelson with amendments responding to the subcommittee's recommendations. Sigler was furious with me. I shrugged and said this was the Senator's wishes.

CHAPTER 5

❧

The Blowup—Or, Do We Have a Lakeshore?

President Johnson, in his 1967 message to Congress, "Protecting Our Natural Heritage," said, "I recommend that the 90th Congress . . . establish the Apostle Islands National Lakeshore in Wisconsin, to add a superb string of islands to our National Seashore System."[1] In spite of this highest level of support, hurdles to the lakeshore remained. The change in presidents to a Republican, Richard M. Nixon, and new debates, including those over the inclusion of tribal lands within the lakeshore boundaries, caused significant headaches for lakeshore supporters and serious concerns over the future of the lakeshore proposal.

Contentious Senate Hearings

Gaylord Nelson's first lakeshore bill on which hearings were held, S. 778, passed the Senate on August 21, 1967, and was introduced on September 26 in the House of Representatives by Congressman Robert Kastenmeier and fifteen co-sponsors as H.R. 13124. House hearings on H.R. 13124 were held a year later on July 29, 1968, when testimony was limited to government officials, although the House Committee on Interior and Insular Affairs indicated that it would receive letters from interested parties. No hearing record was printed, perhaps because the committee was busy with legislation on Redwood and North Cascades National Parks and a national system of trails and wild and scenic rivers. Other than this preliminary hearing, and given the congressional backlog, the Apostle Islands would have to wait its turn in line in the House.

Nelson's third bill, S. 621, was introduced in the Senate on January 24, 1969. The Nixon Administration was now in place. The March Senate hearings on the bill were contentious. The National Park Service threw two bomb-shells into its testimony. The first dealt with funding constraints; the second was the absolute insistence on the inclusion of Native American lands before a lakeshore would be established.

With the change in the administration, from Johnson to Nixon (Democrat to Republican), Nelson and I had lost direct influence with the Department of the Interior. As a consequence we did not know what to expect, although supporters within the agency remained. Appearing for the NPS before the Senate Committee on Interior and Insular Affairs were Edward Hummel, an associate director; Lemuel Garrison, a regional director; James M. "Mike" Lambe from the Office of Legislation; Richard P. "Dick" Wittpenn, a land-scape architect; and Theodore R. "Ted" Swem, an assistant director. Wittpenn was the only witness who had seen the area, having spent some three weeks there working on the master plan. The others had no direct familiarity with the area or the issues, and lengthy testimony and cross-examination by the Senate subcommittee chairman and committee members made it obvious that they were not well informed. Chairman Alan Bible expressed extreme frustra-tion with the NPS representatives and their inability to answer questions: "I have always demanded and insisted that whoever is testifying on a park or recreation area visit it so he knows what he is talking about, not read about it or describe it when he cannot make the grand tour of the area. I do not know how you can know it is breathtaking and everything else having never been there. You cannot develop that by reading about it or maybe even looking at some pictures."[2] He threatened to adjourn the hearings until the NPS could provide witnesses who had actually set foot on the territory.

The letter report of the USDI to the Senate had indicated their approval for the lakeshore.[3] In spite of that, however, Hummel's prepared statement threw cold water on the Apostle Islands proposal. He noted an enormous backlog of authorized parks and recreation areas and insufficient funds to purchase lands throughout the nation.[4] As a member of the committee, Nelson asked him, "Is this specifically an announcement by the Department of the Interior that they will not recommend any further national recreation or park areas this year?" Hummel replied, "I cannot speak for the Department completely, Senator, but this particular statement indicates great concern on the part of the Department for expansion of obligations for acquisition of lands."[5]

Nelson continued, "I think it would be a matter of grave concern and great interest to the Congress and the people of the United States and every con-servationist in the country if this is the beginning of a declaration by this administration that there will be, because of funding, no more national recreation projects recommended to this Congress. . . . Do you not endorse the Apostle Islands?" Hummel responded, "I cannot answer that, Senator." Chairman Bible then declared, "[We] had better find someone who can answer, whether that means we go right to the Secretary of the Interior. . . . But find out who can with authority answer and if necessary we will have Secretary Hickel come."[6] (Stewart Udall had been replaced by former Alaska governor Walter Hickel as the secretary of the Department of the Interior.)

The first bills on the lakeshore had stated that the Congress should establish the lakeshore. Nelson's second Senate bill (S. 778) contained the same provision. In accordance with the USDI recommendation, the bill was amended to state that the secretary of the Interior would establish the lakeshore when there were sufficient lands for efficient administration. Subsequent bills contained this language. Other lakeshore and seashore acts of this era contained similar language. The USDI letter did not address the question of the necessity of acquiring or leasing Native lands before the secretary would establish the lakeshore.[7] The issue had never been squarely faced within that context. The Bad River and Red Cliff Tribes had been assured that they could make a judgment on whether reservation lands were included within the lakeshore after legislation passed. In Hummel's oral testimony, he took a different position, saying, "We will not proceed with the project until we have obtained the consent of the Indian bands to the acquisition of [their] lands."[8] (Udall had made the same statement in oral testimony before the United States Senate Select Committee Hearings in 1967.) Senator Nelson angrily retorted:

> I started working on this proposal when I was Governor in 1961. I have spent hundreds of hours on it during the past eight years. . . . This is the first time the Interior Department has taken the position that there had to be prior approval of the involvement of any Indian lands. . . . I do not understand how this can go on in the Park Service for nine years and then suddenly out of the clear blue you come up with this reservation. . . . The islands themselves are a unique collection within the boundaries of the continental United States, standing alone as a viable park project. Some of the Indian lands on the mainland units of the Lakeshore would be a useful part of the project, but it has never been my contention that they were essential to the establishment of the Lakeshore. . . . [W]e have always had the position that [that] unit stands alone on its own. If it does not, then this Department does not support any islands any place. . . . I want to know why do these islands not stand alone as a unique project that you would buy if I had never suggested the Bad River Band's property or the Red Cliff?[9]

Hummel responded, "I want to emphasize again that, since the use of Indian trust land is essential for establishment of the lakeshore and the bill explicitly bars acquisition of trust land or interests therein without the consent of the Indians, it is clear that the lakeshore could come into being only when and if the Indians support its establishment. . . . It would seem desirable that this committee solicit from the two Indian tribes affected a clear expression of tribal consent before proceeding to report this bill." Hummel's statement was inconsistent with all prior positions taken by the Department of the Interior.

Nelson continued to hammer the NPS witnesses, "This proposal came from me, not the Park Service. . . . And I recognize that it would be ideal to have the Bad River Band . . . and it would be ideal to have the 30 miles of the Red Cliff shoreline. . . . But the project stands alone justified with no Indian lands at all. . . . So, I just say when I proposed this, I added two units to it because I thought that it would be ideal."[10]

Swem was then questioned by Bible, and he promptly confused the issue. Swem indicated that he had never seen the area, and then he further said that it had never been the feeling of the NPS that all of the shoreline had to be acquired by the time the lakeshore was established, but that a minimum acreage of Native land, which mainly comprised access points to the shoreline, would be required. Nelson picked up on the access question by noting that there were good docks in Bayfield and that the purchase of the shoreline was not necessary for access.[11]

Swem responded, "I do not know that in our thinking during the planning process . . . if it ever came down to just whether or not the islands would stand on their own. . . . [We] hope, as you have, that eventually this would be a total complex tied together into one national lakeshore." In deference to the NPS position, the USDI Subcommittee on Parks and Recreation reports on the bills considered earlier by Congress had not addressed this issue in this fashion. Nelson, however, stated that whether it was twenty-five miles or twelve miles of shoreline on the peninsula, there would be more than enough room for the NPS to build a visitor center and "an awful lot of shoreline that you can acquire without the Indian land at all. You can have a visitor center there and hike the whole 30 miles on the beach. Now won't that be satisfactory?"[12]

Wittpenn, the NPS landscape architect, said, "I have worked with the project so long with the boundary as it is, I have come to feel we need every square inch to do what we have proposed to do." Nelson responded:

[But] if you are up here saying you have got to have perfection or you are going to commit recreation suicide . . . you say you have worked with it so long, it is such a great proposal, but if you are going to change one foot or do not get all of it, therefore let us collapse that marvelous group of islands of which there are no others in the continental United States. I do not know why you do not stick to the position we had from the beginning. We will discuss it and negotiate with the tribes. They will approve or not approve. . . . [The] only way to handle this problem is to pass the project and the islands stand on their own whether or not you ever get any Indian land. If you want to wash it down the drain and get rid of the only collection of islands of this kind in the continental United States, you just continue this procedure.[13]

Hummel attempted to deflect the controversy by stating that he wanted to refer the matter to the National Parks and Recreation Area Advisory Board and to the President's Council on Recreation and Natural Beauty to have them re-evaluate whether or not the lakeshore would qualify as a recreational area without the land owned by the tribes. Hummel observed that, in 1967, Udall had indicated that the Native lands were necessary for the lakeshore. However, the Interior secretary had not said at that time that he would not establish the national lakeshore without the tribal land. Nelson responded further. "Secretary Udall stood for saving those islands, as did Mr. Hartzog. . . . They stand for saving those unique islands whether you get the shoreland or not."[14]

Subcommittee Chair Bible commented wryly, "I think you have made your point. I have gotten the message." He asked the NPS witnesses to confer further with their superiors in the Department of the Interior. "If all they got was the islands and not the Indian land . . . will you recommend the bill be passed or will you recommend a veto? You find the answer and come back with it before we finish the hearings."[15]

These two problems raised by the NPS witnesses posed serious obstacles to Nelson's hope that the Senate would act rapidly on the bill. In fact, three months went by before the Senate passed S. 621, which now contained eight amendments worked out between Nelson and the National Congress of American Indians, which made explicit Native American concerns, without yet modifying park boundaries. The Senate committee report on S. 621 did not deal with the issues raised by the NPS.[16] The bill was referred to the House of Representatives.

House Hearings in Ashland

The House Subcommittee on National Parks and Recreation held hearings in Ashland, Wisconsin, on the amended bill on August 19, 1969. Because the hearing was for local people, USDI officials did not testify. Nelson, in his prepared statement, indicated that during the March Senate hearings, "the Interior Department had reaffirmed the merit of the proposal, and the Secretary of the Interior testifying later at a hearing on related matters by a Senate Appropriations Subcommittee said that he would recommend Presidential approval of an Apostle Islands bill if passed by Congress." Nelson also reiterated with emphasis that tribal lands would only be included with the approval of the tribes, confirming the earlier discussions and the Department of the Interior subcommittee's report.[17]

The House of Representatives took no action in 1969 because of the freeze on LAWCON funds that was meant to help dampen inflation, but the NPS position would surface again—with a vengeance—during the 1970 House hearings.

House Subcommittee Hearings in Washington

In his budget message on February 2, 1970, President Nixon freed up LAWCON dollars by requesting $327 million. With funding now assured the House prepared for hearings on the amended version of the bill. The new letter report of the USDI now stated unequivocally that, "it is necessary that the two mainland units be acquired. Without them the area would consist only of the 21 islands, and it could not effectively be administered nor would it meet the criteria for a national lakeshore. . . . [We] do not intend to establish the Lakeshore without these two mainland units."[18] Thus the stage was set for another vigorous debate between the Department of the Interior, Senator Nelson, and the Congress.

Veteran southern Wisconsin congressman Robert Kastenmeier recommended the adoption of the bill and the eight amendments as approved by the Senate. He further indicated that in his judgment, even without the tribal land, the area constituted a viable unit of the National Park System.[19] Congressman Alvin O'Konski concurred: "I think it will be a great national park. I think it would be good for the Indians, but unfortunately, the Indians do not see it that way. So, if it poses a problem or hurdle, my suggestion would be to leave [tribal land] out temporarily and go ahead with the rest of the development, and I think that as the years go by they will see the value of it, and then they themselves will want to become a part of it."[20]

Nelson suggested that the special provisions for the Red Cliff Tribe (initiation by the tribe before any negotiations were held, as well as providing for congressional oversight) be provided to the Bad River Tribe as well. All of the difficulties posed by the Native American issues could have been avoided, he observed, if he had left them out of the proposal ten years earlier. "I was trying to do something for the Indians; I would have left it off and nobody in the bureaucracy would have thought of it. In fact, they would not have thought of the bill." Congressman Roy Taylor agreed.[21]

In his testimony, George Hartzog (whom Hickel had kept on as NPS director) exuded confidence that the tribes would eventually want to be included, but he repeatedly reiterated that the NPS would not establish the lakeshore without the two mainland units. He observed, "This bill has more advantages written into it for Indian tribes than any other piece of legislation I have ever seen presented to the Congress." In the event that the tribes did not choose to be included, he stated that he would return to Congress for advice on what to do with the alienated and allotted land acquired as a part of the project.[22]

Although he continued to insist that he would not recommend the legislation without the Native lands, Hartzog recognized that the policy decision rested with Congress. He wanted all three units but in an about-face said he was willing to compromise and delete the Kakagon–Bad River Sloughs. The shoreline area on the Red Cliff Reservation was, however, critical to the project as it protected the environment as viewed from boats on the water. He advised House subcommittee chairman Wayne Aspinall, "At some point you come to the rock and the hard spot, and then you either have an investment that is worthy . . . of the federal government, or you do not have it."[23]

Congressman McClure pushed Hartzog hard on the need for the mainland units. Hartzog, apparently forgetting his earlier comment on the sloughs, responded, "But you just called for my hole-card and that is it. We are not going to recommend this legislation under any circumstances of which I am aware. If the Congress decides that the mainland should not be in there, then this would be the policy decision of the Congress without our recommendation."[24]

The House subcommittee still was highly uncertain as to how to proceed. In brief, its uncertainty was based on these issues:

- There were no guarantees that negotiations with tribes on trust lands could be worked out after project authorization.
- Native Americans throughout the United States were generating enormous pressure on subcommittee members regarding tribal lands during the Apostle Islands process.[25]

- The NPS had taken a firm stand that all three units were necessary for a viable national lakeshore and that the lakeshore would not be established by the secretary of the Interior until sufficient lands, including the tribal lands, had been acquired.
- Subcommittee members were uncertain of the long-term costs of leases with the tribes; furthermore, a national area had never been established on the basis of leaseholds.
- Non-Native property owners militantly opposed the lakeshore.
- Questions had been raised regarding recreational use and allegedly unsafe boating conditions.

These circumstances, and the NPS position, were described by Kastenmeier in his newsletter to his constituents "as throwing a cloud over the future of the project."[26] And indeed they did.

This debate had been raging before the House subcommittee. A strong minority view developed in the subcommittee, and conservative congressmen Kyle and Skubitz insisted on a full hearing before the full House Committee on Interior and Insular Affairs. Their position prevailed, and the bill was reported without recommendation to the full committee on May 7, 1970.

The Full Interior and Insular Affairs Committee Takes Up the Matter

In the three months between House subcommittee hearings and those at the full committee, my office and those of Nelson, Kastenmeier, and McElvain were sites of furious activity. Stuart Applebaum, a staff assistant to Kastenmeier, suggested that I summarize the situation and pose alternatives. I did as follows:

- Hartzog's position, that he would negotiate with the tribes after the legislation was enacted, was consistent with the Department of the Interior's position since the inception of the proposal.
- The question of whether or not there was a viable project without tribal lands had never been faced.
- Precedents existed regarding Native lands and national parks (Grand Portage National Monument; Big Horn Canyon National Recreation Area; the National Wild and Scenic Rivers Act; and the Nez Perce National Historical Park).

There were alternatives:

- Pass Kastenmeier's bill (S. 621 with its amendments).
- Pass Senate bill S. 621 and amendments, but amend it further to provide the Bad River Tribe with the same options provided Red Cliff (i.e., initiation of negotiations by the tribe with congressional oversight). Moreover, I suggested the following:

    1. the tribes have five years to make a judgment;
    2. the secretary of the Interior would be provided with condemnation power for scenic easements on land 350 feet from the shoreline on the eastern fifteen miles of the peninsula; and
    3. Congress, and not the secretary of the Interior, would establish the lakeshore.

- Establish the islands and the western fifteen miles as a national park, and the eastern fifteen miles of the Bayfield Peninsula and the Kakagon–Bad River Sloughs as a recreation area dependent upon tribal approval.[27]

Nelson wrote Kastenmeier and transmitted various versions drawn up by himself, John Heritage (an aide to Nelson), and me, which included the following options:

- Provide Bad River with the same options as Red Cliff.
- Immediately establish the lakeshore to include twenty-one islands and the western fifteen miles of the peninsula with condemnation powers for two allotments needed for access. Red Cliff and Bad River could, within five years of lakeshore establishment, petition to be included.
- Delete the tribal lands completely with no option to be included at a future date. However, if petitioned by the tribes, Congress could again address the issue.
- Establish the islands and the Kakagon–Bad River sand spit, including Long Island, as a national park. (Nelson observed that, "Jordahl suggests inclusion . . . of the [Long Island] sand spit . . . as it contains no Indian lands and is a unique resource worth protection.") No tribal lands would be involved.[28]

On April 22, 1970, McElvain was preparing alternatives for the House committee that were being reviewed in Nelson's and Kastenmeier's offices. McElvain wrote a confidential memorandum to the House Subcommittee on National Parks and Recreation on May 1 based in part on an earlier executive session of the House committee. The memo stated that the lakeshore would be established by Congress and would consist of the islands, the western fifteen miles of the peninsula including six allotments, and the sand spit (Long Island). Within five years and by petition, the tribes could be included. The allotments would be acquired by successful negotiations with 50 percent of the owners of interest. If the tribes participated, all preferences in the amended version of S. 621 would prevail. Ninety-nine-year leases on tribal lands would be authorized. Rentals would be limited to a percentage of the fair market value of the fee and the average interest rate of federal long-term securities.[29]

From the tribal point of view, this bill, H.R. 555 with amendments, was their best option. The Native lands were identified on NPS maps as "Potential Additions to the Apostle Islands National Lakeshore on Request of the Indian Bands." This was a unique arrangement in the history of national recreation areas. In effect, Congress was saying that if the amendment passed, the western fifteen shoreline miles, Long Island, and the twenty-one islands would constitute a worthy addition to the National Park System; tribal lands could be added later. Kastenmeier described the House committee's action as "neither a victory nor a setback for the [lakeshore] . . . but the future of the Apostle Islands is in doubt."[30] The Republicans on the House committee were still insisting that S. 621 as originally introduced be considered in order to characterize Nelson and Kastenmeier as "anti-Indian."[31]

In the midst of all this Aspinall wrote to Hartzog, "The feeling of most members of the committee was that the testimony which you have given with respect to the Indian lands made a compromise difficult." An amended bill was attached. Aspinall asked, "Would the Administration—including the Interior Department and the Bureau of the Budget—have objection to the enactment of the revised language?" He also wanted a new development plan and cost estimate based on the revised boundaries.[32]

Secretary of the Interior Walter Hickel Expresses Support

In an attempt to create a compromise, Nelson talked with Hartzog on May 19, 1970. Hartzog indicated that he could not speak for the administration. Therefore Nelson decided to visit with Secretary Hickel personally; this was arranged for June 1. Rumors were then circulating in the USDI that the Bureau of the Budget would not approve an amended lakeshore bill. McElvain, however, felt that the Bureau of the Budget would not take that position.[33]

Wisconsin Congressman O'Konski joined Nelson in the meeting with Hickel. After the meeting O'Konski said that Hickel was "solid for it and will send some people up to the hill to make some contacts."[34] The press reported that, "Hickel's enthusiastic support for a bill creating the project without the Indian lands could be the deciding factor in convincing the Committee to move the bill to the House floor."[35]

Kastenmeier and O'Konski now wrote a joint letter to all members of the House Committee on Interior and Insular Affairs explaining in detail the amended version of the bill. Kastenmeier also called Governor Warren Knowles, who indicated that he would send a telegram of support to the House committee. During this period, however, Aspinall was upset and testy. In his opinion, the proposal was rife with too many uncertainties. Further, Native American groups were still actively opposing the lakeshore. The new Bureau of Indian Affairs commissioner, Louis R. Bruce, had not yet taken a position (although two prior commissioners had supported S. 621 in both its original and amended forms). Aspinall was having difficulty achieving a quorum for the committee's June 3 hearings. He and Congressman James O'Hare of Michigan were anxious to dispose of the Apostle Islands and move on to consideration of Sleeping Bear Dunes National Lakeshore in Michigan.[36]

The House Committee Acts: Tribal Lands Are Deleted

Aspinall achieved a quorum, and the committee met on June 3. In his opening comments, Aspinall pointed out that the Department of the Interior had not been consistent regarding the lakeshore.[37] The hearings got off to an amicable start, but proceedings grew more heated as they progressed. Congressman Skubitz asked Hartzog if he would recommend a presidential veto if the lakeshore was reduced in size. Hartzog responded, "I would rather not speculate on that because my recommendation would not be a matter of concern to the President. It would be the Secretary's recommendation, and I have not discussed that issue with the Secretary."[38] Communications had obviously broken down between the secretary of the Interior and Hartzog. Hartzog took the position of favoring the amended bill and said that the administration objected to the recent amendments "because [they] would not permit the acquisition of 2,930 acres of private non-Indian trust or allotted land on the mainland [Bayfield Peninsula]."[39]

Hartzog emphasized the need to acquire the private lands on the Bayfield Peninsula to prevent development that would detract from the lakeshore and said that the Red Cliff Tribal Council did not have the funds to acquire them. If the tribe decided not to participate, NPS would not build the scenic road, and the tribe would be denied an economic development opportunity. In spite of his position in favor of S. 621 Hartzog continued to comment on the bill, "You have included in the committee rewrite this much of the spit and at this point I would like to suggest for your consideration if it be your judgment that you are not going to provide a mechanism for the Bad River Indians to become a part of this proposal, that the spit should be eliminated."[40]

I had not discussed this proposal with Hartzog. It was Hartzog's independent judgment, which would cause a great deal of work in later years to get Long Island included in the lakeshore. Committee members Skubitz and Barton wanted to know if Hartzog would be willing to negotiate with the tribes, obtain an agreement, and then return to the committee before the legislation was passed. Hartzog said, "Well, that in effect is condemning the legislation to defeat, because obviously we are not going to get any agreement out of the Indians this session. And I think the opportunity for doing something to preserve what little remains of Apostle Islands is now."[41]

Skubitz said, "It may take a year, but I am willing to wait another year to get this park properly planned and developed." Hartzog replied, "What do I have to promise them, Mr. Skubitz? I do not have a thing to promise them because in advance of the Congress enunciating a policy to establish the parameters within which I can negotiate, I would be talking with the same forked tongue that . . . we have been talking with for the last 150 years."[42] Hartzog was neatly summarizing the position that I, the subcommittee, and local citizen supporters had maintained throughout the long planning process.

Throughout the House committee hearings, Hartzog consistently took the position that he favored the amended bill S. 621. On the other hand, he reiterated repeatedly under questioning that he could administer a reduced lakeshore, and that was a decision for Congress to make. He indicated his willingness to drop the Kakagon–Bad River Sloughs. Hartzog vigorously sought the authorization to acquire the 2,930 acres of alienated reservation land (land acquired by non-Native private owners) on the peninsula, and he stated that if, within a five-year period, Red Cliff Tribe did not petition for inclusion in the lakeshore, he would do the following:

- retain title to those lands needed for the lakeshore in the vicinity of the proposed administrative site;
- sell the remainder to Red Cliff at a price paid by the secretary of the Interior plus an amount equal to the interest charges incurred by the government for borrowing the purchase price or the fair market value on the date they were purchased by the tribe, whichever was less;
- ask the secretary of the Interior to offer the lands under long-term lease

at reasonable annual rates if the tribe did not exercise its right of first refusal; and

- ask the secretary of the Interior to sell or lease the lands to others, subject to environmental restrictions, to ensure their use in a manner compatible with the objectives of the lakeshore if the tribe chose neither to purchase nor lease. Prior owners would have the right of first refusal.

Hartzog commented, "Under any of these arrangements the Secretary will be able to achieve an important objective of the Apostle Islands proposal with respect to these privately owned lands; namely, environmental protection of the overview from the mainland to the islands consistent with compatible public use and development."[43]

Thus, in the spirit of compromise and accommodation Hartzog built into the proposal another significant opportunity for the Red Cliff Tribe. If they would not negotiate for inclusion, they now would have the opportunity to reacquire alienated land under favorable terms, a course of action not then open to them because of a lack of tribal funds.

Subsequent to the hearings, Kastenmeier and Aspinall conferred on the matter several times. They agreed, finally, that all of the tribal land except for the two allotments would be eliminated as would all language regarding Native American preferences.[44]

McElvain then called me wanting assurances in writing that the state would transfer its lands, without charge, to the federal government. This was a normal process for new park authorizations. After a lengthy debate and discussion, he agreed with my position, that a transfer could be arranged at a later date and that the issue should not be joined at this time. I was still concerned that the Wisconsin Conservation Department could insist on compensation. The sand spit and Long Island were also to be deleted. Although I concurred with McElvain's position on the elimination of the sand spit because of its proximity to tribal lands, I argued with him at great length that Long Island should be kept in the project because it was totally different and unique ecologically from the other twenty-one islands, and that further it was not close to the Bad River Reservation boundary. McElvain's response was that it was too close to Indian country, and Hartzog had indicated that it was too far removed from the administrative site planned for the Bayfield Peninsula for efficient management. McElvain, in a fit of exasperation, finally stated, "Do you want your damn park or don't you!" I acquiesced, and Long Island was deleted.[45]

On June 10, 1970, the House Committee on Interior and Insular Affairs had a thorough discussion on the bill. The committee appeared to arrive at a consensus that it would make the policy decision in spite of NPS reservations, and it would establish a reduced lakeshore. Aspinall was of the opinion that Hartzog and the Nixon administration would not recommend a veto. The revised cost estimate was now $9.25 million.

The House committee was to consider the bill again later that month. Park supporters planned to stimulate letters and telegrams in support. In the meantime the committee was giving further study to the 1854 treaty signed between the United States government and the Bad River and Red Cliff Tribes, especially with regard to land matters. Aspinall said after the review, "If you ever want to see a treaty that gave more thought to tobacco and firewater without taking into consideration what was really involved—the land—this is it."[46] In his newsletter, Kastenmeier reported further on Hartzog's position:

> The Red Cliff . . . have hopes of recapturing these private lands but they probably never will because of economic conditions. While the Indians have these aspirations, they are, at this point in time, essentially dreams and they should not stand in the way when other public interests are involved. Some landowners are happy to promote the Indian position, although they personally oppose it, for they would be no more willing to sell their private holdings back to the Indians than they would be to have their lands within the Lakeshore. Until the time comes when the Indian claims and economics make these dreams a reality, if indeed that is ever possible, there is no justification for blocking this park, the goals of which are compatible with the Indian respect for the land.[47]

The House committee reported on the bill, now identified as H.R. 9306 (the same as H.R. 555), on July 7, 1970, with the recommendation that it be passed as amended. The House committee report included the dissenting views of four Republican members and one Democrat. A number of policy questions were addressed by the majority report:

- All Native lands, tribal or allotted, except for two allotments on the Bayfield Peninsula, were excluded, and those two could only be acquired with the consent of a majority of the owners. The bill explicitly stated that Native land could not be acquired, except with the two exceptions. The Committee described tribal opposition as adamant at the time and indicated that they would not wish to participate in the near future.
- The lakeshore would be established by the act and not by administrative action. The question as to whether or not a reduced area qualified for

national status was unequivocally answered: "The Committee has concluded that it is ludicrous to suggest that a proposed unit of the National Park System is any less viable than it otherwise would be merely because the boundaries are revised. If a proposed unit of the national park is needed, desirable and worthy of national recognition; if it can help meet the outdoor recreation needs of the Nation; and if the general good of the public can be served with a minimal disruption of the localities involved, then it is the responsibility of the Congress to consider it. . . . It is the Congress which must decide what action should be taken."[48] The Committee further noted that although the NPS favored a larger area, it had indicated that a smaller lakeshore would be manageable.

- State lands were expected to be donated and the secretary of the Interior could only acquire them by donation.
- Costs were authorized as follows: $4.25 million for lands and $5 million for development.[49]

In late July, Aspinall, Taylor, and Kastenmeier met with the House Rules Committee in a closed meeting to explain the lakeshore.[50] The Rules Committee reported favorably on August 11 and allowed two hours for floor debate. Letters, telegrams, and telephone calls to the Wisconsin delegation supporting the lakeshore were generated by supporters. Applebaum prepared a letter for the signature of the Wisconsin members of Congress. It was signed in early September by most members. The letter noted that the area had been under consideration for forty years, that all Native lands had been deleted, that the Advisory Board on National Parks, Historic Sites, Buildings and Monuments had approved it (although in its original form), and although the NPS had preferred the larger area, it still supported the project.[51]

Native Americans Urge Defeat of the Bill

Native Americans and their supporters continued to object. For example, Loretta Ellis, the Minneapolis regional vice president of the National Congress of American Indians, wrote to all members of the House of Representatives urging that the bill be defeated. Her primary concern was the authorization to acquire the alienated shoreline along Lake Superior within the small Red Cliff Reservation, which represented a full third of the reservation area.[52] She did not realize that these lands had already been deleted.

Native American groups continued to be active. After their unsuccessful efforts in the House they again pressured the Senate. Michael Connors of the

Chippewa Indian Youth Council called "on all Native Americans to telephone or telegraph their respective Senators in an effort to influence their voting patterns."[53] He objected to the inclusion in the lakeshore of alienated land within the Red Cliff Reservation.

Some Native American communications with Nelson were inconsistent. Some individual tribe members had written him stating their desire to sell their land even as they objected to the lakeshore. Fred Connors, who opposed the inclusion of tribal land, wanted assurances from Nelson that the NPS would hire ten to fifteen Native Americans.[54]

On September 11, 1970, by a voice vote the House approved the lakeshore, although members were "flooded with telegrams from Indian groups across the country urging defeat."[55]

Finally, on September 26, 1970, President Nixon signed Public Law 91-424. There was no signing ceremony. Kastenmeier, in writing to me afterward, commented, "There were times when I wondered whether we would be able to win approval. It wasn't easy, but the effort was rewarding."[56] Nelson reflected on the struggle regarding the tribal land:

> It was at that stage that I decided, okay, we can't get the twenty or thirty miles of the Red Cliff shoreline and we can't get the Bad River Band in it, so I would drop it. George Hartzog was pretty sore about that. . . . It was kind of foolish that they didn't even want the right to petition to be included if they decided to at some stage in their history. It didn't really matter anyway. If they ever reached the stage where they wanted to it wouldn't be very difficult to get an amendment with the tribal council supporting it. . . . You see a lot of people never read the bill and they just assumed the Congress—the white people—was trying to take something away from them. So, if they weren't going to read the bill and you had all this emotion, the best thing was just to leave it out.[57]

Hartzog, in his reflections, noted that the earlier rejections of Apostle Islands had a negative effect on the NPS attitude in the 1960s. There was "great institutional resistance from within the Park Service and a lot of talk about destroying the system, etc. . . . But we had a roll on," Hartzog said. "My objective was to save what was left and leave my successors to sort it out. Congress always corrects. Public policy is like making sausage—messy, but eventually you get good sausage. Apostle Islands would be a much better park today if we had taken it in the 1930s." Hartzog spiced his observations with some choice words about the 1930s NPS "stupidity of rejecting the area because some timber had been cut."

Regarding the debates, he said his own contribution to the Apostle Islands proposal was "finding the consensus that would pass on the Hill." When asked about the hot words he exchanged with Senator Nelson in the hearings and his strong position that without the tribal lands the unit did not meet Park Service standards, Hartzog laughed. "You might call it . . . a negotiating position. Ultimately, you take what you get. . . . In the legislative process, you can't have perfection."[58]

But there finally was an Apostle Islands National Lakeshore, or at least, most of one.

❧

CHAPTER 6

Long Island at Last

In the original proposal for the lakeshore, Long Island had been included as a part of the Kakagon–Bad River Sloughs unit. When the debate in the House of Representatives Committee on Interior and Insular Affairs became fractious, George Hartzog, director of the National Park Service, had, in a few short sentences, recommended that Long Island be excluded. It was. His reasons for this recommendation were valid. However, for equally valid reasons, I and others believed that it should be part of the Apostle Islands complex. Despite the fact that it appeared to be a relatively simple matter to add Long Island, it quickly became very complex. The effort to add Long Island to the Apostle Islands National Lakeshore is explored in this chapter.

Long Island is part of a sand spit that extends from the end of Chequamegon Point in Chequamegon Bay, from a point near the Bad River Reservation to the east of Ashland. It is approximately 300 acres of land, two-and-one-half miles long and about one-quarter mile wide (accurate measures are not available; the North Central Field Committee's subcommittee estimated 400 acres in 1965, the NPS 300 acres in 1991).

In reality, Long Island is not an island at all. A storm in the late 1800s breached the sand spit, creating an island of the spit's northern and westernmost point. The breach, called a sand cut, was deep enough to permit a person to drag a canoe or a light boat from the inner waters to Lake Superior. By the mid-1970s, the sand cut was filled in by wind and water action, and Long Island was once again connected with Chequamegon Point.

Long Island's geologic origins are different from the rest of the Apostle Islands archipelago. It is the only true barrier island in Lake Superior; as a consequence its ecosystem is different from those of the other islands and the adjacent mainland. It was the home of two endangered birds, the common tern and the piping plover. The U.S. Fish and Wildlife Service designated the plover as an endangered species during the period Long Island was considered for inclusion in the lakeshore. Habitat destruction threatened the bird, and the U.S. Fish and Wildlife Service estimated that only seventeen nesting pairs remained in the Great Lakes region by 1985.[1]

Long Island's History

Archeologists speculate that Long Island has had sporadic and oftentimes intensive use throughout history. The remains of early inhabitants are either buried under layers of deposited sand or below the waters of Lake Superior; the island shifts twenty to thirty feet a year. In 1693 Pierre Le Sueur moved an early fort on Long Island to Madeline Island.[2] Later the federal government constructed the second lighthouse in the archipelago on Long Island in 1858 at a site called La Pointe. The remains of that lighthouse are visible. The ship *Lucerne* was wrecked immediately adjacent to the island during a vicious storm in 1886, and its remains are visible in the shallow water.

Developers became interested in lakeshore property early in the last century. Chequamegon Point and Long Island were subdivided into 709 lots in 1912.[3] A street called Grand Boulevard ran through the middle of the subdivision and lots, twenty-five feet wide and averaging 125 feet in depth, faced either Chequamegon Bay or Lake Superior. The *Ashland Daily Press* described the proposed development in glowing terms in an article entitled "Long Island to Be a Mecca for Tourists," noting that Long Island was long a rendezvous for campers, picnickers, and berry pickers, a favorite resort for fishermen, both summer and winter, and an attraction to local people and also to tourists.[4] Many of the lots were sold. With the changes in lake levels, shifting sands, and access difficulties, most of the lots eventually became tax delinquent and ended up in Ashland County ownership. Despite being deleted from the Apostle Islands National Lakeshore proposal during the 1960s, the island continued to be of interest to a number of people and agencies. Because of its uniqueness, the Wisconsin Scientific Areas Preservation Council in 1976 included Long Island on its lists of natural areas that it recommended for purchase by the Wisconsin Department of Natural Resources (DNR). In 1977 the U.S. Fish and Wildlife Service also received a recommendation from the council to the effect that it acquire the island as a unique or nationally significant wildlife ecosystem. Neither recommendation was acted upon, probably because the two major private landowners were unwilling to sell.[5] However, the natural values of the island faced potential threats as new technologies, including on-site liquid waste treatment systems and wind and solar energy systems, as well as improved boat access, began to make private development on such a remote area attractive.

Reasons for Adding Long Island to the Lakeshore

In July of 1983 Apostle Islands National Lakeshore Superintendent Pat Miller discussed with Martin Hanson the possibility of adding Long Island to the lakeshore. Hanson was enthusiastic and discussed it with me; I was also enthusiastic. Miller then discussed it with the NPS regional director in Omaha, who indicated that they were supportive.[6] At this time Martin Hanson was Wisconsin Congressman David Obey's field representative. Obey would be asked to introduce a bill to add the island. The island proponents knew, however, that moving a bill through Congress would take time. Thus it was decided to explore the possibility of securing either Nature Conservancy or private foundation funds to acquire and hold the island until the NPS was authorized to purchase it. The two major owners on Long Island opposed the DNR and NPS efforts to acquire the land and were perhaps more likely to negotiate with a private organization. In lieu of attempting to secure any kind of favorable response from the Department of the Interior, the Obey bill would precipitate a reaction that, it was hoped, would be favorable given the island's small size. Under the anti-park policies of President Ronald Reagan's administration it would be difficult to predict the outcome, but the NPS did favor the idea.

A number of arguments would justify the inclusion of Long Island within the national lakeshore:

- The island had great natural and cultural values.
- Because of its proximity to the mainland, the island would attract more tourists, which Pat Miller indicated would be useful when arguing for budgets.[7]
- The island would provide different forms of outdoor recreation not available on the other twenty islands. Swimming would be especially delightful.
- Increased tourism and boating would have a favorable economic impact in the area, especially in Washburn, where a new marina had been constructed, and in Ashland, where plans were underway for the construction of the city's first marina.
- Miller favored the inclusion of Long Island, and although he might be

constrained by the no-new-parks policies of Secretary of the Interior James Watt and President Reagan, he would provide quiet support.

• Given the earlier history of subdivision proposals, intensive development would always pose a threat.

• Because Long Island was several miles west of the Bad River Reservation, the tribe would probably not object.

All told, the arguments seemed rational and persuasive.

In Congress the political climate appeared to be favorable. The Democrats controlled the House of Representatives. Morris Udall (an ardent conservationist and brother of former Secretary of the Interior Stewart Udall) chaired the House Committee on Interior and Insular Affairs. Moreover, Martin Hanson, who had coordinated Udall's political efforts in Wisconsin during the 1976 Wisconsin presidential primary, would have access to him and his office. Bruce F. Vento, a Minnesota Democrat, chaired the House Interior Committee's Subcommittee on National Parks and Recreation and would likely be supportive, as many of his constituents came from the Twin Cities of Minneapolis and St. Paul and used the Apostle Islands National Lakeshore. Although the Senate was controlled by the Republicans, developing strong bipartisan local support would probably have a favorable influence on Republican Wisconsin senator Robert Kasten, who had defeated Nelson and who would be up for re-election in less than two years. Kasten was a lakeshore supporter, had a good record on environmental matters, and was keenly aware of the importance of the environmental vote in Wisconsin elections. Moreover, his victory over Nelson in the 1980 Reagan-led Republican landslide had been razor thin, less than 1 percent. Senator William Proxmire, who had always been a supporter of the Apostle Islands, was expected to continue that support for the Long Island proposal. However, how the Senate Committee on Energy and Natural Resources (chaired by Idaho Republican James A. McClure) and its Subcommittee on Public Lands, Reserved Water and Resource Conservation (chaired by Wyoming Republican Malcolm Wallop) would react was unknown.

Given the generally favorable climate, explorations with the Nature Conservancy and other groups for interim acquisition were discarded. It was decided to amend the Lakeshore Act to include Long Island. As events unfolded, the original optimistic assessment of the situation proved to be partially incorrect, and the quest for Long Island took a number of unexpected twists and turns during the following two years. Indeed, it was never clear that a Long Island amendment would ever pass in Congress.

Congressman Obey Introduces the Bill

David Obey, with another Wisconsin Democrat, James Moody, as co-sponsor, introduced H.R. 2182 on April 23, 1985. A few days later Proxmire introduced companion legislation in the Senate.[8]

Hanson and I had numerous conversations about whether to include a small tract on Chequamegon Point in the proposal as well. Because piping plovers had historically nested there it was decided to include this small tract.

To set the stage for the eventual congressional hearings, a substantial amount of work needed doing. Obey continued to line up more co-sponsors and was joined by Wisconsin Democrats Les Aspin, Bob Kastenmeier, and Gerald Kleczka and Republican Tom Petri. He released this information to the press and again stressed the economic implications of including the island in the lakeshore. He also reported that the Washburn City Council had recently endorsed the bill.[9]

Tony Earl, who had been secretary of the DNR, was now governor of Wisconsin. I decided to elicit from him a statement in support of the addition of Long Island. Hanson and I also called and wrote members of the Wisconsin environmental community. State government assistance would be extremely important, including that from the Office of Coastal Zones, the State Board for the Preservation of Scientific Areas, and especially the DNR. I discussed Long Island on two occasions with Natural Resources Board Chairman John Lawton, a personal friend.[10] Based on advice received from Obey's office, DNR Secretary Carroll D. Besadny was known to be waiting for the NPS position before acting. I claimed that it was pure and simple obfuscation; Besadny knew full well that the NPS probably would not support additions to its system. Some of the same Wisconsin Conservation Department tactics from the 1960s would be used over the next couple of years to thwart the Long Island proposal.[11]

Support was also needed at the local level. Thus a public informational meeting was held at the Sigurd Olson Environmental Institute in Ashland. The meeting quickly turned into a spirited debate among a capacity crowd. Martin Hanson, a member of a panel, presented the case for Long Island and noted that the U.S. Coast Guard, which owned half of the island, might eventually sell its land to private parties. He stressed the values of preserving the endangered piping plover and common tern. He further suggested that the old Coast Guard buildings could be restored to become focal points in the Chequamegon Bay area. Other panel members, Fred Gould of the Northwest Wisconsin Regional Planning Commission, Dennis Van Hoof of the

Wisconsin Coastal Zones Management Council, and Summer Matteson, a DNR non-game species management specialist, also argued for the addition.[12]

One landowner argued that he did not want his cabin taken away from him and objected to the proposed use of herbicides to manage vegetation and predator control to protect the piping plover (apparently a DNR employee had said that these techniques might be necessary for plover management). Another owner questioned how the plover could be protected while recreational use was being encouraged at the same time. (This would later become a central issue.) Norrie Reykdahl, a Washburn sportsman, and John Sivertson (the Sivertsons had owned land on Long Island since 1888 and had argued vigorously against the original lakeshore legislation) also spoke in opposition.[13]

Hanson and I had erred in not proposing the explicit boundaries for Long Island, especially to the east where it reached the Bad River Reservation. The DNR proposed a major portion of Chequamegon Point for inclusion to support the piping plover; this would cause more problems. I called Natural Resources Board Chairman Lawton and director of the Bureau of Endangered Species Ron Nicotera to emphasize the total values of the island, not just the plover's habitat, but they continued to focus on the piping plover. To deal with the boundary question, Hanson called Obey's office and made explicit that the proposed boundary would include only the tip of Chequamegon Point, which was separated from Long Island by a shallow water channel. At this point, there was no identifiable boundary.[14]

Hoping that the matter could be resolved, the DNR had agreed to review with Pat Miller a proposed letter to Vento. This it did not do, and the letter was sent without change. The letter was a weak statement and did not even state that including Long Island in the lakeshore was a good idea.[15] The DNR proposed an amendment to increase the area to be acquired from 220 acres to 600 acres, including lands extending east three-and-one-half miles from Chequamegon Point into the Bad River Reservation and including both tribal and allotted land. I advised Nicotera that the proposal was sure to result in a dandy fight with the Bad River Tribe and questioned whether he wanted that.[16] Nicotera agreed to check to see if the letter could be changed. After a lengthy series of phone calls between Nicotera, Hanson, Miller, and me, it was agreed that the boundary line of the addition would go to 600 feet east of the boundary of Chequamegon Point. The DNR telexed the agreed upon boundary to Neil Neuberger in Obey's office. Obey was pleased that the matter would be cleared up.[17]

An editorial in the *Milwaukee Sentinel*, which opposed the Long Island addition to the lakeshore, did not help the cause, although valid points were raised. The editorial noted that the island had slipped to 200 acres from the original 400 acres measured when the lakeshore was created. It further argued that the Coast Guard could easily manage for plovers. Finally, it said, "As a sandbar, the island is unlike the rest of the Apostles, which are granite blocks where changes wrought by the waves can be discerned only after years have passed. Long Island just doesn't belong in the park."[18]

The First Congressional Hearings

The first hearings on the House bill on Long Island were held in Washington on June 11, 1985, before the House Subcommittee on National Parks and Recreation, which was chaired by Bruce Vento. Although Gaylord Nelson, having become the counselor for the Wilderness Society, could not personally attend the hearings, Vento had volunteered to read Nelson's statement to ensure that it would have more impact than if a staff person from Nelson's office had read it.[19] Nelson's statement summarized the long history associated with the enactment of the lakeshore and observed that because of Native American objections to having their lands included, he had requested the House Committee on Interior and Insular Affairs delete tribal lands, "and unfortunately at the same time, Long Island [was deleted], which is not Indian land."[20]

Obey's testimony stressed the bipartisan support for the bill, including the fact that Congressman James F. Sensenbrenner, a Wisconsin Republican, had by this time added his name to the bill as a co-sponsor. Obey emphasized the broad base of support, which included Wisconsin governor Tony Earl, the Department of Natural Resources, the State Board for the Preservation of Scientific Areas, the Wisconsin Coastal Zone Management Council, the Sigurd Olson Environmental Institute, the city of Washburn, the *Ashland Daily Press*, the Sierra Club, the Audubon Society, and the Wilderness Society. To clarify confusion regarding the eastern boundary, Obey indicated that the 600-foot terminus had been agreed to by the state.[21]

Bill Bechtel, Nelson's former administrative assistant and now director of the Wisconsin Office of Federal-State Relations in Washington, offered testimony on behalf of Governor Earl. The statement was powerful and warned in strong words that "although there was no specific threat of unwise use or exploitation of this fragile spit of land immediately adjoining a priceless National Lakeshore but as it was easily visible from shoreland communities, . . . the danger seems obvious. It is not inconceivable that effort would be made to develop this strategic, almost exotic spot, either for private use or for commercial, resort type developments. This area has an established history of such efforts. The mere existence of this strip of sand surrounded by the icy blue waters of Lake Superior makes it a potential victim of some ill-considered exploitation."[22]

Tom Klein, former executive director of the Sigurd Olsen Environmental Institute, raised a major issue by stressing that the expansion of the lakeshore was for the birds, not the tourists. "There are twenty other Apostles to play on; protection not recreation, should be the objective of H.R. 2182." He also observed that the Nature Conservancy could adequately protect Chequamegon Point.[23]

Others also testified or submitted letters in favor of the bill, including the Sierra Club, the National Audubon Society, and the Wisconsin Audubon Council.[24]

In general these supporters stressed the following points:

- the need for protection;
- the important ecological values of the spit;
- the spit's importance to two endangered species;
- the fact that the deteriorating Coast Guard buildings were not currently being maintained;
- the danger that the Coast Guard lands would be declared surplus and, under Reagan-Watt privatization policies, would be sold to private parties; and
- the island was now being used by recreationalists and as a result was experiencing problems with litter, damage from all-terrain vehicles, loose dogs, and vandalism.

Some supporters put less emphasis on the plover and noted the potential recreational use of the island: camping, berry picking, hiking, nature study, swimming, and the favorable economic impacts on adjacent communities associated with increased recreational boating. Those interested in plovers and those interested in recreation did not agree; these differences would later threaten the legislation.

Under the Reagan administration, parks and conservation issues were not viewed favorably. Not surprisingly, Mary Lou Grier, deputy director of the NPS, recommended that the bill not be enacted for several reasons:

- The Coast Guard owned much of the island, and the land was therefore protected. Long Island was located at a considerable distance from the other management units in the lakeshore.

- The NPS assumed that the House Committee on Interior and Insular Affairs had deleted Long Island in 1970 because it was part of the Bad River unit, which had been excluded.
- The Coast Guard had some concerns regarding a transfer of land to the NPS.
- Recreational use of the entire lakeshore was low: 127,300 visitors in 1984. Since there were no imperative reasons for acquiring the island, the costs were not justified; "it is important that we not add relatively low priority areas at a time when strong actions are necessary to reduce the budget deficit."[25]

Archie Wilson of Rhinelander, Wisconsin, testified on behalf of himself and the other property owners on Long Island.[26] The statement, given in a professional manner, made persuasive points:

- Keeping Long Island out of the lakeshore was consistent with President Reagan's desire to develop within parks rather than expanding the numbers.
- If the Coast Guard lands were declared surplus, they would have to first be offered to the state and then to local units of government. The chance of a sale to private developers was nil, and even if true, a developer would be faced with strict shoreland zoning, a lack of electricity, a probable inability to install septic systems, a lack of boat facilities, and a short tourist season.
- A day-use picnic and recreational area was not practical on the sandy, infertile, and droughty soils. The vegetation was particularly susceptible to wild fires, and the risks would increase with more recreational use.
- Substantially increased use of the island by marina-class boats would not occur without the development of a safe harbor and day-use areas on the islands; they would be expensive and environmentally damaging.
- Much of the critical nesting area for the piping plover was outside the proposed boundary. DNR data revealed that no more than ten to fifteen plover nests could be sustained under proper management, which might not represent a viable population, at a cost of $16,000 to $20,000 per nest site based on acquisition estimates.

Wilson proposed two alternatives. The first, based on earlier recommendations of the DNR's Bureau of Endangered Species, was to work out land-use agreements with the owners to exclude people from the plover nesting areas during the two-month nesting period. Wilson's second alternative was to lease the Coast Guard lands to the Sigurd Olson Environmental Institute as a shot in the arm to a worthy and deserving institution that would also provide for the learning experiences and environmental preservation desired by the sponsors of the bill. All told, Wilson's arguments were well reasoned, were grounded in fact, and honestly reflected the private property owners' desires to keep their lands.

Obey had hoped to put the bill on the fast track with a suspension of the rules, but because the NPS and the Republicans were in opposition, it would have to follow normal procedures and be debated on the House floor. Although Chairman Vento was still supportive, the bill faced an uncertain future. The five to seven persons in opposition, especially property owners such as the Sivertsons and the boat charter operator out of Washburn, were, according to Obey, still really raising hell. Moreover, Obey was upset with a recent resolution of opposition adopted by the Ashland City Council (on a seven-to-five vote). Neuberger felt that Obey needed more local support. He was concerned that if there were a great deal of debate in the House, even though the bill might pass, the Senate, now controlled by the Republicans, would kill the bill.[27]

To make matters worse, there were now indications that the Bad River Tribe would oppose the bill. Long Island was reputed to have religious significance to the Chippewa. Furthermore, they were afraid that any increased boating use in the area would pose threats to the nearby ecologically fragile Kakagon–Bad River Sloughs.[28] Local non-Native opposition had also increased. By now Obey was not sure how to proceed.[29] Was Long Island going to die in the subcommittee?

In spite of Obey's uncertainty, Vento was persistent in his efforts to pass the bill. Irritated by NPS delays, he sent a curt letter to NPS Director William Penn Mott Jr. requesting a prompt response to his earlier inquiry regarding cost estimates. The response was neither prompt nor informative and indicated that land costs would be available in three to four weeks. It also indicated that developments on Long Island could be handled within the $4.3 million unappropriated balance authorized for the lakeshore. Almost four months later the NPS provided Vento with estimates on land costs: $240,000 for 103.85 acres and two improvements. The remainder of the 241.29 acre island was public land, and no costs were assigned. A 38-acre tract owned by Ashland County was valued at $60,000.[30]

Vento would also not let stand the NPS statement that the Coast Guard had some concern over the proposed transfer of its 137 acres to the NPS. The matter was laid to rest when the Coast Guard responded to Vento's inquiries, stating that it did not own the 137 acres estimated by the NPS but only 1.8 acres surrounding the Chequamegon Point Light, a .75-acre parcel for the La Pointe Light, and a permanent right-of-way for access and utility lines between two lighthouses. The balance of its acreage had been relinquished to the Bureau of Land Management in 1967. The Coast Guard insisted that these remaining rights be maintained. In line with the administration position, it also made clear that the information was "a factual response and does not constitute a commitment with respect to the merits of the proposed legislation by the administration, the Department of Transportation or the Coast Guard."[31]

While Vento was looking for answers, Martin Hanson and I began to use our network of media friends to drum up support for the bill. The *Milwaukee Journal* responded and published a strong editorial backing the bill. It noted that the charges by a handful of property owners that recreation use would conflict with piping plover nesting could be worked out. More distressing, in the *Journal's* opinion, was the NPS's shortsighted opposition to the lakeshore addition. "Congress should take the longer view and preserve a resource that is priceless."[32]

Hanson enlisted the aid of the University of Wisconsin's public television station, WHA-TV, to give Long Island additional coverage. A video was developed and used as a part of WHA-TV's popular weekly news summary, *Wisconsin Magazine*. Although it was nicely balanced in its inclusion of both opposing and supporting views, the visual images of the beautiful sand spit and its flora and fauna could only leave viewers with strong feelings for the preservationists' point of view.[33]

Long Island's coverage in the statewide press, environmental newsletters, and educational television was good. But Obey still wanted strong local support. Hanson made personal visits to members of the Ashland County Board and the Ashland City Council. Working with Mark Peterson (director of the Sigurd Olsen Environmental Institute) and Pat Miller, he also planned a boat tour for Ashland County Board members.[34]

The boat trip and the personal visits, letters, and telephone calls by Hanson and others paid off. In October the Ashland County Board's Committee on Agriculture and Extension Education, with one dissenting vote, approved the sale to the NPS of all the county-owned land on the island if the Obey bill passed. Of course, the fact that the NPS had appraised the county land for $60,000 had been brought to the committee's attention by Hanson. This was a persuasive argument. At the time the county received $172 a year in taxes on the land.

The committee's resolution, as adopted by the board, was the important one. This favorable vote was what Obey wanted, and he told Hanson that he would have the bill out of the House Interior Committee in two weeks and that the full House would approve it. Obey also immediately put out a news release commending the county board for its action.[35]

Obey's prediction on the House Committee was correct. A two-thirds vote was achieved; the bill was placed on the Suspension Calendar and passed on a voice vote.[36] Obey was elated and gave credit to the bipartisan unity expressed by the Wisconsin House delegation.[37]

During the floor debate, Vento reported that except for the two automated lighthouses, the 137 acres of Coast Guard land had been transferred to the Bureau of Land Management. Because the bureau was in the process of eliminating its holdings in Wisconsin, he amended the bill to transfer the land to the NPS, leaving the Coast Guard enough land to maintain its facilities.[38] It was too late in the year to expect action in the Senate.

Although 1985 ended on a high note, 1986 would prove to be the critical and decisive year. The issues and politics associated with this small sand spit would become even more complex, tangled, and confused. At times it seemed that the legislation would fail entirely. The debate on issues would be sharpened by conflicts between encouraging recreation and protection for the plover and tern. Questions also arose over protecting Long Island through acquisition by the Nature Conservancy in lieu of NPS protection, the significance of the island as a Chippewa religious site, potential problems from increased boating in the Kakagon–Bad River Sloughs, and partisan politics.

Bad River Tribal Involvement

Although Long Island was not within the Bad River Reservation, the Native American community became concerned over their interests. Paul De Main (a member of the Lac Courte Oreilles Band of Chippewa and Governor Earl's advisor on Indian affairs), and Steve Dodge (a Menominee and DNR employee), involved themselves in the issues.

De Main wrote to Thomas Vennum Jr., an ethnomusicologist with the Smithsonian Institution in Washington (with family roots on Madeline Island) regarding Long Island and expressed concerns over mass recreation, public intrusions into Native religious ground, and increased boat use.[39]

As their opposition developed, the tribe decided that their position needed to be laid out. Vennum authored a draft letter in opposition to be signed by either the Bad River Tribe or the National Congress of American Indians. The letter outlined the tribe's significant concerns:

- The Bad River Tribal Council had voted on July 5, 1985, to oppose H.R. 2182.
- Converting Long Island into a public park would have disastrous ecological effects on the Bad River Reservation and would violate deeply held Chippewa religious beliefs about Long Island and the peninsula.
- If the proposal went to Congress without full debate in Senate subcommittee hearings, it would be in direct violation of the review process established under sections 106 and 211 of the National Historic Preservation Act. Furthermore, Congress in 1978 had enacted the American Indian Religious Freedom Act (42 USC 1996), which established the policy to protect and preserve traditional Native American religions. In 1980 Congress included Section 502 in the National Historic Preservation Act Amendments, which directs the secretary of the Interior to submit a report to the president and Congress on preserving and conserving the intangible elements of American cultural heritage.
- At the time of the treaty cessions in 1845 there was evidence that Long Island was indeed attached to the mainland and the Bad River Reservation and had been used by the Chippewa in their traditional manner for hunting, fishing, berry gathering, and religious purposes.
- Increased boating would adversely affect the wild rice stands in the sloughs, an important food source for the Chippewa. Bad River had no control over boat use on navigable waters within the reservation.
- The area held tremendous historical and religious significance for Native Americans.

Vennum's draft letter stated, "To convert such a holy and historic place in Ojibwe history into a playground for the non-Indian population, we feel, would be its ultimate desecration. Over the past few years, we have continually been confronted in the Apostle Islands area with attempts to defile our ancient burial grounds by the imposition of development plans on the part of insensitive and unscrupulous entrepreneurs, viz. the recent debacle with condominium plans on Madeline Island adjacent to the resting places of our hereditary chiefs. These intangible cultural resources, are by law to be protected under the *Native American Religious Freedom Act*."[40] My files, and the NPS files, contain no further information on whether this draft was sent to the Senate subcommittee. In any event the arguments were powerful and were advanced in subsequent debates.

Vennum also began to put pressure on Wisconsin Senators Proxmire and Kasten. He noted that he had been a summer resident on Madeline for forty years and was certain that local public sentiment was against the bill. He reminded Proxmire that the Bad River Tribal Council had passed a resolution in opposition. Vennum alleged that Long Island costs would approach a half-million dollars, not the $240,000 the NPS had estimated. He also stressed the religious significance of the island. Unless there was adequate Senate committee review, he believed the legislation would violate federal law.[41] I became curious about Vennum's personal interest in the matter. Vennum had done a great deal of anthropological research on the Bad River Reservation. Apparently he had persuaded Bad River Tribal Council Chair Bob Bender and Bad River tribal attorney C. Candy Jackson to oppose the proposal because the island was an integral part of the Bad River Tribe's history.[42]

Early in 1986, De Main met with the Bad River Tribal Council. Chuck Connors of the DNR (and the son of Fred Connors, a former Red River Tribal Chair who had been a long-time supporter of the lakeshore) joined him. The meeting increased Native American concerns. A delegation from Bad River was to leave for Washington, DC, in a few weeks to raise the issues over Long Island.

To meet their arguments, it was decided that the best strategy was to ensure that hearing records included specific legislative history documenting the fact that the NPS could preserve and interpret Native American historical and archeological values on the island. I was to meet with De Main for further discussions on the matter.[43]

I brought De Main's concerns and involvement to the attention of Governor Earl. In response Earl wrote a vigorous letter to Bad River Chair Bender: "I believe acquisition is the best vehicle to protect the island from private development or destruction of fragile habitat. While the Bad River Tribe has raised concerns, the National Park Service, through rules and regulations, can best designate zones for multiple use, preservation of religious sites and/or other such accommodations. In addition, there are other remedies at hand which would be useful in protecting your lakeshore resources such as motorboat wake laws and prohibition of development on reservation lakeshore land."[44]

These actions were having the desired results. Neuberger had called the Smithsonian and determined that the institution had no position on the bill.[45] After Earl's letter was sent, I met with De Main. The day before he had met with Vennum and had laid out the governor's firm position on H.R. 2182 and S. 1019. However, I still felt that Bad River concerns should be met, but through other ways. Thus I suggested that an exploration be made to determine if the authority to regulate boating could be vested with the Bad River Tribe instead of the town or, as an alternative, to determine the possibility of joint Bad River–DNR surface water regulation. He did agree that the NPS could develop an interpretive program reflecting Native American values on Long Island.[46]

As these events unfolded, the Bad River Tribe began to feel that their opposition was a lost cause. They recognized that the Obey bill in some form would pass. Earlier positive discussions regarding the purchase of Long Island by the Nature Conservancy were no longer realistic. They decided therefore for informational purposes to attend an upcoming Ashland County Board Meeting but not to make a statement.[47]

The Role of the Nature Conservancy

Because of the uniqueness of Long Island and the nearby Kakagon–Bad River Sloughs, the Nature Conservancy had long had an interest in the area but had funded no projects for protection of the island. Before initiating the effort to incorporate Long Island in the lakeshore, I met with Wisconsin's Nature Conservancy director, Russell Van Herrick, in 1984. At that time Van Herrick stated that the organization was not interested in spending money to protect Long Island or to protect piping plover habitat in Wisconsin. He noted that healthy, viable plover populations existed in relatively secure habitat in the West, especially in North Dakota. He felt that it would be prohibitively expensive to keep people and dogs off the island and Chequamegon Point, especially in view of the fact that there was no certainty that a viable population of plovers could be maintained there.

I also discussed Long Island with Clifford Germain of the State Scientific Areas Council, who was supportive of Long Island protection. The island was on the council's acquisition list, but the DNR was not interested and had, in fact, turned down an offer of a land gift by one landowner. Germain was confident, therefore, that the council would support the addition of Long Island to the lakeshore.[48] In January 1986 Vennum again mounted a direct attack on the Long Island proposal by suggesting to Brent Haglund, the new Wisconsin director of the Nature Conservancy, that the Obey bill be killed and that Haglund should initiate alternative measures to protect the area. I sought Germain's advice. He suggested that I talk the matter over with Proxmire, who, given the political sensitivity of Native American issues, could withdraw his support for the bill if there was any tribal blowup. I did not agree. Germain then suggested the development of a master plan for the island that would ensure protection of the plover.[49] No master plan was developed.

Vennum maintained pressure on the Nature Conservancy to get involved both at the national and state levels. Although Haglund was concerned that the NPS could not appropriately manage for plovers, he did not want to become involved in these divisive issues. Haglund would consider getting involved on a win-win basis. He informed me in February that he was going to meet with Vennum, and when we spoke, that was his position.[50] The confusion surrounding Nature Conservancy involvement would increase over the following days.

In fact, the Nature Conservancy had not been consistent in its prior positions and was careless in communicating with Long Island supporters. In part this can be explained by the involvement of both the national and state offices of the Nature Conservancy; each had different views on the matter. In the summer of 1985 the state office changed its position of neutrality to one of considerable interest. That interest was piqued by an inquiry from a summer resident (probably Vennum) on Madeline Island who was interested in keeping the NPS and the state off the island. In particular, he did not want Long Island managed in the same way the DNR was managing Big Bay State Park on Madeline Island. The resident pledged a $10,000 donation to the Nature Conservancy to aid its efforts toward this end.[51] Haglund was not enthused over the prospect of becoming involved in the Long Island question, and later in 1985 he assured Miller that this was not a project he was ready to move on anyway. His recommendation was to move very slowly on the project, but to begin by gathering the necessary information for a suitable project package. But then, perhaps responding to interest from the national office, Haglund said, "Long Island is going to be one of the top forty sites the Conservancy can work on to meet its program needs in Wisconsin."[52] So the Nature Conservancy had flip-flopped on their Long Island position and now had an interest in having some control over the land.

By 1986 it appeared that the Nature Conservancy might be attempting an end-run around the Long Island bill. It was surmised that the Conservancy plan was to acquire the county lands on Chequamegon Point, to negotiate a cooperative agreement with Bad River on the Kakagon–Bad River Sloughs, the state's largest scientific area, and to acquire easements on the two tracts of private land on Long Island (Wilson had, in fact, suggested this in his House testimony) and on land east of the Long Island boundary. Vennum confirmed the Nature Conservancy's involvement in a letter to Proxmire in which he noted, "There is currently some movement between the Nature Conservancy, the tribe, the landowners and other interested parties to come up with a compromise solution, one which would not cost the taxpayers what Obey's bill is going to."[53]

Late in February, Haglund met with Bad River Tribal Chair Bob Bender and tribal attorney C. Candy Jackson. He laid out the difficulties he saw in attempting to block the Obey bill, as the Native Americans were demanding. First and foremost, Haglund insisted that the Nature Conservancy would not block the Obey bill. Instead they would only intervene if there was a more desirable alternative to put in its place.[54] Haglund agreed to accompany Bender to Washington in March to discuss the problem with Obey's and Kasten's staffs. Staff in the DNR, Matteson and Nicotera, were to be contacted by Haglund immediately to discuss their proposed alternative. Haglund would also visit with the landowners to obtain their commitment.

To clarify the uncertain situation, Hanson called Cliff Messinger, chair of the Wisconsin Chapter of the Nature Conservancy, who stated that he was all for the Nature Conservancy getting involved. He felt that the NPS was just interested in getting people to visit the island and was not concerned about bird life, especially the plover, and that in general the agency was not a good steward. Messinger further indicated that the Conservancy had had conversations with Sam Johnson (of Johnson Wax Corporation and a part-time resident on Sand Island) regarding an easement; if it were consummated, Kasten would announce it. Messinger said that the Conservancy had not yet contacted the county, the NPS, the Bureau of Land Management, or Long Island landowners.[55]

A day later Haglund, who apparently was not informed on all of the events that had transpired, informed me that the Conservancy would not oppose the Obey bill. He also advised me of his meeting with the Bad River Tribe at their request to discuss protection of the sloughs, and he had told them that the Conservancy would not oppose the Obey bill.[56] In retrospect it was clear that Haglund had developed an alternative, but the record of his numerous telephone calls and letters to the offices of Obey, Proxmire, and Kasten shows consistent support for the Obey bill. Furthermore, he later supported efforts to work out compromise language on the bill.

I was not the only one confused; the Bad River Tribe was as well. To the tribe, it appeared that there was no plan at all, and they did not know what to do. Kasten, obviously well aware of what was going on, had given Bad River five weeks to come up with their plan. Haglund was trying to help them.[57]

I needed help from Obey's office and called Neuberger. He then called DNR Secretary Besadny, who admitted that he was not familiar with the events going on in his agency but agreed to inform Nicotera of the agency's and the governor's positions. Obey called Gaylord Nelson for help. Nelson agreed to talk with Messinger to get these matters cleared up. Obey was confident that Kasten would support the bill if the deal between Nicotera and the Nature Conservancy could be stopped. Nelson, however, could get little satisfaction from Messinger, who indicated that the Conservancy had serious reservations regarding the Obey bill. He did agree that they would not block the bill without advising Obey in advance.[58] I had a long personal discussion with Messinger on the matter and emphasized my desire to see the Obey bill pass. Messinger subsequently changed his mind, and he apologized to Obey for not maintaining closer communications. The Conservancy, he said, had never opposed the bill either openly or quietly; in fact, they were delighted with it. He suggested an amendment that would require the DNR to give special attention to the natural communities and endangered species on Long Island. The Conservancy could then work with adjacent landowners outside the boundary on easements to protect their land.[59]

Although it appeared now that the Nature Conservancy would not oppose Obey, the alternative of easements and agreements with private owners that they had presented was attractive to the Bad River Tribal Council as a means of blocking the Obey bill. The tribe went before a committee of the Ashland County Board to enlist its support. Jon Gilbert, a wildlife biologist for the Great Lakes Indian Fish and Wildlife Commission, made the case before the full Ashland County Board. According to the *Ashland Daily Press*, "Gilbert was to present the alternative and show how it will work. He will tell about the Nature Conservancy concept, and ask if the county wants to be involved in this alternative."[60]

To deal with this potentially explosive threat, Hanson attempted to elicit a letter from Haglund stating that the Nature Conservancy supported the Obey bill, which he could use in contacts with Ashland County Board members.[61] I urged Messinger to call Haglund and tell him to cool it. Messinger agreed, provided, however, that the Conservancy would continue its work with the tribe on the sloughs. I concurred, provided, in turn, that the Conservancy did not muddy the political waters by engaging in publicity.[62]

With what appeared to be firm Conservancy support for the Obey bill, which would probably pass, Bad River abandoned the Conservancy alternative, with a caveat that the legislation be amended to include strong preservation language.[63] Through some adroit negotiating by Peterson, Hanson, and Miller with Haglund, Nicotera, and the Bad River Tribe, preservation language was drafted for incorporation in the Senate Committee Report. To reassure participants, Miller had developed for Hanson a list and explanations of laws and regulations the NPS had to follow in managing all of its lands. Hanson used this to argue the case for NPS management. The list included

the American Indians Religious Freedom Act; the 1899 River and Harbor
Act; the National Historic Preservation Act as Amended; Executive Order
11593, Protection and Enhancement of the Cultural Environment; the Endangered Species Act; the Coastal Zones Management Act; and the Wilderness
Act.[64] Moreover, the report would emphasize preservation, as indicated by
the agreed-upon language: "Long Island is part of the Chequamegon Point–
Kakagon Slough ecosystem which sustains nationally significant wetland and
terrestrial communities containing rare plants and animals. Therefore, the
primary goal of this legislation is to protect all natural and cultural resources
on Long Island and to enhance habitats as necessary for the well being of the
endangered and unique resources found there. A secondary goal of this legislation is to allow for development of human use and visitation patterns, and
enforcement thereof, which is compatible with the protection of all natural
and cultural resources of the island."[65] (This language was used by Kasten during the Senate debate.)[66]

Peterson set out to sell the bill with the revised report. Two meetings were
held at the Sigurd Olson Environmental Institute. Nicotera agreed that the
bill was fine, unless something better came along. The Bad River Tribal Council stated that it would not oppose the bill, but it might not support it either.
Apostle Islands National Lakeshore Superintendent Pat Miller was most
helpful in providing factual information. He indicated that if the legislation
passed he could live with it. Peterson kept both Proxmire's and Kasten's offices informed of the group's progress. With a consensus apparently in hand,
Peterson observed that the name of the game now was to obtain a public position from Wisconsin Senator Kasten supporting the bill.[67]

In spite of strong public support and the consensus achieved by Peterson
and others, obtaining Kasten's support would not be easy. The information
reaching me indicated that Kasten was still considering the Nature Conservancy's alternative and had requested appraisal information from Haglund.
Proxmire's office had on two occasions contacted Kasten's office and had been
assured that the senator would sponsor the bill; each time Kasten had backed
off. To ensure, once again, that the Conservancy and Haglund were still firm,
I called Messinger (who had made a commitment to Obey) to ensure that he
would keep me informed of any activities or changes in position on the part
of the Conservancy.[68] It appeared that it was firm.

In line with an earlier agreement, Nicotera and Haglund had been meeting
with the Bad River Tribe on designating the Kakagon Sloughs as a state natural
area. The western terminus was to be the Long Island boundary as described
in the Obey bill. The Conservancy would also work to acquire nonreservation

lands on Chequamegon Point and in the sloughs for eventual transfer to the DNR, which would in turn transfer the land to the tribe with deed restrictions. In return the Conservancy wanted a five-year agreement with the tribal council to protect tribal lands, after which they would seek permanent deed restrictions. Most importantly, Haglund told me that Kasten's office had finally called him and indicated that Kasten would support the bill.[69]

On May 6 Kasten finally came out publicly in support of the bill. Proxmire's office now wanted early hearings; a year had passed since the bill had been introduced in the Senate, and it now had the necessary Republican co-sponsorship.[70]

Almost up to the day of the Senate hearings, island proponents were not fully persuaded that the Nature Conservancy would remain firm on the bill, largely because Haglund had not kept them informed of the group's activities. Haglund had met again with Vennum on June 9. These matters were brought to Obey's attention. Obey instructed Neuberger to call Messinger and advise him that not one word or comma was to be changed in the language worked out by Peterson. Neuberger also called the Smithsonian Institution, where Vennum was employed, and "read the riot act" to the undersecretary regarding Vennum and the Smithsonian's apparent involvement. If necessary, Obey's office would request everything the Smithsonian had on Long Island under the Freedom of Information Act. The undersecretary was not pleased with this statement, although he agreed to comply.[71]

There was no need for the paranoia that gripped everyone at this time regarding Haglund's position. The group was, perhaps, overreacting to the long, complex, and confusing positions of the Conservancy. Given the numerous setbacks that the bill had experienced during the legislative process, everyone wanted to make sure there were no further last-minute obstacles. Haglund set people at ease at the hearing by speaking strongly in favor of the bill.[72] Kasten's statement was also strong, emphasizing the cultural, historic, and natural values of the island. He stated: "When the Long Island bill passed the House there had not been any discussions, either formal or informal, about balancing an increased use of the island by recreational users with preservation of the integrity of the island's resources. All apparently wanted to protect the island, but there was no consensus concerning the proper mechanism." He then noted that each interest group felt that its needs had been met.[73]

The record is not clear if any Bad River Tribal members testified in person, but the file contains a statement entitled *Testimony* in which tribal chair Bender said, "We are currently not opposing the addition of Long Island to the National Lakeshore. . . . [We] have been verbally assured that our interests will be protected. We are asking you to ensure that this will be so." He did not want any commercialization of the island. "An influx of people and boat traffic into this area would destroy the unique habitat."[74] Proxmire and Nelson also gave strong statements in support of the bill.

The NPS, consistent with earlier positions and following the directions of the assistant secretary of the Interior, testified in opposition. When Republican Senator Dan Evans of Washington inquired whether the NPS was opposed, the response was that it was the Oversight Management Bureau (in the Office of Management and Budget) that was in opposition.[75] Although the hearing had gone well and the Senate subcommittee had endorsed the bill, it still had to clear the full Committee on Energy and Natural Resources and the Senate.

The Senate Acts

In the waning days of the second session of the Ninety-Ninth Congress, there were deep concerns that political and bureaucratic delays would kill any possibility of the Senate taking up the bill. The assistant secretary of the Interior and the NPS were doing their best to slow down the bill.

Substantial pressure had to be put on Kasten to ensure that he used all of his influence in the Republican-controlled Senate and with the administration to get the bill passed. Kasten was now running for re-election, and in one of his television advertisements he claimed credit for protecting the lakeshore from Secretary of the Interior James Watt's abortive effort to sell NPS land on a portion of Sand Island to the original owners. Hanson and I would exert additional pressure. Hanson made calls, and I contacted the *Milwaukee Journal* in the hopes of eliciting a supportive editorial. Their editorial response, in the September 7 Sunday edition, could not have been better. Under the title "Can Kasten Get Senate to Save Island?" the editorial stated, "In television and radio ads touting his re-election campaign, Wisconsin's Senator Bob Kasten tells how he led the winning fight to prevent former Interior Secretary James Watt from selling off parts of the Apostle Islands National Lakeshore. Now let the Republican Kasten lead a similarly bi-partisan fight to preserve an environmentally sensitive but neglected stepchild of the Lakeshore: Long Island."[76]

The task once again was to distribute the editorial widely throughout the environmental community with requests that letters be written to Kasten urging action. Members of the politically conservative Nature Conservancy would be especially helpful in this regard.[77]

Long Island was approved by a unanimous voice vote of the Senate Committee on Energy and Natural Resources on September 27, 1986. In its report, it said, "Long Island is one of the last remaining habitats in the Great Lakes region of two seriously endangered bird species, the piping plover and the common tern. As part of the national lakeshore, the island would be managed so that these species, as well as many of the island's other shorebirds, would be protected."[78] The $240,000 land acquisition estimate was placed in the record.[79] The original lakeshore authorization of $4.25 million for lands and $5 million for development was not changed.[80]

On October 8, 1986, the full Senate voted in favor of the Long Island bill.

On October 17, 1986, President Reagan signed the bill. Long Island was now part of the Apostle Islands National Lakeshore.

After the act passed, the Samuel C. Johnson family of Racine, Wisconsin, donated to the Nature Conservancy a conservation easement of approximately forty acres on Chequamegon Point and hired a plover warden to ensure that nesting plovers would not be disturbed.[81] Brent Haglund confided to me that he was happy that the NPS had jurisdiction over Long Island. The Nature Conservancy did not have the resources to manage and patrol it.[82]

What had seemed at first blush to be a relatively easy task of protecting one small 300-acre sand spit had, in fact, turned into a major effort. In reflecting upon the chain of events, the obvious conclusion would suggest that Hanson, Miller and I should have conducted a more careful analysis of the natural and cultural resources of the island and a thorough political analysis of those who had either decision-making powers or could influence public perceptions. An informal committee could have worked out most, if not all, of the complexities before a bill was introduced into the Congress. However, the inclusion of Long Island within the Apostle Island National Lakeshore was achieved, and an important public interest was protected.

Governor Gaylord A. Nelson during the Kakagon–Bad River sloughs inspection, June 11, 1962. (photograph by author)

Kakagon–Bad River sloughs inspection, June 11, 1962. Top photo, left to right: Governor Gaylord A. Nelson, J. Louis Hanson, Bad River Tribal Chair Don Ames, Louie Lefernier, Jim Hawkins of the Bureau of Indian Affairs, and Bureau of Outdoor Recreation Director Edward P. Crafts. Bottom photo, rear to front: Martin Hanson, Governor Nelson, Director Crafts, and Tribal Chair Ames. The two people at the front of the boat are unidentified. (photographs by author)

Shack in the Kakagon River Slough with wild rice in the foreground, circa 1962. (photograph by author)

"The Unfinished Task" conference held in Madison, Wisconsin, when the
Wisconsin Council for Resource Development and Conservation ("The Peoples
Lobby") was formed on October 10, 1962. Above, left to right: Wisconsin
Department of Resource Development Director David Carley, Governor
Gaylord A. Nelson, Martin Hanson, Secretary of the Interior Stewart Udall,
and Bad River Tribal Chair Donald Ames. Facing page, left to right: Governor
Nelson, Secretary Udall, and Harold C. Jordahl. (photographs by William
Wollin Studio, Madison, Wisconsin)

Governor John Reynolds and State Democratic Party Chair J. Louis Hanson at Julian Bay on Stockton Island, circa 1963. (photograph by author)

John F. Kennedy visits Ashland, September 24, 1963. Front row, left to right: Governor John Reynolds, President Kennedy, Senator Gaylord Nelson; back row, left to right: Secretary of the Interior Stewart Udall, Secretary of Agriculture Orville Freeman, and tour guide Martin Hanson. (photograph by Carl Wahl, reprinted with permission of the Duluth News Tribune)

U.S. Department of the Interior inspection of the Kakagon–Bad River sloughs, July 10, 1964. Left to right: Marilyn Jordahl, Albert Whitebird and Fred Connors of the Bad River Tribal council. (photograph by author)

Ruth Bresette and Linda and Sherry Gokee ride the Red Cliff Indian Tribal Council float in the Bayfield Apple Festival, October 4, 1965. (Ashland Daily Press)

PART THREE

Issues and Policy Studies

❧

CHAPTER 7

Planning the Lakeshore

In the process of developing the Apostle Islands National Lakeshore several forces were significant factors in the eventual outcome. In the next several chapters, the focus is turned more closely upon certain issues and policies that played a formative role and are essential case studies for those seeking to understand the forces shaping local, state, and federal responses to the lakeshore. In this chapter the strategic role that planning at various levels played in the outcomes of the process is examined. Chapter 8 evaluates how politics at every level affected the choices lakeshore proponents made. Chapter 9 examines the crucial role the press played in creating and shaping public demand and support for a park of some sort in the region. Chapter 10 examines the responses of those most affected by choices, those who resided, permanently or part-time in the region, to the idea of a park in their midst. Chapter 11 looks at the conflicts that arose between state interests and those of the federal government, and mechanisms by which those challenges were addressed. Finally, chapter 12 examines the crucial roles, both positive and negative, that the two Native American tribes, Red Cliff and Bad River, played and the consequences of the lakeshore proposal becoming caught in national-level power plays by Native leaders seeking broader political change.

We begin with the vital role of planning.

In the 1930s Apostle Island enthusiasts urged the establishment of a national park on one or more of the islands. The concept of "recreation areas" had not yet evolved in either the National Park Service (NPS) or congressional policy. By the 1960s, however, the question was, "Should the Apostles be a national park or a recreation area?" It was an important question because of the different uses and management programs engendered in each designation.

Furthermore, the chosen designation would significantly influence public acceptance of the proposal.

Gaylord Nelson's original proposal called for a "lakeshore recreation area" encompassing the Kakagon–Bad River Sloughs and the long sand spit along Chequamegon Bay and Lake Superior. The proposal was strongly influenced by evolving legislation on national seashores, such as Cape Cod, Oregon Dunes, Point Reyes, Fire Island, and Padre Island. Lakeshores at Sleeping Bear Dunes, Pictured Rocks, and Indiana Dunes were all to be recreation areas. Other nonconflicting uses were permitted. To have proposed a national park for the Apostle Islands with restrictions on hunting, commercial fishing, harvesting wild rice, and trapping would have been highly controversial among the Bad River Tribe and local sportsmen who freely used the sloughs and who had hunting and fishing shacks there. When the proposal was expanded to include the Bayfield Peninsula, parts of the Red Cliff Reservation, and twenty-one of the twenty-two islands, there was even greater need to allow Native Americans to hunt, fish, and gather, and to address the desires of both Native and non-Native sportsmen to hunt deer and bear on the islands. To have proposed a national park might well have doomed the proposal from the start. A recreation area would fit the region nicely and avoid conflict. The Recreation Advisory Council's *Policy Circular No. 1* spelled out the concept clearly: "Within National Recreation Areas, outdoor recreation shall be recognized as the dominant or primary resource management purpose. If additional natural resource utilization is carried on, such additional use shall be compatible with fulfilling the recreation mission, and none will be carried on that is significantly detrimental to it."[1] Other uses could occur without major conflicts.

In spite of the obvious need to maintain strong support from the two tribes as well as with local communities and with hunters and fishers, the idea of designating the Apostle Islands as a national park continued to surface during the planning and legislative process. The Bureau of Outdoor Recreation (BOR) initially took the position that judgments on this question should not be made until each island and the mainland units had been evaluated and classified according to the Outdoor Recreation Resources Review Commission (ORRRC) system, leaving open the question, "Is it a national park, a recreation area, or a national monument?"[2] ORRRC had proposed six classifications: high density recreation areas; general outdoor recreation areas; natural environment areas; unique natural areas; primitive areas; and historic and cultural sites.[3] The Apostle Islands proposal would fit under several of these classifications.

Secretary of the Interior Stewart Udall first saw the area while accompanying President Kennedy on his helicopter trip. He told me that he thought the area was of such outstanding quality that it deserved national park status. After I explained the political complexities of such a designation he appeared at the time to be satisfied with a recreation area. Two years later he again suggested designating the Apostle Islands as a national park. I urged the secretary's policy staff to withhold its recommendation on the matter until it was discussed in detail with Udall, Nelson, USDI bureaucrats, and supporters. During these discussions, the idea was advanced that perhaps the twenty-one islands could be designated as a national park while the mainland units could be given recreation area status. Subsequently, Nelson, his staff, Martin Hanson, and I agreed that national park status, even for a portion of the area, would raise too many complex issues. The position that the entire area should be classified as a recreational area was to be maintained.[4]

This was a prudent decision, especially in view of Native American interests regarding their historical rights to hunt, fish, and trap. The need for public protection of the area would have been lost in clashes between preservationists and multiple-use advocates. The case of Voyageurs National Park in Minnesota and the intensity of similar debates there are instructive. Seven years were required (1964–1971) to see Voyageurs authorized as a national park. During this seven-year period, the most divisive debates raged over issues such as hunting and logging. The forest product industries raised the subject of lumber famines. The U.S. Forest Service joined the debate, insisting that they were opposed to any inclusions of their lands in a national park. Early proponents had made a decision that they wanted a national park in the state to demonstrate that the state had natural resources and scenic beauty that, although different from western parks, was every bit as worthy as anything the West had to offer. It was in no small measure a matter of state pride. Had they compromised on the "recreation area" designation, the political path would have been eased considerably. The initial authorization included a highly valued duck-hunting area, and in spite of the congressional authorization, hunters were persistent. In 1983, twelve years after the authorizing legislation for the Voyageurs National Park was enacted, a thousand waterfowl-rich acres were deleted from the park boundary.[5]

Other classifications for the Apostle Islands were explored by a subcommittee of the USDI North Central Field Committee (NCFC) studying the project; these classifications included the establishment of a national wildlife refuge for the sloughs in lieu of including it in the recreation area.[6] In fact, a refuge proposal had been turned down by the Bureau of Sport Fisheries and Wildlife in 1959. At that time bureau officials had noted that although the sloughs were important to waterfowl during migration periods, they were not significant as nesting areas. Furthermore, they did not see any threats of immediate development in the sloughs. Should threats develop they could acquire the area as a refuge using Federal Duck Stamp Funds. They held to this position and recommended that the sloughs become an integral part of a national recreation area. From a pragmatic point of view, the establishment of a refuge in the sloughs would have posed serious conflicts with the Native Americans and their hunting, fishing, and gathering activities and thus was not realistic.[7]

During the final congressional hearing in 1970, George Hartzog again raised the possibility of a national park, stating, "Except for the non-conforming uses of hunting and resource utilization, . . . in my judgment this is a great national park, because it is scientific, has scenic values in every sense of the word, and measures up to that standard."[8] The eventual inclusion or exclusion of tribal land had at that point not been decided upon by the House Subcommittee on National Parks and Recreation. Hartzog had, of course, targeted the primary issue of resource utilization that would be sharply curtailed in a national park and that would have adversely affected its success. It was, however, a nice accolade for the special and intrinsic values of the area. Congress eventually resolved this issue, and the lakeshore was established as a recreation area.

Lakeshore Boundaries

The lines on a map drawn by the planners is one of the most significant steps in the evolution of a park proposal; it determines which lands to include and which to exclude. The boundary should ensure that the project includes an ecosystem protected from the adverse impacts of adjacent human activities. Furthermore, in a park, the boundary should permit the development of necessary facilities, such as visitor centers, ranger stations, roads and trails, and campsites with minimal impacts on the natural resources within the park. Diverse opportunities for recreation are another important consideration. Political questions have to be raised and answered. Total costs must be realistic. Judgments have to be made on potential opposition from private landowners whose holdings fall within the boundary. As planning for the lakeshore proceeded, planners faced these and other difficult choices.

The first draft of the lakeshore bill was envisioned as a federal-state collaborative program. It was broad in its scope and sweep. It included the unique and distinctive Kakagon–Bad River Sloughs and all of the islands but Madeline and an undefined portion of the Bayfield Peninsula, leaving open the question of a national monument on Madeline Island. Further, it included all of the Bad River Reservation land north of U.S. Highway 2, including Long Island and Chequamegon Point, and a buffer strip extending south of Highway 2. A buffer strip on the Red Cliff Reservation extended south of State Highway 13. It also included the Bayfield Peninsula area, including lands within the Bayfield County Forest and the Chequamegon National Forest and other lands south and west of State Highway 13 and north of U.S. Highway 2.[9]

Supporters felt that this draft was too broad and sweeping, so a second proposal was developed, and the size of the proposed lakeshore was reduced considerably. The Bayfield Peninsula unit was limited to the tip of the peninsula from Bark Point to the eastern Red Cliff Reservation boundary; on the Bad River Reservation the sloughs and the land north of Highway 2 were included. The twenty-one islands were included. The proposal now included a study of the feasibility of establishing a national monument on Madeline Island.[10]

The first preliminary NPS plan, prepared by landscape architect Andrew Feil, again broadened the scope considerably. The area now encompassed approximately 294,000 acres—110,000 acres of land and 184,000 acres of Lake Superior. A water boundary was drawn to include all of the islands except Madeline; the boundary extended one-half mile beyond the outermost islands in the group. A total of forty-five miles of Lake Superior shoreline was included. The village of Cornucopia was excluded. The boundary extended south of State Highway 13 and included the Sand River and Raspberry River corridors. On the Bad River Reservation, the boundary included the Kakagon–Bad River Sloughs north of U.S. Highway 2 and extended east almost to Marble Point.[11]

The NPS plan was bold in concept and essentially ratified the first proposal. It recognized political reality by emphasizing that two-thirds of the area was already in some form of public or tribal ownership. The lake bottom, Stockton Island, and acreage on several other islands were owned by the state. The plan further noted that summer-home development was not extensive in the area, and building activity was minimal.[12] Following up on recommendations by the Department of the Interior subcommittee a year later, however, Feil modified the boundary significantly. A proposed narrow corridor along the shoreline would permit the construction of a scenic highway. The amount of land on the peninsula had been reduced from 50,000 to 6,000 acres. The USDI subcommittee believed that although the area west of Squaw Bay and

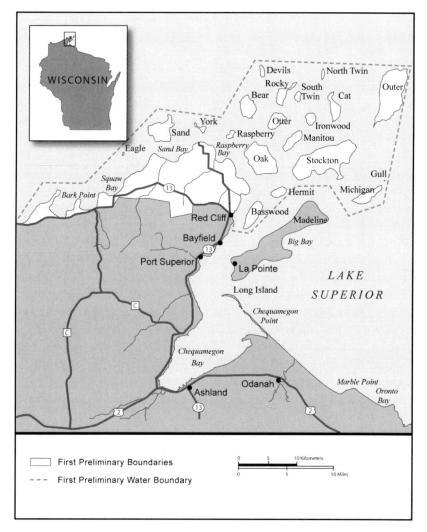

Map 3. First preliminary National Park Service plan boundaries, September 1963

along to Bark Point qualified for inclusion in the lakeshore, these areas would complement the federal area as private residential, commercial, and service centers. As such the local property tax base would be protected and improved. The USDI subcommittee also strongly recommended careful local planning and zoning to protect the private portions of the Lake Superior shoreline.[13]

All of the islands except for Madeline were included. The water boundary had been deleted. State-owned lands on Stockton, Oak, and Basswood Islands would either continue in state ownership or the state could sell or give them to the federal government. In the Kakagon–Bad River Sloughs, the boundary had been moved north of U.S. Highway 2 and reduced in size. Feil recommended that approximately 326 acres of land on Sand Island and 59 acres at Little Sand Bay be excluded because of sizable summer colonies. The total project was now 56,000 acres, a substantial reduction from the earlier 294,000 acres of land and water.[14] Unfortunately, significant and valuable resource areas had been eliminated, perhaps too early in the planning process. However, the lines were becoming fixed.

The USDI subcommittee struggled with the question of including or excluding the two summer colonies on Sand Island and Little Sand Bay. In October 1964 there seemed to be a consensus that they could be excluded and perhaps covered by special provisions; for example, life tenancy for owners who wished to sell, or restrictive covenants and other legal devices to ensure compatible development.[15] However, in November, after substantial discussion, the earlier consensus was reversed and the decision was made to include the summer colonies within the boundary. Life tenure or twenty-five-year tenure with a right of assignment were believed to provide adequate protection of private property rights at the sites. With the inclusion of the summer colonies, the total project acreage was now 56,385.[16] Questions regarding the two colonies would arise repeatedly during the legislative debates.

The Interior subcommittee endorsed the Feil recommendation that excluded the water boundary. Conflicts over water-use regulations were to be worked out cooperatively between the NPS and the state. In spite of the subcommittee recommendation, officials higher up in NPS continued to push for a water boundary, regardless of potential political problems with the state.[17] It would allow the NPS to develop marinas, other docks and piers, float plane facilities, swimming beaches, and similar facilities in the water adjacent to the land area. It would allow for the regulation of public use of the water areas. If and when a water boundary was authorized, it would prevent adverse uses such as commercial fishing adjacent to public use areas. Finally, the control of the water "would preserve the environment of the remote northwoods wilderness, water and island combination which is the great charm of this proposal."[18]

The Washington office of the NPS was pushing for an irregular boundary that would encompass the islands and extend one-quarter mile from the shorelines of the outer islands and one-quarter mile from the mainland units. Superintendent C. E. "Corky" Johnson at Isle Royale National Park believed a quarter-mile boundary was adequate, and the Washington office concurred.[19] Nelson agreed to amend his bill. He also advised Governor Knowles to this effect. Predictably, the Wisconsin Conservation Department reacted adversely. Director Lester Voigt, in a letter to Knowles, cautioned against including the water zone within the boundary because the state and the U.S. Coast Guard had jurisdiction, and adding a third agency could create serious problems.[20] In spite of state recommendations, however, final authorization included a quarter-mile water boundary around the islands and off the Bayfield Peninsula.

The Kakagon–Bad River Sloughs

Once agreement was reached on the lakeshore boundaries, decisions had to be made on classifying the lands for various purposes and associated development. Nelson had initially urged "wilderness preservation" for the sloughs. Lakeshore planners struggled with the issue of achieving that goal while at the same time permitting public use and enjoyment in the area. Could extensive bathing and beach facilities be permitted along the sand spit? Although large campgrounds were not feasible, should primitive camping be permitted on the sand spit or on highlands to the south? How could the wild rice beds be protected while still permitting boating?

These and other issues in the sloughs were resolved by the Interior subcommittee and the Bad River Tribe in the 1965 final report to the secretary. The unit was to remain undeveloped as "a unique shore and marsh area." Limited road access would be provided from U.S. Highway 2, two miles west of the village of Odanah, where a ranger station and visitor center were planned. A parking area would provide access to nature trails, walkways, and observation towers. Docking and launching facilities were to be provided at Bear Trap Creek in addition to the two Native-operated boat facilities on the Bad and Kakagon Rivers. Primitive camping, reached only by water, would be limited to Oak Point, south of the sand spit, and at the mouth of the Bad River. Native Americans were already developing lakeshore campgrounds accessible by car east of Honest John Lake, outside the project boundary.[21]

The Islands

From the beginning, plans called for keeping the islands wild. Minimum docking facilities were planned along with simple campsites, which included Adirondack-type shelters, fireplaces, and toilet facilities on certain islands.

Trails would be constructed. To assist visitors and to serve as a base of operations for patrols engaged in preservation and protection, a ranger station was planned for one of the centrally located islands. The only exception was Sand Island, which was easily accessible from Little Sand Bay. Here a concessionaire-operated lodge and a large group campground was planned to give visitors a readily accessible overnight island experience. Visitors could also enjoy overnight camping on Madeline Island—easily accessible by car ferry—where the state was planning Big Bay State Park.[22]

The NPS summed it up in the Interior subcommittee report: "The islands are the core on which the entire proposal revolves. Collectively, rather than singularly, they form a unique environment for recreation. They should be considered as primitive or wild areas and as such only minimum basic facilities are necessary for their use and enjoyment."[23]

The Bayfield Peninsula

The Bayfield Peninsula posed more difficult questions. Some favored keeping it wild and primitive, with minimal camping facilities and trails. Others favored development. The issues were debated, in part, within the context of plans for scenic roads along Lake Superior. Nelson had been elected to the U.S. Senate by the time the Wisconsin Department of Resource Development's *South Shore Studies* was completed. Local groups had proposed a twenty-two-mile lakeshore drive from Superior to the mouth of the Brule River; the NPS planners did not recommend this choice. Rather, they proposed the improvement of existing roads leading to the most scenic areas on Lake Superior and a conceptual framework for a primary and secondary scenic highway system, called "The Wisconsin Heritage Trail," which included improvements to State Highway 13 west of Brule on the Bayfield Peninsula.[24] That concept was ratified by the Interior subcommittee, and in its final report to the secretary of the Interior it also recommended that the peninsula provide maximum recreation use and development for the entire lakeshore, including a thirty-mile scenic tour. In addition, park headquarters were proposed at Red Cliff Creek, which would include employee housing, visitor orientation services, an interpretive center, and a marina. The site would be the major jumping-off point for trips to the islands and the scenic tour.

The NPS followed the lead of the Interior subcommittee and in their master planning process placed the bulk of the lands, both islands and mainland, within the lakeshore in a "primitive" designation.[25] Lakeshore supporters did not necessarily agree with the development plan's tradeoff between recreation and wilderness. B. L. Dahlberg, an ecologist with the WCD at Spooner, raised concerns that a road on the peninsula would adversely impact scenic and wilderness values.[26] Dahlberg knew the area well, having fished the streams and snowshoed into the numerous deer yards in the deep coniferous ravines. I took some time to respond to his concerns.

> I have, as do you, mixed emotions on the road. The plan is to keep it far enough from the lake so that natural beauty is not destroyed and to permit a continuous hiking trail around the entire area. The road will, however, permit tourists to select views of some of the outstanding scenery. If I had my "druthers," the peninsula should have been kept wild and natural. To do this would have meant national park status, which opens up a whole series of other problems associated with hunting, logging and public use. Keep in mind our recommendation for preserving the islands and the sloughs and this is already giving me considerable problems with the Bureau of Outdoor Recreation. In fact the road was put in to permit mass recreation . . . to help qualify the area of recreation status. Because of dual goals (massive recreation use and preservation), Secretary Udall has already asked Nelson if he would consider the area for national park status. At this point, I am still urging recreation area status.[27]

As the proposal advanced, others raised concerns and objections to the road, including the National Parks Association, the secretary and chair of the State Board for the Preservation of Scientific Areas, and the Michigan, Wisconsin, and John Muir chapters of the Sierra Club. A consultant in leisure living warned of car-deer accidents and severe erosion hazards with road construction on the peninsula.[28]

The tourism industry, on the other hand, offered enthusiastic support for the road. Henry Jardine, president of the South Shore Scenic Drive Association, which included as many as two hundred area businesses, said, "This is one of the best things that ever could happen to the south shore and the whole area."[29]

Because of the controversy that erupted over the road at the hearings in Ashland in 1967, NPS Director George Hartzog personally intervened and brought together those groups opposing the road. A compromise was hammered out consisting of a two-part, one-way drive. The eastern portion had a counter-clockwise traffic flow to an exit near the midpoint of the Red Cliff unit. The western part had a clockwise traffic flow to the same exit. Although this solution lacked unanimous support, the road as a significant issue was defused.[30]

Madeline Island

Madeline Island was the largest in the archipelago. Developments on the island were extensive. Two firms operated ferry services from Bayfield to Madeline. There were a large number of homes and vacation cottages and a network of roads. During the winter cars had access across an ice road. The island in its entirety had been excluded from the lakeshore proposal. However, the Interior subcommittee sought to determine: 1) the potential for a national monument commemorating the significant archeological and historic values of the island; 2) the relationship of Big Bay State Park to the lakeshore; and, 3) the possibility of a long-term lease with the Bad River Tribe for a small tract in tribal ownership on the northern tip of the island where a ranger station could be located.

Big Bay State Park, established by the Wisconsin Conservation Commission in 1962, consisted of 2,732 acres, including 2.5 miles of beautiful beach. At that time local residents had pleaded for the park as a stimulus to the economy of the village of La Pointe.[31] The state park, in effect, obviated any need for direct federal involvement on the island for recreation purposes.

The report of the North Central Field Committee's subcommittee recommend that NPS interpretative programs be cognizant of the historic values of the region and further urged the state and local groups to accelerate their efforts to protect and interpret the history of Madeline Island. It made special note of the need for protection of the "Indian Cemetery," which was "in danger of complete destruction from over-use by the public and curious souvenir hunters."[32]

Recreation and Resource Use within the Lakeshore

Wilderness

Overall the NCFC subcommittee report proposed boundaries and development plans that nicely balanced preservation and recreational use goals for the lakeshore. The sloughs and the islands, with the exception of Sand Island, were to be de facto wild or wilderness areas. In spite of this balance, which recognized the political and economic realities and the special needs of the Native Americans (acknowledged at the first House hearings held in Ashland), environmental organizations, with their more focused agenda, recommended that the legislation be amended to immediately designate the islands and sloughs as NPS-administered units of the National Wilderness System. Those favoring a cautious approach at the time knew that the Wilderness Act mandated that the NPS would have to consider wilderness designation in their master planning process after authorization.

The Wilderness Society sent a special memorandum to lake state members and cooperators urging them to testify at the first hearings to the effect that all of the islands and the sloughs should be immediately designated as wilderness and that the proposed lodge on Sand Island should be deleted. In Wisconsin, the John Muir chapter of the Sierra Club also took this position and urged the elimination of the scenic road. It also urged a substantial broadening of the proposal, with all areas to be considered for special scenic status. The Michigan chapter of the Sierra Club also supported wilderness designation for the sloughs and the islands and argued the need to exercise great care on the construction of the scenic highway.[33] Rupert Cutler, the assistant executive director of the Wilderness Society, expressed concerns that, as a developed recreation area, the lakeshore would attract too many visitors.[34] WCD Director L. P. Voigt also favored wilderness designation because it would fit in with his department's plans for the Apostle Islands State Forest.[35]

With a touch of nostalgia, Sigurd Olson, a well-known conservation writer and president of the Wilderness Society, noted that he had spent part of his boyhood in Ashland and attended Northland College. He urged that the legislation be amended to provide that the "superb string of islands be immediately designated . . . as a unit of the National Wilderness Preservation System." He also raised concerns that because "recreation areas" provide for high recreation carrying capacity, the Park Service would be tempted to overdevelop the area. He felt that statutory limitations would protect the wildland resources of the islands and prohibit overdevelopment.[36] The environmental organization Friends of the Earth took a more conservative position and, in lieu of immediate wilderness designation, suggested an NPS study of wilderness values.[37]

From the first drafts of the bill to the many iterations of the legislation considered by the Congress, explicit recognition had been given to wilderness values, but not to statutory wilderness designation. The NPS's 1968 revised master plan recognized wilderness concerns by designating major portions of the lakeshore as "primitive." Campsites on the islands and in the sloughs would be primitive, although a group campsite was still planned for Sand Island. Perhaps in response to wilderness advocates, the proposed lodge on Sand Island had been eliminated.[38] In 1965, Nelson introduced the first bill, S. 2498. It recognized wilderness values as did S. 778 introduced by Nelson two years later, which passed in the Senate on August 21, 1967, without a dissenting vote. The latter bill defined the goals of the management plan to be developed by the secretary of the Interior as "preservation of the unique flora and fauna and the physiographic geologic conditions now prevailing on the Apostle Islands . . . [and the] preservation and enhancement of the unique characteristics of the Kakagon–Bad River Sloughs." In the sloughs the bill constrained the USDI secretary, mandating "that no such development or plan for the convenience of visitors shall be undertaken . . . if it would be incompatible with the preservation of the unique flora and fauna or the present physiographic conditions."[39] As the House failed to act, Nelson introduced his third bill, S. 621, on January 24, 1969, which was subsequently passed by the Senate.[40] It contained the same strong preservationist language.

The legislation, when finally enacted, reiterated the original language of S. 621. Because Native lands had been deleted in the final law, there were no references to the sloughs. The House Committee on Interior and Insular Affairs report made no specific reference to wilderness per se but did note that the development of docking facilities for private and excursion boats would permit island camping, hiking, photography, nature study, and sightseeing. The greatly reduced area on the peninsula was to be appropriately developed to ensure the protection of natural values. The House committee believed that the peninsula would "serve the greatest portion of the visiting public to the lakeshore."[41]

Although Nelson had empathy for those who had urged immediate designation of the islands as a part of the National Wilderness system (he personally favored keeping the islands wilderness), such an amendment would have created substantial political problems with local people. In a recreation area the Native Americans would be permitted to hunt, fish, trap, and harvest wild rice within the reservation. They would have preferential rights to any timber harvests. Hunting, trapping, and fishing (both sport and commercial) would be permitted in the entire lakeshore for both Native Americans and non-Natives. Such usage was inconsistent with formal wilderness designation.

In spite of the substantial changes in boundaries in the final legislation, the record is clear that Congress made no changes in the NPS plans for the islands. With the exception of Sand Island, they were to be kept essentially wild and primitive. The peninsula was to be appropriately developed with attention paid to protect natural values.

Logging

Although timber harvest in recreation areas was permissible if it did not interfere with recreation, the House Subcommittee on National Parks and Recreation, following the recommendations of the Interior subcommittee, recommended that logging not be permitted in the lakeshore for reasons related to maintaining the "wilderness-like condition" of the area. The House subcommittee further noted that there was a surplus of wood products in the region and, in fact, throughout the lake states, and that eliminating timber harvest within the lakeshore would not adversely impact the local economy.[42]

Mining and Mineral Rights

Fortunately little potential existed for metallic and nonmetallic mining within the lakeshore, thus mining was never an issue in the legislative process. It still needed to be addressed, and the NCFC subcommittee was mindful that an earlier mining history, particularly brownstone for buildings, should be acknowledged as some future mining might take place. Also, at the western end of the range, near Mellen some twenty-five miles south of the lakeshore, substantial deposits of magnetic taconite existed. The U.S. Bureau of Mines believed these deposits had high mining potential. Mining here could pose a problem to the lakeshore; large quantities of water would be drawn from the Bad River Basin for grinding and beneficiating the low-grade ores. Although 95 percent of the water used in such mining operations would be returned to surface waters, it might be degraded and could adversely impact the Bad River Slough within the lakeshore.

The Bureau of Mines stated "existing geologic evidence and interpretations lead to the conclusions that the Apostle Islands and adjacent Lake Superior shore areas have a very limited mineral industry potential."[43] However, the Bureau of Mines in Washington, ever mindful of its mission to maintain a vigorous mineral industry, wanted to keep mining as an option and suggested that the NCFC subcommittee report be modified to read: "Should mining [in the lakeshore] become in the national interest, arrangements for operations would be made to provide adequate and reasonable protection to recreational features and still permit the enjoyment of mineral benefits."[44] This suggestion, however, was not included in the report.

Harvesting Wild Rice

Plans for the lakeshore envisioned continued harvesting of wild rice in the Kakagon–Bad River Sloughs. During good crop years, approximately 6,000 to 10,000 pounds of rice were gathered by as many as forty harvesting teams during a six- to twelve-day harvest period. Bad River Tribe members were the main harvesters; they used the rice for family needs and for sale. Although the total value of the crop was not great, harvesting rice was an important element of the Chippewa culture and lifestyle. The lakeshore would not interfere with that tradition. To protect rice stands from adverse wave action, the NCFC subcommittee recommended restrictions on outboard motors and proposed "no-wake" speeds in the Kakagon Sloughs portion of the lakeshore.[45]

Trapping

As with wild rice, the trapping of furbearers, although not commercially important, was symbolically important to the Native Americans and would continue to be permitted in the lakeshore. At the beginning of the twentieth century, more than an estimated two thousand muskrats and lesser numbers of mink, beaver, and otter were trapped in the sloughs. With management, biologists estimated that an annual harvest of some twenty thousand muskrats would be possible. At the time of the Field Committee's subcommittee studies, only a handful of muskrat were being trapped, and without a significant increase in fur prices, future trapping was not viewed as significant.[46]

Sports and Commercial Fishing

The only significant sports fishing within the lakeshore area was in the sloughs on the Bad River Reservation; this activity could continue for both Native Americans and non-Natives. Overfishing and the invasion of the parasitic sea lamprey had practically eliminated sports fishing in Lake Superior by the mid-1960s. Although sixty commercial fishermen still operated out of Washburn, Bayfield, Cornucopia, and Port Wing in the 1960s, the bulk of their catch consisted of low-value herring, chub, and smelt. No significant increases in commercial fishing were expected until the lake trout fishery was, if it could be, restored.[47] Even though the area was to be established as a national lakeshore, commercial fishing was expected to continue. The NCFC subcommittee carefully investigated methods of eliminating potential conflicts. At the time, a water boundary for the lakeshore was not envisioned. However, the responsibility of the NPS for public use, safety, and enjoyment was explicitly recognized. The subcommittee recommended collaborative efforts with the state and local governments to deal with conflicts. The final report recommended that the secretary of the Interior regulate hunting, fishing, and related activities where there existed a threat to public safety, use, or enjoyment on lands and waters under the secretary's jurisdiction. As no serious conflicts existed then (nor were anticipated) on surface waters, the responsibility for surface water control would continue with the state government, and conflicts would be resolved through cooperative efforts. The state retained the right to regulate commercial fishing, to open and close seasons, and to determine the manner in which fish might be taken and the types of gear that might be used.

One commercial fishing family, the Hokensons, opposed the lakeshore because their home and base of operation were within the lakeshore boundary and would be acquired by the NPS. Other commercial fishers generally remained neutral. Roger Bodin, a well-known commercial fisherman, was a strong advocate for the lakeshore, but he urged that commercial fishing be regulated by the state, the one-quarter mile water boundary be eliminated, and "the use of roads and landings within the Lakeshore for getting on and off the winter ice continue as they have done for hundreds of years in this area."[48]

The NCFC subcommittee report concluded that "the potential conflicts . . . do not appear at this time to be sufficiently serious to the Subcommittee to warrant major changes in the historic roles played by the state and federal governments on these matters. Moreover, if a national lakeshore is established, state officials have indicated their willingness to cooperate fully with the Department in resolution of conflicts over which they have jurisdiction."[49]

Hunting

Hunting within the lakeshore would continue. At the time of the proposal, the sloughs were recognized as one of the better waterfowl hunting areas in the area; twenty-four species of ducks had been observed there. Long Island and Chequamegon Point were often good spots for hunting Canada, snow, and blue geese. Ruffed grouse were important game birds on the mainland, although they were not found on the islands. Deer had shown an eruptive population behavior on the islands in the 1950–60 era and provided marvelous hunting. By the 1960s populations were rapidly declining.[50] Louis Hanson summed up the political realities of hunting in the lakeshore, and especially in the sloughs in 1985: "I think the hunting thing was brought up by concerned citizens. . . . [But] after the Apostle Islands proposal . . . [Nelson's] popularity dropped markedly. They didn't want this to be done."[51]

Sportsmen, primarily from Ashland, many of whom had hunting shacks in the sloughs, did raise some strong opposition to the lakeshore through signed petitions. They were appropriately afraid that what they viewed to be their private hunting grounds would be infringed upon by outsiders attracted to the sloughs as a result of national designation and publicity. Although hunting did not become an important substantive issue in the debates before Congress, hunters did use their influence with Bad River Tribe members to enlist their support to oppose the lakeshore proposal.

General Observations on Resource Use

The overall strategy on the part of the NCFC subcommittee had been to permit most traditional uses within the lakeshore and to enlist the various user groups to either remain neutral or to support the proposal. In general, the strategy worked. In part because state jurisdiction over hunting, fishing, trapping, and harvesting wild rice would continue, Governor Knowles and WCD Director Voigt eventually supported the lakeshore.[52] The national and Wisconsin chapters of the Wildlife Federation and the Izaak Walton League also came out in support if these activities would continue.[53] As a matter of principle, the National Parks Association objected to continued hunting, although it supported the proposal in general.[54] In the end, the language in the act explicitly allowed a variety of activities:

> The Secretary shall permit hunting, fishing, and trapping on lands and waters under his jurisdiction within the boundaries of the Lakeshore in accordance with the appropriate laws of Wisconsin and the United States to the extent applicable, except that he may designate zones where, and establish periods when, no hunting, trapping, or fishing shall be permitted for reasons of public safety, administration, fish or wildlife management, or public use and enjoyment.[55]

Careful planning had resulted in a successful, and generally accepted, proposal.

CHAPTER 8

The Role of Politics in Establishing the Lakeshore

Obviously to set aside an area of land and water the size of the Apostle Islands National Lakeshore would impact private ownership, Native American lands, both tribal and allotted (alienated to non-Native or private owners), as well as local, state, and federal government lands. The proposed use of that land would be fraught with political considerations, both partisan and practical. This was reflected in the debates that occurred at the local, regional, and state levels, within the communities of the Red Cliff and Bad River Tribes and their governing bodies, within the conservation communities of the region and nationally, as well as in the U.S. Congress. Many government bureaucracies had or would have jurisdiction. Congress had the final authority. Fortuitously, within our democracy we have numerous agencies, ranging from small relatively simple town boards to highly complex institutions such as the U.S. Department of the Interior. The lakeshore proposal had to find its way past many of these agencies, small to complex, in its ten-year odyssey through a bewilderingly complex system. Along the way, special needs developed and new organizations and solutions were created to meet these. This chapter examines these challenges and their influence on the Apostle Islands story.

The Apostle Islands and Congressional Politics

In addition to partisan considerations, Wisconsin Senator Gaylord Nelson would be continually frustrated with procedural issues in Congress, in spite of the fact that both the House of Representatives and the Senate were controlled by Democrats. For, example, it had taken Nelson a full two years just to get a draft bill out of the USDI that he could introduce in the Senate.

To start the legislative process, Nelson, along with Senators William Prox-mire and Paul Douglas, an Illinois Democrat, introduced S. 2498 in the Senate (the Interior's draft bill) on September 7, 1965. Congressman Alvin O'Konski introduced companion bill H.R. 10902 in the House of Represen-tatives a day later.

Because of the bill's late introduction, no hearings were held in 1965. Fur-thermore, President Johnson had called for more study of the Apostle Islands; a year would pass before any action would be taken. Thus, Nelson had to reintroduce the old bill, now numbered S. 778, in January 1967. He met with Alan Bible, chairman of the Senate Subcommittee on Parks and Recreation, but was unable to obtain a commitment for early hearings.[1] By this time Nel-son's frustration was evident, and he told reporters, "The bill has been two years in Capitol Hill doldrums."[2] In spite of the inaction, he was still unrealis-tically hopeful for successful passage of the bill by early summer.

Nelson finally secured Senate hearings in May and June. The lakeshore pro-posal received overwhelming support, and it was not difficult for Nelson to move the bill through the Senate. The Senate Subcommittee on Parks and Recreation approved it on August 16, followed by the full Committee on Inte-rior and Insular Affairs two days later. On August 21 Nelson was able to place it on the Consent Calendar, and it passed on the same day.[3]

Action in the House of Representatives was to be a much more difficult matter. Before Nelson introduced the bill in the Senate he had conferred with Wayne Aspinall, chairman of the House Committee on Interior and Insular Affairs. Aspinall told Nelson he would have to get in line; numerous proposals for new parks, seashores, and lakeshores were already before his committee. Although Nelson went out of his way to develop strong collegial and social relationships with Aspinall, his turn in line would not come up for two more years. Nelson, reflecting on it later, said, "I also did a lot of talking about it with Wayne Aspinall. I had him out to my house on his birthday and was pushing both the St. Croix Wild and Scenic Riverway and the Apostle Islands bills, and without his consent, nothing passed that committee. Finally, he agreed that both were good ideas. So finally it did pass in 1970."[4]

Lack of money for the Land and Water Conservation Fund (LAWCON) in 1968 further delayed House action on the Apostle Islands and other lakeshore proposals. Aspinall did not want additional authorizations until funding was secure. The House acted on the funding issue in midsummer by doubling the money available to assure funding of $200 million a year. Aspinall then promptly scheduled hearings on the Apostle Islands for July 29.[5]

Richard F. Fenno Jr., in his book *Congressmen in Committees*, provides an excellent analysis of House committee processes and the reasons why the Apostle Islands and the scenic rivers bills passed easily in the Senate twice before Aspinall would even hold hearings.[6] Fenno points out that senators reflected both rural and urban interests, with the latter playing a predominant role in their re-election probabilities. Urban people were significantly more interested in environmental matters, conservation, and outdoor recreation. The Senate Interior Committee was willing to let a member of the committee, such as Nelson, gain something for his state that did not have significant national policy precedents. Although dominated by western senators, the Senate Interior Committee normally took a pro-park position and acted far more quickly than did the House Interior Committee. For example, between 1955 and 1966, of the thirteen major parks and land bills reported by the House committee, the Senate committee had reported the bill first in ten instances, sometimes more than once, before the House chose to act.[7]

Aspinall, a former school teacher, had been in elective politics continuously since 1931, first as a state legislator and, after 1948, as a congressman. Aspinall's Committee on Interior and Insular Affairs was the hardest-working committee in the House and reported on more substantive legislation than any other.[8] He maintained absolute control over the committee and its agenda. He decided when matters were to be taken up, when hearings were to be held, and when decisions were to be made. He hired the staff and kept it attached to his office and the full committee; aides were not assigned to subcommittees. Although Aspinall maintained tight control, committee members found him to be "fairness personified."[9]

Bills were carefully and thoroughly scrutinized in his committee, and all interests were given an opportunity to present their cases. As one member characterized him:

> Wayne Aspinall is an old schoolmarm. He gives us civics lectures up there in the committee about the three coordinate branches. He tells us we don't have to accept the administration bill or the Senate bill—that we are going to take our time and do it our own way. We are schooled in that philosophy of independence. This committee is pretty independent. I don't think it's an arm of the executive department. We make the policy, we are the policy makers. That's a right that's very jealously guarded by the committee.[10]

The fact that Aspinall was thorough and orderly and insisted on full and complete reviews of legislation accounted for the long delay before he would take up the Apostle Islands bill. The committee simply had too much other business before it. As one committee member observed, "You can't keep up with the Senate if you want to do a thorough job."[11] And Aspinall insisted on a thorough job.

Another significant factor was the view that Aspinall and the committee had of their policy responsibilities. He continually reminded committee members that they made the policy, not the Executive Branch. This posture had significant implications for the Apostle Islands when NPS Director George Hartzog kept insisting that the project would not be viable without the tribal land. The committee, in its report to the House, addressed the issue squarely: "After considering all of the arguments and weighing all of the competing interests, it is the Congress which must decide what action should be taken."[12]

The House Interior Committee was not split along partisan or ideological lines. Its members' primary interests were projects for their own districts. Aspinall and the ranking minority member, John Saylor of Pennsylvania, worked well together. In Fenno's analysis, "Saylor shared a desire to maintain the committee's reputation for careful, expert and independent handling of its legislation and consequently the confidence of the House. Saylor's support on the House floor helped legitimize the committee product in the eyes of non-westerners."[13] This was certainly true for the Apostle Islands.

Although preservationists attacked Aspinall for holding up House action after the Senate had passed legislation on wild and scenic rivers, a Redwood National Park, the Apostle Islands, and a bill on wilderness, an astute Department of the Interior official observed that Aspinall knew what his committee would do and how to reconcile competing interests. Had the Senate-approved versions not receiving substantial modification in the House committee, they would not have passed on the floor. The House respected Aspinall and the thorough work of the committee. Consequently, when bills from his committee finally reached the floor, they passed.[14]

The Apostle Islands and the Congressman from Northern Wisconsin

To enact park bills, support from the state district's congressional representative was typically required. The Apostle Islands were in Republican Alvin E. O'Konski's sprawling Northern Wisconsin District, which he had represented since 1942.

O'Konski recognized Nelson's popularity in the north and did not challenge him while he was governor and later senator. In fact, he had supported many of Nelson's programs. O'Konski was not a strong legislative leader and typically "tested the winds" in his district before taking positions. Constituent relations and service was his political forte. Provided there was strong local support, he would not be a direct threat to the lakeshore. Even though O'Konski was a member of the minority party, the veteran congressman's tacit support in the House would at a minimum be necessary. Of course, strong support would be even more helpful.

Although Nelson had not informed O'Konski when he made his first proposal in 1961, it posed no problem. The governor was simply responding to a request for planning from the Bad River Tribal Council. Thereafter, I made sure that O'Konski was informed of every step in the process. William Bechtel in Nelson's office also had excellent relations with O'Konski and made it a point to keep him informed. Nelson and his staff did not ask the congressman to take a position. Evidence of local support would be a stronger stimulus for him to take action.

O'Konski's initial posture was one of caution. In 1963 he had reservations because he viewed the project as controversial. But, he added, "If the federal government really means business and will spend $5 million or so really making it a park of consequence, I am all for it. If, however, the government purchases the land to call it a national park and does no investing other than buying the land, I do not foresee where the project would help our economy very much."[15]

By 1966 pressure from a new organization, the South Shore Property Owners, caused him to revise his position. O'Konski then felt, as did many local people, that the federal government was taking too much land in Bayfield County. He claimed that more than half of the county was now federally owned land on which no property taxes were paid. Local owners viewed taxes as breaking their backs. O'Konski reassured them and noted that the park proposal was running into trouble in Washington.[16] A year later, when substantial property owner opposition had developed, O'Konski suggested dropping the mainland units.[17]

Supporters of the lakeshore provided countervailing pressure, and in May 1967 O'Konski reported that he was receiving twenty-five letters a day in support of the lakeshore from within and outside the district. His stock reply was now generally supportive. He urged the letter writers to attend the upcoming hearings and to "make a good case for the project. If this is done, I am sure that the members of the [House] subcommittee will come back to Washington sold on the idea . . . The success or failure of the project will depend on the enthusiasm or lack of enthusiasm of the people in the area."[18] When the first hearings were held in Ashland in 1967, O'Konski pleaded business in Washington and was absent. The hearings, held at Northland College, were jammed with people, most of them supporters. During the hearings, O'Konski called John Chapple of the *Ashland Daily Press* and asked him to read a surprisingly strong statement on his behalf. "I have studied this project for the past ten years. I have concluded that the establishment of an Apostle Islands National Lakeshore is good for the area, good for the state and good for the nation. Furthermore, it is the only opportunity for this area to get substantial federal assistance."[19]

Nelson maintained the pressure on O'Konski. After overwhelming support was demonstrated during the Ashland hearings, he wrote letters to every supportive organization and individual urging them to write to O'Konski and the members of the Senate Committee on Interior and Insular Affairs. O'Konski responded by stating that "his mail was running overwhelmingly in favor of an Apostle Islands National Lakeshore."[20]

In 1968 when the first House hearings were held in Washington, O'Konski was enthusiastic. He had had oral surgery only hours before the hearings but showed up to say, "It's of utmost importance to my district. I would be here if I'd had to come on a stretcher." The *Milwaukee Journal* noted that it was the first time O'Konski had appeared in person to testify and had turned out to be an enthusiastic co-sponsor. Any loss in property taxes, he felt, would be offset by positive economic impacts.[21]

From that point onward he never wavered in his support. In spite of the intense national concern that was developing over the proposed inclusion of tribal lands, O'Konski wanted action after all these years. He made an eloquent statement dealing with the long-standing vacuum local property owners with lakeshore boundaries had faced for many years. He felt that tribal lands could now be excluded with the belief that the tribal members eventually would support the project. Moreover, he directly challenged his Republican colleague from Kansas, Joe Skubitz, by stating that the Apostle Islands were quite safe for recreational boating.[22] O'Konski and Congressman Kastenmeier (southern Wisconsin) signed a joint letter to all members of the House committee. The letter pointed out that even though the tribal lands were deleted, the proposal still constituted a viable project.[23] O'Konski also joined Nelson in a personal visit to Secretary of the Interior Walter Hickel to make the case. Hickel indicated his full support even with the deletion of the tribal lands. He also promised to send people to make congressional contacts and urge support. After meeting with Hickel, O'Konski said he "was confident the Interior Department would agree to develop the lakeshore as proposed by the House Committee. Hickel wants to move full speed ahead on the project."[24]

At the time, House members were under intense pressure from Native American groups throughout the country to defeat the proposal. However, O'Konski continued to support the project without the tribal lands, and when the bill was debated on the House floor, he declared that he

> could find no Indian opposed to the project. No one is more concerned about Indian welfare than I am. I happen to be an honorary chief of the Chippewa Tribe of the Bad River Indian Reservation and I have been an honorary chief of that tribe for 20 years. [I] held office hours in Ashland last month and no one expressed opposition. . . . Twelve Indians queried me about where all this opposition was coming from. They couldn't understand why they were being quoted as saying they were opposed to this bill.[25]

Congressman John Kyle, an Iowa Republican who was trying to stall the bill, said he had a telegram from the chief of Red Cliff in opposition. O'Konski responded, "The chief who sent you that telegram is no longer chief. They changed chiefs."[26]

Developing a Bipartisan Coalition

Enlisting support for the lakeshore from Democrats was not difficult. Congressmen Henry Reuss and Clement J. Zablocki, both Democrats from urban Milwaukee, submitted strong statements in support at the initial hearing. Senator William Proxmire also testified in favor and suggested naming the scenic shoreline drive in honor of Senator Nelson.[27] Vice President Hubert H. Humphrey gave Nelson a ringing endorsement and applauded the Apostle Islands National Lakeshore at a dinner attended by 1,100 people in Nelson's home town of Clear Lake, Wisconsin.[28]

When hearings were held in Washington in 1968, the base of congressional support had broadened. Kastenmeier testified that the legislation had strong bipartisan support. He listed as its backers:

- Wisconsin Republicans Alvin E. O'Konski, John W. Byrnes, Melvin R. Laird, and William A. Steiger, and Democrats Clement J. Zablocki and Henry Reuss;
- Minnesota Republican Albert Quie and Democrats Donald Fraser and Joseph Karth;
- Illinois Republicans John Anderson and Robert McClory; and
- Michigan Democrats John Conyers and John D. Dingell, and Republicans Jerry Ford and Martha Griffiths.[29]

Letters and telegrams from the Wisconsin Council for Resource Development and Conservation and the Citizens Committee for the Lakeshore to Wisconsin's Republican members of Congress had been important in building this congressional support.[30] The fact that the three Republican governors from Michigan, Minnesota, and Wisconsin, as members of the Upper Great Lakes Regional Commission, had supported S. 778 was also emphasized at these hearings.[31] By 1969 Nelson could justifiably say that the bill had been endorsed by a solid bipartisan majority of the Wisconsin congressional delegation and "has received support as well from members of the Minnesota and Michigan delegations."[32]

However, as opposition from Native American groups intensified, this bipartisan support would weaken. Given Native American unrest and opposition, Kyle and Skubitz insisted on a full House Interior Committee meeting on the proposal. Stuart Applebaum, in Kastenmeier's office, believed the congressmen were attempting to force full House committee consideration of S. 621, the original bill that included the tribal land, to paint both Nelson and Kastenmeier as anti-Indian.[33] (S. 621 was not "anti-Indian"; amendments had made Native American interests more explicit.) Because the USDI had not taken a position on the bill that deleted the tribal land, the Kyle-Skubitz strategy worked. The House subcommittee did not take action but forwarded the bill to the full committee without recommendation.

Kyle and Skubitz kept the pressure on Hartzog and on the full House committee at the June 3, 1970, meeting. The House committee acted by deleting the Indian land and recommended full House support by a vote of twenty-two to two on June 17, 1970. Republicans Kyle, McClure, Skubitz and Sam Steiger of Arizona were joined by one Democrat, James A. Haley of Florida, in submitting a dissent to the committee report.[34]

The Wisconsin bipartisan coalition held together, and on September 9, 1970, four Wisconsin Republicans joined four Wisconsin Democrats in a letter to each member of the House urging the support of H.R. 9306 (Wisconsin Republicans Vernon Thompson and Glen Davis did not join in).[35] The House debate that followed underscored the importance of this bipartisan support.

Saylor made an eloquent speech in favor of H.R. 9306. David Obey, the new Democratic congressman from northern Wisconsin (who had defeated O'Konski), spoke in favor of the bill. Phillip Burton, a California Democrat, said, "Mr. Chairman, after the profound and moving address of the gentleman from Wisconsin there is little that anyone can add. I rise in support."[36] Opponents attempted to kill the bill. The bill passed on a voice vote. A motion to reconsider was laid on the table.[37] The *Milwaukee Journal* summed it up: "A strong coalition of Wisconsin congressmen and leaders of the House Interior

Committee whipped a small group of opponents led by Representative John Kyle (R-Iowa) in gaining passage."[38]

The bill moved back to the Senate, where immediate concurrence was expected. During the week that this issue was debated, Native Americans again marshaled opposition to Senate action.[39] In spite of their pressure the bill was placed on the calendar for September 16, and with nineteen senators present Nelson declared that "the Apostle Islands is an idea whose time has come." The bill passed.[40]

The Apostle Islands National Lakeshore bill now moved to the White House. Robert Kahn, appointed by President Nixon to the newly formed Council on Environmental Quality, advised Nelson that an environmental impact statement would now have to be filed by the NPS under the recently passed provisions of Section 102 of the National Environmental Policy Act. Nelson's aid John Heritage and I were concerned that such a step might give the NPS an opportunity to say once again that the project was not viable without the tribal land, thus providing Nixon a rationale for a veto. The record is not clear as to how it was accomplished, but the impact statement requirement was avoided. Given the votes in the House and the Senate and strong bipartisan support, a presidential veto would probably not have been realistic.

The Apostle Islands and Presidential Politics

The Apostle Islands were under consideration during three presidential administrations, those of Kennedy, Johnson, and Nixon. The role of a president and his staff in the White House, and especially in the Bureau of the Budget, would in no small measure influence passage.

Kennedy visited the area late in 1963, and although he pledged the support of the federal government to Wisconsin and the upper Great Lakes region, he did not endorse the lakeshore per se. To receive presidential support required the backing of the Department of the Interior and the approval of the Bureau of the Budget. Four years would pass before those hurdles were cleared.

I worked within the Department of the Interior to develop a bill that would satisfy the myriad interests that were affected. Nelson would work from the outside on the Secretary's Office, the Bureau of Outdoor Recreation, and the White House. Late in 1965 Nelson and Bechtel met with Joseph Califano, a key aide to President Lyndon Johnson. Califano was encouraged but noted "that money is going to be a terrible problem." Nelson argued the low cost of the lakeshore, but all Califano would promise was a call to Secretary of the Interior Udall to determine his recommendations on the matter.[41] Later, Nelson was invited to the president's ranch in Texas. Bechtel commented on the trip:

> We loaded him up with material, we primed him and briefed him. We said again, since we were so totally preoccupied with this, we thought, my goodness, if you are going to Lyndon Johnson's farm, this is an opportunity to talk about the Apostle Islands bill. So he went down and he made the visit and when he came back we all pounced on him and asked him, "How was it??" And he said, "Oh, great. We got in that old car and drove across those farmlands and everything like that." We kept saying, "But, but, what did he say about the Apostle Islands?" "Oh," he said. "It really wasn't convenient or appropriate so I never brought it up." We could have lynched him.[42]

Clearances from within the USDI came slowly, and when they were finally achieved the Bureau of the Budget held up approval in spite of Nelson's pressure.[43] Nelson again visited Califano: "Then I went over . . . to the White House to see Joe Califano, who was on Johnson's staff. There was, as always, money problems. . . . I talked with Joe for an hour or so to persuade him to get the president, in the message to the Congress, to endorse the idea of the Apostle Islands. I told him it wouldn't cost very much . . . so Joe wrote that up and put it in the president's speech. So now we had two presidents that had endorsed it."[44] President Johnson, in his 1967 "Message to Congress," recommended four new parks and recreation areas and the establishment of the Apostle Islands National Lakeshore.[45]

President Johnson again included the Apostle Islands in his 1968 legislative program and in his budget message. Nelson said, "The president's firm support of these vital Wisconsin conservation projects [the National Rivers System, including the St. Croix, Namekagon, and Wolf Rivers] should be of real help in getting them through the House. The budget recommendation gives them a priority rating which is very helpful."[46] The president followed up a year later in his message "To Renew a Nation," which called for the enactment of Redwood National Park and "two other major additions to the Park System that I sought and the Senate approved last year: North Cascades National Park . . . and Apostle Islands National Lakeshore, along Wisconsin's most scenic water areas."[47] A few weeks later, at a White House reception held during the president's Conference on Scenic Beauty, Johnson again called for the enactment of the Apostle Islands National Lakeshore and the reservation of a million acres for the Wilderness System, saying, "The aim was to preserve the solitude and splendor of the land as God made it."[48] Within the span of three short months the president had given the Apostle Islands ringing endorsements on four occasions. In spite of that support, the House Interior Committee was not to be hurried. Hearings on the Apostle Islands would not come until LAWCON problems were cleared up later that year.

A nation divided over Vietnam, however, caused Johnson to decide not to run in the 1968 presidential election. The following January, Richard Nixon took office.

With a new Republican administration, the Apostle Islands suddenly faced new uncertainties. The divisiveness over Vietnam had dominated the campaign. The environment had not been debated, and there was no clear sense of how the new president would view such issues, especially those left over from the Johnson administration.[49]

George Hartzog remained as director of the NPS and Edward Crafts as director of the BOR. They too were pondering an uncertain future and how and in what way they might respond to new leadership. Udall had departed. Walter Hickel, former governor of Alaska, had been nominated by President Nixon to be his secretary of the Interior. The department submitted to Congress the same Apostle Islands bill that had died the year before. So the momentum developed for the Apostle Islands in 1968 carried over into the initial days of the Nixon administration. But within a few months the Senate's Subcommittee on Parks and Recreation received new signals. The associate director of the NPS, Edward Hummel, who had no prior direct involvement with the Apostle Islands, suggested that the Nixon administration would probably not favor additional parks at this time because of a shortage of funds. The *Milwaukee Journal* reported that an incredulous angry Nelson fired back with the harshest language he had ever used with Department of the Interior officials: "If you're not going to fight for conservation, I think we should move these responsibilities to some other department. . . . Your position would mean suicide for the Apostle Islands National Lakeshore."[50]

The Aspinall House committee began to seek more definitive answers on the new administration's position on parks and called for informal briefings by NPS and BOR. The two agencies did not completely shut the door to new authorizations but indicated "that it is unlikely that new conservation areas will be established this year."[51] Indeed, the administration was recommending slashing $30 million from the LAWCON Fund. Senate subcommittee members indicated that "there is little point in authorizing new areas and adding to the backlog."[52] In spite of these negative signals the Senate passed the Apostle Islands in June, and the House subcommittee held hearings on it in August.[53]

All committee action ceased in September when Bureau of the Budget Director Robert Mayo, in an attempt to curb inflation, imposed a federal spending limit and recommended the halt to all new park authorizations involving land purchases. Aspinall stated that the House Committee on Interior and Insular Affairs was faced with a half-billion dollar backlog of requests for new authorizations and development projects. He canceled all House hearings and said, "The administration isn't willing to go ahead and spend the money. It's about time to quit fooling the people by authorizing more. What we need is closer cooperation between the two departments of government [legislative and executive], and until I get it, I'm not willing to be the legislative scapegoat."[54] Important new pending authorizations included the Apostle Islands, Voyageurs National Park, Big Thicket National Park, Sleeping Bear Dunes National Lakeshore, Sawtooth National Recreation Area, and Buffalo National River.[55] Ironically, while the Bureau of the Budget imposed spending curbs, Hickel said he was considering a new $6.3 billion, five-year park and recreation program to relieve social pressures in big cities. This was a follow-up to his initiative of "urban parks," which included a proposed Gateway National Recreation Area in New York and New Jersey of approximately 15,000 acres, much of which was already in public ownership.[56]

The BOR sent out further budget warnings by pointing out that the acquisition program for the NPS after fiscal year 1970 would cost about $275 million, without any new authorizations. These constraints meant that the NPS would not be able to complete land acquisition on existing projects by 1973, when the current augmented fund authority would expire. The only accommodation the Bureau of the Budget was willing to make was to approve those requests presently before the House Interior Committee for increased authorizations for the national seashores at Point Reyes and Cape Cod. But the Bureau of the Budget warned that such action meant that already programmed land purchases elsewhere would be extensively curtailed.[57]

Both Aspinall and Henry Jackson, who chaired the Senate Interior Committee, charged the Nixon administration with bad faith. They pointed out that in 1968 Congress had authorized a minimum of $200 million for LAWCON each year for the next five years regardless of any other budgetary consideration. Johnson's request of $154 million had been reduced by Nixon to $124 million. However, the House and Senate Appropriation Committees did not agree with the $200 million figure and accepted a $124 million recommendation.[58]

Conservationists took exception with apparent inconsistencies between Hickel, who was recommending expensive new urban parks, and Mayo's no-new-authorizations posture.[59] Mayo's optimism was justified when the House took no further action on the Apostle Islands in 1969.

The inconsistency on the part of Nixon's advisors was resolved, obviously in Hickel's favor, in the president's first "Environmental Quality" message to the Congress on February 10, 1970. Nixon recommended "full funding in fiscal 1971 of the $327 million available through LAWCON for additional park and recreational facilities, with increased emphasis on locations that can be easily reached by the people in crowded urban areas." He also proposed legislation to protect LAWCON, "ensuring that its sources of income would be maintained and possibly increased for purchasing additional parkland."[60]

Hickel had managed to gain presidential support for his urban parks without jeopardizing pending new authorizations in rural regions. The House Interior Committee could now go back to work. Aspinall then wrote Hickel and requested USDI reports on the Apostle Islands, Sleeping Bear Dunes National Lakeshore, Voyageurs National Park, and the Gulf Islands National Seashore.[61] The next time the White House would address the Apostle Islands occurred after Congress passed the bill and the president had to decide whether to approve it. Nixon signed the Apostle Islands National Lakeshore into law on September 26, 1970, without public ceremony.

The Support of Political Leaders

Governor John Reynolds, Lieutenant Governor Patrick Lucey, and Attorney General Bronson LaFollette, all Democrats, provided support for the lakeshore and for Nelson. In addition, I was then a federal representative, and alternate cochair, to the Upper Great Lakes Regional Commission and the three participating Republican governors of Minnesota, Wisconsin, and Michigan. The commission gave the lakeshore their support and a bipartisan legitimacy. And, of course, President Kennedy's visit to Ashland and President Johnson's final endorsement of the national lakeshore were critical events. Special mention, however, should be made of Secretary of the Interior Stewart Udall's visits to Wisconsin.

From its inception, Udall was supportive of the Apostle Islands National Lakeshore, and he went out of his way to publicly support Nelson. They became good friends. He came to Madison to launch Nelson's Wisconsin Resource Development and Conservation Council during the 1962 senatorial election campaign. He accompanied President Kennedy on his visit to the area in 1963 and became even more enthusiastic, believing then that the area was so outstanding that it qualified for national park status. He joined Nelson in speeches before the Madison Press Club in 1964 and was visibly influenced after viewing a movie about the area. On that same trip, he and Nelson made major speeches to a statewide audience of six hundred people attending the University of Wisconsin's annual "Farm and Home Week Conference." Udall lauded Wisconsin's conservation initiatives under Nelson's leadership, and he gave the lakeshore another boost by announcing the formation of the North Central Field Committee's (NCFC) subcommittee to develop plans.[62]

Udall also joined Nelson in an aerial tour of Wisconsin the day after President Johnson signed acts approving the Redwood and North Cascades National Parks, and a system of National Trails and Wild and Scenic Rivers. The trip was notable in that Nelson was responsible for bringing to fruition the inclusion of three Wisconsin rivers in the National Rivers System: the Wolf, St. Croix, and Namekagon. Although the lakeshore legislation languished, the Wild and Scenic Rivers victory demonstrated to voters that Nelson could be effective in Congress in bringing to Wisconsin significant national projects. On this trip, Nelson and Udall rafted the Wolf River and met with the Menominee Tribe. They viewed the Apostle Islands and the Namekagon and St. Croix Rivers from the air and ended up before a crowded, emotionally charged group of supporters at the Hudson House in western Wisconsin. Re-election to the U.S. Senate was only weeks away. Nelson went on to win a smashing electoral victory.

Given Udall's enthusiasm and personal knowledge of the lakeshore, he made a special effort to testify in person before the House subcommittee in 1967, declaring for both himself and Hartzog, "We are here today because of our enthusiasm and keen interest in this particular area."[63] His sustained personal support for the lakeshore was critical in the eventual success of the proposal.

State and Local Political Support

The Wisconsin Council for Resource Development and Conservation ("The People's Lobby")

When Nelson left for Washington to assume his Senate seat, he left the Wisconsin Department of Resource Development staffed by persons supportive of his long-term interests. Planning for the lakeshore by that agency would continue. Moreover, the State Recreation Committee, Nelson's creation, would continue to guide recreation expenditures and would support statewide recreation planning. The "South Shore" studies, then underway, would support plans for a lakeshore.

To ensure an organized base of citizen support for his programs, Nelson had also formed the Wisconsin Council for Resource Development and Conservation, also known as the "People's Lobby." During his tenure as state senator and governor, he had long believed that support for conservation programs was fragmented and ineffective. A coalition of conservation groups could, however, marshal sufficient political strength in the Legislature to obtain passage of new initiatives that he had called for as governor. Moreover, a new coalition would also serve as a useful check on other statewide organizations over which the Wisconsin Conservation Department exerted considerable influence; for example, the Wisconsin Conservation Congress, an advisory group to the WCD and the Conservation Commission; the Wisconsin Wildlife Federation, a coalition of hunting and fishing clubs; and the Citizens' Natural Resources Association, which was formed in part through WCD leadership in the 1950s.

To form the new coalition, Ralph Hovind and I, in the Department of Resource Development, extended several thousand invitations for a meeting not only to conservation organizations but also to civic groups, labor unions, and the like. Staff papers were prepared for the session. The kick-off conference, entitled "The Unfinished Task," was held in Madison on October 10, 1962. Four hundred people representing 139 organizations attended. Secretary of the Interior Udall was the featured speaker. Nelson also addressed the group and in his speech outlined the emerging needs in the decade ahead. He described the conference as "the broadest range of conservation interests ever assembled in our state; united in a 'People's Lobby for Conservation;' the participants would counterbalance special interests and could lead to the most powerful force for preservation of outdoor resources that has ever been created in any state."[64] Substantive workshops were held on topics such as land use, pollution, outdoor recreation, and planning. Martin Hanson narrated a showing of the Apostle Islands movie, which he had filmed. Out of this flurry of activity came the Wisconsin Resource Development and Conservation Council. Its primary purpose was to promote sound conservation legislative proposals. The use of the phrase *resource development* also made it clear that the organization supported the State Department of Resource Development and the numerous Nelson initiatives underway at that time.

After the Senate election, one of Nelson's last actions as governor was to call together a small group of leaders from the larger October conference to formalize this council and to elect officers. I developed a full list of his conservation achievements as governor. Nelson chaired the initial session. Historian Thomas Huffman described this meeting: "His speech before the group sum-

marized every important environmental idea he had proposed as chief executive. . . . Beginning in 1963, the new council could safeguard the integrity of
the environmental achievements of the past four years . . . and 'promote responsibility in natural resource use by action as a watch dog.'"[65] Huffman further suggested that the council would serve as a political base for the senator.

In many ways, this group proved a forerunner of the Wisconsin environmental organizations of the 1970s. It joined other earlier reform-oriented
Wisconsin groups like the Izaak Walton League and the Citizens' Natural
Resources Association in establishing an intellectual perspective involving
the issues of the "new conservation," an approach considerably broader than
hunting, fishing, and forestry, concerns of the traditional state conservation
community.[66]

Martin Hanson was put in a leadership position as secretary. He served
well, contributing substantial time, energy, and money to the council. In
addition to chairing quarterly meetings, he made frequent appearances before
legislative bodies to advance council positions. In 1969, when he testified for
the lakeshore before the House subcommittee, he indicated that the council
then consisted of thirty-three organizations, including thirteen sportsmen's
clubs, of which three were themselves alliances of other groups; seventeen
conservation groups, including the Izaak Walton League and the Sierra Club;
two forestry groups; and the Wisconsin Federation of Women's Clubs. All
told, it was a formidable organization with statewide roots.[67]

Under Hanson's leadership over the years, the council was responsible for
a continuous flow of press releases, resolutions, and letters to the press, to
agency staff, and to Congress. In no small measure they served well in the
cause of the lakeshore and in Nelson's efforts to shepherd it through Congress.
Reflecting on the council, Martin Hanson observed, "Well, it's easy to turn up
people to be against something, but for people that are for something to turn
out is always more difficult. . . . So that organization was very helpful in getting people to come to the hearings, . . . to be for it; it worked especially well
at the Senate hearings, and when the House hearings came about [we] had to
get the same people again, and the opposition wised up that they had to do
some work; so the House hearings weren't as successful as the Senate hearings
were initially."[68] Although the council could not completely counteract all the
adverse testimony at this House hearing, its continuous support over the years
made a significant difference.

Nelson has noted the importance of the involvement of brothers Martin
and Louis Hanson: "They were deeply involved in helping with the politics of
the bill. . . . When we had hearings in Ashland, they always had a reception

out at their house and we would have senators and congressmen out there for the evening or for all night."[69]

Historian Kathleen Lidfors describes NPS Director George Hartzog's view of the Hansons' role this way, "He was impressed by their workings on behalf of the park and their great enthusiasm for the area. He allowed that bringing people up to their beautiful place, taking them out on the houseboat for cocktails and not bringing guests back in until they were good and ready—sometimes more than ready—was good strategy."[70]

The Citizens' Committee for an Apostle Islands National Lakeshore
To stimulate local support for the lakeshore, the Citizens' Committee for an Apostle Islands National Lakeshore (CCAINL) had been formed. Membership consisted of influential local citizens. Culver Prentice, a local physician, was the chair. At an early meeting of the NCFC subcommittee, Prentice made a presentation that indicated that his "committee" consisted of community leaders from Ashland, Washburn, Bayfield, Mellen, and other local units of government, including members of the Bad River and Red Cliff Tribes. During Senate hearings in Ashland, Prentice described the CCAINL as follows:

> The Citizens' Committee for an Apostle Islands National Lakeshore was conceived late in 1962. This was a purposely small and quite loosely formed group of 38 responsible men about the two counties whose purpose was to keep informed of the nature and the progress of the proposal and to aid wherever possible in furthering its progress. Its membership has fluctuated. . . . A good many of the people you will hear in these two days have never actually been a part of our committee, but have become so enthusiastic in their attitudes and actions that we have come to regard them as a part of it; for example, Dr. Richard Bailey, the president of Northland College, and Mayor Harry Perrin of Ashland, and others. The enlistment of the support of such responsible people is a basic purpose of the Citizens' Committee. We feel we have achieved much in this direction with a minimum number of highly responsible citizens.[71]

Prentice noted that the CCAINL had been meeting in small informal groups over the previous few years and strongly favored the idea of a national lakeshore.

Prentice operated in an informal and quiet but highly effective manner. For example, the *Midland Cooperator* reported that he was working quietly behind the scenes to drum up support for the lakeshore. Prentice was quoted as saying, "The only thing we have here is recreation. The people want places to go for recreation and the government wants to create more places where they can go. What could be more logical!"[72] He was highly respected in the community and was especially effective in public meetings. He and Martin Hanson covered most of the organizational and operational costs of the CCAINL.[73]

At the first House subcommittee hearing in Ashland, Prentice said, "I have been privileged to work with the Interior Department Task Force. . . . This association has convinced me that this is a clearly conceived, forward-looking proposal. I strongly endorse the intent and the purpose of the present House bill and urge its passage."[74] Prentice and the CCAINL were enormously useful to me in my position as a representative of the Secretary of the Interior's Office. Over the years Prentice kept up a steady stream of correspondence with me, his membership, the press, and the community at large. He encouraged and stimulated local citizens and officials and state representatives to attend CCAINL meetings and congressional hearings. He was especially effective in chairing a meeting at Northland College when the NCFC subcommittee report was made public. Following that meeting, he generated a flurry of letters to Udall and members of Congress urging early action. Moreover, Prentice made presentations to local groups and urged their support for the lakeshore. When controversy and conflict erupted, Prentice, as a respected local physician, had a calming influence. He provided the NCFC subcommittee with useful advice on planning, policy, and local political considerations, and he urged the establishment of lines of communication with the Land Committees of the Ashland and Bayfield County Boards. He also kept pressure on me to move the proposal along and supported my efforts in dealing with the oftentimes obfuscating bureaucracy within the USDI.

The CCAINL and Prentice helped to legitimize lakeshore efforts and plans with the local community. Prentice was also useful to Nelson and his staff as an influential local contact, arranging for and participating in local meetings attended by Nelson. Importantly, Prentice sustained local support over the many years that the lakeshore was debated in Congress.

His sense of commitment to the lakeshore is best illustrated by a phone call he made to me from his hospital bed in Milwaukee, a day after open-heart surgery. Deeply concerned over the proposal by the owner of Michigan Island to log the island, Prentice told me that he would be willing to pay the $1,815 annual property tax on the island until the Nature Conservancy or the NPS could buy it.[75]

Of the CCAINL, Louis Hanson said, "Martin and a good friend of ours, Dr. Culver Prentice, set about putting together an organization, and the doctor spent many, many evenings talking to all kinds of groups in a four- or five-county area about this, as did my brother. . . . You really can't—you can, but it's not wise—place something upon an area if they don't want it. So through an educational process, they built support, and it was strong support. It was witnessed by the attendance of those who testified at both the House hearings and Senate hearings."[76]

Martin Hanson also reflected on the CCAINL, "Well, we talked and met with people in the bank and various interests . . . to explain the park idea, and there were endless amounts of meetings. . . . There were lists, there were answers and questions. . . . And so that committee got people to be for it. As with anything, there's always a few percentage of people that are for something, and a few percentage of people against something, and then you have this other large group of people—the highest percentage—that really haven't thought the matter through, . . . but you needed a vehicle to get that big majority of people . . . informed of what was really being proposed . . . and that's who you had to work on."[77]

CHAPTER 9

❧

The Sellers of Dreams

THE ROLE OF THE MEDIA
IN SUPPORTING THE LAKESHORE

[T]hey intrigue the minds of people (like us) who pore over maps and dream.

GORDON MACQUARRIE, *Milwaukee Journal*, November 15, 1954

The media played a huge role in establishing the Apostle Islands National Lakeshore. While politicians and conservationists argued over the future of the Apostle Islands, all in the name of the people of Wisconsin, those most responsible for bringing the Apostles to the attention of the average Wisconsin citizen were the newspaper writers. The first time that many people in Milwaukee or Madison, or elsewhere in the state, heard about the islands was through a press that was able to generate popular support for an Apostles park. This the writers did through skillful imagery. When the lakeshore became a national issue, it was again the press, as well as the use of other media by the major players, that was instrumental in placing key issues, both in support of the lakeshore and against, before the public and the politicians. This chapter focuses on the use of media over the course of the debate.

The Early Role of the Press

Long before Gaylord Nelson introduced the first lakeshore bill, an early base of local support had been built by three energetic news people in the area: John Chapple and W. B. "Bud" Koons of the *Ashland Daily Press* and Charles "Chick" Sheridan, a reporter for the *Superior Telegram* and the *Washburn Times* and a well-known freelance photographer.

Sheridan's pictures of the region appeared frequently in the local press and often in the large metropolitan papers of Milwaukee, Madison, Chicago, and Minneapolis–St Paul. Over a forty-year period these journalists printed thousands of words on the beauty of the area. Chapple had also done a lengthy series on the region in the *Ashland Daily Press* that was later reprinted as a booklet and given wide distribution over many years.[1] His family owned the *Press* until 1945, but John's career as a writer and reporter spanned seventy-five years. Sheridan had done a series on the islands for the *Superior Telegram* that he placed in a "blue booklet" that was also widely distributed.[2]

Koons and Sheridan, representing Ashland and Bayfield Counties, respectively, had driven to Washington in the 1930s and appeared before the Congressional committee that was considering authorization of an NPS study on the Apostles. Sheridan presented his "blue booklet" of photographs and text to the committee to familiarize its members with the beauty of the region. I interviewed Chapple shortly before his death at the age of eighty-nine. We talked about his participation in the early negotiations with the NPS regarding a study:

JOHN CHAPPLE: I spent all my summers on the island. I'm an islander, second nature. I spent my time for ten years trying to throw this idea of at least one island [probably Stockton] has got to be a national shrine or something like this so I will accept a certain amount of credit for being one of the chief figures and I would say that [Congressman] Peavey and Chick [Sheridan] [and I] were a trio. . . . Well, anyway, we were very red hot for this idea; they had to protect this pristine beauty of the islands.

JORDAHL: But you did have a lot of local support up here.

CHAPPLE: Oh, I say we not only had it, we developed it. We rammed it down their throats.

JORDAHL: You were writing, Chick Sheridan was writing, Koons was writing, and you people built a base of political support, John.

CHAPPLE: That's correct . . . Well, then the great thing about it was my idea that we got to protect one of these islands and I never dreamed that we could take the whole damn thing, you know.

JORDAHL: Are you happy the way Apostle Islands ended up?

CHAPPLE: Oh, happy . . . Heaven on earth.[3]

By and large, most newspaper coverage between 1950 and 1960, as the state of Wisconsin considered whether to buy the Apostle Islands for a state "park," was sympathetic toward state acquisition. The *Milwaukee Journal* was especially important not only in affecting public opinion but in influencing political thinking. The newspaper's editorial staff had close relationships with the wealthy, influential conservationists found in organizations such as the

Milwaukee County Conservation Alliance. Furthermore, the paper was a significant force in supporting conservation programs and had a favorable attitude toward the idea of a park in the Apostle Islands. The *Journal's* position led many smaller Wisconsin papers to follow.

The press carried both feature and news stories on the Apostle Islands throughout the decade. This chapter does not offer a comprehensive survey of that newspaper coverage; rather, it intends to create a sense of the flavor of that coverage.

One of the most loyal supporters of the Apostles was the *Journal's* long-time outdoor editor, Gordon MacQuarrie. A native of Superior, Wisconsin, he was familiar with the area and set an early standard for writing about the issue. MacQuarrie was the first to report the Conservation Alliance's 1950 request that the state consider the acquisition of the Apostles. Even before the Wisconsin Conservation Commission had formally considered the request, MacQuarrie ran a story strongly in support. After noting approvingly that the alliance had suggested the acquisition of all twenty-two islands before development caused land prices to skyrocket, MacQuarrie astutely commented:

> It would be difficult to argue that state acquisition of the Apostles would not be a good thing, in the long haul, for Wisconsin. . . . But to argue that because the big lumber is now gone, and therefore the state should not acquire the islands, would be to argue against the established policy of the state in previous land acquisitions, such as the thousands of acres picked up to form Flambeau State Forest. . . . Any consideration of state acquisition must be on a basis of long range thinking, if timber is the deciding factor, as it was with the National Park Service people [in the 1930s]. Nevertheless, as they stand today, largely denuded of the big sticks, those islands are still mighty fetching and this reporter has nothing but sympathy for the Alliance proposal to study the idea. Furthermore, there are men on the state [conservation] commission who are thinking not particularly of today, but of forty or fifty years from now, and that's the only kind of thinking that could justify purchase of the Apostles.[4]

While supportive, MacQuarrie was keenly aware of potential difficulties, including the largest stumbling block: "The problem will be to determine where the money is to come from. . . . One of them, Madeline, is so developed by private owners that it seems unlikely the state will ever find enough money to buy it for the public."[5] MacQuarrie's early observation proved to be correct. Finances remained a long-term problem, and Madeline Island was never acquired by either the Wisconsin Conservation Department or the NPS (although the state did establish Big Bay State Park on part of the island).

While MacQuarrie argued the Apostles' aesthetic appeal, another *Journal* writer saw other potential. In 1950 Mel Ellis chose to describe the Apostle Islands as a hunter's paradise, teeming with birds, bear, and deer but very few hunters. Winningly, Ellis concluded, "[A trip to the Apostles] could be something like a trip to Africa or Alaska at a small percentage of the cost. There's an idea for a 1952 hunting trip."[6] After the 1954 decision by the state to attempt to acquire four or five of the islands, Ellis again described the Apostles as a deer hunter's paradise, well worth preserving.[7]

Statewide press also took note of the state of Wisconsin's interest in purchasing the islands. The *Green Bay Press-Gazette* was quick to report on the 1952 meeting of the WCC when the Apostles were discussed, and described the islands as "among the leading scenic attractions of Northern Wisconsin." Aware of its audience's interests, the article also described the islands as a deer hunter's dream, with success rates of 80 or 90 percent.[8]

As discussions on the Apostles went on, newspaper descriptions of the islands became more romantically inclined. A 1953 "On Wisconsin" column in the *Milwaukee Journal* described them as a place to attract dreamers.[9] *Journal* writer Arthur Fellows devoted three columns to the wonders of the Apostles in 1954, observing that with the growing movement to turn some of the islands into a state preserve, the area's unique features deserved to be recognized:

> Here the inexorable glaciers planed off the red-brown sandstone usually found at depths of 3,500 feet. Through centuries, the battering wave cut out great caves—some big enough to hold a sixteen-foot speedboat easily. The most impressive are on Devils Island, the northernmost land in Wisconsin. Jumbled rocks give the impression that giant hands have smashed a jigsaw puzzle of stone into even more complications. Huge blocks lean at all angles, thin layers are stacked like lumber, great peaks suggest no modern architecture but that of Karnak and Ur, or its feathered serpent stairways of Mayan temples. The rocks are probably much older. Rock colors range from deep cream through blue-green, to somber red. Tints come in stripes, patches, swirls, stipples—every way. Above the rock spreads a green mantle of pines with birch for lace. Trees cling where it seems even a fern could find no foothold. Towering above all, is the lighthouse whose red and white flashes can be seen from Castle Danger on the north shore. Below, singularly clear, cold water of Lake Superior permits a peek at depths that range down to some 1,200 feet.[10]

What romantic heart would not be stirred?

But it was MacQuarrie who returned again and again, figuratively at least, to these northern islands. In August 1955, while the WCC was at last giving serious thought to the possibility of acquiring some of the islands, MacQuarrie wrote two columns unabashedly in favor of acquisition. The first began by poking fun at the undeniably cool nature of the northern climate through the reminiscences of famed University of Notre Dame football coach Knute Rockne, who visited Superior one August. Climbing off the train from Chicago, dressed for the ninety-degree Illinois heat, Rockne reported: "I was in a temperature near the low forties. I walked down the platform looking for a cab. I had a tennis racket strapped to my bag and as I passed the locomotive I saw the engineer point to my tennis racket and remark to his fireman, 'Look at that man, coming up to Superior in August with only one snowshoe.'" MacQuarrie concluded his column on a more thoughtful note: "The value of the Apostles may not be immediately apparent to this generation, but as more and more of Wisconsin changes from rural to urban living, and as people with more leisure seek additional places of recreation, the Apostles most certainly will have to be considered."[11]

MacQuarrie's second piece played up the support for acquisition of the Apostles among the state's own employees: "If you chat long enough with the state's game managers about the twenty-two Apostle Islands in Lake Superior, they finally get down to hardpan and confess what they want to see done for this fetching archipelago in the world's biggest lake. They want Wisconsin to buy the islands; or all of them they can get, and as soon as possible. [District Game Manager George A.] Curran has studied the islands as a man reads a newspaper. He has fallen in love with them. That is why he is willing to go beyond a mere presentation of a deer report and declare: 'We shouldn't let a thing stand in the way of getting these islands.'"[12]

MacQuarrie died late in 1956, but he lived long enough to see Wisconsin take the first steps toward acquiring a part of the Apostles when the Conservation Department signed a five-year lease for Stockton Island in March 1956. He applauded the decision in an article that went on to warn of the chance of losing the rest of the archipelago through government inaction. He wrote: "The Apostles are of Wisconsin, yet they are not. These islands . . . have crept into the news occasionally in this century, hardly at all before that. They are, rather than subjects of news, relics of history. . . . Everybody seems to be in favor of somebody doing something about buying the Apostle islands, or a part of them, but the commission's action [leasing Stockton Island] was the first state move in a direction which might lead to eventual acquisition."[13]

Later, it was clear that MacQuarrie despaired of the state ever taking action on the Apostles (his article was entitled "The Islands Wisconsin Forgot"), and if he had known how long it would take for the Apostle Islands to finally find the protection he thought they deserved, his critique might have been harsh indeed. MacQuarrie would have approved, however, of the *Milwaukee Sentinel* article that trumpeted the actual purchase of Stockton Island by the state in 1959: "Purchase of Stockton Island . . . as the nucleus of an Apostle Islands state wilderness area is the beginning of the realization of a long-cherished dream in the Chequamegon Bay area."[14] It was a dream that would not be fully realized for another ten years.

Media Strategies in the 1960s

Gaylord Nelson was popular with reporters. An irrepressible and delightful raconteur, especially over an after-hours drink, he instinctively attracted reporters to him. He was accessible, forthright, and candid. During his ten years as a state senator and four years as a popular governor, Nelson went out of his way to court members of the press. Given Wisconsin's strong conservation tradition, his bold conservation initiatives were widely reported in the media. He exploited media coverage. On one occasion he used a voluminous scrapbook of news clips on conservation programs enacted while he was governor to persuade Attorney General Robert Kennedy to convince the president to make a National Conservation Tour. Nelson argued that conservation was not only good, solid public policy, but also good politics. His record as governor demonstrated that fact. President Kennedy made the tour in 1963, and his speech at Ashland generated enormous favorable media coverage for the Apostle Islands as well as for the president.

When Nelson went to Washington as a U.S. senator, he left behind a press corps of admirers. As a senator, he continued to cultivate the press and staffed his Washington office with skilled reporters. Bill Bechtel, former chief of the Madison Bureau for the *Milwaukee Journal*, was his administrative assistant during the years that the lakeshore was under consideration. Bechtel knew media professionals throughout Wisconsin. Moreover, his family owned a cottage on the Bayfield Peninsula; thus, he was intimately acquainted with the area. John Heritage, formerly an environmental reporter for the *Minneapolis Tribune*, was also on Nelson's staff during much of this period.

To launch the initial lakeshore proposal in 1962, careful preparations for media coverage were made. For his formal presentation to Secretary of the Interior Udall, Nelson had in hand the Bad River Tribal Council resolution requesting a state and federal study of the area. Philip Lewis, a state government landscape architect, had prepared a set of dramatic maps in color. I prepared descriptive text that outlined the potential of the area as a national lakeshore. Nelson presented these materials to Udall and Bureau of Indian Affairs Commissioner Philleo Nash. Photographers were on hand for this first important session. Statewide press coverage was substantial. The wire services—Associated Press and United Press International—published favorable reports. Pictures of the Kakagon–Bad River Sloughs appeared in many newspapers, as did photographs of Udall and Nelson holding up Lewis's maps.[15]

Immediately following the meeting, dates were arranged for an inspection of the area to be made by Nash and Bureau of Outdoor Recreation Director Edward Crafts. With press interest running high, a second series of releases from Nelson's office announcing the trip again received substantial coverage.[16] Local residents Martin and Louis Hanson and Bad River Tribal Chairman Don Ames made arrangements for the inspection. Although WCD participation was important, no one wanted them to control the trip. Thus, boats from private parties were secured for the trip through the sloughs. The Department of Resource Development plane was used for an aerial inspection of the islands and the Bayfield Peninsula. The press was invited to join the tour. Harvey Breuscher, an Associated Press reporter, described the trip: "A northern Wisconsin wilderness tract fringed by the white sand shore of wind tossed Lake Superior was host Monday to state officials who want the federal government to preserve it as a national recreation area. The unblemished natural beauty of the land . . . was the strongest testimony in support of the appeal."[17]

These initial strategies in dealing with the media on the lakeshore proposal provided a model that was consistently followed thereafter. Almost every summer, an "official inspection," announced in advance by Nelson and arranged by the Hansons, generated media attention. The WCD would participate, but Nelson's staff controlled the agenda and the guest list. Governor John Reynolds joined one trip.[18] Lieutenant Governor Patrick Lucey visited the area and commended Nelson for his leadership on the lakeshore.[19] Native American leaders and local officials frequently joined in these inspections. Fortunately for lakeshore proponents, the major daily papers normally assigned their political and state reporters to cover these trips, rather than the outdoor writers who were much more dependent upon and supportive of the Conservation Department. Moreover, the political reporters were often the people who had covered Nelson as governor and had long-standing, established relationships with him.

The charm and the beauty of the Apostle Islands and the Long Island spit would virtually sell themselves. Some reporters who consistently attended meetings and joined in tours became almost as knowledgeable about the area as those involved in planning for the lakeshore. Favorable stories and pictures were the normal result. (Dissent, when it did appear, was also reported; this is discussed later in the chapter.)

Nelson also used his periodic newsletter, which was sent to Wisconsin voters, the media, and local, state, and national organizations, as an effective method of maintaining high visibility for the lakeshore. Every significant step in the long process was reported in the newsletter. For example, in 1965 Nelson reported that the proposed lakeshore had had an enthusiastic reception in the *New York Times*, the *Chicago Tribune*, the *Chicago American*, and in newspapers in Minneapolis and St. Paul. He reprinted editorial support from the *Ashland Daily Press*, the *Wisconsin State Journal*, the *Milwaukee Sentinel*, the *Milwaukee Journal*, the *Eau Claire Daily Telegram*, the *Portage Daily Register*, the *Appleton Post-Crescent*, the *Chippewa Herald Telegram*, the *Superior Evening Telegram*, and the *Mellen Weekly Record*.[20] He also noted local support.[21]

Nelson also found the newsletter useful for clarifying misunderstandings or misinformation regarding the proposal. In 1967 he announced in the newsletter the upcoming congressional hearings and noted local concerns regarding property tax losses, hunting and fishing, and the tenure rights of owners of improved property. Each concern was carefully addressed in a thorough and sensitive manner. One of the newsletters was devoted exclusively to questions and answers regarding the lakeshore. Others described important events (such as the president's visit) or summarized government reports.[22]

In October 1965 the *Milwaukee Journal* featured the area in its Sunday supplement, "Picture Journal." The front page was a full-color photograph of the Bad River region in fall colors followed by five additional color pictures of the islands and the sloughs.[23] The *New York Times* devoted a full page to the proposal in a September 1967 Sunday edition, including aerial and ground pictures.[24] The *Ashland Daily Press* declared, "A full page in the Sunday *New York Times* is the latest proof that the entire nation is turning its interest in this direction." It reprinted the entire article.[25] Martin Hanson escorted *Minneapolis Tribune* reporter Ron Way on a boat trip through the area in 1969. The result: two full-color pictures and a long, favorable story.[26]

Bechtel recalled the efforts to gain favorable press:

> We did speech after speech on the subject . . . and when [Harold] Bud Jordahl finally came up with the bill, we had maps prepared. I got them to the *Milwaukee Journal* in advance, which I formerly worked for. I remember I was back in Wisconsin when the story broke and I rushed into a drugstore in Madison and

bought a copy and, to my delight, I think it was a top story at top of page one in the Sunday newspaper with a color map. John Wyngaard, the distinguished [state] capitol correspondent for the Appleton and Green Bay papers, and, I would say, the most prestigious reporter in the last twenty-five years in Wisconsin, wrote once that he had never seen an issue as effectively developed for publicity purposes as the Apostle Islands National Lakeshore. I take a certain amount of pride in that.[27]

When Nelson introduced his Apostle Islands Bill (S. 2498) on September 2, 1965, it received substantial media coverage. In a letter to the editor, the local assemblyman, Gehrmann, supported the concept but suggested that Nelson amend his bill if the people wanted change.[28] The *Superior Evening Telegram* wrote that the economic impact was significant, and "the lakeshore development plan would appear at this time to be a highly desirable project."[29] The *Mining Journal* of Marquette, Michigan, reprinted an editorial of support from the *Green Bay Press-Gazette* and suggested that the poor economy of the region would be helped by a lakeshore.[30] The *Badger Sportsman*, a monthly newspaper for Wisconsin hunters and fishers, came out strongly in support.[31] Nelson summarized this editorial and citizen support in his fall newsletters.[32]

Public information efforts were sustained and vigorous. Nelson recorded a four-and-a-half-minute tape that was sent to forty-two radio stations. Molly Sulewsky of the Wisconsin Federation of Women's Clubs distributed a hundred copies of the North Central Field Committee (NCFC) subcommittee report to local chapters.[33] I mailed a release and copies of the report to all the major national conservation organizations. The University of Wisconsin printed and began distribution of an additional 2,500 copies of the "Fine Study" (which presented the case for a park in the Apostle Islands).[34] The National Parks Association gave the lakeshore prominent coverage in the December issue of its magazine.[35]

Because the lakeshore was held up in the Department of the Interior and later in the Bureau of the Budget, press interest was muted in 1966.

In preparation for the Ashland House Subcommittee on Parks and Recreation hearings in 1967, Nelson reissued his "Questions and Answers on the Lakeshore." He also sent to the press a list of the organizations that supported the lakeshore. The *Minneapolis Tribune* reported that 200 people had asked to testify during the hearings, while the *Capital Times* of Madison estimated the number at 240.[36] Miles McMillin, editor of the *Capital Times*, gave the lakeshore and Nelson strong support in his weekly statewide radio program.[37] The efforts paid off. The *Milwaukee Sentinel*, reporting on the hearing, described it as "an almost monotonous parade of witnesses representing thousands of Wisconsin residents supporting the establishment of a [national lakeshore]."[38] Some coverage was also given to the opposition.[39] The *Ashland Daily Press* estimated that lakeshore supporters outnumbered opponents ten to one: "Coupled with strength in the House and with President Johnson's personal approval and with Congressman O'Konski's approval . . . it is possible that the Apostle Islands measure may become law before Congress adjourns in the fall. The impressive thing about the two-day hearing was the large number of persons who came all the way from Milwaukee, Madison and elsewhere, just for a five-minute opportunity to go on record in favor of the legislation."[40] The writer, probably John Chapple, then listed the numerous organizations in favor. Two months later, when the Senate approved the bill, the press was laudatory.[41]

The massive effort had depleted the supply of colorful reports. To provide the public with a continuous flow of information, the NPS printed thousands of copies of a new two-page, two-color summary of the proposal.[42] This summary, along with a sustained public relations effort, was the payoff for some sixty public meetings with local people that had been held in prior years.[43] When Senate hearings were held again in 1968, Nelson could now point out that the list of organizations in support had grown to 150.[44]

Nelson, reflecting on these efforts, said:

> Well, there were a lot of hurdles. You ended up with the Indian hurdle. You ended up with the Park Service against it without the Indian lands in. We were . . . going at it year after year after year, and then, of course, there were the Sand Island people who stirred up a big fuss and came to Washington and lobbied. The Ashland Rod and Gun Club raised hell about it. There was a lot of ferment going on and you just had to keep batting it down and fighting. There was one reason we went to the great lengths we did to get endorsements. We were sending stuff to every single newspaper in the state, including Minneapolis, which gave us editorials. We were contacting chambers of commerce, labor unions and everything you can imagine around because you had to offset that opposition. It just took a lot of time to do it.[45]

Key Media Tools

Nelson was able to effectively employ two key media tools to generate support for the Apostles proposal: a reprint of a magazine article from *Wisconsin Tales and Trails* and a movie, *Apostle Islands Region.*

The Wisconsin Tales and Trails *Reprint*

In 1964 Howard Mead, editor and publisher of *Wisconsin Tales and Trails*, a quarterly Wisconsin magazine with a circulation of twenty thousand, proposed to me that the 1964 summer edition be largely devoted to the Apostle Islands region, including an article on the Kakagon–Bad River Sloughs. Mead's editorial staff published the edition in such a way that it could be easily reprinted.

The issue contained five dramatic color photographs, a detailed colored map of the region describing twenty-seven points of interest, a state location map, thirty-two black and white pictures, and a solid body of prose carefully juxtaposed with graphics. It made a splendid twenty-two page reprint. Much of the prose was written by George Vukelich, a popular Wisconsin radio personality and environmental writer. The issue also included an interview with Nelson by Vukelich accompanied by a photo of Nelson framed by dramatic pieces of driftwood on an island shore. In the interview, Nelson warned that the area was vulnerable to unwise and unplanned development that might trigger a small-scale, short-term tourist boom at the cost of "the loss of a great national treasure . . . a national recreation area, clearly labeled on the maps of American travelers [that] would identify this area for the entire nation. . . . We must have something worth seeing, and we must protect what we have so that it can be enjoyed by many people over a period of many years."

Nelson tied the Apostles proposal into a series of developing national recreation areas—Sleeping Bear Dunes and Pictured Rocks National Lakeshores, the Great Circle Route around Lake Superior, the "awesome bridge" spanning the Straits of Mackinac, Voyageurs National Park, the Quetico-Superior Wilderness Region, and Isle Royale National Park. These areas, he noted, could stimulate related commercial development of taste and dignity and lasting economic benefit. He commented, "Slowly and carefully, we are developing a sound proposal to preserve much of the best of this priceless area and make it available to all our people and their children."

The reprint also included

- articles by Howard Mead on the history of the region including early Native American history and culture, French exploration, the geology and ecology of the area;
- "Fisherman's Cover," a story by Fred Morgan that included the delightful reminiscences of John Hagen, an eighty-two-year-old fisherman who had fished the Apostles for sixty-five years (Morgan was a freelance writer and photographer who lived in the north);

- an article by me that dealt with the history of Native Americans in the area, including the movement of the Chippewa people to the sloughs of the Kakagon and Bad Rivers and the nineteenth century treaties, and that also stressed outdoor recreation opportunities; and
- the decision by the secretary of the Interior to conduct a study of the feasibility of a national lakeshore in the area.

Some twenty thousand reprints were published. Nelson used them effectively in presentations before Senate and House committee and subcommittee hearings. All key officials in the Department of the Interior, at both the Washington and regional levels, were provided copies. Press packets were mailed to key newspapers. The reprint was used effectively at the many public meetings held in Ashland and the surrounding communities and was enclosed with replies to route requests to Nelson and to me for lakeshore information. The regular circulation and the reprint reached some forty thousand homes and offices including every important organization and individual in Wisconsin interested in the lakeshore.[46] This skillful and beautifully illustrated publicity piece did exactly what it was intended to do: it created a highly visible and favorable image of the Apostle Islands region and the proposed lakeshore.

The Apostle Islands Region Movie

Martin Hanson was a professional wildlife photographer with great sensitivity to the impacts of visual images. He created a fifteen-minute silent color movie of the area, which he presented and narrated to various state groups early in the lakeshore planning process.[47] He presented it at a meeting called by Nelson in 1962 with some four hundred conservation leaders from across the state. Fortunately, Secretary of the Interior Stewart Udall, who had been invited by Nelson to address the group, was in attendance and saw the movie. His response was as enthusiastic as that of the audience.[48]

In 1963 at Isle Royale National Park, Hanson presented the film at the first meeting of the regional directors of Department of the Interior bureaus, who made up the NCFC. It was an excellent introduction for them and their staff, who would soon be deeply involved in lakeshore project planning.

Fortuitously, another film producer, Stuart Hanish of Ash Film Productions in Madison, became interested in the region. He had already contacted Congressman Kastenmeier's staff regarding the production of a movie on the Apostle Islands region. He wanted to present the history of the region, its beauty, and the story of the Native Americans and to offer a message that stressed the need for preservation for the people of the area. He also saw that a film could serve as a potential inducement to tourists and the money they would bring.[49]

Kastenmeier brought it to my attention and to the attention of Nelson's staff, and they joined forces with Hanish. Hanson wrote Nelson, outlining the idea for a longer movie; being sensitive to costs, he suggested that Nelson's friend, well-known radio commentator Edward P. Morgan, do the narration. Nelson obtained the free services of Morgan.[50]

As Nelson's office had no access to a budget per se for film productions, Hanson agreed to donate his film footage to Hanish along with assistance on filming, boat trips, travel expenses, and the like. To raise money for the film and to obtain broad support and commitment, local, state, and federal agencies were approached. State support came from the Department of Resource Development (DRD), which would become the primary sponsor. Hanson obtained $650 each from the Ashland and Bayfield County Boards. I obtained $650 each from the Bureau of Indian Affairs and the National Park Service. All told, and because of Hanson's generosity, the final cost of the film was slightly less than $3,000.[51] Each participating agency was given credit in the film, thus helping to ensure their support for the lakeshore.

George Vukelich wrote the script. He plowed through several feet of background reports and other materials I provided and in a few weeks completed a marvelous narrative. (Part of the emphasis in the movie had to be shifted during the production period because of the assassination of President Kennedy.)

With the script in hand, Morgan, in silence, viewed the film, made several notations, looked up and said, "This is good copy, let's go." Without a pause or a break, he completed the narration. The film was introduced by Morgan accompanied by shots of waterfowl in flight and panoramic views of the unspoiled beauty of the region. The camera then focused on Nelson, who talked about the marshes, blue-winged teal, sand spits, and, using wall maps of the Midwest and Wisconsin, located the Apostle Islands region for the viewer. Nelson said, "Within a few hours distance of this area live some fifty million people. This magnificent outdoor resource should be preserved for their enjoyment and for the enjoyment of posterity."

He stated that only 2 percent of Wisconsin's shoreline was in public ownership; the rest was privately held, and the public had to keep out. Nelson said, "It would be nice to leave—this lakeshore area—their unspoiled back yard, unspoiled." These statements were the only direct and explicit references to a national lakeshore. We had made the decision to emphasize the beauty and the values of the region and rely on the visual images to sell the viewer on the importance of preserving the area.

The film presented the geologic origins of the region, native plants and animals, the human history, the exploitation of the area's resources and its subsequent economic decline, as well as the current recreational use and seasonal cycles. In poetic words and in pictures, the Chippewa were introduced:

> The sons of the Chippewa are still here. They live on the reservation and the living is not easy. The annual gathering of the wild rice crop is one source of income. By itself, it could provide only a marginal existence. But in guiding fishermen and the rental of boats, there is some hope of a better future. The old chiefs and leaders understand the problem. They have lived with it all their lives. They must learn new ways; new skills; a new life. They do what they can to prepare the young ones; schools, books, education, skills. This is the country of their fathers. Now these young ones face an uncertain future in their own lands. And sometimes it seems as though there will be no future for them. Sometimes it seems as though no one cares.

The film led into President Kennedy's visit.

> A man came to this country in September of 1963. A man who did care for their future and for the future of this land. He was the president of the United States. The people shook his hand and thanked him for coming and they had new hope. The people had come to Ashland from Bayfield and Cornucopia and Madeline Island and Mellen and all around. They had come to hear their chief and what he would say. It was not a political speech. A lot of people who listened on this day had not even voted for him. But after he finished speaking, they shook his hand. In the sloughs, the Canadas and the mallards rested and formed their great living rafts. In Ashland, Wisconsin the president of the United States spoke with the sons of the old settlers and the sons of the Chippewa Nation. And then the president was gone.
>
> The Wisconsin winter would be lonelier this year than any winter within the memory of man. The red cliffs standing mute and forlorn, against an ice field covering the land and the water, the great long silence of winter wrapping this land in a white winding sheet. But life goes on.
>
> In hutches and burrows, nervous twitchings and watchful eyes alerted for flight; beneath the snows, seeds in secret places waiting for warmth. A land—an idea—lies fallow here.
>
> Many things die in a Wisconsin winter. It is the way of nature. To say nature is cruel is half true. To say nature is kind is half true, too. Nature is nature and some will die. The strong ones will live to see the spring.

The film concluded with a shot of Chippewa lads biking down a long hill.

> Down the hill the sons of the Chippewas come gliding on balloon tires, silent as the very shadows, dreaming of yet another summer in the sun.
>
> A man can return to these islands time and time again and never get his fill—never know it all. There is the wind and the water and the feeling of eternity. This is how it must have been in the beginning of the very first beaches.
>
> A man—walking—and looking—and knowing that he is alone.
>
> And yet not ever really feeling alone—at all.

These were powerful words joined with powerful images.

The first showing of the film was before the Madison Press Club. Fortunately, Udall was once again present. John Patrick Hunter, a veteran reporter for the *Madison Capital Times*, summarized the response in an article titled "Film of Apostles Steals Show from Nelson, Udall."

> A cabinet member and a U.S. Senator spoke at a luncheon meeting . . . of the Madison Press Club . . . and they drew the largest crowd in the group's history, but a movie stole the show. The cabinet member was Secretary of the Interior Stewart Udall. The senator was Madison's own Gaylord Nelson. The film captures the eloquence of loneliness that caresses the northland area that includes the Bayfield Peninsula, the Chequamegon Bay region and the sloughs of the Bad River near Odanah. . . . The "Apostle Islands Region" is a masterpiece and with it, its sponsors hope to draw national attention to that special corner of the Lake Superior region that is rich in Wisconsin history dating back to the earliest French explorers and the Jesuit missionaries.[52]

Hunter made note of the fact that several agencies had sponsored the film. And with 260 persons present, including many media reporters, the Apostle Islands received tremendous publicity.

Nelson then called the national conservation organizations together in Washington to view the film in order to garner national attention.[53] Prints were made for the Bureau of Indian Affairs (BIA), the NPS, the DRD, and the Bureau of Audio-Visual Instruction at the University of Wisconsin–Madison. National distribution and publicity on the film were secured through Sterling Movies-USA.[54]

The film was in immediate demand. Howard Potter of the BIA Office in Ashland literally wore out his print showing it to audiences in northern Wisconsin. Hanson and I used it frequently before state conservation organizations. The film was awarded a "Certificate of Acceptance" by the San Francisco International Film Festival. The Michigan Outdoor Writers' Association awarded it an "Honorable Mention" in their Outdoor Travel Adventure Category. The national Izaak Walton League of America, after viewing it at one of its monthly roundtable sessions, felt that an Apostle Islands bill should be introduced immediately. The group "really wanted to get behind it."[55]

As Democratic Party chair Louis Hanson later described one impact of the movie:

> I used to use it going around to various meetings. The largest local in the state is what I call the 'Nash Local,' which is American Motors—and that's how old I am—and there must have been 1,000 people in all at a regular union meeting. There were at least ten or fifteen people who came up to me after showing the film and said, 'Louis, why didn't you get a picture of so-and-so?' They were all from the Hurley-Ironwood area who knew the Apostle Islands backwards and forwards, who had lost their jobs as miners and were working at American Motors. Showing that film down there all of a sudden got support from a bunch of labor leaders because some of their guys knew about it. It got used. And, of course, when you get it on television, and it was shown several times, you reach a lot of people.[56]

The movie, viewed by thousands of people, gave the lakeshore a powerful boost, and it garnered highly favorable coverage for Nelson. (Even today, Hanish still receives several requests for prints each year.)

The Use of Government Reports

Nelson, as governor, had skillfully exploited the fourteen reports dealing with natural resources and conservation that had been prepared by his DRD. The reports furthered his programs and also advanced his public image as Wisconsin's "Conservation Governor."

The pattern would continue when the reports on the Apostle Islands prepared by the USDI became available, but first the reports were needed. The NCFC subcommittee report, with 116 pages, 9 figures, 6 maps, and 8 appendixes, was obviously much too bulky for public distribution and had been condensed in a popular report. Furthermore, the "Fine Study," a twenty-one-page document, succinctly and incisively made a persuasive case for the lakeshore.[57] It was printed in four colors and included 2 large foldout maps, 58 photographs, and dramatic graphics. It was an attractive report indeed for public distribution.

With the two reports in hand, Nelson distributed them to the media along with a press release. As they were Department of the Interior reports, he also arranged to have Secretary Udall present them to him in a ceremony, which was recorded by photographers; the photos and release were given wide distribution. To ensure that Nelson had first crack at media coverage, his staff arranged for Wisconsin's congressional delegation to receive the materials the day after meetings in Ashland, when the reports were first presented to the public. In addition to the published reports, staff also prepared several thousand four-page summaries. A packet of the materials was prepared for the state press and released a day after Nelson's Washington office release. The University of Wisconsin News Service also summarized the "Fine Study" and released it at the same time through its news system.[58]

This carefully orchestrated strategy paid handsome dividends in media coverage. The *Ashland Daily Press* reprinted most of the materials and included extensive photo coverage of the August 28 meeting when the reports were made public.[59] The Sunday *Milwaukee Journal* carried a five-column banner that proclaimed, "U.S. Proposes $11 Million Plan for Apostle Islands." Maps and photos were included with substantial text explaining the proposal.[60] The *Duluth News Tribune* gave it front-page coverage in its second news section on Sunday, including maps and photos.[61]

The newspapers nationwide carried stories of the proposal focusing the attention of recreationalists on the region.[62] The *Wisconsin State Journal* gave it editorial support.[63] The *Mellen Weekly Record* called it a "must" for the northern Wisconsin economy and stated: "The sincere approach and extensive work in compiling data and information that went into Saturday's meeting and the enthusiastic and almost feverish willingness of U.S. Senator Gaylord A. Nelson to '. . . see it through . . .' has kindled a amazing interest for the project. This is by far the soundest of any proposal to help the north that has been presented in many years."[64]

The *Bayfield County Press* editor, heretofore negative, said, "Although I have generally opposed intervention of our government into affairs that have previously been left in the hands of 'people,' I must conclude that there are situations which call for action of this kind."[65] The *Milwaukee Journal*, although discounting some of the visitor and economic estimates, lent it editorial support.[66] The *Ashland Daily Press* reprinted the *Milwaukee Journal* editorial. The *Iron River Pioneer* also supported the project, stating that it "will help the area economy."[67] The *Vilas County News-Review* printed a strong editorial in support.[68] The *Milwaukee Sentinel* ran an editorial strongly supporting the lakeshore along with the proposed St. Croix-Namekagon National Wild and Scenic Riverway.[69] A Milwaukee television station, WTMJ-TV, also gave it editorial support.[70] The *Milwaukee Journal* followed its editorial with a marvelous story and photographs in its Sunday "Picture Journal."[71] The Bayfield Chamber of Commerce publicly endorsed it.[72] And the *Sawyer County Record* declared, "Apostle Islands Plan Merits Support."[73]

The Opposition's Use of Media

The forces in support of the lakeshore weren't the only ones to use the media to influence public opinion. The state Conservation Department, initially in opposition, effectively used the press to advance its position. For example, the *Milwaukee Journal's* veteran conservation writers, John Baker and Russ Lynch, both department supporters, would not be easily swayed. Baker, and sometimes Lynch, wrote a daily editorial entitled "On Wisconsin," printed in the out-of-state edition on the lower-left corner of the front page. At the time, the *Journal* was Wisconsin's most influential paper, and Baker's and Lynch's words carried weight. Lynch was an unabashed supporter of Lester Voigt, then the WCD director. Lynch's conservatism later earned him an appointment by Governor Warren Knowles to the Natural Resources Board, where he would wield a powerful influence.

Nelson's initial meeting with Udall early in 1962, and the subsequent inspection by Bureau of Outdoor Recreation Director Edward Crafts, was coolly greeted by the *Journal*. Editorials declared that the proposal raised "mixed feelings; weather makes the season short. Bathing is for a Polar Bear club. . . . The Conservation Department long has wanted control of this area [the Kakagon–Bad River Sloughs]; Indian retention of hunting and fishing rights needs attention and they should abide by state regulations."[74] Another editorial stated, "It will be questioned whether the campers, boaters and fishermen attracted to this very cool and very beautiful area on Lake Superior will spend much locally to help the economy. The proposal must be looked at realistically and the possibilities . . . judged from the standpoint of total public needs and benefits, not what will especially help this group or that area or win local votes in some coming election."[75] (Nelson was running against Alexander Wiley for the U.S. Senate.)

The WCD also took initiatives to stake out its claims in the Apostle Islands. Shortly after Crafts' visit in July 1962, the Wisconsin Conservation Commission (a six-person policy board) and staff inspected the islands. In spite of the fact that they were well aware of Nelson's interest in the area and that he had assigned the planning task to the DRD, Nelson's staff was not advised of the trip. Lynch covered the event with a major story on the front page of the "Men's Section" in the *Milwaukee Journal's* Sunday edition. The headline read,

"State Recreation Area Planned in Apostles." "Within ten years the Apostle Islands may be dotted with wilderness campsites, docks for island-hopping boaters and a few beaches for public picnicking and bathing. [Earlier the *Journal* had indicated bathing was fit only for the Polar Bear Club!] These are the Conservation Department plans approved by the Commission."[76]

Lynch became poetic in his description of the islands, the land, and sky-scapes. Lynch did note Udall's interest in the area and the fact that BOR Director Crafts was impressed with the region after flying over the islands. But the state's position was made clear in a statement by Roman Koenings, the superintendent of forests and parks: "'But the state can't wait,' said Koenings. 'The National Park Service has rejected the islands twice. We will go ahead and the Commission can decide what to do if the federal people want the islands.'" Koenings also proposed to acquire two miles of fine beach at Big Bay on Madeline Island for picnicking and bathing and to begin the construction of a new dock, campsites, and toilets on Stockton Island. The article further suggested that a national area could include other portions of Madeline Island.[77]

On a positive note, the state's inspection did generate publicity for public protection of the area. Importantly, the WCC demonstrated its willingness to spend more money for protecting and managing the area, a laudatory step given the long delays in securing federal approval. The trip also served as a warning to Nelson and his staff that they could expect more difficulties regarding federal involvement with the WCD.

The *Milwaukee Journal*'s "On Wisconsin" column periodically dampened public enthusiasm for federal involvement. It posed questions: "Is the area too remote from mass population centers to justify extensive developments? Despite some superb sand beaches, is the big lake too cold for swimming? Can the rights of the Indians on the Bad River Reservation be protected?" The editorials also noted that the area needed more careful study, that there was a potential for vocal opposition from property owners on Madeline Island, and that many residents preferred the state's less sweeping plan for a 2,731-acre park at Big Bay.[78]

Not all of the publicity and reporting by the national conservation organizations was favorable either. Even before the release of the NCFC subcommittee report, a blast came from Ernie Swift of the National Wildlife Federation (formerly director of the WCD and a strong Republican supporter). Swift believed strongly in his brand of conservation: the scientific management of natural resources using sound and efficient organizational methods.[79]

Given Swift's national stature, his articles in the National Wildlife Federation's *Conservation News* had a wide readership. In an article on the Apostle

Islands he took umbrage with the federal proposal and the film, stressing that the advocates were "promoting politics and gross commercialism."[80] Ralph Hovind of the DRD responded to Swift with vigor, noting the ongoing USDI study and the emphasis being placed on preservation and wilderness. In letters, he stated that project supporters were not promoting "hurdy-gurdy fringe establishments." Swift's response was prompt: he further criticized the planning reports of the DRD as being much too commercial; he claimed, for example, that the proposed Ice Age National Scientific Reserve was being promoted by Congressmen Henry Reuss and Nelson only because of its potential commercial tourism value.

In a flurry of letters between Hovind and Swift, Swift moderated his position but said, "I think the total effort, federal and state, is too much commercial in relation to recreation. All state agencies including [the Conservation Department] emphasize that too much. The *Sand County Almanac* [by Aldo Leopold] describes my feelings better than I can say it."[81]

Editorial comments in the *Milwaukee Journal's* "On Wisconsin" column were muted in 1965. Dick Kienitz, a veteran reporter who covered conservation on a statewide basis, reported on lakeshore meetings with accuracy and without editorial comment. It took until September 5, 1965, after enthusiastic meetings in Ashland, for the *Journal* to come out in support: "The important thing is to preserve portions of this superb region, while it is still available at such a bargain price and develop it wisely as a whole in the future public interest."[82] Thereafter the *Journal* was steadfast in its support, using even stronger supportive language after that date.[83] When Senator Walter Mondale, a Minnesota Democrat, inserted into the *Congressional Record* a statement in praise of Nelson, he included six editorials from the press, including the *Journal's* editorial of September 13, 1970 (after the bill had passed), which declared: "Senator Nelson may take the bow in the starring role. It was he who picked up the old cause nine years ago. . . . The 20 rocky wilderness islands in the preserve, with 11 miles of mainland shore, make a necklace in Lake Superior around Wisconsin's Bayfield Peninsula. Just a day's drive from Milwaukee, our treasure looks secure at last."[84]

The *Bayfield County Press*, situated next door to the Little Sand Bay and Sand Island property owners, predictably opposed the lakeshore in the beginning. In an article entitled "Think before You Leap," the writer suggested that there were arguments pro and con on the proposal. When local people were told "time after time that they live in a depressed area and that their standard of living is below normal, some are inclined to believe it. They become susceptible to promises of an improved economy. Unfortunately, these handouts always require a sacrifice. Any time the federal government 'gives' it also 'takes'!"[85] The writer went on to suggest that the proposal was politically motivated, and that federal involvement would mean a loss of local freedom. She suggested letting the federal government have half of the islands followed by an evaluation of that decision and whether the federal government delivered on its promises.

Reporter and editorial writer Eleanor Knight continued to run negative stories in the *Bayfield County Press*. Because much of the shoreline in Bayfield County was included in the lakeshore, "the howl went up, for that is a mighty large chunk off the tax rolls. . . . We would rather add taxpayers than lose them. I have no reason to howl, but I will howl with you . . . out of loyalty." With tongue in cheek she suggested legalizing gambling on York Island as an inducement for people to use a tourist passenger rail line from Hayward to Bayfield proposed by Tony Wise, a major tourism developer. It was not until 1965 that the publisher of the *Bayfield County Press* finally endorsed the proposal.[86]

The South Shore Property Owners' Association also capitalized on the media's interest in reporting conflict. At one of the group's early meetings, members made sure that a reporter was present; the first significant opposition to the lakeshore was reported in the *Ashland Daily Press* when all sixty-five people in attendance at a 1965 meeting voted against the proposal.[87] Members wrote "letters to the editor" that were frequently published.[88] One owner wrote an especially bitter and lengthy letter to U.S. Representative Wayne Aspinall, which was reprinted in the *Bayfield County Press*. In his letter he attacked Nelson, accusing him of stacking the hearings, and claimed that the bill had been sneaked through the Senate, that the scenic drive wouldn't work, and that the Indians would be given menial jobs.[89] Local supporter Culver Prentice later wrote to Aspinall, "My real reason for writing to you is to apologize to you for the utterly shocking tone of the letter written to you by a man in our community."[90] Aspinall's response to Prentice was unperturbed: "This is not the first time I have been favored by such a letter. . . . You will find a few people in any community . . . willing to blow off steam in this fashion. Such letters do not bother me very much over the long run, though I must admit that my immediate reaction to them often falls short of being a model of Christian charity."[91]

The Property Owners' Association also used the Senate and House hearings in Ashland to dramatize its case, even picketing the House session. The press picked up on the controversy, and the *Ashland Daily Press* included photographs of the pickets.

The attempts of the opposition to defeat the lakeshore failed for a number of reasons. The opposition was never well organized or well represented at the hearings; it frequently did not use legal counsel. Simply put, it was up against a formidable array of talent and agency capability dedicated to creating favorable media coverage for the lakeshore. Moreover, reporters were attracted to the area; they truly liked the proposal and reported with that bias. Native American opposition was a different matter. As the Red Power movement grew, Native American leaders became sophisticated in using the media. Moreover, they were increasing their capacity through the establishment of organizations such as the National Congress of American Indians and in hiring educated, committed, and skilled staff. Given the many injustices of the past, and the legitimacy of their claims for justice and equality, their story attracted sympathetic national and even worldwide coverage. The lakeshore became caught in the middle of these larger forces and issues (see chapter 13 for this discussion). As Native American opposition mounted, it became inevitable that the inclusion of reservation lands within the lakeshore would become politically difficult, if not impossible.

By 1970, as the final hearings on the proposal ended, Nelson, given the high media visibility and support the proposal had generated, was able to insert into the House hearing record a list of organizations in support of the lakeshore:

- thirty-seven businesses;
- seventeen civic organizations;
- twelve national organizations, including all major conservation groups;
- sixteen farm organizations;
- two labor organizations;
- six regional organizations;
- twenty-four newspapers;
- two state magazines;
- Duluth and Milwaukee television stations;
- thirteen government agencies; and
- fifty conservation clubs.

After Nelson had submitted the list for the record, Congressman Don H. Clausen, a member of the House Committee on Interior and Insular Affairs, said, "I am concerned, you have not mentioned the Green Bay Packers." Nelson responded, "That was a winning year too; I should have had them."[92] In his campaign for re-election to the Senate in 1968, Nelson did receive a marvelous endorsement from the successful and popular Green Bay Packer coach, Vince Lombardi.

CHAPTER 10

The Local Citizens and the Lakeshore

The very nature of a park proposal will inevitably cause friction with the local citizens with well-established patterns of land use, which will be affected. Lands will be removed from tax rolls, which are a major source of local government budgets. Some residents will be forced to sell or give up their private property through condemnation. "Outsiders" will be the new users of the land and will be resented and viewed with suspicion by residents. The park planner needs to have a great sensitivity to these understandable human emotions and must treat owners and other residents with sensitivity and honesty. Where possible they must try to soften the impacts. In the case of the Apostle Islands, planners made their best efforts to so do.

Dealing with local units of government was another matter entirely. Because the region had been economically depressed for decades, some private owners had simply abandoned their land without paying the taxes. State and federal governments had bailed out those local governments in the 1920s and 1930s with massive transfers of tax delinquent lands to establish the Chequamegon National Forest, a number of county forests, and infusions of new money to support forestry, fire prevention and suppression, road construction, and so on. In other instances, land titles often ended up with the county or town governments. This was the history underlying the Apostle Islands proposal, and not too unexpectedly local governments used their leverage to either resist the proposal or insist upon untenable conditions. Historically, with good cause, the federal government had always insisted that local (and state) governments should be willing to give up their lands to the federal government in exchange for the national investment and recognition that the areas would receive, as well as the increased tourist spending. However, as this chapter demonstrates, local citizens and governments do not always act in predictable ways.

County Governments and the Apostle Islands National Lakeshore

Ashland County rather parochially resisted donating lands to the federal government for the lakeshore. It had also previously resisted a sale to the state. For example, in 1962 the state offered the county $80,000 for Oak Island. A Wisconsin Conservation Department staff member even flew to Ashland to present the check to the county board; it was rejected.[1] A year later the Ashland County Board asked for private bids on the island, again turned down a state offer, and reviewed with favor a tentative offer of $50,000 from a developer. Obviously they did not view parks with any great favor.[2] In 1969 the state finally succeeded with the purchase of Oak Island and five additional parcels on Stockton and Basswood Islands for $201,000. The state was the only bidder on all six parcels; the Basswood Island parcels drew bids from three private individuals, including William C. Brewer of Chicago, a staunch opponent of the lakeshore.[3]

Ashland County's opposition to either the sale or donation of its lands went further: the county initially opposed the entire lakeshore proposal. The chair of the board, Ken Todd, pointed out that 48 percent of the land in the county was owned either by the state or the federal government. Todd stated, "I can't imagine how they can make a national park out of those islands."[4] Over the next several years members of the Citizens' Committee for an Apostle Islands National Lakeshore lobbied county board members with little effect. In fact, in 1966 the county board voted against the taking of any privately owned developed property within lakeshore boundaries. It further resolved that the county be compensated for any loss of property taxes (ignoring state "in lieu" policies regarding tax payments by local governments).[5]

The parochial view of Ashland County was brought clearly into focus in 1967 when C. E. "Corky" Johnson, the superintendent of Isle Royale National Park, and I engaged in a contentious discussion with the county board. The *Ashland Daily Press* headlined the meeting "Island Park Sizzles: Meeting Called." Although the proposal was carefully explained, the county board was not prepared to act. One board member declared that Oak Island was worth $160,000 and that "we better get some money for Oak Island." Another meeting was called for a month later in preparation for the upcoming June hearings.[6] Perhaps in response to the publicity and pressure, the county board shifted its position. A few days before the Senate hearings, Senator Nelson's assistant William Bechtel and I appeared before the county board urging support. This time, on an eleven-to-six vote, Board members favored the sale, but with conditions. The first condition required a trade of Oak Island for a marina in Ashland or equivalent land in the Chequamegon National Forest in Ashland County, or a purchase of Oak Island by the state with subsequent transfer to the NPS. The second condition opposed any further acquisition and development by the state on proposed Big Bay State Park until the lakeshore was authorized, at which time the size and type of park on Madeline Island could best be determined.[7]

With a favorable resolution now in hand, county board chair Ken Todd could now testify with enthusiasm: "Mr. John Rybak, Ashland County Board Vice Chairman and myself have proudly delivered to this inspired committee . . . a certified copy of a resolution . . . passed by the County Board . . . endorsing and supporting the Apostle Islands National Lakeshore in the setting up of this great nature's wonderland of America, for the world to see and use; [it] will be infinitesimal as compared to the exhilaration and joy that will fill the hearts of endless thousands when they witness and partake of this outdoors treasureland."[8]

The Bayfield County Board also endorsed the proposal, but with a proviso that no privately owned or developed land could be acquired for the lakeshore and that the sale of county land to the federal government be withheld until further action by that county board.[9] The proviso regarding private land was an attempt to accommodate the chairman of the town of Russell. It did not work; he was the only member of the county board to vote against the resolution.[10] The Bayfield County Board held to this position at the House hearings in 1969.

In spite of the caveats of the two boards, only some of which could be met, their resolutions were significant statements of overall support. Other local governments were also supportive, including Ashland, Washburn, and Bayfield City Councils, Iron and Polk County Boards, the towns of Iron River and Bayview, the Washburn Planning Commission, and the Bayfield Harbor Commission. At the time of the 1967 and 1969 Senate hearings, such support from local government was impressive and important.[11] Of course, these government units had no land affected directly by the proposal!

Town Governments and the Apostle Islands National Lakeshore

Town governments were responsible for property value assessments, tax collection, refuse disposal, and roads. Within the lakeshore were four town governments: Russell and Bayfield in Bayfield County, and La Pointe and Sanborn in Ashland County. Among town governments, support for the lakeshore was mixed. They traditionally represent rural, conservative constituencies that resist state and federal interference in their affairs.

When hearings were held, supervisors from the town of Russell on the Bayfield Peninsula expressed themselves in no uncertain terms. Robert Hokensen stated, "Speaking as a supervisor for the town of Russell which the park takes in over 95 percent of our shoreline, I have to take a stand in their favor against the park. We have a lot of private property in each one. . . . I understand the government won't buy lands owned by a municipality, they want them donated. I am here to tell you our town is not going to sell, lease or donate any land for this park. This shoreline as of now is one-third of our tax base, $3,000 a year and getting bigger."[12]

A Bayfield County Board member declared, "I'm writing . . . so I just can't sit back and take all this without a fight." A third town supervisor said, "I am one of the town supervisors. Our township will lose in taxes based on the 1968 valuation . . . $9,469 . . . I would like to know how the taxpayers . . . can pick up this amount of tax loss. . . . Where are we going to get this money? I also found that the town of Bayfield will lose from $5,000 to $7,000 in taxes. Also the town of La Point, excluding Madeline Island, will lose $22,487."[13]

The Russell Town Board remained adamant in its opposition and on April 11, 1970, advised House Committee on Interior and Insular Affairs Chairman Wayne Aspinall to that effect. Town Board Chairman Arthur Meierotto declared, "As chairman of the town of Russell, I oppose the proposed national lakeshore park. The federal government already owns some 250,000 acres of national forest in Bayfield County. . . . When and where will this land acquisition stop?"[14]

The town of La Pointe in Ashland County contained all of the islands except Eagle, Sand, York, and Raspberry, which were in the town of Russell, and Long Island, which was in the town of Sanborn. Except for a small park on Madeline, the town owned no lands in the archipelago. In spite of the fact that the town would lose some of its tax base, Elmer Nelson, La Pointe town chairman, took an enlightened view and in 1963 favored the lakeshore proposal.[15] Four years later, town chairman Daniel B. Angus, after taking a "person-to-person" poll, found that the majority of the electors were still in favor of the lakeshore. He further noted that town responsibilities would in effect be reduced to one island, Madeline. Despite these reservations, Angus stated, "I am in favor of including our islands in the Apostle Islands National Lakeshore, fully understanding the county-wide urge to set aside lands for public use."[16] Thus, the town of La Pointe broke ranks with the town of Russell, in spite of the fact that the Ashland County Board had called for a moratorium on state land acquisition at Big Bay State Park on Madeline Island.

The Petition as an Opposition Technique

Until the boundaries were identified, property owners had found it difficult to take a stand on the matter and organize. Even after the release of information, opponents would face formidable resources; the professional staff of the state and the Department of the Interior, the resources of a popular U.S. senator, and the local Citizens Committee for an Apostle Islands National Lakeshore. They also faced enormous statewide support for the project and a press that was highly favorable.

Landowners' concerns and opposition took several predictable forms. Petitions in opposition were circulated. Owners formed an association to oppose the proposal. They made direct appeals to federal officials and to Nelson, requesting that their lands be excluded. On the other hand, some owners indicated their support and their willingness to sell their lands to the federal government.

In 1965 the Chequamegon Outboard Boating Club and the Ashland Rod and Gun Club, led by a member named Fred Huybrecht, began to circulate petitions opposing the lakeshore. They most likely saw it as a threat to their favorite hunting and fishing areas in the sloughs where they had shacks. Club members claimed (in letters to Secretary of the Interior Udall, Senators Proxmire and Nelson, and Congressman O'Konski) to have collected more than 1,095 signatures on their petitions, representing forty-two communities and cities in the state. They opposed the inclusion of the Kakagon–Bad River Sloughs and Long Island in any federal or state park.[17] When public hearings on the proposal were held in June 1967, the clubs indicated that they now had 2,000 signatures on file and that about 500 south shore property owners had signed the petition. Although one member testified that the petition was in opposition to the "park," the wording of the document limited the opposition only to the Kakagon–Bad River Sloughs.[18] He did, however, note the strong opposition of the Chequamegon Outboard Boating Club and the Ashland Rod and Gun Club to the lakeshore proposal.

The impact of the so-called Huybrecht Petition on the Senate Subcommittee on Parks and Recreation had been substantially softened by earlier testimony by members of the Citizens' Committee for an Apostle Islands National Lakeshore. To further reduce the impact of the petition, this committee had encouraged the Social Studies Division of Northland College to study the petition. Dr. B. C. Prentice submitted its report, "A Study of the Validity of the Huybrecht Petition," which concluded:

- that the Huybrecht Petition as of February 24, 1966, had diminished in reliability and/or validity by 61.7 percent since March 29, 1965;
- that this discrepancy might have been much larger had this survey sampled those "remotely concerned" petitioners who resided far from the areas of direct impact of the proposed project; and
- that this discrepancy may be due to changes in the minds of the petitioners or to a large-scale invalidity originally involved in the signature-gathering process.[19]

Although the petition continued to be used by those in opposition, the credibility of the document had been so weakened that it had no significant influence on the House or Senate committees.

The South Shore Property Owners Association also used petitions to argue against the lakeshore. In the 1969 Senate committee hearings, the vice chairman of this association, William C. Brewer, indicated that he had a petition in opposition signed by more than 300 permanent area residents, which seemed to belie the "overwhelming support" in the area for the lakeshore that promoters alleged. In a subsequent submission to the Senate, the petition contained signatures of 478 residents.[20] Both the Senate and the House subcommittees attempted to relate the signatures on the two petitions to the number of members in the association and the number of private property owners within the boundary. (In earlier testimony, Willard E. Jurgens had indicated there were 156 owners along the thirty-mile strip.)[21] In the 1969 House hearings, Congressman Roy Taylor asked Jurgens how many homes were in the south shore area within the park. He replied, "I do not have those figures." Under further questioning, Jurgens indicated he could not differentiate between permanent homes and seasonal residences.[22]

A year later in House committee hearings, Jurgens again indicated that the South Shore Property Owners Association had 300 members. Congressman Kastenmeier noted that Jurgens's numbers were at considerable variance with data provided by NPS Director George Hartzog. There were 14 year-round residences within the lakeshore boundary, 135 seasonal residences, 16 commercial rental units, and 28 docks and miscellaneous structures.[23] As with the "Huybrecht Petition," the inaccurate and frequently vague responses to committee members weakened the property owners' petitions.

The South Shore Property Owners Association appointed Donald F. Schumacher, an attorney from Illinois and a south shore landowner, to represent its interests at the first Senate hearings in Washington on May 9, 1967. The group had joined with the Chequamegon Outboard Boating Club and the North Wisconsin Rod and Gun Club in vigorous opposition to the project. Schumacher argued:

- Too much public land existed in the northern Great Lakes, and additional land for recreation was not necessary.
- The area should be developed commercially and with small businesses to provide year-round employment in lieu of seasonal employment associated with tourism.
- The thirty-mile scenic highway would violate the wilderness character of the Bayfield Peninsula and cause serious erosion of the unstable red clay soils.
- Treaties and agreements with the Indians were once more being broken by the government.
- Federal acquisition would take additional land off the property tax base, worsening the economic conditions of local government.
- The proposed park would attract too many people, thus destroying the tranquil nature of the Apostle Islands.
- Seasons were short and the water was cold and unsuitable for swimming and unsafe for recreational boating.
- The project was costly and would further strain the federal budget and the American taxpayer.
- The University Economic Impact Study [the Fine Study] was grossly inflated.[24]

In addition to having Schumacher testify, the South Shore Property Owners Association persuaded property owners to testify in opposition. They would continue their efforts to block the proposal, and at the second Senate hearing in March 1969 they restated their arguments and provided the Senate Committee on Interior and Insular Affairs with numerous opposition calls and letters. The owners had become more strident, and they made personal attacks on committee members, Nelson, and myself and alleged a lack of due process. Their discourteous behavior weakened their effectiveness with the committee.

Between the March 1969 Senate hearing and the August 1969 House hearing, property owner opposition intensified. Members of the House subcommittee were greeted at the entrance to the hearing room in Ashland with picketers carrying signs that read, "Keep Land on Tax Roll—Vote No, No. No," "Nelson's Proposal Unfair to Indians and Landowners," "Lakeshore Proposal Unconstitutional," "We Oppose The Federal Land Grab," and "A National Lakeshore Means Higher Taxes."[25] Fourteen landowners vigorously testified in opposition.[26]

A new organization, the Apostle Islands Residents Committee, based in Minneapolis, had been formed in the interim. William G. McFadzean, president of a public affairs consulting firm, was the Residents Committee's executive director. McFadzean was not a property owner in the Apostle Islands region, but he indicated that he owned land within the proposed Voyageurs National Park in Minnesota, which he would be willing to sell for park purposes. McFadzean stated that he "had cause to have developed a little booklet on questions and answers on the Apostle Islands." Portions of the booklet had been prepared by Lieutenant Robert E. Evans of the U.S. Coast Guard Reserve in Excelsior, Minnesota. Another author was James N. Brodie of Brodie Engineering Corporation of St. Paul. Brodie had testified in 1967, at that time arguing that costs would be "1,000 percent higher" than NPS estimates.[27]

Although the booklet had been prepared in 1967, it was not brought to the attention of the House committee until 1970, when Brodie, McFadzean, and Evans formally presented it with their arguments.[28] The booklet emphasized the hazards of recreational boating in the archipelago, claiming,

- that fetches and occasional seiches were dangerous;
- most recreational boats were too small and inappropriately designed for safety on Lake Superior;
- "the extreme cold of the water will cause death from exposure at any time of the year within a short time. Superior is known as the lake that does not give up its dead. Because of the cold, bodies tend to sink to the bottom and are rarely recovered";
- iron ore deposits in the region cause error in the use of magnetic compasses; and
- rapid shifts in weather and erratic winds made most shorelines dangerous.

They reprinted the federal Recreation Advisory Committee criteria on recreation areas in full and in an analysis indicated that the lakeshore did not qualify as a national recreational area. Their arguments were based on the premise that recreation would not be the dominate use because the islands were inaccessible, boating was dangerous, and the Kakagon–Bad River Sloughs were to be kept wild and primitive. Unless the NPS subsidized boat tours, they contended, recreational boating would be limited to rich persons owning large boats suited to Lake Superior.

During the hearing, the question of boating safety was taken up in detail with Lieutenant Evans by Lee McElvain, the counsel to the House committee. Supplemental information was provided to the committee.[29] This had indicated that in 1969 three accidents had occurred in the Apostle Islands region: a collision between two vessels with no injuries or fatalities, resulting in $700 damage; a collision between two vessels with no injuries or fatalities, resulting in $165 damage; and a capsizing of a vessel with no injuries or fatalities, resulting in $1,000 damage.[30]

Brodie also erred in his exaggeration of costs and was sharply rebuked by House committee member John Saylor, who said, "I knew it just as sure as the sun rose in the east this morning. You have used the Corps of Engineers approach to projects. . . . While I have disagreed violently sometimes with the figures that have been presented by the Park Service as being an underestimate, this is the most fantastic estimate I have ever seen presented to this Committee in 21 years, even by representatives of the Corps of Engineers. I would not say that I am heartily in favor of this project in all aspects, but if there was ever any testimony that convinces me we ought to buy it, your testimony has made me the outstanding advocate of this park, with or without Indian lands."[31]

Saylor noted that the road plan had been changed in 1967, that the federal government did not charge interest on costs associated with park investments, and that Brodie's estimate of annual operating costs of $6 million was totally unrealistic when the NPS had managed to operate 274 parks the previous year at a cost of $53,343,000. Further he noted that the state had managed to acquire two islands for a modest $250,000.

Because of grievous errors and downright misrepresentation, the credibility of the booklet and the Apostle Islands Residents Committee was largely destroyed, although some of the information was used in the dissenting views of five members of the House committee in the report of H.R. 9206 which recommended passage of the lakeshore bill.[32]

The Cape Cod Formula

To soften the blow to private landowners, the subcommittee explored the utilization of what was known as the Cape Cod formula. The Cape Cod

National Seashore in Massachusetts, authorized in 1961, was the first major addition to the National Park System in many years. Moreover, it was the first time Congress had authorized funds for land acquisition in the act authorizing a natural or recreational park. Early additions to the National Park System had been based on withdrawals from the public domain or land purchases by private persons or foundations.

Cape Cod included numerous villages and small communities that made up an important part of its seashore charm. To purchase these communities would have been prohibitively expensive and politically unacceptable. The question seashore planners and Congress faced was how to permit these communities to remain private, protect their integrity, and yet ensure that they would not adversely impact the seashore. Because the federal government lacked zoning powers, a novel approach was used. The boundaries of the seashore included the communities, but the secretary of the Interior's powers to acquire lands within these communities was suspended as long as local zoning ordinances that met federal standards were in effect. Thus the communities would remain private while their charm, so important to the mystique of the cape, could be ensured.

Planners of the Apostle Islands lakeshore explored carefully the application of this concept to the developed portions of Little Sand Bay and Sand Island but discarded it for two reasons: the number of improved properties was not large; and eventual federal ownership was deemed necessary for the lakeshore. To give owners of improved properties some protection the legislation drew upon another Cape Cod innovation providing that buildings and a modest amount of land could continue to be held privately for either twenty-five years with a right of assignment or for the life of the owners without assignment rights. The owners could select either option.

A careful review of the record suggests that had the property owners been better informed and organized, and had they been represented by a person who understood the application of the zoning provisions used at Cape Cod, they might have succeeded in excluding the developed portions of Sand Island and Little Sand Bay from the lakeshore. Senators Alan Bible and Frank E. Moss (a Utah Democrat) brought the matter up on a number of occasions. Bible, in fact, suggested in 1967 that the "Cape Cod Zoning" might be used and that "the committee could take care of [opposition by owners] if that develops to be the main problem of opposition to this particular national lakeshore bill."[33] It was an open invitation for owners to organize, draw boundaries excluding the developed areas, and testify in an informed manner. Although Schumacher, the South Shore Property Owners Association attorney, and

S. W. Jensch, another property owner, had suggested using this formula at the first Senate hearing, their presentation had not been effective. Schumacher had not been clear on what the formula actually meant, and Jensch, by stressing his adamant opposition to the lakeshore, had failed to capitalize on Bible's observation that the formula had worked well in other areas. Bible closed the Washington hearing by indicating he wanted more testimony on the issue at the upcoming Senate hearing, to be held in Ashland, after which the committee would make a decision.[34]

At the Ashland hearing, property owners continued to stress their overall opposition to the lakeshore but failed to recognize that perhaps some compromise was possible. Even during the 1967–69 hiatus, property owners failed to see the potential for a compromise and kept up their vigorous opposition to the lakeshore. Nelson gave Brewer an opening by bringing up the Cape Cod formula in 1969, but Brewer's response was that he did not want it if it provided for twenty-five-year or life-tenure rights. Jensch pleaded for the Cape Cod formula but failed to provide maps or supporting documents suggesting areas that might be excluded. The effectiveness of his arguments was compromised when he concluded by stating that the bill was unconstitutional.[35]

At the time of the final House hearing, property owners were represented by the South Shore Property Owners Association, the Apostle Islands Residents Committee, and a newly formed organization, the Apostle Islands Wilderness Council. The council's spokespersons— Brewer, Brodie, and Eric P. Westhagen, a property owner—provided no new arguments in their opposition to the lakeshore; however, they did emphasize Native American opposition, recognizing that the House committee was struggling with the issue of whether a viable lakeshore could be created without the tribal land.

The Concerns of Private Landowners

Many of the people protesting the inclusion of private land within the lakeshore boundary had a deep love for their property and the environment of the Lake Superior region. For many, their land had been in family ownership for decades. Their pleas to the House and Senate were often highly emotional, heartfelt, and honest. The dilemma Congress faced was summed up by the *Bayfield County Press* as a choice, "where one may suffer a crushed dream— hundreds, for generations to come—will be there to dream, to realize their dream of a vacation in a very beautiful section of our country."[36]

The depth of many landowners' anguish can be found in their letters and statements on the matter:

James H. Brodie: I am the owner of Ironwood Island, it is one of the smaller islands, roughly 600 acres. One of the most beautiful islands in the group. . . . This Ironwood Island has been the property of my family for 65 years. My grandfather acquired it and we have held it through three generations, with the idea in mind that this was a treasured spot of the nation and we feel as owners of this land, we are entitled to some of the credit for preserving this great natural beauty. . . . The owners of this land have been the ones who have kept its beauty intact and maintained it to a point where . . . I think that many of us who are the old time owners feel our great propriety [interest] towards this project.[37]

Harold L. Palm: [T]his is a plea for mercy. I am [a] lifelong resident of Sand Island. . . . My children are the fourth generation to enjoy this beautiful area. Our roots are deep. . . . One of the pathetic results created by the confiscation of land is the unhappiness which is instilled in the hearts of people who are forced to leave the land they all love so dearly.[38]

Melvin Dahl: I am a property owner on Sand Island and have been since 1940. My father and mother lived there for many years and I was born and raised on Sand Island and attended school there. . . . If Madeline can be excluded because it has been developed, why can't Sand Island and Little Sand Bay be excluded because we have kept it the way our fathers and forefathers developed it and that was to keep it the way they found it. . . . As we inherited from our fathers and forefathers so would our children like to inherit from us.[39]

Property owners' opposition never truly died, although they came to accept the reality of the lakeshore after its creation.

❦

CHAPTER 11

The State and the Apostle Islands

The state of Wisconsin was frequently hostile toward and uncooperative with federal interests in the Apostle Islands. In part this was due to the state's own interests in acquiring some or all of the islands as a state forest or park, interests that the state pursued during the 1950s. This initiative failed, largely due to financial constraints. After Congress established the Apostle Islands National Lakeshore the state continued to show its displeasure by dragging its feet over the transfer of state lands to federal ownership. This chapter examines the state of Wisconsin's interests in the Apostle Islands from 1950 on, including the federal negotiations with the state to accept the lakeshore and the final political maneuvering necessary to see the transfer of state lands into federal hands during the 1970s. The early period, while the state contemplated acquiring some of the islands for its own use, was characterized by a great deal of uncertainty as to how to protect the islands for some future and unspecified purpose. Budget constraints played an important role in creating that uncertainty. The middle period, characterized by the sometimes unkind debates between the federal and state governments, focused on determining the long-term best use of the lands, including the modest state holdings. The final period, as the state dragged its heels over legal transfer of land title for state-held acres on four islands, serves as a primer on relationships between a state and the federal government and their challenges.

Wisconsin's Interests in the Apostle Islands, 1950–60

After the inconclusive nature of the debate during the 1920s and 1930s, when northern residents had been very interested in and active in trying to establish a national park in the Apostle Islands, with time off during the Second

World War, it was a lack of money and opposing ideologies that plagued the state in its deliberations over the Apostle Islands during the 1950s. Although citizen interest in and support for public ownership of some or all of the archipelago was increasing, the Legislature, the Wisconsin Conservation Commission, and the Wisconsin Conservation Department were highly uncertain as to what course of action to take, if any. Having no clear goals or objectives, these institutions reacted to external forces. In spite of their confusion and uncertainty they would, near the end of the decade, take steps to establish an Apostle Islands State Forest.

But what should Wisconsin try to establish? While in Wisconsin (as in many states), parks and forests were administered by the same bureau, there were substantial differences between a park, a forest, and a forest that was designated "wilderness." They were essentially distinct yet related and complementary management units, and each had different goals and uses implicit and explicit in its definition.

State forests were (and are) primarily natural resource reserves; their present and future lay in use through timber harvests. Gifford Pinchot, who argued this before the Wisconsin Legislature, said "that the planned and orderly *development* of the natural resources for the general welfare is the very essence of national common sense."[1] But by 1954 Wisconsin had officially modified this definition to meet changing public demand: "State forests are areas set aside primarily for timber production but managed under the principle of 'multiple use'. . . . Although the primary use of state forests is the growing of recurring forest crops, scenic values, scientific and educational values, outdoor recreation, public hunting and fishing and stabilization of stream flow are important extra benefits. Under the principle of multiple use, forests contain special use areas such as recreation sites, wilderness areas, scientific areas, game refuges and canoe-ways within which specific uses take precedence over timber production."[2]

Multiple use had been endorsed by the State Planning Board as early as 1939 in recognition of changing public values.[3] Yet the term *multiple use* was confusing. While by consensus certain forests, or areas in forests, might have scenic or other values worth consideration, by legal definition a state forest's *primary* purpose was to produce trees for harvest. Other values, while important, were distinctly secondary. Thus, while a certain level of protection might be afforded an area such as the Apostle Islands if designated as state forest, that protection was only as strong and long lasting as public pressure and support and agency compliance. Nothing in the statutes precluded logging of even scenic areas in state forests.

State parks, on the other hand, were intended first and foremost to be protected and preserved. The *1947 State Parks Act,* influenced by National Park Service precedents, defined parks as areas with unique cultural, historical, biological, or geological features, or areas of great scenic beauty. Their intended use was principally recreational: hiking, camping, and nature watching. The intent was to *protect* rather than to *use* in an exploitative sense. In 1954 the WCD defined parks as follows: "The main purpose of state parks is to preserve the unusual or unique scenic or historic places of the state for all time, in a manner consistent with the legitimate use of such areas by the public. It is, therefore, necessary that the use of these parks be regulated in such a manner so as to preserve the qualities that justified the selection of the area for state park purposes."[4]

Although public use could be regulated, recreational development was necessary. Thus, parks could contain picnic shelters, flush toilets, parking lots, concession and souvenir stands, extensive road systems and graded trails and other human-made features that "aided in the legitimate use of such areas by the public."[5] A park designation aided in the protection and preservation of some natural values in some ways but not in others.

The designation of wilderness areas was generally limited to state forests, since most of the parks had been too changed by human activity to merit such a title. What was meant by designating an area such as the Apostle Islands as *wilderness,* however, was open to question, a problem frequently noted by Apostle Island advocates. Wildernesses clearly contrasted with well-developed parks, which had extensive facilities such as toilets and picnic shelters. Whether the idea of wilderness meant "untouched" or "unmanaged" was unclear. It was not until the 1960s that a National Wilderness Act was passed.

Between 1949 and 1955 the WCC and WCD debated the issue of designating state forests, or portions of state forests, as wilderness. The Conservation Department generally interpreted wilderness in two related but distinct ways. First, wilderness was not to be managed. In the Wisconsin Flambeau River State Forest, for example, in designated areas, this meant that downed trees and dead timber were left to rot rather than hauled out. "Cleaning it up" was seen as tantamount to turning it into a park.[6] The second interpretation was essentially the restoration of wilderness in areas that had been developed and used. Again in the Flambeau, this meant relocating and obliterating forest roads and locating new roads away from river banks.[7] Thus the WCD saw no problem in designating an area as wilderness, in spite of earlier logging activity, if the area could be returned to "natural" conditions (although the definition of *natural* opened an entirely different sort of debate). Within this definition, the logged-over Apostle Islands qualified as wilderness, but purists could argue against such a designation. Within the context of the Apostle Islands debate, however, the distinction rested between a *developed* park and an *unmanaged* wilderness.

There were other vital differences between parks and forests in Wisconsin. For one, their funding came from different sources, and the forestry budget was greater and more stable than that of parks. And while parks often involved a great deal of financial outlay, not only for the original purchase but also for facility development and maintenance, forests, particularly wilderness areas within forests, required very little capital investment other than the cost of the original purchase. Thus, for many reasons, the decision on how the Apostle Islands would be classified was important.

The Beginnings: 1950–1954

In the 1920s and 1930s, initiatives on behalf of the Apostle Islands had come from local residents. During the 1950s the interest originated in southern Wisconsin. The Wisconsin Duck Hunters' Association had raised the issue and was most likely interested in the hunting and fishing opportunities the islands and sloughs presented, although the proposal called for a park, where hunting was not permitted. The proposal passed unanimously, and the Milwaukee County Conservation Alliance (MCCA) sent it to the WCC with a resolution.[8] The alliance proved to be the only organization ambitious enough during the decade to suggest that all the islands be acquired. No one else ever took seriously the possibility of securing all twenty-two islands, given the potentially substantial cost, especially when Madeline Island was included.

WCD Director Ernie Swift presented the MCCA proposal to the WCC, which in turn approved the suggestion that the islands' ownership be investigated.[9] Six months later Swift presented to the WCC the results of the investigation into ownership of the islands; it was a mix of public (state, federal, and county government) and private. The Conservation Commission's early response to the alliance proposal was decidedly unenthusiastic. Swift was concerned that unless definite plans were formulated, little would be gained by spending any more time or money. Forest and Parks Superintendent Harrington questioned whether the islands could be used for a park; past explorations had concluded that, "for general public use . . . these islands were impractical for such purposes." The WCD conclusion in 1950 indicated its low level of enthusiasm for any further action.[10]

A year later, the Conservation Department wrote to Ashland County regarding the possible purchase of Oak Island for a state forest. The chair of the town of La Pointe estimated the value at two dollars per acre.[11] At a subsequent meeting of the Ashland County Board of Supervisors, one supervisor argued against selling Oak Island, and the matter was tabled.[12]

In 1952, the MCCA again recommended that the Apostle Islands be publicly acquired, this time in much stronger language. Earl May of the Legislative Council appeared before the WCC to emphasize the MCCA's interest and support. He specifically called for the establishment of public hunting and fishing grounds and proposed the use of public hunting and fishing budgets for the purchase.[13]

When the Wisconsin Legislative Council Conservation Committee (LCCC) reported on its inquiries into the Apostle Islands in 1952, it reported widespread grassroots interest in the islands as public hunting grounds and recommended the adoption of the MCCA proposal.[14] Deer were abundant; new woody plant growth on the cutover islands provided ideal habitat.[15] Bear hunting was also good. The islands had no inland lakes or streams; however, fishing was excellent on Lake Superior.

Still, the Conservation Commission's interest in the Apostle Islands continued to be modest. It took up the question of the MCCA proposal in July 1952 at a meeting in Ashland heavily attended by Conservation Department personnel, conservation organization representatives, and local business people. During lunch on Stockton Island, the possibility of using the Apostles for recreation was discussed; however, the Conservation Department was most interested in Oak and Stockton Islands, both fairly large islands, as potential additions to the state forest system.[16] After the meeting, the Conservation Commission presented a progress report to the Legislative Council noting the public interest in seeing the Apostles turned into hunting lands, but no action was taken.[17]

Given the caliber of those supporting some sort of state acquisition of the Apostle Islands, it was surprising that the Conservation Commission members and Conservation Department employees failed to express much more enthusiasm for the idea at this meeting than they had in 1950. Instead, during discussion over lunch, Charles "Frosty" Smith, the commission chair, stated that any proposal for acquisition should go straight to the Legislature for approval. Swift quickly agreed. No clear plans or time lines for acquisition were discussed. Essentially, the Conservation Commission and the Conservation Department were saying they wanted no part of the scheme unless specifically ordered to do so by the Legislature.

At the time both the WCC and the WCD had good cause for referring the question to the Legislature. In 1952 the financial situation of the state parks system was deplorable, and short of an outright donation of the islands, funding for a proposed park would have to come through a special appropriation from the state's general fund, a move only the Wisconsin Legislature could authorize. Some funding could have come from the state forestry budget, but the WCD had other uses for these funds.[18]

In the meantime, the University of Wisconsin was attempting to pursue an interest in acquiring Stockton Island. In 1953 the agricultural agent for Ashland County, Dave Holt, presented to the Ashland County Board a university proposal for the purchase of Stockton. The county board unanimously passed a resolution objecting to the university's effort to purchase Stockton Island.[19]

In 1954 the LCCC began to plan a tour of the Apostles to again evaluate requests that the islands be purchased.[20] When the LCCC met on August 23, 1954, it focused on the possibility of a state park in the islands. John Beale of the WCD, however, strongly advised against establishing a park, arguing that a forest was a more financially feasible option. He was also concerned that if the state were to purchase some of the islands, as a park or a forest, public pressure would force the development of extensive recreational facilities, including accessible and inexpensive transportation to the islands (an incredibly expensive undertaking). The WCD was reluctant to commit to such expenditures using dollars earmarked for forestry purposes. The possibility of using state general funds was dismissed early after a lively discussion.

During an interview with the press after the meeting, one legislative committee member, Senator Melvin Olson, stated that the LCCC would recommend the purchase of four or five islands. While considerable debate had focused on the nature of the proposed acquisition (some spoke in favor of a park, others a forest), by the time of the press conference these distinctions were lost. Senator Olson was quoted to the effect that the LCCC would probably be recommending the "[p]urchase of four or five of the Apostle Islands . . . as an addition to the state's *park and forest system. . . .* Olson said plans call for one of the islands to be devoted to park purposes and others to be used as wilderness areas."[21] However, not surprisingly given the lack of clear goals on everyone's part, nothing was to be done about the Apostle Islands until the following year.

The Turning Point: 1955

The year 1955 would be a key period for the Apostle Islands as public, legislative, and Conservation Commission interest in some type of public acquisition mounted. Continued local interest was evident when the Bayfield County Board passed a resolution calling for the state to establish either a park or forest reserve in the Apostles.[22] Early in the year the Legislative Council replaced the Interim Committee on Conservation with a permanent body designated as the Conservation Committee. The new Conservation Committee was given four study topics, including the possible acquisition of the Apostle Islands for game management, park, or forestry purposes.[23]

Although Senator Olson had stated in 1954 that the Interim Conservation Committee was recommending the purchase of four or five of the islands for a park and wilderness, it chose not to send a complementary recommendation to the Wisconsin Legislature regarding an appropriation for the purchase.[24] On reflection, the Conservation Committee's decision seems to have been politically shrewd. Aware of past and current public support for state acquisition, especially by such influential and powerful groups as the MCCA, the LCCC could not help but acknowledge that support. A decision clearly against acquisition of the islands might well have been viewed as a politically poor position to take. Instead, the LCCC supported a nicely balanced compromise of acquiring four or five islands to be kept as both park and wilderness. This action seems to have been neatly calculated to insulate LCCC members from public disappointment. Yet the committee, taking care not to irritate the WCC and WCD, left them an escape route. They waffled. In a formal letter dated February 2, 1955, Earl Sachse, the committee's executive secretary, wrote to Guido Rahr, the chair of the Conservation Commission: "At a recent meeting of the Legislative Council's Conservation Committee, the committee went on record in favor of your purchasing or making preparations to purchase the islands of Hermit, Manitou, Oak and Stockton [Basswood was inadvertently omitted and added later]. . . . The Committee's action was taken with the understanding that *if sufficient funds are not available to your commission at the present time, an option should be taken and the purchase consummated as soon as the money is available.*"[25]

Notable by its omission was any suggestion that the Legislature should consider a general fund appropriation. Thus, for the time being, everyone concerned was neatly off the hook for an expensive acquisition, while the public was left with the impression that action would be forthcoming. The Conservation Department's response to the committee recommendation was predictable. Beale, at a Conservation Commission meeting, requested a specific sense of direction. The WCC told him to advise the Legislative Council that the WCD budget lacked sufficient funds for the acquisition of the five islands, and that if any such purchase were to take place in the near future it would have to be financed by the Legislature. However, other interests in the Apostle Islands were starting to emerge. Beale had reported in February that Ashland County was now interested in selling Oak Island to the state, and that the Vilas Estate (which owned most of Stockton Island) had contacted the WCD to determine its interest in the island.[26] The trustees for the estate were more interested in receiving a payment than in giving the land to the University of Wisconsin.[27]

The Legislative Council Conservation Committee finally responded to the Conservation Commission's request for funding. The committee's executive secretary informed Voigt that it was very unlikely that any recommendations on acquisitions in the Apostles would be made, and that it was also unlikely that a request for an appropriation from the general fund for such an acquisition would succeed in the current session.[28]

Voigt was also aware of the university's interest in Stockton. The university had completed a report on Stockton and had concluded that forestry, wildlife, marine, and entomological research possibilities existed there; that was encouraging news to the professional resource managers in the Conservation Department. One comment in the university report is worth noting. WCD Director Swift had indicated that the WCC was interested in the islands and had also suggested that the Wisconsin Legislature might want to provide the funds for the purchase of all of the islands, except Madeline, over a period of several years, to create a state forest for future logging and recreational use.[29] Oddly, this comment by Swift never was recorded in WCC minutes or other WCD records and was never raised in later years. When the lawyers for the Vilas Estate indicated their willingness to lease Stockton to the department, the university's interest ended.[30]

In 1955, Victor Wallin, a Bayfield County resident and state assemblyman, appeared before the WCC and urged the use of hunting and fishing license funds for land purchases in the islands. One key event coming out of his appearance was his request that the commissioners prepare a summary of their position and the WCD position on the acquisition of the Apostles.[31] In May the commission adopted a draft resolution that

- directed the Department divisions to examine their roles and participation in acquiring land in the archipelago;
- directed that land appraisals be initiated;
- stated that major assistance might be required from the state general fund; and
- urged that contributions from local sources be encouraged if they endorsed the program.[32]

At this time the Conservation Commission also authorized attempts to seek a lease on Stockton Island. Within a few weeks Voigt reported that the trustees of the Vilas Estate had agreed to a five-year lease on Stockton Island for $1,000 a year, subject to a purchase option. Land values were yet to be determined.[33] On June 10 the commission met to discuss the possible purchase of Stockton.[34]

There were, interestingly, internal differences and perceptions in the Conservation Department regarding the use and values of Stockton. Chief Forester Beale favored designating the island "wilderness" for the time being because an acquisition would require few improvements and, therefore, little cash outlay. Voigt and Shorger discussed the possibility of logging the island to pay for the purchase. However, WCD wildlife ecologist Burton Dahlberg (highly regarded within the department) supported the wilderness view. "The value of an undeveloped area where it is possible to get away from the hustle and bustle of modern living cannot be overestimated. There are very few places left in the middle west that offer an opportunity to establish a natural area, where future generations may know the value of natural things. . . . One of Stockton Island's greatest assets is its inaccessibility. The fact that a vacation on the island requires some planning and the possibility that one may be stranded for a few extra days makes it all the more desirable."[35]

The internal debates within the WCD continued and were resolved only when, in August 1955, the WCC met to present and approve a formal *Policy on Acquisition of an Apostle Island Wilderness Area*. The meeting was held in Bayfield and, by special invitation, was attended by members of conservation organizations, local organizations, business people, and the press. The commission's policy stated:

> Because of the continuing interest of many citizens and organizations in the desirability of public ownership of some of the Apostle Islands in Lake Superior, and because the Legislative Council's Conservation Committee is on record in favor of purchase by the state of several of these islands, the Conservation Commission deems it advisable to adopt a general policy regarding an acquisition program of this nature. Therefore, it is the policy of the Wisconsin Conservation Commission to:
>
> 1. Recognize the importance of the Apostle Islands in Lake Superior to the future welfare of the citizens of Wisconsin for preservation of unusual historical, geological, plant and animal resources, for unique research opportunities, and for specialized recreational values, by establishing an acquisition unit to be known as the Apostle Islands Wilderness Area.
>
> 2. Encourage all citizens and organizations to work toward the accomplish-

ment of this desirable goal and recommend increased scientific and social studies by departmental divisions and educational institutions of the human, forestry, fish and wildlife resources in this area and their potential aspects for multiple-use and wise management, and especially for their specialized wilderness-type recreational values.

3. Declare that although this acquisition program is most desirable, it is not immediately attainable and may be realized slowly because of already established commitments and priorities in the use of available funds. It also points up to the citizens of the state, their various organizations and their legislators the opportunity here presented for public service by helping to dissolve this financial barrier to a worthy social, educational and recreational project of importance to themselves today, but especially to the citizens of tomorrow who will need this type of recreational opportunity in the presence of greatly increased population pressures.[36]

The policy statement fudged nicely on what, precisely, this area was to be, and not incidentally on who was going to pay for it. An interesting mix of key words was used: "preservation of unusual historical, geological, plant and animal resources" and "specialized recreational values" in one paragraph, clearly draws upon the 1949 State Parks Act, and in the next paragraph "multiple-use and wise management," key forestry terms, are used. The final paragraph neatly emphasized the enormous financial hurdles the project would have to clear.

Further, the statement conveyed the impression that the WCC was supportive of land purchase, but without identifying what islands would be acquired and without committing any division to taking the responsibility of paying for it. Because forestry values were noted, forestry mill-tax revenues could be used to finance the purchase. However, the commission was skirting this possibility and instead was urging several departmental divisions to support it with their funds.[37] In the end the commission left the financial responsibility to Wisconsin citizens, their conservation organizations, and the legislative representatives. On the one hand the policy statement highlighted the values of the Apostles. On the other it was a polite, political "put-up-or-shut-up" challenge that offended no one. Meaningful decisions would have to come later.

Although the policy did not identify the islands to be included in the wilderness area, a consensus existed within the Conservation Department that Madeline Island was to be excluded. Local people were, however, interested in a park on that island, and a few weeks after the commission action, the Ashland County Board, at the request of La Pointe Town Chair Elmer Nelson, adopted a resolution favoring the establishment of a state park at Big Bay on the island. At the same time the county board expressed considerable frustration with the department's failure to move decisively on the islands and the state's insistence on a forest over a park.[38]

By September when the LCCC met to again consider the Apostle Islands, supporters pushed strongly for an Apostles park. Frank Dexter of the *Bayfield County Press* argued that the Apostle Islands should be designated as a park rather than wilderness because a developed park would attract more visitors. George Sprecher told the committee, in no uncertain terms, that there was no money to be appropriated from the forestry fund for a park (a legally questionable action anyway). The Conservation Department's financial priorities were clear: defend the state's forests from the threat of insect infestation, a legitimate concern that year.[39]

Signs of Progress: 1956–1960

Early in 1956 the Legislative Council Conservation Committee met again to discuss the islands. A committee member noted that not all islands were available for purchase but stated that Ashland County was willing to sell Oak Island for $5,000, a splendid opportunity. Public support for the acquisition was again stressed, this time by Les Woerpel of the Wisconsin Federation of Conservation Clubs. Woerpel favored an acquisition that would turn some islands into playgrounds while leaving others as wilderness for a variety of recreational opportunities. During the discussion Sprecher indicated that using one island for park purposes and leaving the rest as wilderness, "in the raw," as he put it, for fish and game purposes had some support in the WCD. Some participants debated the merits of the islands for game management or for forestry; another argued that recreation was best in a wilderness park. It was clear that after six years of discussion, the Legislative Council Conservation Committee, the Conservation Commission, the Conservation Department, and Wisconsin citizens had yet to reach a consensus on how to acquire and manage the Apostle Islands.[40]

Local residents were, however, quite clear. They wanted a park, and a nicely developed park at that. But the Ashland County Board was making the acquisition of county lands in the islands a serious problem for the WCD. The board, initially willing to part with Oak Island and the seventy-two acres it owned on Stockton, suddenly turned difficult. At an LCCC meeting in March, Dexter spoke about his concern that private individuals would acquire the most scenic spots in the islands. He indicated that it was possible that Ashland County had been offered $75,000 from a private party for Oak Island but that he had been unable to confirm that report.[41]

The Ashland County Board was clearly frustrated with WCC foot-dragging. In April it passed a resolution authorizing the sale of 9,000 acres on Oak and Stockton Islands. The board placed no restrictions on who might purchase the land.[42] Although the county board never carried through on this resolution, it was a source of concern for WCD staff.

In August 1956 the LCCC met in Ashland, and local residents again argued that northern Wisconsin already had enough wilderness; what was needed in the Apostles was a well-developed park. When Frank Dexter tried to soften the comment by pointing out that the definition of wilderness was rather vague, Ashland County Board Chair Todd retorted that the people of Ashland wanted a moneymaker that would give the locals something new to look at and pull in tourists.[43]

Although the funding question had not been resolved, the LCCC decided to direct the Conservation Department to acquire purchase options on county-owned lands on Stockton, Hermit, Manitou, Oak, and Basswood Islands by December 15, 1956. The options would then provide the stimulus for legislative debates and, hopefully, funding.[44]

Ashland County continued to maintain a hostile position toward the WCD and unanimously adopted a resolution to deny the state purchase options on the islands because it would remove the land from the county tax rolls.[45] In its *Final Report to the Governor and the 1957 Legislature*, however, the LCCC recommended only that the department purchase Stockton Island. Further acquisitions would depend on the availability of funds.[46]

By 1958 the Conservation Department was again considering some action on the Apostle Islands, specifically the purchase of Stockton Island (with $40,000 taken from the reforestation fund) and its establishment as a state forest.[47] Apparently, funding issues were easing. A state forest was the most logical designation; Stockton had not been logged since 1918, and the island's principal value was in its $170,000 worth of timber. Wildlife research, hunting, fishing, boating, and camping would be secondary values.[48] At its first meeting in 1959, the WCC supported this action. It approved the purchase of Stockton Island and the creation of the Apostle Islands State Forest and directed that public hearings be held on the Stockton Island Forest Boundary.[49] Press coverage was favorable.[50]

During the public hearings on the proposed forest boundary, held in both Madison and Ashland, the public not only supported the Stockton Island purchase but specifically called for the acquisition of other islands as well.[51] Emboldened by this public support the WCD recommended in March that the forest be enlarged to include Oak and Basswood Islands. (Basswood at the time was owned by private parties who were willing to sell to the state.) Voigt then drafted a formal order including all three islands in the proposed Apostle Islands State Forest. The order was subsequently approved by the Conservation Commission.[52]

During this period the entire area received a great deal of attention. The Wisconsin State Senate, following up on the earlier interest in a park along the south shore of Lake Superior, in March passed a joint resolution advocating an investigation of the "desirability of establishing a state park or forest in the area of the south shore of Lake Superior and adjacent to and including the Apostle Islands," with a recommendation that the acquisition not be delayed.[53] The Assembly amended the joint resolution to direct the Legislative Council to study the possibility of acquiring land on the south shore of Lake Superior for a park or forest. The matter was referred to the Conservation Committee.

The area also received national attention following the publication of the NPS's *Fourth Shore Reports* early in 1959. These reports recommended that Wisconsin establish seven areas as state parks or forests on the south shore of Lake Superior. In response to a follow-up inquiry by the Ashland County Board, NPS Region 5 Director Daniel J. Tobin described the entire Apostle Islands group as an "outstanding feature" and recommended that the Conservation Department purchase Stockton Island.[54] Not everyone shared this view. Former WCD Director Ernest Swift was highly critical of the later diversion of $75,000 from the forestry fund for parks purposes, a portion of which was later used to buy Stockton.[55]

Unfortunately, by 1960, Stockton was the only island to have been purchased. Negotiations for the purchase of Oak and Basswood Islands had bogged down in a lack of cooperation from the Ashland County Board.[56] In March 1960, still angered by difficulties in dealing with the state, the board adopted a report from its Land Committee that recommended *not* selling county lands on Oak or Basswood Islands until the WCD was able to demonstrate a suitable development program for Stockton.[57]

In his summation to the LCCC in October 1960, Beale reported that the Conservation Department simply could not afford to develop Stockton Island and that the two other islands proposed for the Apostle Islands State Forest were now likely to cost $48,000.[58] In the meantime, and quite oblivious to the fiscal constraints of the department, the committee was still exploring the idea of another new park in the region along the south shore of Lake Superior.[59] It was not an auspicious beginning for the new decade.

State Activities: 1960–1970

Gaylord Nelson's initiatives as governor had invigorated planning for the state and especially for the north. Not since the 1930s, with the work of the National Resources Planning Board and then the Wisconsin State Planning Board, had the north received such intense attention. And the planning would be sensitive to Nelson's policy initiatives: the Wisconsin Department of Resource Development's State Recreation Plan, the "South Shore Studies," the planning for the lakeshore, and the plans being developed for the State Recreation Committee by the DRD. To have assigned the Conservation Department planning responsibilities for a national lakeshore, given its interests in some of the islands and its antipathy to both federal involvement and Nelson himself, would have presented the proposed lakeshore with enormous difficulties. In contrast, the state's planning programs supported and reinforced a national lakeshore.

Recommendations to protect important recreation and scenic resources in the state would be joined with persuasive arguments that tourism spending was important to the state's economy. The Fine Study reported that during one twelve-month period (1959–60), individuals who spent at least one night away from home spent a combined total of $581,295,311 in Wisconsin on vacation-recreation activities.[60] Slightly more than half of this revenue was derived from nonresidents. The number one attraction to tourists was scenery and sightseeing (40 percent), with fishing ranking second (23 percent).[61]

This data, and data developed in subsequent studies, attracted a great deal of media and public attention and support. Recreation and tourism were becoming major elements in the state's economic development strategy, especially for the north. But more than just promoting commercial tourism development, the studies repeatedly demonstrated the importance of protecting scenic beauty, the single most important reason for tourists to recreate in Wisconsin. Tourism proponents and parks advocates saw the wisdom of joining forces to support Nelson's recreation initiatives and national lakeshore dream.

Although the WCD had numerous interests in the region, and in spite of the fact that new ORAP dollars were available for outdoor recreation, the WCD's capacity to meet needs statewide was still limited. State Parks Director Koening, who had rather expansive plans for the Apostle Islands, was simply not being financially realistic. The department was committed to completing state acquisition on Stockton and acquiring Oak and Basswood Islands, and it had also initiated a new Big Bay State Park on Madeline Island. The WCC's earlier adoption of the *Policy on Acquisition of an Apostle Islands Wilderness Area* indicated that its limited acquisition goals could only be realized slowly because of established commitments and other priorities in the use of available funds.[62] This was adopted prior to ORAP but would continue to hold true.

The first iteration of the DRD's comprehensive recreation plan would further emphasize that Wisconsin needed to address outdoor recreation needs in other parts of the state. Facilities were severely limited in the populous southeastern and east-central Wisconsin; an additional 1,000 acres of beach lands were needed in these areas immediately, and by the year 2000 needs would reach 7,050 acres. Of the Great Lakes shoreline in the state, only 28 miles out of 820 miles were in public ownership, and most of that was on remote Stockton Island. Acquisition needs on the Lake Michigan shoreline were especially critical, and because no sites met national criteria, state action was vital. Although the emphasis for state action was placed on the Lake Michigan shoreline, the DRD plan recognized the high recreational and aesthetic qualities of the Apostle Islands region.[63]

Both the preliminary and final "South Shore Studies" also emphasized the need for federal action in the Apostle Islands region. "[The national lakeshore] will provide an economic stimulus to a region which is financially depressed, will meet the social goals of providing Americans with valuable outdoor recreation amenities in a unique area, and will materially assist the members of two tribal councils to improve their economic and social status. The department heartily concurs in the foregoing federal proposal and is working closely with the agencies concerned to promote this concept."[64]

The final South Shore Report further recommended that the state abandon its plans in the Apostle Islands region in the event the federal proposal materialized, and focus instead on the north on a number of new land acquisitions for parks, forests, and wildlife habitat.[65] These were formidable planning goals and would require substantial funds. The WCC was already beginning to struggle with the fiscal demands of a greatly enlarged state recreation program. In 1963 it estimated that its established program would take twenty-one years to complete at a cost of $150 million; acquisition costs alone were $50 million. The massive infusion of new funds had brought about a sense of euphoria within the Conservation Department, but its expanded goals were not in keeping with the fiscal realities of the times. Thus, in October of that year, the commission adopted a new policy of completing established projects while initiating no new major projects and dropping low-value projects.[66]

In spite of the "South Shore Studies" and the work of the federal North Central Field Committee's subcommittee, the WCD remained cool to federal involvement in the region. In 1964 I reviewed with top department officials the outlines of the lakeshore proposal. Although interested, they would make no commitments. They also advised me that they planned to continue their acquisition and development plans for the islands, a park at Big Bay on Madeline Island and land purchases at Raspberry Bay and other areas on the Bayfield Peninsula.[67]

In addition to recreation planning, the state was engaged in economic development planning for rural regions. The Overall Economic Development Plans (OEDP) prepared by the DRD proposed investments in public recreation as one mechanism to attract tourists and tourism spending to the Apostle Islands region. County-level OEDPs made similar recommendations. Both drew upon the conclusions of the Fine tourism studies. Earlier, on September 25, 1963, at the "Land and People Conference" in Duluth, Minnesota, the conferees agreed that recreation and tourism offered the northern Great Lakes region its greatest undeveloped economic opportunity.[68]

The first phase plan stated the following:

> The results of the DRD recreation and economic studies in the Apostle Islands region could only lead to the conclusion that the state did not have the fiscal capacity to undertake the Lakeshore and that Federal involvement was necessary. This conclusion was summarized in the first phase of the state recreation plan as follows:
>
> The [Lakeshore] area conforms with the first phase of the Wisconsin Comprehensive Plan. It conforms with the Preliminary Report on the South Shore Area and the unpublished final report on the region. The proposal is consistent with the policy position of the Wisconsin Conservation Commission. The proposal conforms to findings of landscape architects, consultants to the Wisconsin Department of Resource Development, who made a complete Lake Superior shoreline survey, that the environmental resources within the proposed area have high recreation potential.[69]

In spite of the fact that the state had changed governors, from Reynolds (a Democrat) to Knowles (a Republican), civil service planners in the DRD had continued the momentum with the second phase of the recreation plan, which echoed and reinforced the first phase: "The Apostle Islands offers a unique potential as a recreation area. The creation of a national lakeshore in the Apostle Islands area is consistent with this plan on the assumption that this federal facility will be established, and that no state or local funds will be involved. No allocations are made in this plan for the acquisition or development of this area."[70]

The plan further noted that the state had 690,000 acres of potential park land, of which more than 250,000 acres were rated "top quality." Needs were greatest in the southern and eastern counties, and DRD plans called "for protection and development of these sites close to where large numbers of people live. It recommends against expansion of public recreational lands in sparsely settled northern counties."[71]

The Apostle Islands and Substate Regional Planning

Centralized state recreation planning and support for a lakeshore was one thing. As importantly, substate regional planning—after careful analysis of the data—should likewise show consistency with state planning and state goals. The Northwest Wisconsin Regional Planning Commission (NWWRPC) would serve that role. The Department of Resource Development provided planning assistance. During the 1960s the NWWRPC was struggling with pervasive problems of economic stagnation and decline. It elected to make tourism an important element in its economic development strategies. Fortunately, the University of Wisconsin tourism studies were partially completed. Others were underway. The analysis of the economic implications of a lakeshore would predict that when fully developed, the area would attract 920,700 visits, resulting in a $7.25 million economic impact on the local economy.[72] These persuasive data were made available in preliminary form to the NWWRPC and were useful in enlisting its support for the lakeshore.

Members of the NWWRPC staff met with the NCFC subcommittee in 1964 to review the relationship of the proposed lakeshore to their tourism and economic development strategies. They were urged to designate the Apostle Islands region as a special study area in their forthcoming comprehensive plan.[73] Because the NWWRPC had in part been organized in response to Nelson's charges in 1957 and 1958 that the state had done nothing on regional planning, I was concerned that there might still be some political antipathy vis-à-vis Nelson. This was not the case; instead, the Conservation Commission reiterated the following recommendations emanating from the state: "Local residents, the Regional Planning Commission and private promotional groups should press for the establishment of the . . . Apostle National Park

Area. Such a project would draw many vacationers into the region."[74] The NWWRPC members were appointed by county board chairs, so it had significant influence on tourism groups and local residents in the five northwestern Wisconsin counties, including Ashland and Bayfield.

In addition to planners, the commercial tourism industry also saw the wisdom of large-scale regional efforts. For example, Tony Wise, an imaginative and innovative developer in Hayward, reflected this recognition in a statement to the press: "Regional development is essential to succeed as opposed to local development. No one is big enough to cope with the demand for recreation facilities. We must pool our resources and our attractions for developing them."[75] Wise was a highly visible and respected leader, and his staunch support for the lakeshore was significant. He understood the importance of public protection of significant natural resources in the region, resources that would attract large numbers of tourists, and the development of appropriate private tourism facilities nearby.

With the defeat of Reynolds in the 1964 campaign, planners now had to work with Warren Knowles, the new governor. He would serve an unprecedented three terms well into 1970. He was a popular governor and fortunately had a strong personal interest in conservation. Moreover, he was willing to be innovative. During his governorship, Knowles signed into law a complete reorganization of the resource agencies in Wisconsin that resulted in the creation of an integrated umbrella agency, the Department of Natural Resources (DNR). Knowles eventually gained influence over the policy-making Natural Resources Board through his appointments. He also took the lead in strengthening the role of the state in water resources. Furthermore, he greatly expanded funding for outdoor recreation programs and for the first time got the state directly into funding water pollution programs.

As a conservationist, Knowles did not wish to directly oppose Nelson on the lakeshore proposal. It simply had too much public support, and to commit the state to accomplishing the same goals would have been a substantial drain on state recreation budgets. His strategy was to keep pressure on Nelson and congressional committees to commit federal funds for the project and to make the best possible deal with Congress on matters of direct concern to the state—matters such as hunting and fishing and the recapture of the state's investment.

There were three important considerations with which to deal: Knowles as governor, with all the substantial powers of the office; Knowles as chief executive, with strong influence over state agencies; and, Knowles as a political leader. When governors speak, the media report. The early strategy of lakeshore proponents, simply put, was to maintain and increase the base of citizen support for the lakeshore and to keep Knowles informed without formally asking for his endorsement of the proposal until it was absolutely necessary. To this end, I met with him in July 1965, in advance of the public release of the NCFC subcommittee report and the "Fine Report" on the economic implications of the lakeshore, so he did not read about the proposal in the press.

I briefly outlined the proposal. Knowles knew the area well, having frequently fished and vacationed there. He had three concerns. First, he wanted to know if the lakeshore would be patterned along the lines of the Wisconsin Ice Age Scientific Reserve, which provided for national designation and state management. However, Congress had directed the state to use federal grant funds allocated under LAWCON. Understandably, state officials took umbrage with federal direction on how they were to use what they believed to be state funds. The Ice Age Scientific Reserve had, in fact, been hung up in Congress for several years over this issue. I assured Knowles that this would not happen with the Apostle Islands. Instead it would be a federal project using LAWCON funds allocated to federal agencies.

Second, Knowles was concerned about private property rights. I explained that owners of improved property would have options of immediate sale, life tenure, or a twenty-five-year tenure with a right of assignment. His third concern was the availability of LAWCON funds to the state. I advised him that $194,669 would be available as soon as the state's comprehensive plan was approved by the federal Bureau of Outdoor Recreation.[76]

Knowles did, however, continue to hammer on the issue of federal funding; "The plan of Senator Nelson for the Apostle Islands is a meritorious one, but I'll be anxious to see the bill to find out where the money is coming from. I hope he doesn't take it out of the land and water fund as they did on the Ice Age Park bill. That caused real headaches."[77] He also told representatives of nine northern counties to "think big" in asking for federal dollars for the lakeshore.[78] Nelson, finally responding to Knowles's criticisms, stated that the lakeshore would be funded with federal LAWCON dollars, and this would be in addition to the amounts Wisconsin was already receiving for state and local parks.[79]

At the June 2, 1967, congressional hearings, Knowles went on record in support of the lakeshore with caveats laid out by his representatives, Voigt and "Frosty" Smith.[80] Late in 1968 he said, "We at the state level have also endorsed this national area. . . . The former Conservation Commission and now the Natural Resources Board have also favored its creation, but it takes the federal government years to move while Wisconsin has moved on the Apostle Islands State Forest."[81] A few days later he was more negative in his comments before the Executive Committee of the Natural Resources Committee of State Agencies, when he said, "The dream of Apostle Islands as a recreation area right now is rather remote. When you go up there and see the remoteness of those islands . . . my opinion is that the recreational usefulness [of federal designation] of the islands is nothing more than the identification of an area. . . . It would be better to look for more 'inland parks' to develop than to rely on the Apostle Islands Lakeshore."[82]

Knowles also kept the pressure on the congressional committees. In 1970, in a strongly worded telegram to Congressman Roy Taylor, who chaired the House of Representatives Subcommittee on National Parks and Recreation, he stated: "The state of Wisconsin has already acquired extensive areas for public use within the proposed National Lakeshore boundaries while awaiting federal action. Your committee has the opportunity and I believe the obligation to take the first federal step . . . by taking favorable action on H.R. 555. . . . As governor of the state of Wisconsin I endorse this bill."[83]

Although Knowles had varied his positions, in 1970, when the legislation was in serious trouble in the House, the governor eventually came through with strong support and indicated to Congressman Kastenmeier that the Upper Great Lakes Regional Commission, which Knowles cochaired with me, would be meeting on other matters, and the commission sent another telegram reiterating its earlier support.[84]

To obtain support from leading Democrats in Wisconsin was easy. For example, the Hansons conducted a tour of the islands for Wisconsin Attorney General Bronson LaFollette, after which he wrote Stewart Udall a strong letter of support. Udall responded, "In 1963, I visited this area with the president and share your admiration for the natural charm and wilderness quality of the islands."[85] In addition to his letter to Udall, LaFollette presented a strong supportive statement during the first congressional hearing. His support (especially his concerns regarding Native American rights) reassured the Senate subcommittee.[86]

Lieutenant Governor Patrick Lucey also visited Ashland, where he applauded Nelson and said, "It goes beyond anything which can be accomplished by local governments or the state." As a pragmatic politician, Lucey recognized the need for more formal action and urged a joint resolution of the Wisconsin Legislature to Congress indicating support, but the Republicans controlled the Legislature and did not act. Lucey also urged local residents and organizations to pass resolutions and write letters in support.[87]

David Carley, former head of the Wisconsin Department of Resource Development and now a candidate for governor, urged bold action by the state in calling upon Congress to act on the lakeshore and on Nelson's St. Croix National Wild and Scenic River bill. Carley recognized the important role of the state and local governments and urged that their full capabilities be immediately mobilized to deal with land-use issues and the threat of overcommercialization. "We cannot expect the federal government to invest a predicted $17 million in these areas if the parks are surrounded by billboard clutter and trash on the one side and polluted waters on the other," said Carley.[88]

Because conservation was strongly supported by coalitions of voters from all political spectrums, obtaining support from Republicans was achieved, although not as easily achieved as from Democrats. This support made it possible for the Republican assemblyman from the area, Bernard Gehrmann, to speak strongly in favor of the lakeshore. At the same time he urged Congress "to listen closely to the people who testify both for and against the proposal . . . so that in your wisdom you can proceed . . . in a well planned program, which even our children's children can live proudly with in the years to come."[89] Gehrmann's statement was important. He had served as a city councilman and a county board member and now was a congressman. His father, a Progressive, had represented northern Wisconsin in Congress for many years, and voters placed their trust in the name. His successor, Democrat Ernie Korpela, continued to support the lakeshore.[90]

Vic Wallin, a highly respected former Republican assemblyman from the area, was likewise supportive during House hearings and urged Congressman O'Konski to be favorable. Wallin noted that even though some private property owners would be hurt, the option of life tenure provided some economic protection.[91] He further stated his strong belief in capitalism and private property rights, but said the lessons of unshackled exploitation of northern Wisconsin had led him to conclude that strong government involvement in the region was necessary, including a national lakeshore. Wallin said: "The Apostle Islands and lakeshore lands are not man made. Created in ages past, they are a gift, an inheritance. . . . We can preserve this large scenic natural resource area and offer enjoyment through wise use, to those of us now, and to those who come."[92]

Land Acquisition Issues in the Apostle Islands

Ownership and improvements within the proposed lakeshore in 1967 are listed in the following table:

Public Acreage
    Federal (largely for lighthouses)   1,213
    State (largely Stockton Island)   9,920
    Local (largely Oak Island)   10,325
        Total   21,458
Private Acreage   25,186
Reservation Acreage
    Red Cliff Reservation
        Tribal   1,724
        Allotted   535
        Total   2,259
    Bad River Reservation
        Tribal   3,178
        Allotted   5,430
        Total   8,608
Total acreage in lakeshore   57,511

Number of facilities undergoing improvements
    Year-round residences   14
    Seasonal cottages   115
    Lodges   1
    Rental cottages   11
    Restaurants, stores, taverns   3
    Docks   27
    Airstrip   1
        Total number of improvements   172

Outside of the reservations, 46 percent of the land was already in public ownership. There were only fourteen year-round residences within the lakeshore boundaries. Seasonal cottages were located at Little Sand Bay, on Sand Island, and at scattered locations throughout the islands; hunting and fishing shacks, largely owned by non-Native Americans, were located in the Kakagon–Bad River Sloughs.

Given the large amount of public land, the modest number of year-round residences, the mixed land tenure pattern within the reservations, and the outstanding natural resources, a persuasive case could be made for the establishment of a national lakeshore in the region. Although the case was persuasive, land issues, including those concerning Native American lands, would dominate much of the congressional debate over the lakeshore. Also, private property owners made sustained and understandably emotional arguments that they not be included, in spite of the fact that they would continue to have use of their property for either twenty-five years or their lifetime.

Reactions on the part of government officials varied from the state, county, and town levels; they also changed over time. The posture of these officials would strongly influence the debates. The House and Senate committees believed that state and local government lands within the boundaries of recreation areas should be donated to the NPS as a contribution to the public benefit. In the case of the Apostle Islands, the field Office of the Solicitor and I argued that an exception should be made for the economically hard-pressed town and county governments, that town and county lands would be purchased by NPS, and that state lands would continue to be managed by the state or could be donated at a future date.

Thus bills S. 2498 (1965) and S. 778 (1967) contained language specifying that "any property or interests therein owned by the state of Wisconsin, or any political subdivision thereof, may be acquired only with the concurrence of such owner." No mention was made of donation; however, donation was hoped for. The House subsequently changed the language to explicitly provide that lands owned by the state be acquired only by donation. No mention was made of locally owned land.

During the 1960s the Wisconsin Conservation Department consistently maintained a position that it would vigorously pursue land purchases within the established Apostle Islands State Forest and on other islands as the opportunities presented themselves. In addition, during this period the Conservation Commission approved the establishment of the 2,732-acre Big Bay State Park on Madeline Island.

The Department of the Interior supported state land acquisition within the proposed lakeshore boundary, and in its reports and public testimony it stated that the WCD could manage its lands in a manner consistent with NPS standards when the lakeshore was approved. Lakeshore proponents stressed that the state lacked the fiscal capacity to accomplish the larger goals envisioned for the lakeshore. With help from the Wisconsin DRD, I successfully persuaded the WCD to drop plans for selected acquisitions on the Bayfield Peninsula.[93] The arguments for joint management of existing state land worked reasonably well although the state raised concerns from time to time.

Another issue repeatedly raised by state and local officials was in-lieu-of-property-tax payment of thirty cents per acre made by the WCD to local units of government for state-owned land in their jurisdictions. The response was to stress that new private development associated with increased tourism would offset the modest tax losses. In spite of this reassurance, the department effectively represented local government concerns on this issue and repeatedly urged that federal legislation be amended to include a comparable in-lieu payment by the Department of the Interior to local units.[94]

As NPS staff assigned to the Apostle Islands changed over time, it was continually necessary to advise them not to join the arguments over state land donations. Nelson's staff refused to be drawn into arguments regarding the donation of state lands and noted that joint federal-state management would be consistent with lakeshore goals.

The first formal position by the state was articulated at the first Senate Subcommittee on Parks and Recreation hearings in 1967, when Voigt said: "for, and at the request of Warren P. Knowles, Governor of the state of Wisconsin, . . . I would like to say that we strongly recommend passage of this bill. We are strongly in favor of an integrated and well-coordinated state-federal program for the area." Commissioner "Frosty" Smith put the WCC on record as supporting the governor and the bill. He noted that a joint state-federal study might suggest that the long-term public interest would best be met by the *sale* of state lands on Stockton and Basswood Islands. The issue of the sale of state land was now on the table, but fortunately the senators did not join the issue. For two and a half years the state maintained that it would continue land purchases and that the land would be sold in the event of a transfer.[95]

By 1970 the DNR had made considerable progress on its land-purchase program; 96 percent or 16,609 acres of the state forest on Oak, Stockton, and Basswood Islands had been acquired at a cost of almost $250,000. A dock and public-use facilities on Stockton had cost $120,000. Voigt had no fears regarding joint management and cautioned that the transfer of state lands to the federal government would take legislative action, "which of course cannot be predicted."[96]

During the 1970 House Committee on Interior and Insular Affairs hearings, NPS Director George Hartzog shifted from favoring joint state-federal management to favoring the donation of lands owned by the state and local governments to the NPS. In direct response to a question by the committee chair, he indicated that the NPS would not pay for these lands, and he was not expecting any problems over a land donation. Representative James McClure, an Idaho Republican, was uneasy over the fact that Ashland County had had attempted to market their land to private parties. Representative Abraham Kazen, a Texas Democrat, was also concerned about the lack of commitment to donate state land. Nelson indicated that he was not worried and believed the state would eventually donate its lands.

That ended the discussion of state and local government land ownership during House hearings. However, a few days before final markup of the legislation in the House in 1970, the issue resurfaced. At the request of Chairman Aspinall, Lee McElvain, a House committee staff member, called me and requested that I obtain a letter from the state indicating that it would be willing to donate its lands. In fact, the DNR had written the congressional delegation to oppose the language requiring donation. If a transfer was to be made, the DNR wanted reimbursement. I assured McElvain that even though a letter from the state indicating its willingness to donate its land could not then be secured, a donation could likely be accomplished after enactment. A further negative public response from the state at this critical time would certainly muddy the political waters.

In the interim, joint management was feasible. McElvain agreed with my arguments, and the language in H.R. 9306, as reported by the House Committee on Interior and Insular Affairs and as enacted into law, provided that state lands could be acquired only by donation. Any reference to the donations of lands by local governments was kept out of the bill.[97]

The issue of state lands in the archipelago was ever-present in the lakeshore debate. The state took careful, conservative positions vis-à-vis Nelson and a federal proposal. No state lands had been involved in the initial Nelson proposal. WCD officials, in fact, were not advised of the proposal; they read about it in the newspapers. When the islands were included, great care in dealing with the state would be required; in fact, the first unsure steps in developing legislation were based on the idea of a joint project. The federal government would provide the funds; the state, under joint agreements, would manage the area. Such an arrangement posed few problems for the state. As the proposal evolved and the need for direct federal involvement became apparent, the state informally warned that the Legislature would have to enact enabling legislation to permit the federal government to establish a lakeshore. I did not argue this dubious point; it was simply side-stepped. Joint management of the islands by NPS and the DNR was a satisfactory solution. By the mid-1960s political and popular support for a lakeshore had risen to the point where direct state opposition to it would have been politically damaging to the agency and the state.

An objective analysis of the situation might lead to a conclusion that state support for a national lakeshore and a free transfer of state lands made eminent good sense. The islands could continue as "wilderness areas" under federal management and would be available for public use. The substantial annual budget savings that would accrue to the WCD could be allocated to the new Big Bay State Park and other substantial needs identified in the "South Shore Studies" and the State Comprehensive Outdoor Recreation Plan. But objectivity does not necessarily lead to a reasoned conclusion. There were numerous reasons for the state to choose a different course of action.

The state had a history of dealing with its own problems. The state had been addressing conservation issues since before the turn of the century, drawing on its strong tradition of independence especially in matters relating to natural resource management. In the central and northern "cutover" lands, the overwhelming economic, fiscal, and social crisis in the 1920s and 1930s forced the state to permit the federal government to establish national forests and national wildlife refuges (including the Horicon Marsh, Upper Mississippi, and Necedah refuges) and large Farm Security Administration land utilization projects in the central Wisconsin conservation areas at Black River Falls and Meadow Valley. However, the Apostle Islands region was not of sufficient import to the state for any serious attention. It had been given at best only lukewarm support in the 1930s for a national park in the Apostle Islands. And when the NPS at that time rejected a national park, the state made no effort to have the decision overruled; and, in fact, it resisted NPS pressure to establish a state park there.

Independence, self-reliance, and a distrust of federal agencies and programs accounted for the state posture toward the 1960s lakeshore proposal. Moreover, human emotions played a part. The state had made a substantial fiscal commitment to the area. It persisted in its attempts to acquire Oak Island from Ashland County; it took eight years of effort, innumerable personal contacts and communications with local citizens and officials, and five formal appearances before the county board before it succeeded. In addition, the state had made a substantial effort to obtain local support for Big Bay State Park. Field staff, administrators, and policy makers were justly proud of their accomplishments. This independence and pride of accomplishment was to resurface when it came time to transfer state lands to the established lakeshore.

The Transfer of State Lands
to the Apostle Islands National Lakeshore

President Richard M. Nixon signed the Apostle Islands National Lakeshore Act in the fall of 1970. At that time the state owned 16,609 acres on Oak, Basswood, Stockton, and Michigan Islands, almost 40 percent of the land mass in the archipelago. The NPS obviously had a considerable interest in adding these lands to the lakeshore; the Wisconsin DNR preferred to keep them under its ownership and management. The process of getting the state to agree to transfer the lands was long and tricky and would not be accomplished until 1976. Numerous issues and problems arose over what at first appeared to be a simple property transfer.

The state's position had been made eminently clear during the long legislative history on the lakeshore. It would consider a sale of the land to the federal government, or it would continue to manage the islands in a manner compatible with NPS policy. The latter position was consistent with the pragmatic political position Nelson and the NCFC subcommittee had taken regarding state lands during the debates on the lakeshore. Joint management would avoid outright opposition from the DNR during the legislative process. In addition, Congress would not deviate from its long-standing policy of not paying for state lands to be included in the National Park System.

At the time Congress approved the Apostle Islands National Lakeshore a number of political changes were occurring in Wisconsin. After six years of Republican rule under Warren Knowles, Democrat Patrick Lucey swept into the governor's office with 55 percent of the vote. Lucey would be the first governor to serve the four-year term that had been recently approved under a state constitutional amendment. In the third year of his term Lucey would have a majority of appointees on the new, and powerful, Natural Resources Board (NRB). The NRB had been created to assume the functions of the WCC as well as major new responsibilities for pollution control. The NRB would set policy; the DNR would carry it out. In 1970 this new board was still controlled by members of the former WCC and was dominated by appointees who had caused Nelson trouble in the establishment of the lakeshore. They would make the initial decisions regarding a land transfer.

During his first year as governor, Lucey nominated Charles H. Stoddard, former director of the U.S. Bureau of Land Management, to a seat on the NRB. Stoddard, a distinguished conservationist and a lakeshore supporter, was also a partisan Democrat. The Wisconsin State Senate refused to confirm him. Immediately after the negative vote on Stoddard, Lucey nominated me to the NRB, and I was confirmed in March 1972.

Although DNR officials recognized my influence and were realistic enough to see the eventual impact Lucey would have on the NRB, they still balked at new initiatives emanating from the governor or myself, especially if such measures represented dramatic shifts from long-established policy. Lucey nominated a second member, Lawrence Dahl, who was readily confirmed by the Senate. Two more Lucey appointees were confirmed in his first term, but it would not be until May 1975 that three more Lucey appointees would bring the NRB fully under his influence. That same month, L. P. Voigt, the WCD secretary, resigned. Voigt had followed the direction of the WCC and the NRB on the Apostle Islands from the inception of the debate. With the appointment of Anthony Earl, a close associate of Lucey, to head the DNR, the ownership of the islands would be more readily transferred. But before that was to happen, the island transfer would be delayed for years by NRB and DNR obfuscation.

During the 1970 political campaign, I had discussed with Lucey the desirability of transferring the state-owned islands to the NPS. There was no urgency, however, as it would take a few years before the NPS had a staff and program in place in the lakeshore. Furthermore, given the history of the NRB and its predecessor, the Conservation Commission, Nelson's staff expected resistance. It would be better to wait until they had a more powerful presence on the NRB. I also set the stage for a transfer in discussions with Norman Anderson, a Democrat and the Assembly Majority Leader, and Lewis T. Mittness, who chaired the Assembly Committee on Natural Resources. Their response was favorable.

Although I had good working relations with Clifford W. "Tiny" Krueger, the Republican chair of the Senate Committee on Natural Resources, the Wisconsin Senate was still controlled by the Republicans, and it would have been risky to bring the matter to their attention until lakeshore proponents had a stronger position. The DNR had considerable influence with Krueger and the Senate, and a partisan squabble over the land transfer could easily occur.

Arguments for a transfer made good sense. The islands would be under unified NPS management, and the state would save money by relinquishing its management responsibilities. Moreover, it would contribute to the national recognition of the values of the Apostle Islands region. Bureaucracies, however, seldom respond to logical arguments when their power and, in this instance, their lands are threatened.

Gaylord Nelson later reflected on the transfer:

The Conservation Commission started out with the viewpoint that they had to be paid for the [state lands] which, of course, would destroy the whole project. . . . [We] did a lot of work in persuading the conservation people to change their mind, but when you look at all the editorial support, you can see, politically, there was all along the line a lot of heat on the people in state government. . . . [So] there was a lot of political pressure on the Conservation Department and they finally gave up on their idea that they had to be paid for those state lands. . . . I explained to them, how foolish can you be, that it would release money for other projects that you have. What sense does it make to be spending money managing Stockton and the other parcels you own when you have the federal government willing to take it off your hands? . . . [And] I guess, at some stage, they were convinced that they either were beat or what have you. I think they were beat.[98]

But it would take five years to beat them.

The Debate over the Transfer

The DNR stated its position on the transfer of land:

- the state could retain its islands and agree to a management plan with the NPS;
- a transfer should not be considered until the federal government had made a serious and substantial commitment through appropriations to the lakeshore; and
- the NPS had to make a persuasive case that a transfer would benefit the state.

If, however, the DNR should consent to the transfer of the islands, it wanted a number of concessions first:

- reimbursement for the state's investment of approximately $400,000 in the islands;
- free access by Wisconsin residents to the lakeshore in recognition of their contribution (legislation on the Ice Age National Scientific Reserve contained such a proviso);
- a formal agreement between the secretary of the Interior and the state on master plans for the islands and on subsequent revisions;
- an "in-lieu" payment to local units of government to compensate for lands removed from property tax rolls, as the state was currently doing;
- reservation of mineral rights on all transferred land or the right to approve any future mining;
- a clear statement that the state retained the power to enforce fishing (both sports and commercial), hunting and trapping, and that the NPS confer with the state on any closures for purposes of public safety;
- boating should be regulated by the state and the U.S. Coast Guard and not the NPS;

- an assurance that the donated lands would be kept primitive, wild, and scenic; and
- an agreement that, if the transferred lands were not used in accordance with the Lakeshore Act, they would revert to the state.

These elements were not minor, were contrary to a number of existing federal laws and policies, and would require careful negotiation over the next several years.

The DNR took a position that would ensure that the transferred islands would not be overdeveloped. The department was arguing on behalf of sports and commercial fishers, hunters, and trappers and for minimizing the number of agencies that had jurisdiction over boating. It was arguing against mining (which could be conducted under the Lakeshore Act as long as mining did not interfere with the primary purpose of the lakeshore). The DNR put up a long fight to force the federal government to meet these demands; compromises were finally achieved.

The first formal action by the NRB came in 1970 with a resolution that insisted on the need for compatibility between NPS and state plans for the islands. It declared that a transfer would not be considered until the lakeshore had been adequately funded and a persuasive case had been made for the necessity of a transfer. The NRB was, at that point, comfortable with joint management in the area.[99]

A year later Voigt still argued, in a letter to Lucey, that a persuasive case for a transfer had not yet been made. Furthermore, he felt that a new NPS draft master plan was seriously flawed. He wanted the governor to respond to NPS Director George Hartzog regarding the master plan and attached a draft of a harshly worded letter of criticism.[100] I redrafted Voigt's letter, using more conciliatory language, and stated that Lucey was ready and willing to assist the NPS in a transfer.[101] I also advised the NPS that a transfer could be made when they had the full capacity to manage the lakeshore.[102] At the same time the new lakeshore superintendent, William Bromberg, a newcomer to the area, was pushing for a transfer of Stockton Island because it was of major importance in the archipelago.[103] Moreover, a transfer of Stockton would give the NPS a presence in the area that it did not yet have, given the slow process of federal land acquisition. In response, the NRB voted against transfers until the NPS was able to demonstrate substantial progress in its work on the other islands.[104]

By mid-1972 Bromberg, who continued to be anxious for a transfer of all state lands, advised me that the NPS now had the capacity to manage the lakeshore, and that the development plan for 1974 had been approved. He asked for the transfer of the islands to be approved by the spring of 1973; it was to include all of the state land, including mineral rights, and the submerged lands extending one-quarter of a mile from the island shores.[105]

At the start of the new year, after a flurry of correspondence, I reviewed a draft of a letter from Lucey to the NPS assuring them that Lucey had a personal interest in the islands and that his staff was drafting the necessary legislation.[106] The drafting was referred to the DNR for action, but trouble was brewing.[107] The NRB took up the question again, and in a neat bit of sidestepping was advised by staff that the question of transfer was a matter for the Legislature, not the NRB. A point was also made of the $5,000 in-lieu-of-taxes state payment to the town of La Pointe, a payment that would not be made if the lands were transferred.[108] This was a neat way of stirring up local interests to oppose a land transfer. Although the NRB took no action at this time, Voigt submitted a draft bill to Lucey. It contained the DNR's earlier caveats: free admission to the lakeshore for Wisconsin residents; state regulation of hunting, fishing, and trapping; maintenance of the islands in a natural condition under a wilderness concept, with any changes in management requiring the prior approval of the governor; and, a reversion to the state if the islands were not used for lakeshore purposes.[109]

The NPS objected, contending the following:

- the legislation did not mention "wilderness purposes." The meaning of "wilderness purposes" was not defined and could conflict with the Lakeshore Act and should therefore be deleted;
- free admission for Wisconsin citizens was discriminatory, and the federal government could not discriminate against its other citizens;
- public hunting and fishing were already permitted in the lakeshore; therefore, state legislation should not mention it;
- prior approval by the governor of any changes in NPS land use plans was objectionable; and
- the reversionary clause was contrary to Department of Justice requirements if funds were to be used for development of the area. The basis for reversion was too nebulous and was contrary to law and policy.

NPS officials, not having read the lakeshore hearing records, assumed that the governor or his representative had testified on the act and had concurred in the donation of state-owned lands for the project.[110] The NPS transmitted a revised bill.[111]

Lucey then considered taking the matter up personally with a visit to Department of the Interior Secretary Rogers Morton. I advised him that the issue was too contentious for a discussion between the governor and the secretary and that disagreements should be thrashed out with Voigt.[112] Voigt submitted another draft to Lucey in September that still contained language that the NPS had found objectionable.[113] Because a compromise had not been reached, the bill was not introduced in the fall legislative session.

The following year, the NPS began to work on compromises. It agreed to allow state law to reiterate the purposes of the lakeshore and to permit state regulation of hunting, fishing, and trapping and reversion of lands except where the federal government had made a capital expenditure.[114] In spite of these compromises, the DNR remained adamant on its other conditions.[115]

Department of the Interior staff, responding to pressure from the governor's office and me, finally met with the USDI field solicitor to try to hammer out compromises on the bill.[116] At the same time, they noted that the state's "in lieu" payment would rise to $5,869. Furthermore, they claimed that they spent $1,900 annually for the operation and maintenance of the Apostle Islands State Forest. These arguments suggested continued state ownership and management. A lengthy memorandum from the DNR's chief legal counsel, submitted to the governor's office, restated all of the earlier objections and in addition urged a strict prohibition on any mining, a new and tricky issue not raised before.[117] Voigt wished to resolve the matter and asked the governor's office for help. It appeared that an agreement might have been reached that spring.[118]

The transferred islands would be "managed in a manner that will preserve their unique primitive and wilderness character"; the state would retain regulatory authority over hunting, fishing, and trapping; and except where the federal government had made a capital improvement, the lands would revert to the state if not used for the lakeshore. Funds were also to be appropriated to the DNR for the acquisition of 9.06 acres on Michigan Island, which was owned by the state commissioner of public lands. They would later be transferred to the NPS. (The state constitution prohibited the commissioners from giving away lands under their jurisdiction.[119]) In spite of concurrence, the rest of 1974 was to pass without further consensus or action.

The 1974 fall elections significantly changed the political composition of the state Legislature. The Democrats maintained their comfortable control of the Assembly (sixty-three to thirty-six) and more importantly took control of the Senate (eighteen to thirteen). For the first time in decades, the party controlled the governorship and both legislative houses. Mittness would continue to chair the Assembly Committee on Natural Resources, and Jerome A. Martin of Manitowoc would chair the equivalent Senate committee.[120]

The NRB took the matter up again early in 1975. At this time Lucey appointees controlled the NRB, and I was chair. I noted that there was, at that point, concurrence on the transfer between the DNR, the governor's office, and the USDI field solicitor. I emphasized that Nelson wanted the donated islands to be used for their "unique primitive and wilderness character." The NRB subsequently approved the transfer of the lands by a vote of six to one.[121]

Mineral Rights Issues

Unfortunately, in spite of the appearance of a consensus, the case was not yet resolved. The DNR's legal counsel again raised a question with the Department of the Interior's field solicitor regarding mineral rights on the islands. The resolution was quite different than either federal or state ownership of the rights.

The field solicitor was willing to compromise on the question of mineral rights. However, he commented to the DNR legal counsel that the USDI secretary had to acquire an interest sufficient for him to utilize the lands for the stated purposes. Accordingly, the lands could be donated subject to a reservation of the minerals—provided the NPS could certify that the mineral interest was not needed in order for the agency to manage the area in accordance with the enabling legislation. It would seem that such certification could be made, particularly if the state were prepared to subordinate its mineral interest to the federal government's right to manage the area as part of the lakeshore.[122]

The NPS was receptive toward the field solicitor's position. The NPS regional director stated: "While we would hope that the lands would be donated without any reservation of mineral interests, if the state sees fit to donate with a reservation we would be agreeable to the procedures set out in your letter of February 12, 1975. It appears that this procedure would be analogous to the situation involving the state of Michigan at Sleeping Bear Dunes National Lakeshore, where we are handling the matter with certification and subordination agreements."[123]

The Legislature Acts

In spite of the unresolved debate on mineral rights and at the request of the NRB, Bill 381 was introduced with bipartisan sponsorship by Representatives

Mittness and Lawrence Day, a Republican. There was agreement on language regarding hunting, fishing, and trapping; that the islands' management would preserve their unique primitive and wilderness character; and that the lands would revert to the state if the lakeshore was abandoned or not used in accordance with stated purposes. No mention was made of mineral reservations. However, Mittness raised concerns in the Assembly debate that indicated that a transfer was not a sure thing. In addition to issues that had been raised over the past five years, Mittness asked if the Department of the Interior could lease the islands for a consideration based on the amount of the state's investment, if land exchanges were possible, and what the impacts would be if there was no donation. Fortunately the DNR adhered to the NRB position affirming the transfer and responded that the USDI would probably not agree to leases, that the Lakeshore Act precluded land exchanges, and that the impacts of not transferring the land would require further study.[124]

These concerns were set to rest, and in April the Assembly Committee on Natural Resources recommended the approval of A.B. 381 by a vote of eight to three.[125] Both houses subsequently passed the measure. On August 13, 1975, Governor Lucey signed A.B. 381 and declared: "The federal government's recognition of the Apostle Islands as gems to be preserved in the purest of our great lakes deserves applause and support from the state of Wisconsin. In transferring these four state islands to federal care we are not only facilitating the completion of Lakeshore acquisition, but contributing to the overall recreation and economic development of the northland."[126]

Lucey had raised again one of the underlying arguments for the lakeshore—economic development—and in his statement reinforced it with an announcement that Pat Miller, who had replaced William Bromberg as the lakeshore's superintendent, had advised him that the transfer would speed the use of $300,000 in economic development funds that had been pledged to the lakeshore. These funds would be used to employ forty-five people to repair facilities, rehabilitate trails, and build campgrounds. Preservation and economic development went hand in hand.

Lucey also noted a partial veto of the section of the bill that provided that the state would continue to make perpetual in-lieu-of-tax payments to the town of La Pointe, as "this would establish a precedent whenever state lands are transferred to another level of government" and was therefore not good public policy.[127]

The state act provided for concurrent jurisdiction by the state, including state laws and regulations governing hunting, fishing, and trapping. Furthermore, the Federal Lakeshore Act was explicit in stating that the Department of the Interior secretary's authority to regulate such activities in the interest of public safety, administration, fish or wildlife management, or public use and enjoyment could be exercised only after consultation with the state (except in emergencies). Thus, the DNR retained regulatory powers for those activities in the lakeshore.[128]

Mineral Rights Again

The question of mineral rights had not been raised in legislative debate. Moreover, the state act did not address the issue. The DNR and the NRB would have to once again struggle with and decide the issue when a quit claim deed (a private mining stake) was approved. Lakeshore Superintendent Pat Miller had serious concerns regarding a state reservation of mineral rights and was not willing to accept the prior agreements worked out by his agency, the state, and the USDI solicitor. Thus Miller wrote to me and observed that although there appeared to be little evidence of metallic minerals in the region, the removal of sand, gravel, and ballast stone from the lakeshore could pose problems. He noted that such had been the case at Isle Royale National Park. The legislative language of the act—"it is the policy of the legislature that the Apostle Islands be managed in a manner that will preserve their unique primitive and wilderness character"—would be inconsistent with any further sandstone quarrying in the lakeshore. To set the matter to rest, Miller urged that the NRB transfer the mineral rights to avoid future conflicts because of divided jurisdiction.[129]

Early in 1976, I brought Miller's concerns to the NRB when the quit claim deed for the islands was to be approved. The DNR came up with a neat compromise on the issue; a transfer of rights, but a reservation of state approval over any future mining activity. The DNR's Bureau of Legal Services attorney said, "The reservation was a compromise, since the Park Service expressed disagreement with the [NRB's] policy of severing the mining rights from the surface fee ownership."[130] He stated that this should cause no problem since the enabling legislation had made no mention of mineral rights. I observed that the reservation would provide a role for both the state and federal government and that it was a good method of handling the issue; it would avoid the problems Michigan had encountered when it reserved mineral rights on the land that became Isle Royale National Park. The NRB's fears were allayed, and it voted unanimously to approve the quit claim deed transferring mineral rights but reserved to the state "the right to approve any and all prospecting and mining activity prior to its commencement on the above described lands."[131]

Although the transfer was not easily achieved and took more than five years to accomplish, the debate was healthy. The Legislature reinforced the congressional statement of purpose: that the lakeshore would be managed in a manner that would preserve the islands' unique primitive and wilderness character. And the debate on mining and the quit claim deed made it clear that the state would have a role in any future decisions on mining on the transferred lands.

CHAPTER 12

The Apostle Islands National Lakeshore and the Native Americans

O n May 10, 1962, a resolution of the Bad River Tribal Council requested that the secretary of the Interior and the governor of Wisconsin initiate studies into the feasibility of "the establishment of a National Shoreline-Recreational Wildlife Area consisting of approximately 20,000 acres of land within the Bad River Reservation north of the Village of Odanah and U.S. Highway 2." The resolution opened up a complex series of legal, institutional, and political issues regarding the Chippewa (also referred to as Ojibwe in some documents) with which the state of Wisconsin, the U.S. Department of the Interior, Congress, and the two Wisconsin tribal councils grappled for eight years. These issues were rooted in the history of the Chippewa people, the treaties they signed with the U.S. government, and the experiences of the two reservations, Bad River and Red Cliff, that were involved in the establishment of the lakeshore.

History of the Chippewa

The Chippewa call themselves the Anishinaabeg (First People) and currently occupy areas of Wisconsin, Minnesota, and Ontario in Canada (where they are known as Ojibwe). They are not the original residents of the area but relocated sometime between the late 1500s and early 1600s from an area along the northeast Atlantic coast, likely the mouth of the St. Lawrence River. Anthropologists state that they were driven out by more aggressive members of the Five Nations (the Mohawk, Oneida, Onondaga, Cayuga, and Seneca Tribes) securing their hold on the fur trade with the new European arrivals.[1] The Anishinaabeg say that the tribe was led by a vision to follow the intermittent appearance of the sacred Miigis shell, which rose from the eastern sea, giving life and warmth to the people, only to sink and rise again further west. The sun reflecting off the shell gave the people both wisdom and the color of their skin. The people followed the shell to the Straits of Mackinac, in Michigan, where the tribe split into three groups: the Ottawa remained at the straits, the Potawatomie turned south along the eastern shore of Lake Michigan (where they live today), and the Chippewa continued on west and north.[2]

It is likely they arrived on the shores of Madeline Island in Chequamegon Bay in Lake Superior, which they called Monjngwunakuaning—the place of the golden-breasted woodpecker. Some spiritual leaders state that they were returning to their original home, rather than a new place.[3] They later moved east, where Jean Nicolet found them living around the eastern end of Lake Superior in 1643.[4] By 1679, however they had returned westward and established villages along the south shore of Lake Superior, along Chequamegon Bay, throughout the Apostle Islands, and in Keweenaw Bay in Michigan, having displaced the original inhabitants in battles still talked about (the original residents moved further west and are now known as the Lakota, or Sioux). The Chequamegon Bay area was a clear power base for the tribe by the turn of the century. French fur traders found small, semi-nomadic bands connected through extensive clan linkages. In the winter they hunted and trapped. In the spring they harvested maple syrup and in the fall wild rice, carefully returning a third of the harvest to the waters to ensure the next year's crop. Some crops were planted, to be gathered green if necessary, and berries and plants were collected and preserved. The Chippewa became keen participants in the fur trade and by the eighteenth century were dependent upon regular trade for their livelihoods, a trade that survived battles between European countries over whose colonies these were.[5]

Most tribes in the Midwest backed the French over the British in the 1740s and the British over the Americans in the War of Independence. At the end of each war, they were essentially considered by the victors as "conquered," because in each case their former allies made no treaty provision for their native troops. After the British surrendered the colony to the new American government, the Native Americans became subject to the American government's disposition. The Americans were not interested in the potential for trade, although the tribes most certainly were, given their dependence upon trade goods for many basic necessities. Instead, the Americans were far more interested in the land as private property for a growing American population.

After the Americans had established their presence in the Lake Superior region (1812), government policies toward the tribes followed two themes: removal and assimilation.[6] Removal took two forms. First, it was a deliberate policy of extermination, leading to the great Indian Wars of the 1830s, 1850s, and 1860s. This had little effect on the Chippewa, however. They were more subject to a removal from their traditional lands to restricted reservations after signing their lands away through treaties. By the time these tribes began signing treaties, however, there were no places for them to go (eastern tribes had been removed entirely from their lands and shipped, or force-marched, west of the Mississippi River, including into Chippewa territory), and western tribes, including the Chippewa, generally were given reservations that were drastically reduced parts of their own former territories.

The treaties were essentially legally binding agreements between two sovereign independent nations. Once signed by representatives of the tribes, treaties were ratified by the U.S. Senate and became part of U.S. federal law. They remain binding into the present day, although often subject to legal reinterpretation.

The Chippewa ceded their lands in the Wisconsin Territories over a period of several years. They were divided into different bands by U.S. government decree; one band ceded a large piece of land, including the Apostle Islands in 1837. The treaty did not require the Natives' removal, and the band retained its rights to hunt, fish, and gather on the ceded territory. In 1854, a second treaty authorized the establishment of several reservations in northern Wisconsin, which were to be held in trust for the tribes by the secretary of War. (Later, responsibilities for the tribes were transferred to the secretary of the Interior.) The Lake Superior Band, which had been living principally on Madeline Island and on the mainland, was split. Some of this band was settled on the 124,000-acre Bad River Reservation on Chequamegon Bay, while some went to a second reservation at Red Cliff, 14,902 acres of land on the Bayfield Peninsula, although Red Cliff boundaries were not settled until 1863. The split was essentially along religious lines, with converted Protestants settling in Bad River and the Catholics going to Red Cliff. Significant differences existed (and continue to exist) between the two reservations, and each acted independently in all further negotiations.

The second focus of "Indian" policy was assimilation. Essentially this meant converting Native Americans to lifestyles comparable to those of non-Natives. Religious conversion had come early in the nineteenth century and was well under way by the time the two Lake Superior reservations were established. Other efforts included sending children to boarding schools to learn how to "be white," and turning their parents from roaming hunters to settled agriculturalists. Making a living off natural resources by hunting and fishing was by then quite difficult; many species were scarce, and many adults were taking day jobs in the fishing, mining, or lumber industries. However, the U.S. government contended that the best means of encouraging rapid assimilation was to turn the Native Americans into farmers. The General Allotment Act of 1887 was designed to do just that.

Allotment affected tribes across the country. Under the act, each male of the tribe (subject to certain restrictions) was allotted a piece of land for which he was to hold title and which he was to farm. Family heads were given 160 acres, single men were given 80 acres, and minors under the age of eighteen received 40 acres. The lands left over on treaty-established reservations were termed "surplus," and the "surplus" lands—and there was usually a lot of "surplus" on the reservations—were often sold to non-Native settlers. These lands are known as "allotted" lands. Many tribes lost almost three-quarters of their original reservations. Tribes continued to see their land base erode away as individuals sold their holdings to meet short-term needs.[7]

Further complicating the situation was the fact that the tribal population began to expand significantly after the turn of the century, but those not given allotments in the 1880s were not entitled to land later on. The next generation to come along had to depend essentially upon inheriting land from the original allottees. Unfortunately, dividing a land inheritance of perhaps 80 acres between several heirs over a few generations quickly resulted in impossibly confused land tenure patterns and individuals holding rights to tiny portions of useless land. Allotments frequently ended up in non-Native ownership, and on the Bad River Reservation lands frequently became tax delinquent, along with many other northern Wisconsin properties.[8]

The Indian Reorganization Act of 1934 stopped allotment and its subsequent land alienation, but it did not repair the original damage. Allotment was no longer allowed, but alienated land was not returned. If tribes had the financial resources and the opportunity, they could attempt to buy back alienated reservation land. Most, however, had to compete on the open land market and had limited resources to begin with, so the re-acquisition of land was neither quick nor comprehensive.

The act also took some powers away from the U.S. government (and its Bureau of Indian Affairs) and returned them to the tribes—if they were willing to establish tribal governments based on the American model, complete with constitutions and official elections every two years. The act was well intended, but its results were less than successful; many elected tribal councils stood against traditional organizational structures and power hierarchies, often leaving tribes torn between "official" and "unofficial" (traditional) leaders and policies.

In part the inability of the federal government to deal successfully with the tribes resulted from certain inaccurate assumptions. First, it was assumed that the "Indian problem" would eventually disappear. Initially it was thought that the people might simply die off. Instead, for a number of complex reasons, their populations increased. Later it was assumed that the government could eventually get out of the "Indian business" as the peoples became assimilated into the American culture. The federal government worked hard during the 1950s to get rid of its responsibility for Native Americans through relocation to urban areas and termination of trust responsibilities on reservations. The urban relocation policy resulted in a new problem: large numbers of unemployed Native Americans who lacked the ability to turn to community and government services available only on the reservations. And the policy severely disrupted the social fabric of the tribal communities as the younger generation was drawn away from its culture.

Under the policy of termination the U.S. government simply declared that the special trust status that existed between the federal government and the tribes was ended. The tribes, as independent legal entities, would cease to exist. In 1954 the policy was carried out, using the Menominee of Wisconsin as a test case. The results were disastrous, and the Termination Act was repealed in 1973. The Menominee were again granted reservation status.

Thus, when Gaylord Nelson first proposed the Apostle Islands project in 1962, there was already a two-hundred-year history of bad blood and poor faith dealings between the U.S. government and the tribes, both in Wisconsin and across the country, as well as a legacy of economic hardship and social disruption on the reservations, including Bad River and Red Cliff. Unfortunately the lakeshore was to become a victim of that legacy. It ran up against a tide of rising militancy on the part of Native Americans across the country, particularly among urban populations, the Red Power movement.

Social and Economic Conditions on the Red Cliff and Bad River Reservations in the 1960s

Given federal land policies, from the signing of the treaties in 1854 through to the mid-1950s, it is not surprising that much of the Bad River and Red Cliff reservation lands had been alienated. The Bureau of Indian Affairs (BIA) reported the following land ownership pattern as of 1989:

Bad River Reservation
   Total reservation area   124,434.50 acres
   Alienated (non-Native owners)   67,616.95 acres
Red Cliff Reservation
   Total reservation area   14,092.81 acres
   Alienated   6,211.69 acres

Given the fractured nature of Native land tenure and the problem of multiple heirs on allotted lands, a cohesive resource management strategy for lands on reservations within the lakeshore boundary was not possible without a number of special provisions, which were accommodated in the congressional bills put forward.

The Bad River Tribal Council resolution on a national lakeshore proposal strongly emphasized improving the economic well-being of the tribe through development; the economic conditions of the tribal members were deplorable. More than 500 Native Americans lived on the Bad River Reservation in 1965; only 29 percent of them (147 people) were in the employable age group (ages 18–55). Of this group, only 21 percent (31 people) were permanently employed; an additional 18 people held temporary jobs during the course of the year. The average family income of those employed ranged from $1,500 to $2,000 annually, considerably below that of other rural Wisconsin residents.

Conditions on the Red Cliff Reservation were comparable. More than 300 people resided on the reservation. About 10 families obtained their livelihoods through the timber industry, 12 adults were employed as machine tenders in a Bayfield manufacturing plant, 10 were employed at a tribal garment factory at Red Cliff, and 2 were commercial fishermen. The average annual income for a household head was approximately $2,250. Unemployment was especially severe in winter months. Housing consisted of deteriorating frame or log construction buildings. Many lacked indoor plumbing and relied on community wells for their water supply.[9]

Department of the Interior Secretary Stewart Udall was specific in his instructions that the economic plight of the tribes be addressed in any Apostle Islands proposal; Native American interests were to be equitably treated.[10] The USDI North Central Field Committee (NCFC) and its subcommittee, which did most of the work on early proposals, hoped that these goals would be met by recommending two primary purposes for the lakeshore: the improvement of social and economic conditions for the two bands and the improvement of the local economy in general as a result of tourism expenditures.[11]

Legislation Would Be "Permissive"

The first draft of lakeshore legislation, prepared in 1963, envisioned a collaborative federal-state program. The draft called for the state to eventually own and manage the lakeshore under federal standards and criteria. However, given the complex nature of tribal rights and land tenure within the two reservations, a subsequent decision was made to make the lakeshore a federal project, with the state managing the islands in a collaborative fashion. Congress could then enact the many special provisions designed to improve Native American conditions through the delegation of authority to the secretary of the Interior as trust officer.

The NCFC subcommittee recognized the unique relationship between the tribes and the federal government:

> No other group of citizens stands in precisely the same relationship to the federal government as do Indians. The unique nature of this relationship is rooted in treaties and laws which provide that the Secretary of the Interior has a responsibility for the protection of Indians and their resources. The subcommittee was ever aware of the strategic location of Red Cliff and Bad River Indian Reservations. Thus, the proposed development gives credence to Indian ownership and occupation with a marked degree of national indebtedness to the Indians for preserving a significant portion of the Lakeshore. The subcommittee believes that the recommendation provides for a means whereby the Secretary can meet his trust responsibility to the Indians while at the same time achieving his other responsibility of providing Americans with significant outdoor opportunities.[12]

Early in the NCFC subcommittee's deliberations and in discussions with the tribes, a decision was made to structure the proposed legislation for a lakeshore in such a way that the tribes could decide whether they wished to be included *after* the legislation was enacted. This judgment was based on several factors. First, only Congress and the president could make the *final* decision on the legislation and the special provisions for the tribes. Second, the NCFC subcommittee's report was only a field-level report. It would not become an official policy of the Department of the Interior or the president without the approval of the regional and Washington office directors of eight USDI bureaus, the Secretariat (Offices of the Solicitor, legislative counsel, assistant secretaries, and the secretary), and the Bureau of the Budget. Third, the report would also require the approval of the Senate Subcommittee on Parks and Recreation and the House Subcommittee on National Parks and Recreation and their full committees, as well as full House and Senate backing. Finally, the president would have to give his approval.

The transmittal letter for the NCFC subcommittee report acknowledged the formal participation of seven Native Americans in the development of the document. Don Ames, who chaired the Bad River Tribal Council at the time of the 1962 resolution, was most favorable regarding the study. Alex Roye, the Red Cliff chair, wrote to Udall in 1964, "It is very encouraging to know of your concern for the interests of the Red Cliff Indian community in regard to this development."[13] Responses from the other Native American participants during the course of the studies were also favorable. They pointed to a number of problems but believed these could be worked out.[14]

Prior to the release of the report, the NCFC subcommittee met with representatives from the Red Cliff and Bad River Tribes and agreed that the tribes would not take a formal position on the proposal until after the legislation passed.[15] Throughout the legislative process, the permissive nature of the legislation was emphasized with the tribes. Secretary Udall made this clear in his testimony in 1967, during the first hearings on the bill in Washington, when he stated: "The bill provides that the lands within the Lakeshore held in trust for the Red Cliff or Bad River Bands may be acquired only with their consent. Some of the Indian tribal lands are essential to the proposed lakeshore, and we will need to acquire them before the Lakeshore is established. We will not proceed with the project until we have obtained the consent of the Indian tribes to the acquisition of these lands."[16]

At a continuation of the same hearings in Ashland, Nelson also emphasized that the tribes would have options with regard to the inclusion of their lands within the lakeshore.[17] During the final hearings on the bill in 1970, I addressed this issue:

> I would like to emphasize that since the inception of this proposal, it has always been my position and the position of the Department of the Interior when I was employed by that agency, that the legislation as drafted did not do anything to Indian people and Indian land. All that it does is to provide them and the federal government with an opportunity to sit down and negotiate acceptable arrangements for including their lands in the Lakeshore. I have consistently urged them not to take positions until the Congress has acted and mutually agreed to terms ratified by tribal referenda. In my opinion it would be a tragic mistake to foreclose to the Indian people the opportunity to negotiate with the federal

government for a proposal which potentially will have a significant impact on their economy and which will provide them with job opportunities related to their cultural heritage; guiding; sale of native crafts, naturalists, park rangers, etcetera, and hopefully in the not too distant future, a Chippewa Indian Lakeshore superintendent.[18]

Land Issues

Tribal Land

The NCFC subcommittee recommended that the tribes be provided several alternatives for the use of tribal lands as part of the lakeshore (1,724 acres on Red Cliff and 3,178 acres on Bad River). They could sell the lands to the Department of the Interior secretary, lease the lands to the secretary (this would provide annual income to tribal treasuries), or exchange the lands for other suitable lands within the reservation boundary (this would help maintain the tribal land base and would also permit ownership consolidation within the reservations but outside of the lakeshore boundary).[19] Nelson's bills on the lakeshore, S. 1498 and S. 778, included these provisions.[20]

Allotted Land

The NCFC subcommittee also recommended that alternatives for dealing with allotted lands within the proposed lakeshore be included in any proposal (535 acres on Red Cliff and 5,430 acres on Bad River). It recommended a land sale to the secretary of the Interior, the exchange of the lands for other suitable lands within the reservation boundaries (this would permit the allottee to continue to own land and be eligible for trust benefits), or sale to the secretary and purchase by the secretary of substitute land within the reservation boundary.[21]

In addition, to deal with the difficult problem of tangled heirships on allotments, the bills provided that the secretary of the Interior could acquire allotments if 50 percent of the owners agreed, when there were ten heirs or fewer (when there were more than ten heirs, 25 percent of the owners had to agree); and the secretary was authorized to represent any tribal owner who was a minor, who was *non compos mentis*, or who could not be located.

Leasing of Indian Lands

The NCFC subcommittee also made two innovative and highly controversial recommendations with regard to tribal lands within the reservations inside the proposed lakeshore boundary. The first provided for long-term leasing of tribal lands for lakeshore purposes. The second provided that alienated and allotted lands acquired by the secretary of the Interior could then be acquired by the tribes and in turn leased to the secretary for lakeshore purposes. The secretary in effect would act as a "banker" for the tribes by providing the capital for land purchases, capital that the tribes lacked. This interest-free loan would be amortized with the lease payments. This provision would result in the restoration of tribal ownership of ancestral lands and, once paid off, would provide a stable flow of income to the tribes. Lease prices were to be adjusted every five years to meet changing economic conditions.[22]

These provisions were agreed to by regional and national Department of the Interior bureau chiefs and, after numerous meetings, were found acceptable by tribal leaders. Unfortunately, Lewis A. Sigler, the legislative counsel in the Office of the Solicitor, who was responsible for the final form of an acceptable bill, did not agree to the provisions. This difference of opinion held up the lakeshore bill for months. The secretary of the Interior, in his memorandum of instructions to the NCFC subcommittee, requested that provisions be made "for the necessary equitable treatment of Indian interests." Sigler argued that equity meant "fairness" not "advantage." My position was that anything that lakeshore proponents could do to return alienated lands to the tribes and to provide some semblance of stability in the flow of income to the tribal treasuries constituted "equity." I further argued that these provisions had been discussed on numerous occasions with the tribes. To change the USDI position at this time would be to break faith. This was argued both orally and in writing. Within the USDI, however, Sigler's position prevailed.

In any event final clearance within the Department of the Interior was achieved when this issue was resolved, and Sigler, representatives of the Bureau of Indian Affairs, the Bureau of Outdoor Recreation, the National Park Service, and myself met with the Bureau of the Budget to obtain the approval of the administration. The BIA representative again raised the leasing provision. Sigler quickly dismissed this, saying it was not the Department of the Interior's position. Had Nelson become involved in a lengthy discussion with Bureau of the Budget officials, it might well have held up approvals once again. Instead clearance was obtained. Walking back to the Department of the Interior building, Sigler was furious that the leasing provision had been mentioned, recognizing that it would have jeopardized approval.

The bill had provided for the acquisition and leaseback of alienated and allotted lands. In accordance with the agreements on leases, the Department of the Interior's letter report to Congress stated that leaseholds were not a satisfactory basis upon which to administer a lakeshore. The letter further pointed out that the sale and leaseback of alienated and allotted land could result in the federal government paying rentals that exceeded the amount it received from the sale of the land to the tribes. The Department of the Interior proposed an amendment that would authorize the secretary to acquire tribal land and to pay the purchase price in either a lump sum or in installments that in the aggregate would equal the purchase price plus interest on unpaid balances. The amendment would enable the tribes to receive an assured annual income for a number of years. By the time the payments were completed, the lakeshore would be fully developed, and the tribes would be able to capitalize on the economic potential associated with providing visitor accommodations and services.[23]

Purchase of alienated and allotted land, sale to the tribal councils, and subsequent lease to the secretary of the Interior was thus stricken from the bill. The Senate passed S. 778 on August 17, 1967, and accepted the Department of the Interior's amendment on sale and leaseback. Although the department argued against ninety-nine-year leases of land already in tribal ownership, the Senate kept that provision in the bill. The Senate also authorized capital expenditures on land leased from the tribes, a provision to which the department objected.[24] Sigler, who later joined the staff of the House Committee on Interior and Insular Affairs, was furious with me over the insertion of the lease provisions for tribal land. I could only shrug and note that the Senate, acting within their prerogatives, had made a value judgment.

Although Department of the Interior officials preferred to acquire the fee simple title to tribal land, they eventually and reluctantly accepted the lease provision, and in their letter report to the House of Representatives on S. 778 and H.R. 13124 (the complementary House bill sponsored by Kastenmeier and fifteen others), indicated that they would lease the lands for ninety-nine years with an option to renew. Sigler's conservative fiscal position became evident, however, with a clause that provided a negotiated fixed annual rental with the tribes for at least the initial ninety-nine year period.[25] Thus, the leaseholds made no provision for either rising land values or inflation. Almost two years later, S. 621, passed by the Senate on June 2, 1969, contained the same language regarding leases as did Kastenmeier's H.R. 555 and H.R. 9306, which were then being considered by the House Committee in March and June 1970.

Sigler persisted in his opposition to leases of tribal land. During the March 1970 House Committee Hearings, as NPS Director Hartzog was answering questions, Sigler made the point that no prior national park had been established on the basis of leaseholds. Hartzog indicated that he preferred to

acquire the fee simple title to tribal lands, or a scenic or development easement, in lieu of leases. However, though leases would be less desirable in his
opinion, he would find them acceptable. Sigler then tried to include lease
costs in the ceilings on land acquisition costs normally imposed on the NPS
by Congress. Hartzog argued that lease costs should not be a part of a ceiling
but indicated that he would be happy to return to the House when such costs
were determined for the committee to exercise its oversight function. During
initial questioning he would not agree to limits on lease costs. In subsequent
testimony he shifted positions and indicated his willingness to limit lease costs
over the ninety-nine-year period to no more than the appraised fair market
value of the fee.[26] With the eventual elimination of the tribal land from the
lakeshore, leases and their costs became subsequently irrelevant.

Natural Resource Issues

Hunting, Fishing, and Trapping
The May 20, 1962, Bad River resolution requested "that the old and historic
Indian treaty rights and customs be allowed the Indians such as hunting, fishing, trapping and gathering wild rice." In its early discussions on hunting,
fishing, and trapping, the North Central Field Committee subcommittee uni-
laterally proposed that these rights be extinguished within that portion of the
reservation included in the lakeshore boundary. This issue, though inconsistent with the Native American position, was further explored at both the state
and federal levels. Max Edwards, an assistant to the secretary of the Interior
and a legislative counsel, advised Nelson that the rights could be terminated
by legislation, but such a provision might provide the tribes with the basis for
a claim against the United States for the value of the rights terminated.[27] Thus
the matter of extinguishing their rights was dropped from draft bills and the
NCFC subcommittee report. Questions then arose regarding alienated land
to be acquired as part of the lakeshore and Native American rights to hunt
and fish. Fortunately, Emil Kaminski, the legal counsel for the Wisconsin
Conservation Department, took the position that it was not necessary for the
Wisconsin Legislature to grant Native Americans these rights when alienated
lands came into tribal ownership as long as they were within the reservation
boundary, where Native Americans were not required to abide by state laws
regardless of ownership.[28] The BIA commissioner took the opposite point of
view, that state law prevailed.[29]

Given these complex and conflicting views, the NCFC subcommittee
reached a prudent decision that an Apostle Islands National Lakeshore Act

could not solve the complex issues of hunting, fishing, and trapping. Therefore, the draft legislation provided that no new rights were created, but that existing rights, whatever they were, would not be diminished. The only exception in the draft was a provision for the secretary of the Interior to establish zones where such activities would not be permitted for reasons of public safety, administration, or public use and enjoyment.[30]

The WCD continued its long-held position of obfuscation and occasional hostility. In spite of Kaminski's position two years earlier, state enforcement of rice-harvesting laws paralleled the state's insistence on regulation of hunting, fishing, and trapping on reservations. Wisconsin Attorney General George Thompson, a Republican, responded to a formal request for an opinion by WCD Director Voigt and declared that the Native American rights to hunt, fish (and trap) on reservation lands without regard to conservation laws no longer existed even on nonpatented (tribal) lands. It was his opinion that the Wisconsin Legislature should enact new laws to extend state regulations to reservations.[31]

This opinion, at this time, was unfortunate, as it understandably prompted the Bad River Tribe to indicate that it now wanted to stay out of the lakeshore. Nelson attempted to soften the impact by noting that his legislation in no way affected tribal hunting and fishing rights, and expressed the hope that the dispute would soon be settled.[32] The Conservation Department, however, kept the pressure on. A Bad River member, Mike Neveaux, set a net in Lake Superior within one mile of the mouth of the Bad River and was arrested by the local conservation warden. Judge Lawrence K. Blanchard of Bayfield found him guilty on two counts; he had no state license and he was in violation of state fishing seasons.[33]

Two years later, Bronson LaFollette recouped his loss of the governorship by being re-elected attorney general; having a lakeshore supporter in that position was a delight, and I urged him to re-examine Thompson's earlier opinion.[34] In the spring of 1966 LaFollette reversed the opinion and declared that the WCD did not have the authority to regulate hunting and fishing on nonpatented tribal land.[35] Bad River Chair Albert Whitebird said he "was very happy that [Jordahl] had presented some of the facts to the Attorney General . . . and that Bad River would now be more receptive [to the lakeshore]."[36]

Whitebird's position was important, as a petition against the lakeshore by local hunters and fishermen had caused considerable concern at Bad River. Persons circulating the petition, at Bad River and among factory workers at Munsingwear and other firms in Ashland, alleged that hunting and fishing would be banned on the Kakagon–Bad River Sloughs. BIA Superintendent Riley had pointed out to Whitebird that members of the local rod and gun club responsible for the petition had taken action against the lakeshore for their own selfish reasons and that their agitation among Bad River members was not in the best interest of the tribe. Whitebird agreed and indicated that band council members were now disenchanted with the actions of the rod and gun club. Tribal leaders wrote Nelson, O'Konski and Proxmire, saying, "The people of the town of Sanborn [which included Bad River] and members of the Bad River Indian tribe do not choose to oppose or support a national lakeshore until we know all the facts. . . . This will be forthcoming when the Secretary's task force makes public its findings. Thus the . . . petition is premature. We will appreciate your disregarding this petition as it is the feeling of our people that this proposal could be very meaningful to the people in this town, members of the tribe, people of northern Wisconsin and all of the mid-west."[37]

In spite of the attorney general's new opinion, the Conservation Department still insisted on the strict enforcement of state laws on reservations and arrested two more Bad River tribal members for trapping fish.[38] In part the WCD position might be traced to its antipathy for the lakeshore and its generally unfavorable attitudes toward Native Americans on the part of some state game wardens.

Wild Rice

Wild rice held considerable cultural, as well as economic, value for the Chippewa peoples. The Kakagon–Bad River Sloughs contained wild rice beds that were harvested yearly by the Bad River Tribe. Their May 10, 1962, resolution called for propagation of additional rice beds and the NCFC subcommittee recommended additional detailed planning for wild rice management and preservation and a restriction on use of the sloughs by small pleasure craft and canoes to prevent large motorboat wakes that injure rice stands.[39]

Questions with regard to the ownership of wild rice were more complex. In general the state took the position that rice ownership on lakes rested with the state and on navigable streams with the riparian owner. Attorneys with the state suggested that in the event the alienated lands within the sloughs were acquired, the title to the rice should rest with the secretary of the Interior, and in turn the secretary could give the tribe exclusive rights to harvest the rice. The state would, however, continue to insist that anyone harvesting rice purchase a state permit.[40] The BIA concurred with this position, especially regarding the permit requirement, and stated, "We likewise are not aware of any special right granted by treaty, statute or agreement whereby Indians are exempted from the licensing requirement to harvest wild rice on the Bad River Indian Reservation."[41]

To deal with the question of rice ownership, I conferred further with Bad River leaders, state attorneys, and Assemblyman Norman C. Anderson. Martin Hanson called Attorney General Bronson LaFollette and requested that he introduce legislation granting the Mole Lake, Bad River, St. Croix, and Lac Courte Oreilles Reservations in Wisconsin exclusive rights to the rice within their boundaries. The legislation would be patterned after a Minnesota law that gave Native Americans exclusive rights to harvest rice on certain lakes and streams. BIA Superintendent Emmett Riley and I also enlisted the aid of the Wisconsin Judicare (established under the Federal Office of Economic Opportunity to represent economic minorities in dealing with legal matters) to pursue the matter for Bad River through the courts and to assist in drafting suitable legislation that Anderson then introduced.[42] Through the efforts of Anderson and LaFollette, the legislation passed the Wisconsin State Assembly in 1967 and was to be reintroduced in the 1969 legislative session.[43] Before the Wisconsin Legislature could act, however, Congress had passed the lakeshore law, which deleted all tribal lands from the lakeshore. Consequently, interest in state wild rice legislation was dropped.

With the advent of the August rice-harvesting season on Bad River, the local conservation warden had arrested members of the tribe when they started harvesting one day in advance of the state season and without permits. I suspected that this was to be a direct challenge to state harvesting laws by the tribe. The matter was referred to both the county judge and the Ashland County district attorney. Given these actions, Fred Connors, an ardent supporter of both Native American rights and the lakeshore, resigned as tribal chair.[44]

The Shacks in the Kakagon–Bad River Sloughs

The NCFC subcommittee and the Citizens' Committee for an Apostle Islands National Lakeshore made substantial efforts to assist the tribes on other problems. The Bad River Tribe had repeatedly brought up the matter of white-owned hunting and fishing shacks in the sloughs, which were built on poles or rested on floats. The new Bad River chair, Bernard Lemieux, brought the shacks to the attention of the House Interior Subcommittee, noting that the shack owners were squatters, paid nothing for using tribal land, and were polluting the water.[45] Fred Connors noted that shack owners who were using the area without charge were also spreading false propaganda and pressuring the tribes to oppose the lakeshore.[46]

To help the tribes, Culver Prentice raised the issue of the shacks with the Wisconsin Public Service Commission, which had jurisdiction on navigable waters. Because of these pressures and tribal action, the shacks were removed a few years after the lakeshore was established.

Economic Development Issues

In initial discussions the Bad River and Red Cliff Tribes had stressed their need for economic development and jobs. This need was coupled with the need for economic development in the northern Great Lakes region in general. The lakeshore was not only to "preserve" a significant national resource on the south shore of Lake Superior; it was also meant to attract tourists and tourism spending to the region. To help meet the employment needs of the tribes a number of special provisions were recommended.

First, Native Americans were to be granted preferential rights to harvest timber within the reservation boundary included in the lakeshore. The first Nelson bill, S. 2498 (introduced in 1965), and the subsequent S. 778 (1967), clearly spelled out this provision, which was reiterated in every subsequent House and Senate bill.

Second, Native Americans wanted preferential employment rights. This was recommended in the NCFC subcommittee report and the draft legislation. Bills S. 2498 and S. 778 stated that Native Americans would be "granted, to the extent practicable, a preferential privilege of providing such visitor accommodations and services, including guide services, as the Secretary [of the Interior] deems are desirable [as long as secretarial standards are met] and granted employment preference for construction or maintenance work or for other work in connection with the Lakeshore for which they are qualified."[47] Comparable language was included in all subsequent bills.

Even when they were opposed to the lakeshore in 1970, and perhaps because they may have had second thoughts after the legislation passed, members of both tribes still wanted preferential employment rights even though tribal lands and Native American preferences had been deleted.[48]

Third, the NCFC subcommittee recommended that Native Americans be permitted to traverse the area within their reservations without charge. Provision was made for this in S. 2498 and S. 778; the latter bill stated that recognized members of the Bad River and Red Cliff Tribes would be "permitted to traverse such areas in order to hunt, fish, boat or gather wild rice or to obtain access to their homes or businesses." There were to be no charges to tribal members for use of dock facilities anywhere within the lakeshore. Comparable language was included in all subsequent bills.

Fourth, the final boundaries of the lakeshore were purposefully drawn to put both tribes in an excellent position to develop ancillary tourism facilities on their lands next to the lakeshore. The eastern terminus of the thirty-mile scenic road on the Bayfield Peninsula was situated next to the village of Red Cliff. Here it would have been possible for the Red Cliff Tribe to have developed facilities—motels, restaurants, and gift shops—to capitalize on what would have been the most heavily visited portion of the lakeshore.

At Bad River, the tribe would have been able to develop facilities for boat and canoe rentals, access to the sloughs, and guide services on the Bad River and Bear Trap Creek, which led into the Kakagon Sloughs. Other tourism facilities, such as motels, could have been developed between the lakeshore boundary and U.S. Highway 2 to the south within the reservation.[49] The successive lakeshore bills also provided consultative or advisory assistance to the tribes with respect to planning facilities or developments on tribal lands outside of the boundaries of the lakeshore.

Shifting Tribal Positions

Over the years frequent meetings were held with the tribes to explain and discuss the complexities of the legislation as it evolved and to secure their advice and counsel. Also, at the request of tribal leaders, Howard Potter, a staff employee with the BIA office in Ashland, met with them frequently to explain the proposal and to assist them in the preparation of statements for presentation to the Senate and House subcommittees. The tribes were open with him; on several occasions they reported to him that members of the South Shore Property Owners Association had hosted parties for members of Red Cliff where alcohol flowed freely. Potter recalled these events: "At the time of the first Senate hearings the white men had thrown a party for the Red Cliff Indians. These investors . . . were opposing us, trying to talk the Indians out of going along with it, and there was a big booze party and the next morning we didn't have Indians [for the hearings]. I went out and picked up a few; I think we had only three or four of them that first day; on the second day it picked up a little bit, but they had convinced them at the party that [opposition] was the thing for them to do." At the time, Alex Roye was chairman of the Red Cliff Council, and Potter observed: "He worked very closely with me all the time I was out there. . . . We had a lot of [supportive] Indians out there."[50]

In July 1965 Henry Daley, the Red Cliff chair, did not take a position but said, "The park would be a great benefit in some ways, creating employment, . . . but it might also hurt because timber could not be cut."[51] (This was an incorrect statement; timber could be cut if it did not interfere with recreation.)

Later that fall, the Red Cliff Tribal Council went on record as unanimously in favor of the lakeshore; its float in the Bayfield Apple Festival proclaimed Red Cliff as the "Gateway to the Apostle Islands National Lakeshore." Three tribal members, Ruth Bresette and Linda and Sherry Gokee, dressed in traditional attire and rode on the float. At that time, Red Cliff leaders were concerned that opposition from Bad River would jeopardize the project.[52]

In 1967 the Red Cliff Tribal Council engaged attorney Elizabeth Hawkes from Washburn to represent its interests. She raised ten questions dealing with hunting and fishing, use of federal funds, land matters, concessions, and job qualifications. After a visit with Red Cliff Tribal Chair Ken Andrews, Hawkes said, "I am satisfied that with just a few reservations, all members of the council are definitely in favor of the proposal. Kenneth has been doing an excellent job of reasoning with the various members of the tribe who have been opposed to the plan by discussions rather than broad-axe agreements, but he tells me that the questions listed above are unanswerable by him in detail." Hawkes urged that Nelson, Bechtel, or I meet with the Red Cliff Tribal Council to discuss the questions.[53] I did so on April 18, 1967, and discussed their questions and the proposal in detail. Their response was favorable.

During the June 1, 1967, Senate Subcommittee on Parks and Recreation hearings, members of the Red Cliff Band articulated their positions.[54] Alex Roye, a former tribal chair, felt it would be beneficial if Native American rights were protected. Irene Duffy expressed opposition because of past broken promises as well as job qualification requirements that would preclude Native Americans from park employment. Fred Bresette, a Red Cliff tribal council member, favored leasing and wondered why it had been removed from the bill. He was also concerned that Native Americans would not qualify for jobs. Ken Andrews, the chair of the Red Cliff Tribal Council, stated that the council had voted to remain neutral, although he personally favored the project. He favored leasing tribal land and wanted hunting and fishing rights protected; if the recreation area was ever terminated, he said, the land should revert to Red Cliff.

Two years later the Red Cliff position had shifted again.[55] Philip Gordon, a strong opponent in 1967, was the new Red Cliff chair, and at the 1969 Senate subcommittee hearings he said: "It is the opinion of the overwhelming majority of the Red Cliff people, and, therefore, the unanimous opinion of the tribal council, that the proposal for a national lakeshore park which takes away any of our tribal land be turned down."[56]

The council had, by formal vote, unanimously turned down the proposal on March 13, 1969. Gordon further noted that the people had earlier voted on a referendum on July 5, 1967, three to one in opposition. He did, however, state that they were not opposed to a national park in the area, including non-Native lands on the Bayfield Peninsula, but opposed inclusion of any tribal land. He further objected to the secretary of the Interior representing tribal members who owned allotted land. He also raised concerns over state enforcement of state hunting and fishing regulations.[57]

John Belindo, executive director of the National Congress of American Indians, had been requested to provide the tribes with assistance. He recommended the deletion of the Red Cliff reservation lands because of tribal opposition. However, he also provided a possibility for future action by stating that if the amendments proposed were enacted, along with those proposed by Rodney Edwards (a Duluth attorney), Red Cliff would in his opinion support the bill.[58]

The Bad River band changed its position in 1965 when five council members voted in opposition. At that time, Tribal Chair Albert Whitebird said, "We as a tribe of Indians in the past have ceded large areas of land to the U.S. government and what we have reserved for ourselves under treaty we aim to keep. . . . It's another step by government to acquire Indian lands and destroy Indian hunting and fishing and gathering wild rice without just compensation. The band hereby opposes any and all bills to create within the original boundaries of the Bad River reservation any part or parcel of the so-called Apostle Islands National Lakeshore."[59] Not all members of the tribe agreed with this position, and they initiated a petition among the Bad River people favoring the proposal.[60]

In 1967 the Bad River Tribe also hired Rodney Edwards to represent its interests. The funds to hire Edwards had been made available to the tribe through Nelson's efforts.[61] The Bad River Tribal Council shifted its position indicating that if the bill were amended, the council would favor the lakeshore.[62] Edwards took this position to the Senate subcommittee and reiterated that the Bad River Tribe would support S. 778 if it were amended to

- provide that the tribes would be parties to negotiations on any land within the reservation boundary;
- strengthen hunting, fishing, trapping, and rice-harvesting provisions;
- hold in trust for the Bad River Tribe the alienated land acquired by the secretary of the Interior, which would be leased for lakeshore purposes; and
- provide for the leasing of tribal land (the Department of the Interior at this time opposed leasing).[63]

In addition to Edward's testimony, individual Bad River Band members testified. Albert Whitebird stated, "The people of the nation are entitled to a playground, a place they can come to and enjoy themselves and relax on vacation and time off away from their workshops. I am highly in favor of this park but only under the conditions that the wishes of the Chippewa and their tribal government are met." Whitebird wanted all reservation lands acquired within the lakeshore boundary to be placed in trust for the tribe and leased to the government.[64]

Non-Natives continued to pressure both the Red Cliff and Bad River Tribes to repudiate the lakeshore. Fred Connors noted that shack owners were putting pressure on Bad River; the same techniques had been used by big landowners or cottage owners on Red Cliff.[65] The South Shore Property Owners Association, a local group opposed to the lakeshore, also encouraged Red Cliff members to visit Bad River and urge its members to oppose the lakeshore.[66] These efforts bore results, and a resident of Bayfield County, a lakeshore supporter, was "shocked" at the newly developed vociferous objections on the part of the Chippewa to the proposal:

> If they are successful . . . it will be a victory *not* for the Indian tribe, but *for* the South Shore Owners Association, a group of individual selfish interests. . . . Recently they have had meetings with the tribe. In confusion and lack of complete and accurate information about the national lakeshore proposal, the Indians have been easy prey to this small group of antagonists who have had time to organize and strengthen their position and have successfully talked the Indians over to their side while the rest of us, a silent majority, remained completely silent in the belief that the Indians were maintaining their position of being neutral. . . . It is my fervent hope that you will be able to recognize this devious tactic of using the power of the Indian tribe to further the interest of a selfish few.[67]

In a letter to the editor of the *Chicago Daily News*, William Brewer, a non-Native, said the Department of the Interior "was poised to confiscate *our* reservation and the lands of the owners."[68] Donald Schumacher, a south shore property owner, had met with Bureau of Outdoor Recreation officials and members of the Red Cliff Band and claimed that the twenty-one planned park service positions would be filled on a competitive basis that would exclude Native Americans. He further claimed that their hunting and fishing rights would be taken away in the interest of public safety.[69] Elizabeth Hawkes observed that there had been considerable attrition in Red Cliff support, which in almost every instance had been due to the efforts of the cottagers. But she added, "The Indians are now being satisfied that the white cottagers were merely using them to serve their own cause and are rapidly resuming support of the plan."[70]

Members of the South Shore Property Owners Association were also instrumental in getting Red Cliff members to vote on the issue at a tribal meeting; 30 voted in opposition while 14 were in favor. Although 280 eligible voters lived on the Red Cliff reservation and thus this vote could hardly be considered representative, it further fueled the opposition of the South Shore Property Owners Association.[71] The same techniques were being used at Bad River but at times were not successful. Albert Whitebird, the former Bad River chair, reported to Nelson that taxpayers (non-Natives) were strongly objecting to the lakeshore and were influencing the members on Bad River to oppose it. He did not think this was the time to take a referendum vote at Bad River as "the peoples' minds are confused with agitation."[72]

Given the long period of time over which the lakeshore proposal evolved, shifting circumstances, the Wisconsin Conservation Department's position on the enforcement of state laws, the reversal of the North Central Field Committee's subcommittee recommendation regarding purchase and leaseback, and the confusion and pressure caused by non-Natives, it is not surprising that tribal opinions shifted. They were continuously urged not to take positions until the lakeshore legislation was enacted; then they could make a decision. BIA Commissioner Robert Bennett reinforced this position, stating, "As Senator Nelson cogently stated before the recent hearings, . . . the purposes of the legislation is to establish Congressional authorization on terms that permit the Indian people to consider whether and with what modification they wish to take advantage of its provisions. We recommend support of the proposed legislation."[73] The tribes, however, would not follow this advice.

Negotiations with the National Congress of American Indians

During the course of the Senate and House subcommittee hearings, Nelson had repeatedly emphasized the fact that the legislation did absolutely nothing to the tribes other than to give them an opportunity to negotiate with the federal government. If they did not wish to be included in a national lakeshore, their wishes would be respected. Second, he was willing to negotiate with the tribes regarding further amendments and clarifications to the legislation. During the 1969 hearings, at the request of the Red Cliff and Bad River Tribal Councils, John Belindo of the National Congress of American Indians

(NCAI), claiming he represented 105 tribes and more than 350,000 individual Native Americans, filed a lengthy written statement. To deal with the issues raised, Nelson invited Harold Gross, NCAI legal counsel, to meet to discuss and negotiate further amendments. From March through May 1969, Gross met with Nelson and Nelson's staff assistant, John Heritage, to work out changes. The initial discussion on March 28 was amicable. Nelson was willing to accommodate tribal interests further, and Gross was optimistic that the tribes would approve S. 621 if it were amended as per their discussions.[74] They agreed on changes to several amendments to the Senate bill.

Amendment 1: The bill would specifically find that "the culture, heritage, homeland, and rights of native Chippewa Indians, who have so greatly contributed to the preservation of such shorelines, beaches, sandspits, and other natural and historical features in their unspoiled and natural condition, should be preserved and protected."

Amendment 2: No tribal lands within the Red Cliff unit would be included in the lakeshore unless the tribal council of the Red Cliff had so petitioned. Specifically, after authorization, it would be up to the tribal council to consider the matter of including its land, if it chose to do so. If it did not, the matter would rest there. If an agreement were reached with the council, the matter would go to a referendum vote by the tribe. If there were no congressional objection, tribal land would be included in the lakeshore ninety days after the plan had been transmitted to Congress.[75]

As the Red Cliff Tribe was opposed to the lakeshore at that time, this amendment was directed specifically to meet its needs. It did not deal with Bad River because at that time, "the members of the Bad River Band appear to be of the consensus that some use of their reservation land for this project might be in order, provided that the land was leased rather than purchased or traded to the federal government."[76] Bill S. 621, as always had been the case, still stated that no tribal land could be taken without a favorable tribal referendum. Further, it provided for the leasing of tribal land (the bulk of tribal lands were in marshlands and not susceptible to development; therefore it was not that urgent to include these lands within the lakeshore).

There were two other key amendments:

Amendment 6: Within the reservation boundaries within the lakeshore, the *only* regulations that the secretary of the Interior could prescribe regarding the rights of recognized members of the tribes to hunt, fish, trip, gather wild rice, or gain access to their homes or businesses dealt with the discharge of firearms, and then only to ensure public safety.

Amendment 7: Employment preferences for Native Americans in lakeshore jobs extended, where the person was qualified, to all employment, not just to menial jobs.

In total, eight amendments helped to clarify and make explicit the protection of tribal interests. Nelson, in a letter to Gross, transmitted the amendments. Gross responded: "I hope to have a favorable report from Wisconsin, since I think the corrected bill has important favorable implications for the future of Indian affairs."[77]

Gross also noted that the amendments were subject to ratification of the two tribes and that he planned to meet with the Bad River and Red Cliff Tribal Councils in June. At the Red Cliff meeting, Council Chair Philip Gordon agreed to call for a secret ballot one week later. Only a handful of eligible voters cast ballots; twenty-four voted no and two voted yes.[78]

Gross advised the Senate subcommittee that although the amendments were approved by the NCAI, the Red Cliff Tribe had voted against them. Gross explicitly said, "The form of the bill, as a procedure *for establishment of a park where Indian or allotted lands are concerned, has our support.*"[79] After meeting with Gross, the Bad River Tribe requested three more amendments. The first dealt with leasing. The second required more specific language regarding Native American employment. The third required explicit recognition of Native American contributions to preservation of the area and their significant role in the cultural history of the region. The Bad River Tribal Council put off further comment on the bill until more information was available on their amendments.

Senate Bill S. 621 with the amendments agreed to by Gross and Nelson passed the Senate in June and was referred to the House. The additional Bad River amendments would be considered there.

1969 House Hearings

In spite of the thorough and careful negotiations between Nelson and Gross and the eight substantive amendments to S. 621 approved by the Senate, the August 19, 1969, House Subcommittee on Parks and Recreation hearing was contentious with regard to Native American matters. Edwards, representing Bad River, said in a confusing statement:

> The Bad River Band has to some extent in the past, felt some inclination to support some legislation that would put up a park, but in their pleas for changes in the proposed legislation, they have been pretty well ignored. . . . [S. 621] makes no mention of preserving their right to control and license and regulate this

hunting and fishing and these rights that were reserved under P.L. 280 to them. And P.L. 280 specifically mentioned it, ending up with that they shall have the right to control the licensing and regulation thereof. . . . The Indians have attempted to control and license and regulate the hunting, fishing and ricing activities on their reservations. They passed regulations under P.L. 280. The state of Wisconsin law enforcement people are supposed to enforce those laws. They took on criminal jurisdiction on that reservation under P.L. 280.[80]

(The issues raised by Edwards in this statement could only be addressed by the state of Wisconsin, not by Congress.) Given Bad River Tribal Council's position, Edwards therefore opposed both H.R. 555 and S. 621.[81]

Bernard Lemieux, chair of the Bad River Tribal Council, stated that the council, on August 18, 1969, had voted four against, none for, the lakeshore with two members abstaining. He planned to hold an advisory vote with the members of the tribe on September 13, 1969. He stated that harassment by Conservation Department wardens was a major concern to him.[82]

Philip Gordon, the Red Cliff chair, expressed his satisfaction with Nelson's amendments but indicated that they had not gone far enough. He reiterated the vote of the Red Cliff Tribal Council on June 8, 1969, that had unanimously voted to oppose the inclusion of any tribal or allotted land in the lakeshore. In addition, he stated that he was now opposed to a national park in this region.[83]

Victoria Gokee, a member of the Red Cliff Band and a great-great-granddaughter of Chief Buffalo, a signer of the 1854 La Pointe Treaty, appeared in vigorous opposition. "I would like to dispute the man who welcomed you to God's country. This is not God's country. It is Indian country. We already gave you everything we had—Wisconsin, Michigan, Minnesota—I do not know where you are going to push us—out in the lake?"[84]

1970 House Hearings

The crucial 1970 House hearings were highly contentious regarding Native American issues. Bad River had referred the matter for review to the Great Lakes Intertribal Council, which had acted in opposition. The council declared, "Be it resolved that the Great Lakes Intertribal Council and its ten member bands serve notice of their intent to give the Bad River and Red Cliff member bands their full, active and continued support throughout their opposition to the Apostle Islands proposal."[85] The primary reason for this opposition was the proposed deprivation of the two tribes of their Lake Superior lakeshore territory and their wish "to develop themselves in the creation of a national park."[86]

Congressman Kastenmeier, a member of the House Interior Committee, asked about past Bad River positions; they had first supported the bill, then opposed it, then supported it, and finally again opposed it. "Is that a correct characterization of the band's position?" Sam Livingston, the new Bad River chair, replied, "No sir, that is not correct. We had a referendum vote on this particular bill and the majority of the people voted against it. I consider that one [an] official [position]. But as far as the others, that is all . . ."[87]

Jerome Arbuckle of the Bad River Tribe urged that they be allowed to control the park so that the tribes could raise revenue. "Permit us to operate the park, giving us technical assistance." It was a worthy suggestion, but not realistic at the time, given the long legislative history of the proposal. Alma Peterson, a Red Cliff council member, representing the tribe, said, "We oppose any proposal to take any lands within the original boundary of the Red Cliff reservation. . . . This has consistently been the position of the Red Cliff Band."[88]

Martin Hanson commented later that it was the younger Native Americans who started with treaty rights and felt that the white man shouldn't be running their reservations. He observed that although Red Cliff and Bad River had endorsed the idea, "they changed their minds, that's all."[89]

Reflecting on the tribes' opposition, Louis Hanson said:

> The Indians became radicalized in the 1960s with the American Indian Movement; the younger people in the tribes who were mainly responsible for it were fighting their elders at the same time. This was a proposal backed strongly by their elders and the young [Native Americans] didn't like the idea. This wasn't confined to the Apostle Islands question at all. Wounded Knee and the takeovers of various places and so forth coincided with this. There was no way they were going to get a consensus on this with the Indians once the opposition arose. It's just ironic that it did because I think it would have been helpful to them. It's too bad that that chunk of land isn't a part of it, but there was no sense letting the whole thing go down the tube in order to have the original plan in total. You never get that anyway.[90]

Given the conflicting and frequently inconsistent and confusing positions of the two tribes, it is no small wonder that the House Committee was uncertain as to an appropriate course of action. The issues being raised were relevant not only to the lakeshore but also to the larger issues of past and contemporary injustices to Native Americans. The context for the lakeshore debate can be better understood within the framework of the Red Power movement.[91]

The Red Power Movement

The Red Power movement followed the civil rights movement of the mid-1960s. Native Americans and Native organizations became more militant in asserting their rights and insisting on redress for the many injustices of the past. The Apostle Islands National Lakeshore was, to a great extent, caught in the rising tide of Red Power militancy. Regional and national Native American organizations, and non-Natives concerned with the injustices of the past, seized upon the lakeshore proposal as a significant national symbol of continued Native repression. They made little or no effort to examine the legislation or to attempt to understand the long, arduous planning process that went into the proposal. The success of the 1960s civil rights movement, with its freedom riders and dramatic marches, gained power for disenfranchised African Americans. Native American leaders also began a series of dramatic and militant demands for greater control over their own lives. "Red Power" and "self-determination" became rallying cries across the country, and actions similar to those of the Black Power movement became common. Historian Alvin Josephy described the Red Power movement:

> In the new climate, the strongest and loudest voices are those that speak selflessly and patriotically of Red—or Indian—Power. Their numbers are swelling, particularly among the younger Indians. In substance, their message is no different from what it has been for decades, but it is more challenging and insistent. It demands, rather than pleads for, self-determination; the right of Indians to decide programs and policies for themselves, to manage their own affairs, to govern themselves, and to control their lands and resources. It insists on the inviolability of their land and on the strict observance and protection of obligations and rights guaranteed the Indians by treaties with the federal government.[92]

A number of different organizations grew up between World War II (when returning veterans brought back to the reservation an expanded sense of world affairs) and the 1960s, including the NCAI and the American Indian Movement. Perhaps the most significant feature of these new movements, besides their breaking away from tribal council governments, was the reflection of a pan–Native American alliance. For the first time Native Americans from vastly different tribes and cultures were joining together and presenting a united front.[93]

The NCAI was the more conservative of the new organizations. Formed in 1944, the NCAI worked through negotiations to try to reach compromises acceptable to both sides. It was active, for example, in attempting to reach compromises on the proposal to incorporate tribal land into the Apostle Islands National Lakeshore proposal. By 1961 younger Native Americans grew dissatisfied with NCAI's negotiated positions. They formed an offshoot organization, the National Indian Youth Council. A participating chapter, the Chippewa Youth Council, actively opposed the lakeshore.

The urban relocation policies of the 1950s had produced a large group of displaced, restless, and economically disadvantaged younger Native Americans residing in large urban areas and cut off from the social support networks of the reservations. Nearly as many Native Americans lived in cities by the 1960s as were on the reservations. They had little organized representation; the BIA limited its services to the reservations. The NCAI was working, again, mostly on the reservations, including fighting against termination. In the fall of 1966 many of the more militant Native Americans came together and formed the American Indian Movement.[94] It was American Indian Movement activities that, in many peoples' minds, remain representative of Native American militancy.

Activism first focused on treaty rights issues. During the early 1960s, fishing conflicts between Native Americans and non-Natives in the Pacific Northwest resulted in well-publicized "fish-ins" that garnered nationwide attention for the failure of the U.S. government to honor the treaties.[95] In the fall of 1969 another group took over the abandoned former federal prison on Alcatraz Island in San Francisco Bay to dramatize and call attention to Native American grievances. Again the event fostered national media coverage.[96]

Two positive events of the 1960s also helped strengthen the call for Native American self-determination. During the Kennedy administration, the Area Redevelopment Act was passed; it increased federal spending on the reservations and gave Native Americans a greater role in how it was spent. Then, through the lobbying of Native activists, President Johnson's War on Poverty Program was amended to specifically target Native American reservations. For the first time, Native Americans were asked to propose and work on plans for programs that they thought would alleviate conditions on their reservations. Once proposals were approved, funds were handed over to tribal councils for local implementation and program administration. For the first time, councils demonstrated that they were capable of managing funds and taking responsibility for their own affairs. With the success of this initiative, many Native Americans began to demand the transfer of responsibility for other vital programs, including education and health care, from the paternalistic BIA to the tribes themselves.[97] This was refused. Government–Native American hostilities were at their height when the lakeshore proposal was before Congress in the 1960s. It was to prove an irresistible target for Native Americans and their sympathizers.

Standing on Principles: Native American Activism and the Apostle Islands National Lakeshore

The lakeshore issue drew fire from across the spectrum, both locally and nationally. For example, in 1969 I was asked to appear before a group of Native American students at the University of Wisconsin–Madison to explain the lakeshore proposal. As a prelude to the discussion I asked the small group of about a dozen people where they came from. There were Canadian Athabascan, Alaskan Tlingit, New Mexico Apache, Nevada Navajo, and others. Not one was a Chippewa. After a detailed explanation of the complex options provided to the tribes, the group concluded it was just another "white man's land steal" and voted to oppose the proposal.

Opposition to the lakeshore took other forms. When Nelson spoke at a federal conference in Milwaukee on Lake Michigan pollution, he had to negotiate his way through a group of picketers at the hotel entrance carrying signs with messages such as "Stop Land Grabs" and "Would You Like to Live in a Park?" "Earth Day" speeches given by Nelson in Madison, Milwaukee, and other places in Wisconsin in 1970 were also disrupted by Native American and non-Native militants protesting the federal "land grab." Nelson recalled these events:

> On Earth Day, I traveled across the country and I spoke at Madison at eight o'clock and I spoke at ten o'clock at night at the University of Milwaukee to a full house. I had a group of Indians [chuckle] from maybe both Red Cliff and Bad River . . . and they had a sack full of tin cans, trash, which they threw upon the stage while I was talking. They were arguing that we were taking their land away. So I interrupted my speech to tackle them right on, to tell them they were wrong. . . . But once the Indians got attacking it, they were blind to what we had drafted and worked out . . . and were claiming it was unfair. So I tackled them head on, to a big audience . . . and the students gave uproarious applause to my position because when I got through explaining it, they could see that the claim of the Indians and the literature they were passing around was simply false.[98]

Michael Connors, a Bad River member residing in Milwaukee and the first secretary of the Chippewa Indian Youth Council, kept the pressure on and declared that Nelson had lost control of the bill and that the NPS was now looking covetously at all tribal lands.[99]

Systematic, organized Native American opposition was also being mounted at meetings of the House Subcommittee on National Parks and Recreation, where discussions on the lakeshore were beginning. Opponents recognized that the ambivalence of subcommittee members left them vulnerable to pressure. In April 1970 the House subcommittee debated the issues for more than two hours in closed session. In May, responding to subcommittee sensitivity, Lee McElvain, a House Interior Committee staff member, prepared two additional alternatives for the subcommittee to review. The first was S. 621 with amendments, as passed by the Senate. The second declared that except for six allotments on the Bayfield Peninsula all tribal and allotted land on both reservations would be excluded. This alternative still included 11.75 miles of shoreline, averaging a half mile in width on the northern boundary of the Bad River Reservation and the sand spit known as Chequamegon Point and Long Island.[100]

Members of the Red Cliff and Bad River Tribes, however, were in Washington at that time and were lobbying against S. 621. Some Republicans on the House Interior Committee wanted to stay with the bill in its original form to "hang Gaylord Nelson and Bob Kastenmeier as 'anti-Indian.'"[101] Gross, who now served on Vice President Spiro Agnew's Council on Indians, had taken a more favorable stand and had indicated that he might use the Apostle Islands National Lakeshore as a classic case of Native Americans trying to reacquire alienated lands within their reservation.

The impact of the mounting Native opposition was keenly felt at the June 3, 1970, House subcommittee hearing. Representative Joe Skubitz, a Kansas Republican, noted that the subcommittee had received a dozen telegrams in opposition just that morning. James A. Haley, a Florida Democrat, said that practically every tribe in the country opposed the bill. He had had calls and telegrams from Native Americans in Florida, California, North Carolina, and "every other place throughout the United States." Ed Edmondson observed that, "unless there was some moderation in the [Department of the Interior] position, you are going to have an Indian uprising on your hands. The messages that the gentleman from Florida [Haley] has received—and I have received many of the same messages—are coming from all over the country." Roy Taylor expressed the opinion that Native Americans were being used and were fronting for non-Natives. Kastenmeier observed that the subcommittee had been through a series of crises, more or less, on the Native question but said, "I hope you [Mr. Chairman] are sensitive to at least the political difficulties we find ourselves in with respect to accommodating to the so-called

Indian problem. I do think you are correct in pointing out that this is not a land grab of the Indian lands and that any stack, whether it is 200 telegrams . . . from every state in the Union, does not express any information about this bill, or the problems involved, but rather, I am sure, are at the direction of some central person or group that has decided to oppose the bill."[102]

Wayne Aspinall, the chair of the House Interior Committee, was also present and summed up the problem succinctly:

> If you get this bill to the floor with the Indians of the United States against it, you are not going to pass it. Let us just be realistic. Today the people of the United States are sympathetic towards the Indians. They would rather take care of the Indians than a park proposal., . . . Our colleague from Wisconsin [Kastenmeier] cannot carry it on the floor successfully and I will just be perfectly honest with you, the chairman of the full committee, who has not yet lost a bill on the floor, cannot carry this on the floor with the Indians of the United States against it. . . . The chairman of this committee is not afraid to confront the issues and principles involved. We have never taken a step backward on that, but we also have never walked into a fire that we knew would consume all of us.[103]

The Native Americans kept the pressure on long after the June 1970 hearings. Red Cliff members sent numerous letters and telegrams in opposition. The chair of the Nez Perce Tribal Council telegraphed his opposition to the House Interior Committee.[104] (On May 19, 1970, Secretary of the Interior Hickel had dedicated the Nez Perce National Historical Park; two units included tribal land. The first would be administered jointly by the tribe and the NPS, the second, jointly by the tribe and the BIA).[105] The Mutual Radio Network News out of Washington, DC, summed up the situation by declaring that the "Indians were on the warpath" again and were converging on Washington because of the lakeshore legislation; they believed that the House committee was not telling the truth and that tribal land would be taken.[106]

While the debate over tribal land and the lakeshore raged in Congress, the Native Americans took an action that was inconsistent with their strong feelings in opposition to inclusion of any tribal lands into the lakeshore, even if under lease arrangements. They embarked on a new program of leasing reservation lands on Madeline Island and other areas to non-Natives for recreational purposes. This inconsistent position further confused Congress regarding the question of tribal lands and the lakeshore.[107]

A BIA spokesperson at Ashland admitted in a public statement that some of the land proposed for lease was within the lakeshore boundary. He said that Red Cliff and Bad River had made their lands available "only recently."

Nelson and Kastenmeier were quick to request a Department of the Interior explanation of the apparent contradiction in Native American policies. The BIA's regional director in Minneapolis sidestepped the issue by refusing to comment on the controversy except to say that "the authority to lease had been turned over to the tribal councils."[108] The question of tribal leases would come up again in House debates.

When the lakeshore bill went to the House, excluding all tribal land except several small allotments on the Bayfield Peninsula, Aspinall dealt with the Native American opposition:

> The Indians involved in the area, in my opinion, desire to have their cake and eat it at the same time. They do not desire any development to take place that would serve anybody else except themselves. If we are going to serve the public in this area . . . it is my opinion that it is about time the Indian population is fitting itself into the general complex of the general population. We have seen that in the past, that the tribe involved has seen fit to sell their land to non-Indians. The lands in the proposal are not Indian. The great opposition that we currently have simply comes from the fact that the Indians would like to have back the lands they have heretofore sold to non-Indians. How they are going to get it is not apparent to me after hearing the testimony.[109]

Regarding Native American opposition, John Saylor, a Republican from Pennsylvania, said:

> Now I was impressed, as were a number of other members of the committee when they began to get telegrams from all over the United States from all the Indian tribes and Indian councils to the effect that they were opposed to this bill. I would like to tell you that somebody slipped along the line after all; you sometimes think that these Indians in the west and in the south and in the central part of the country have a common interest and, therefore, it was because they belonged to the National Association of Indians that they got the word. But lo and behold, the Western Union one day made a mistake. I found out about one of the telegrams . . . was to be charged not to the Indian tribe out in California that sent me the telegram, but it was to be charged to a man who is a white man and lives in the area, and who, in my opinion, is trying to use the Indians. In other words, this is not a spontaneous group of telegrams that have come from the Indian tribes who are looking out for their Indian brethren. These are telegrams that have been inspired by a white man who is in the real estate business up in that area and who is trying to use the Red Cliff Band of Indians for his own use and benefit.[110]

Kastenmeier pointed out to his colleagues in the House the inconsistency of the Native American position: "If the Indians are so anxious to repurchase alienated lands, why are they engaged in leasing tribal lands for fifty-year periods for vacation home sites? The wish of the Indians to reacquire alienated lands, however admirable, is based on vague hopes and dreams." Representative Kyle dissented, arguing, "I do have messages from Indians, from New York to Wisconsin to New Mexico and to Alaska. I have talked with some of these people, and they certainly were not being led around by the nose by some white developer."

Congressman Taylor characterized his view of what the Native Americans were saying: "'Do not create a park on this land because we may someday want to buy the land back.' In my opinion this is going too far. I believe the Indian hostility has been encouraged, to a great extent, by white property owners for whom the Indians work. . . . These Indians are being used for selfish purposes."[111]

While the Red Power movement and Native American activism in general were reacting to long-standing, deep, and legitimate grievances against treatment at the hands of the federal government and "white" society, its opposition to the lakeshore proposal seems more a question of standing on principle rather than taking action against a deliberately hostile "white" policy.

It is important to remember that both Bad River and Red Cliff peoples generally supported the lakeshore proposal early in the process. In fact, the Bad River Tribal Council had made the initial request for a study on a possible park in the area. Support for the proposal was strong until the mid-1960s when non-Native residents opposed to the lakeshore began agitating on the reservations, claiming that the proposal was a land grab, that it would result in the loss of hunting, trapping, gathering rights, and so on. The simultaneous rise of general Native American activism picked up on these "introduced" concerns and used them without evaluating the safeguards and benefits built into the lakeshore legislation. When the proposal was challenged by Native American activists on both reservations, additional benefits and safeguards were worked out, which *at the time* were accepted by the tribal councils, although Bad River wanted even more amendments. These concerns were exacerbated by the continuous action by the Wisconsin Conservation Department in its insistence on enforcing hunting, fishing, and rice-harvesting laws against tribal members. By 1969, at the height of Native American activism across the country, the lakeshore was widely criticized. Some critics may have had legitimate concerns and an understandable reluctance to accept good-faith initiatives by a federal government that in the past had been unfaithful. Others may have been responding to self-serving manipulation by outside concerns.

The Apostle Islands, circa 1970s. (photograph by Fritz Albert)

Winter in the Apostle Islands, circa 1960s. (photograph by Clarence Carlson)

Chequamegon Point sand spit looking northwest, with Lake Superior on the right, Chequamegon Bay on the left, and Long Island in the background, circa 1963. (photograph by author)

Rock formations along the east shore of Sand Island, circa 1965. (National Park Service)

Hermit Island has always been difficult to access because of its rocky shoreline. The island is named for a hermit who lived in a log cabin on the remote outpost during the 1850s. (photograph by Arnold Alanen, 1981)

After mooring his sailboat by Devil's Island, this man uses a dinghy to explore the caves. (photograph by Arnold Alanen, 1994)

During the winter months, ice formations develop at the Mawikwe Bay (formerly Squaw Bay) Sea Caves, which are part of the Apostle Islands National Lakeshore mainland unit. (photograph by Arnold Alanen, 1994)

The Sand Island lighthouse, constructed of sandstone quarried from its immediate site in 1881, is a popular destination for Apostle Islands' visitors. (photograph by Arnold Alanen, 1994)

The Raspberry Island lighthouse, built in 1862 and expanded in 1906, serves as the primary structure in a complex that also includes a dock, fog signal building, barn, oil house, two outhouses, and kitchen garden. The National Park Service recently restored the main building with its keeper's quarters below and the square lighthouse tower above. (photograph by Arnold Alanen, 2004)

Julian Bay Beach. (courtesy of Apostle Islands National Lakeshore)

PART FOUR

Conclusions

❧

CHAPTER 13

Reflections

The long effort to establish the Apostle Islands National Lakeshore was instructive. The Apostle Islands had intrinsic natural and social values worthy of becoming an addition to the National Park System. Timing, continuity, planning, media coverage, and strong local, state, and national support were critical elements in securing enactment of lakeshore legislation. Also, insights might be gained from the experience of working with two sovereign minority groups, the Bad River and Red Cliff Chippewa Tribes. Finally, there are some interesting observations to be gleaned from observations on the lakeshore in the twenty-first century: how much of what was imagined in the 1960s by advocates actually occurred? This chapter first examines the lakeshore's circumstances forty years after its establishment. In conclusion, some reflections on lessons learned from the long process are offered.

The Apostle Islands National Lakeshore at the Start of the Twenty-First Century

Since 1970 the National Park Service has worked to establish and develop its management agenda, to institute interpretive programs and visitor facilities, and to fulfill a mixed mandate of public recreation and resource protection. The public that the NPS serves has changed, as have the communities that surround the lakeshore, providing new challenges for managers. Many of the problems originally predicted by lakeshore opponents never emerged, but inevitably questions never envisioned by lakeshore advocates arose in their place. And yet much remains the same, including the Apostle Islands themselves. They remain a landscape, an ecosystem, to catch the dreamer, the poet, the naturalist. They speak of mysteries and natural wonders and human history.

Lakeshore Visitors

During the 1960s, while drawing up plans, testifying before Congress, or publicly lobbying, lakeshore proponents made certain assumptions about the type of visitor it would appeal to, how many would be drawn to it, and what they would do during their visits. Over the decades since the national lakeshore's establishment some of these assumptions have proved to be correct while others missed the target.

Lakeshore proponents had to fend off the charges that the lakeshore would be a "rich person's park," and they did so with reasonable success. It was originally anticipated that many people would come to the Apostles to enjoy the unique boating environment. This has essentially remained true, but in the past few years, the lakeshore has witnessed a change in user group preferences, including increased usage by the nonboating public.

One visitor study, found that 68 percent of visitors arrived by private car.[1] Of those arriving by boat, the greatest percentage used a kayak (25 percent). Twenty-one percent came by power boat, and 15 percent used a sailboat. The fact that more are now visiting the lakeshore by car keeps it from being a "rich person's park"; 67 percent of respondents to the survey had an income below $60,000. They are well educated, however; 64 percent had an undergraduate or graduate degree. Most are in their forties and fifties and arrived with families in tow. More than a third (36 percent) had visited before. Forty-eight percent had come specifically to visit the lakeshore, suggesting its reputation is a significant factor. Most visitors, however, are drawn from Wisconsin and the nearby states of Minnesota and Illinois, suggesting the lakeshore is a regional attraction for those within a day's drive.

Most were attracted by the natural beauty and the solitude of the area, suggesting that visitors are not seeking a highly developed park experience. Kayaking was the most popular reason for visiting the Apostle Islands (23 percent), sightseeing was considerably less of an interest (14 percent; although once visitors arrived, it was a very important at 80 percent), while sailing and motor boating each attracted 13 percent of visitors. This is a considerable difference from what was predicted back in 1970; keep in mind that a thirty-mile scenic road had been deleted. Visitors are clearly being drawn for different activities than were anticipated by early planners, and services need to be allocated accordingly.

Visitors are easier to count when they visit the mainland facilities; unfortunately there is rather limited data regarding island visits. As anticipated by early planners, Stockton and Sand Islands receive the vast proportion of island visits; Stockton is more developed than the other islands and Sand is close to the mainland. Most visit only one island; Stockton is by far the most popular, possibly because it possesses most of the development in the lakeshore and has safe boat docking. Oak and Sand are the next most popular islands (although they rank noticeably below Stockton in numbers). When asked why they chose not to visit the other islands, most visitors cited a lack of time, suggesting the more difficult access remains a drawback to usage. On the other hand, this ensures that those willing to spend a little more time can easily find solitude and uncrowded spaces.

Camping on the islands is a less popular activity than predicted by the lakeshore planners; however, collecting data on camping activities is challenging. More than 110 miles of hiking trails exist on the mainland and the islands. An improved mainland trail extending the length of the lakeshore's shoreline is being planned, but the number of people seeking hiking opportunities appears to be declining from earlier surveys.

Another recreational activity that has developed, although not envisioned by lakeshore planners, is scuba diving, particularly to view the shipwrecks, sea caves and cliffs, and historic docks within lakeshore boundaries. It remains, however a limited activity, for only 2 percent of visitors scuba dive. While diving parties often go out on their own, charter services now operate out of Bayfield. The NPS has begun to monitor both private and charter diving parties through a required permit system, both to ensure diver safety and to protect the shipwrecks and other underwater features from vandalism. However, because the NPS does not own the bottom of the lake, their direct enforcement capacity is limited, and some shipwrecks of interest to divers are outside of the park boundary.

Finally, the lakeshore, as well as the surrounding region, is experiencing increasing numbers of visitors during the winter months. The peak season remains June through September, with August the most popular month. However, winter attracts people every month, largely to the mainland areas. In 2007 Little Sand Bay and Meyers Beach on the mainland received an average of 2,000–3,000 visits per month in January and February. Downhill and cross-country skiing and snowmobiling are popular on the Bayfield Peninsula. New trails have opened in the past few years. Local residents come to ice-fish. The spring and fall also attract visitors for hunting and fishing or viewing the spectacular fall colors.

Most visitors are arriving for short visits, three days or less (57 percent). This again suggests the lakeshore attraction as a regional experience, perhaps as part of a driving tour of other areas or for an extended weekend. Visits to areas outside the park were relatively high, with 68 percent spending at least one day in towns or areas adjacent to the park. The city of Bayfield was the most popular site to visit, although Madeline Island (with its easily accessible ferry) was also popular. As increased tourism in the region was one of the promises made in the lakeshore proposal, this is an encouraging trend.

Visitors are contributing to the regional economy, as proponents promised, although not quite as much as was suggested by Fine.[2] A NPS study undertaken in 2004 indicated that total visitor spending in 2004 within a thirty-mile radius of the lakeshore was $15 million, 22 percent of which was spent on lodging, 21 percent on restaurant meals and bar visits, and 16 percent in boat rentals, guide fees, and transportation. Overnight visitors were responsible for about half of the amount spent. Almost 70 percent of the spending public were explicitly in the region to visit the lakeshore.[3] The study suggested that the dollars spent as a result of the lakeshore supported 264 jobs and generated $4.9 million in personal income and $6.8 million in value-added income, such as wages, profits and rents for area businesses, and sales tax. The amount of revenue generated by the lakeshore increased to $18.1 million in 2005, suggesting the park will remain a very respectable source of revenue for the region in the future, if appropriate attention is paid to protecting scenic beauty and ensuring a high-quality visitor experience.[4]

Number of Visits

The 2007 visitor statistics indicate that the park received 182,396 visits (as opposed to visitors; visits consist of one person per day), considerably less than the 920,000 anticipated by Fine, an estimate that was developed based on a very different lakeshore proposal than what Congress approved.[5] This number is, however, representative of steady growth; 1996 saw 167,432 visits (2002 was the peak year with 208,263 visits).

Management Issues in the Lakeshore

The Apostle Islands National Lakeshore was established in 1970; the NPS began management efforts in 1972. Its congressional authorization stated that the lakeshore would be managed "in order to conserve and develop for the benefit, inspiration, education, recreational use, and enjoyment of the public" and would include twenty islands and a strip of the mainland, and their "related geographic, scenic, and scientific values."[6] The NPS's efforts in the lakeshore can be documented through a number of perspectives and issues, only a few of which are considered here.

The successful operation of any national park or other unit requires money for staff, facility construction and maintenance, and staff support services (other expenses such as land purchases or large capital improvement projects are covered by special congressional appropriations not reflected in the annual budget). In 1972, its first operating year, the lakeshore had an annual budget of $141,200.[7] Since then, the budget has increased substantially; $816,900 in 1983, $1.38 million by 1993, and $2.856 million in 2007.[8]

While operating funds have substantially increased over the years, inflation and changing management issues have eroded the budget capacity. Facilities maintenance requirements were a critical issue in 2007, given both the increase in visitors (and thus increased wear and tear on facilities), the change in visitor usages with a concomitant change in the services required and the area in which they are required (including the more remote, previously less well used islands), and an increase in the number of buildings requiring maintenance. While the 1986 transfer of the six historic lighthouses into the lakeshore significantly increased the cultural and historical artifact base in the park, no increase in maintenance budget occurred to assure appropriate conservation of the buildings. This has led to a not unusual management challenge for NPS staff.[9]

Also increasing operational budget requirements is the challenge created by the 1960s decision over the lakeshore's boundary. The official boundary, one-quarter mile off all land masses included within the lakeshore (excluding lake bottom), leaves much of the adjacent lake outside the park boundary. In fact, both visitors and park staff must traverse this unofficial park space to utilize the lakeshore. For the staff, this means to perform their duties they incur greater travel times and costs without budget allocations recognizing that requirement. For visitors, it means that while they might be outside lakeshore boundaries, if they run into trouble on the water, it is park staff who must come to their rescue in the absence of any closer agency; the DNR does not maintain any public security capability. According to the 2008 lakeshore superintendent, Bob Krumenaker, these circumstances result in what is termed the "effective area" of the lakeshore, the area they must oversee, being four times as large as the "official" lakeshore, for which they are funded.[10]

Staffing is also a critical management issue. In 1972 the lakeshore employed eight people in permanent positions ranging from superintendent to maintenance chief, along with two seasonal park aids.[11] In 2007 the lakeshore had 34.46 total permanent full-time equivalents (almost 45 employees) and 10.19 full-time equivalents (37 people) as seasonal employees.[12] The arguments made by proponents that staffing the lakeshore would have direct economic impacts on local communities have been proven. However, the staffing levels have, again, not kept up with increased maintenance and visitor demands.

Safety was one of the issues raised frequently by opponents of the lakeshore during the many hearings on its establishment. Of particular concern was Lake Superior. Superior is well known for its dangerous and sudden storms, and many argued that the large number of inexperienced boaters likely to be drawn to the area following the lakeshore's establishment would form a lethal combination. It has turned out to be an empty argument.

While the lakeshore has attracted its share of inexperienced boaters (a 1985 survey showed that 41.4 percent of those questioned rated themselves as having no boating skills) accidents are relatively few and far between.[13] In 1990 park rangers responded to thirty-five reported incidents. Most were to assist with boats accidentally going aground, losing power, or having other mechanical difficulties. There was one reported sinking, one fire onboard, and one report of a man overboard. Rangers assisted with searches for three lost people and responded to ten medical emergencies. When one considers that there were almost 18,000 visits involving boats in 1990, the safety record is excellent.[14]

Park personnel attributed this astonishing safety record to a number of factors. They noted that the lakeshore did not attract problem visitors in general; it experienced few of the problems found in other national parks. Instead, lakeshore visitors appear to be quiet, law-abiding, and responsive to public safety information. The latter factor, the rangers believed, resulted in low accident statistics. The lakeshore rangers spend a great deal of their time in safety education efforts. Brochures and ranger contacts emphasize awareness of the changes in weather and the need for adequate preparations and precautions. Weather information is made available at all ranger contact points. The results appear to speak for themselves.

Another concern that has proved groundless was the question of allowing commercial fishing within lakeshore boundaries. The argument was made that recreational boaters might interfere with or injure themselves on the equipment used for pound nets, which are large nets anchored to the lakebed with poles. Lakeshore staff report that only a few collisions have occurred in recent years, with no fatalities within park boundaries.[15] Commercial fishing ventures and recreational boaters appear to coexist reasonably in peace. The greatest threats to commercial fishers have not come from the lakeshore but from declining fish stocks, introduced diseases, ecological changes (including warming water temperatures due to climate change), conflicts over catch allowances, and a weak national economy, all of which make it financially difficult to make a profit. One superintendent has noted that while it is clear if one reviews the Apostle Islands National Lakeshore history, the act made no mention of the fact that commercial fishing is allowed.[16]

Managing Resources and Managing People

The lakeshore legislation includes recreational goals and the protection of the area's natural resources. However, achieving both these goals, which can be in conflict, has been a concern. These concerns may become sharper after the 2004 designation of the lakeshore as the Gaylord A. Nelson Wilderness by President George W. Bush, by which 80 percent of the lakeshore was formally protected as wilderness.[17] Management has, therefore, concentrated on preserving wilderness through limiting development. Excluded from the designation were Long Island (in part due to opposition from the Bad River Tribe and its high use rate by residents), Sand Island, and parts of Manitou, Rocky, and Stockton Islands, where lighthouses are located.

Much of the appeal of the Apostle Islands has been their "natural" qualities, but beginning with the early debates in the 1930s, a pressure has been exerted, particularly by local people, for developments that were more extensive than mere "wilderness." These developments would draw large numbers of tourists and tourist spending, and this pressure continues today. Local residents have argued for developments that would allow the "ordinary" person to enjoy what some view as a park for the rich.

To date, the NPS has responded to these demands in a number of ways. The NPS, for example, often suggests to visitors less expensive options. Taking the public ferry to easily accessible Madeline Island, although not cheap, can meet the needs of the casual visitor while providing local economic opportunities. Other tourist developments, such as adjacent motels, provide an alternative to wilderness camping. The NPS cooperates with the town of La Pointe and Ashland County in promoting Madeline Island by providing information on the island (and on other regional attractions) and by directing visitors to an experience along the lines of their expectations.[18]

The possibility of subsidizing transportation within the lakeshore has been addressed in the current management plan, but given the natural limitations (travel over water over long distances), the NPS has been reluctant to implement a potentially costly subsidy. Currently, private concessionaires offer both cruises that make regular stops at a number of islands to discharge campers and a private water taxi service.

One aspect of "recreational" use in the lakeshore has been the development of commercial activities oriented to the needs of visitors. These include the cruise operators, kayak outfitters, sailing charter operators, fishing charter operators, scuba diving shops, and camping outfitters. The businesses are located principally in Bayfield, but their activity occurs *in* the lakeshore. To manage these uses, the NPS issues permits for those offering services within lakeshore boundaries. While some operators view regulation as an irritant, the NPS considers it important; it ensures some reliability and responsibility on the part of business owners, protecting visitors and owners alike. Prior to the establishment of the permit system, considerable concern arose over potential problems, but the system has functioned from the start without significant problems.[19]

Preserving the natural values of the Apostle Islands National Lakeshore has presented different challenges. Superintendent Bob Krumenaker argued in 2008 that one of the challenges of the lakeshore is the difference in intent for the lakeshore encapsulated in the 1970 lakeshore act and public values of the new century. While ecological values were peripherally acknowledged by the act's creators during the 1960s, the lakeshore was valued for its ability to provide recreational opportunities to an underserviced midwestern populace, albeit of a rougher nature than at, for example, Cape Cod. The planning, congressional hearings, and final enabling act all reflected recreational values. The 2004 congressional decision to designate much of the lakeshore as official "wilderness" reflected the change in national public values, from favoring developed recreational opportunities to opportunities to experience untrammeled nature and to provide increased protection for wilderness for its own sake, in the face of ongoing erosion of wilderness areas in the continental United States. While some development will become necessary to appropriately deal with human uses—pit toilets, designated fire pits, erosion-proof trails and campgrounds—they will detract from the more "natural" feel and wilderness character of an area. Their presence can also increase usage, starting a cycle where increased usage demands more facilities, which will potentially increase usage, and at some point the NPS will be forced to ration usage. A significant discussion of the issue of wilderness in the Apostle Islands and the potential management challenges, as well as the politics, can be found in James Feldman's 2004 dissertation.[20]

A new issue not considered by the authors of the act is the appropriate conservation and management of cultural and historical artifacts within the final lakeshore boundaries. These include the historical lighthouses, various artifacts from early settlers, and, although not formally within lakeshore boundaries, the various shipwrecks found off the islands. Management requires both staff and funding.[21] Maintenance or development, however, such as access trails or interpretive signs, can conflict with the interest in preserving the "natural" aspect of the islands and its official designation as wilderness. Interpretative materials, such as signs or plaques, can overshadow or detract from the artifacts and, if placed poorly, from the natural beauty of the area. Environmental historian William Cronon has looked specifically at the challenge of integrating cultural history into a "wilderness" setting in the Apostle Islands and concludes that although difficult, doing so is essential as it preserves and integrates natural and cultural ecologies while instructing visitors on that possibility in other places.[22]

Threats to the Lakeshore

Overall, the lakeshore faces fewer threats from its own users than do other parks, largely due to the remoteness of the islands and the buffer provided by Lake Superior. Crowding and overuse have raised concerns in some areas, such as Stockton Island, and the NPS has responded by monitoring sensitive areas for ecological impacts and by limiting the number of camping permits it issues for developed sites. Almost all camping on the islands is undesignated and primitive, meaning that there are no established and maintained campsites. So far, unregulated camping in undesignated sites, which still requires a permit, has not been a problem, in part because campers need more equipment and skills that tend to limit their numbers. Those seeking more "developed" campsites concentrate on Stockton and Oak Islands or make use of mainland hotels and motels or private campgrounds. However, with unregulated, undesignated camping, the potential remains for future ecological impacts, particularly on sensitive areas such as the beaches and sand spits.

The real threats to the ecological integrity of the lakeshore come from outside, particularly from pollution drifting in from the atmosphere, or from sites in the Lake Superior watershed and from the threat of global climate change. The Lake Superior basin is threatened by contamination, such as pollution from waste dumps and industrial developments on both the Canadian and American sides of the lake. Acid deposition (acid rain) also contributes to pollutant loading, and toxic chemicals such as PCBs and mercury drift through the atmosphere. Hazardous toxins *are* present in lakeshore waters, as blood tests on bald eagles in the area demonstrate, even though some contaminants have been banned for many years. Because the pollutants show up in the bodies of fledglings, which have been fed on Lake Superior fish by their parents, it is clear that the contamination is in local waters.

Global climate change can significantly threaten existing ecosystems in the area, whether terrestrial or aquatic. Warming in temperature affects the plants and animals that thrive in the area. For example, lake waters have warmed by an average of 5 degrees since 1980.[23] While this makes swimming more pleasant, the warmer waters increase disease outbreaks in resident fish and

encourage invasive species. Local fishers currently report scarcities in populations of whitefish. On land, increased insect outbreaks bring challenges
for forest management. Warmer temperatures (and the early extermination
of larger predators) have also exacerbated the problem of deer populations;
greater numbers of deer have significantly impacted plant populations on the
islands, including those under stress from warmer temperatures. Dealing with
these threats will require a long-term, bi-national effort.

One unexpected outcome of climate change may be the drawdown in lake
water levels.[24] Under severe water drawdowns, the result might be that some
islands will cease to be islands and will become attached to other land masses.
This attachment would create land outside the park boundary, resulting in
jurisdictional and encroachment concerns.

Protecting the cultural resources in the lakeshore has been another concern
of the NPS. Protection has been both costly and administratively complex.
Protecting the lighthouses has meant protecting the shoreline from erosion, an
expensive undertaking. Protecting the shipwrecks from treasure-hunting divers has been rendered more difficult since the ownership of the lake bottom,
and the wrecks themselves, remains with the state of Wisconsin. While relations with the state have been good, administrative and legal policies still need
to be hammered out. Warming water temperatures are also increasing the rate
of decomposition of the shipwrecks, creating a conservation challenge that
few today have the resources to address.

Bad River and Red Cliff Reservations Today

The relations between the two reservations and the lakeshore have been mixed
over the years. It was the Bad River Tribal Council that initially called, in
1962, for a study of the sloughs by the secretary of the Interior. By 1970 tensions between the local tribes and Congress ran high, and tribal lands were
excluded from the lakeshore.

Fairly or not, some bitterness remains on the part of the tribes today over
the establishment of the lakeshore. The initial proposal and its elaborations
and the inclusion of reservation lands were carefully designed to ensure that
the lakeshore would result in considerable benefits for the two tribes. George
Hartzog, when testifying in Congress, noted that the benefits to the Indian
people were the best that he was aware of in the entire National Park System.
When these lands were deleted, the special preferences for Native Americans were also deleted. Conditions on the reservations have shown some
improvement, largely due to tribal initiatives, but considerable problems
remain.

Red Cliff Reservation

Of the two reservations, Red Cliff, because of its proximity to the lakeshore, has benefitted most;[25] relations between the tribe and the NPS are correspondingly better. Of the original 14,092.81 acres within the reservation, the tribe and individual members today hold 8,351 acres, the rest is owned by nontribal people. There are, however, ongoing efforts to recover these alienated lands. As the lands come up on the real estate market, the tribe has made an effort to acquire them. Bayfield County, in particular, has cooperated in these efforts, offering the tribe first option on tax-deed lands. They have had some success in acquiring alienated land on the eastern portion of the reservation within the original boundary of the lakeshore.

In 1991 Red Cliff recorded 5,312 members, 2,513 of which reside within the reservation. When the tribal lands were deleted, the configuration of the lakeshore changed dramatically. As a consequence, Native American preferences and opportunities for employment provided for in the original legislation were eliminated. However, the NPS has made a conscious effort to employ tribal members. For example, in 1972, five members were employed in the lakeshore, two permanently (including a maintenance foreman), one temporarily, and two seasonally.[26] In the summer of 2007, there were five permanent, full-time workers on the lakeshore staff who were Native Americans, with an additional five temporary staff who were Native American (17 percent of total lakeshore staff). While the overall numbers have not changed much in recent years, three of the permanent positions held by Native Americans were in professional or senior administrative positions.[27]

The lakeshore's presence has proved a benefit to the tribally owned campground and marina (both located in excellent locations with magnificent views of the islands), and there is usually a waiting list to get into the marina during the season. However, the tribe has kept no records of precise economic benefits, and it remains cautious of NPS intentions. As Richard Gurnoe, the 1991 tribal chair, commented, relations with the NPS are fine as long as the agency is not thinking of infringing on the tribe's lands and treaty rights, a view echoed by several other tribal members.[28] The roots of that concern are based, in part, on the legislative history of the lakeshore. Professional relationships between the lakeshore staff and the tribal council, as of 2008, remain cordial.

Bad River Reservation

Of the original 124,434 acres within the Bad River Reservation, the tribe and tribal members retain title to 57,884 acres.[29] The tribe is in the process of acquiring additional acres with the assistance of The Nature Conservancy. In

2008, of the over 6,945 members on the tribal rolls, about 1,500 were resident on the reservation or lived nearby. Within the reservation a number of initiatives have been completed or are underway to improve reservation conditions and generate employment, including a lodge and casino, and a cultural center. The tribe has also instituted one of the first reservation recycling programs in the state. Because the lakeshore is located a considerable distance from Odanah (except for Long Island), employment opportunities within the NPS have been more limited, and there has been little direct economic benefit. Instead, the tribe views the establishment of the lakeshore as creating some problems, especially with regard to natural resource management.

Relations with the NPS, both sides admit, have been less mutually profitable. In part this has been due to the tribe's past skepticism over NPS's goals for the region, which the tribe believes were biased toward tourism and recreation. One source of tension was the 1986 acquisition of Long Island, part of the Chequamegon sand spit that protects the sloughs. Private ownership of the island had afforded some protection from indiscriminate tourist use of the spit and the adjacent sloughs. With its inclusion in the lakeshore, the tribe claims, use has increased, not just on the island but also in the sloughs, leading to management problems. Official management, they felt, had been unnecessary prior to 1985; however, the inclusion of Long Island resulted in the need for an official management plan for the sloughs.

Bad River remains uneasy about the lakeshore and the NPS, although work between the NPS and its biologists on wildlife issues, particularly on the endangered piping plover, has been individually productive.

As of 2008 the lakeshore superintendent has been hammering out memorandums of understanding with both tribes to ensure that recently recognized treaty rights (the right to hunt, fish, and gather) can occur within lakeshore boundaries while protecting lakeshore values. This memorandum of understanding, it is hoped, will improve lakeshore-tribal relations into the future.[30]

Lessons Learned

The creation of the Apostle Islands National Lakeshore took years to accomplish. It called for persistence up to and through the addition of Long Island to the lakeshore in 1986. Careful planning was required, yet unanticipated external forces threatened the proposal from time to time: state arrests of Native Americans for violating state fishing and wild rice–harvesting laws, the Red Power movement, the freeze by the Bureau of the Budget of funding for new national park authorizations, and the insistence on the part of the NPS that the tribal lands were necessary before the lakeshore would be established. These situations and others called for patience and flexibility.

The addition of Long Island was, in a sense, an end to a process started almost a quarter century earlier with the 1962 Bad River Tribal Council resolution calling for the first study for a national lakeshore. Yet Long Island was not an ending. Additional steps will be needed in this part of northern Wisconsin—as elsewhere—to set aside natural and cultural resources for preservation, research, aesthetics, and outdoor recreation, through public and private actions and collaborative programs. Past struggles and future efforts form a continuum. The task will be complex, will take time, and will never be complete.

The Validity of an Idea

Although local proponents of a national park in the Apostle Islands in the 1930s recognized the disastrous impacts that logging and fires had had on the aesthetics of the archipelago, they intuitively felt that something special here deserved national recognition. Given the exploitive and short-term nature of natural resource extraction that had occurred, national park proponents also believed that capitalizing on the natural beauty of the region through tourism offered long-term benefits to their depressed economies.

When Governor Gaylord Nelson made his proposal to Secretary of the Interior Stewart Udall in 1962, the islands had naturally re-vegetated; the scars of the past were cloaked with new growth of northern hardwoods and conifers. In contrast to the short-term view of national park leaders in the 1930s, the planners and administrators of the 1960s were quick to recognize that the natural beauty of the area and its cultural values would make it a worthy addition to the National Park System. (Park planners should take a lesson from this experience. Landscapes, especially in humid regions, re-vegetate in reasonably short periods of time.) And although the unique Kakagon–Bad River Sloughs and a significant portion of the Bayfield Peninsula were eventually deleted, the lakeshore still consists of twenty-one islands with 154 miles of shoreline (one of the largest public shorelines in the entire Great Lakes system and substantially longer than any other lakeshore or seashore authorized during this era). NPS Director George Hartzog had argued with vigor that all three units—the islands, the sloughs, and the peninsula—were necessary for a worthy NPS project. He claimed this was a bargaining position, and although he and other proponents were disappointed, the final authorization still made up a magnificent area and one well worth working for.

Timing

The timing in the 1960s could not have been better. Gaylord Nelson was in his second term in the governor's office and was establishing himself as Wisconsin's "Conservation Governor" and as a national leader in that arena. John F. Kennedy had been elected president in 1960 and had appointed Stewart Udall to head the Department of the Interior. Fortuitously, Udall, early in his tenure, had made a personal commitment to double the National Park System. And Nelson, because of his conservation initiatives as governor, had come to Udall's attention. They readily became personal friends.

Some of the building blocks for what has been called the "third wave of the American conservation movement" were ready to be put in place and had relevance to a lakeshore in the Apostle Islands region: the Senate Select Committee on National Water Resources; the Outdoor Recreation Resources Review Commission; the 1930s NPS studies on vanishing sea coasts followed by shoreline studies in the Great Lakes in the 1950s; calls for a new federal grants-in-aid program for outdoor recreation (LAWCON); a public that perceived a crisis in outdoor recreation; the establishment of the Cape Cod National Seashore in 1961; and a host of new national seashore and lakeshore proposals.

Udall moved with alacrity. A new Bureau of Outdoor Recreation and a presidential Recreation Advisory Council were established; comprehensive outdoor recreation was the order of the day at the national, state, and local levels, and substantial new funds were available for outdoor recreation projects. All of these actions, and earlier building blocks, had high salience for the Bad River Tribal Council's call for a study of the Kakagon–Bad River Sloughs. Udall was quick to embrace Nelson's proposal for a study of a national recreation area in the sloughs. And when Bureau of Outdoor Recreation Director Edward Crafts a short time later suggested that the area for study include the islands and the Bayfield Peninsula, the idea was readily accepted. Also, both Udall and Nelson knew that in addition to the substantive issues of great interest and concern to them, conservation was good politics; it appealed to politicians on all sides of the political spectrum from conservative to liberal with strong, sustained support from the middle. In fact, Nelson had been elected to the U.S. Senate in no small measure with support from independents who liked his conservation programs.

One can only compare the environment for a new national park proposal in the Kennedy-Johnson-Udall era to that which existed in the Reagan-Watt era. An Apostle Islands National Lakeshore, in spite of its merits, would have been highly unlikely in the latter period. In fact, Reagan appointees in the USDI worked diligently to keep Long Island out of the lakeshore.

One last point with regard to timing: Nelson's staff (including myself) should have used their relationships with Secretary Udall more effectively to accomplish the planning task more rapidly. Because of our inexperence at the federal level, more than a year was lost (1962–63) testing various alternatives before the decision was made to establish a federal lakeshore. Two more full years (1963–65) would elapse before the planning documents were released to the public and Nelson introduced the bill. The goal during this period was to deal with each problem as it arose and to achieve consensus with the many bureaus in the USDI that would influence the final form of the legislation. Given their close association, Nelson could have prevailed upon Udall to cut through the numerous bureaucratic delays and obfuscation within the Department of the Interior that were experienced. This would have reduced the planning period by several years, which in turn might have meant that President Johnson would have endorsed the bill one year earlier and before he became increasingly entangled in the Vietnam War. Earlier action might also have avoided the conflicts with the Red Power movement, and the Red Cliff and Bad River Tribes would have had the opportunity to explore in detail with the NPS their most favorable options based on facts and the law, not on allegations and mis-truths.

Participant Continuity

Had there not been continuity on the part of participants supporting the lakeshore during the entire period that it was debated in Congress, the outcome might well have been different. Given the shoals and sometimes dangerous reefs the proposal had to navigate, it may well have floundered and sunk. This was especially true when the Red Power movement seized upon the lakeshore proposal as a cause célèbre, and when the presidential administration changed from Lyndon Johnson to Richard Nixon, who brought on board a pro-development secretary of the Interior, Walter Hickel. The new administration effectively stopped for a full year the Apostle Islands and other pending new park authorizations. However, Congress was still controlled by Democrats; committee chairs were the same, and key participants behind each new proposal, including the Apostle Islands, were still there. The momentum was slowed, but not stopped.

Gaylord Nelson as governor had sponsored the original proposal. He had been elected to the U.S. Senate in 1962 and even more successfully re-elected six years later. Nelson had a strong personal love for the area and devoted innumerable hours to the proposal over the years, and when the lakeshore was in serious jeopardy in the House of Representatives, he was there fighting every step of the way. Nelson, more than any other individual, provided the essential continuity and the tenacity to see the proposal through to completion.

Years later he reflected, "I was on the Interior Committee. If I hadn't been on the Interior Committee, we wouldn't have passed either the Apostle Islands bill or the St. Croix [Wild and Scenic River] bill because it just requires too much daily, monthly, yearly persistent pushing. Since I was on the committee, I could get hearings scheduled. . . . I could persuade the members that it was a good concept. That is probably one reason why it didn't get passed in the previous forty years, since there was no follow up."[31]

Continuity came through other critical participants in the process, including USDI Secretary Stewart Udall, BOR Director Edward Crafts, NPS Director George Hartzog, Senators Jackson and Bible, and Congressmen Aspinall and Taylor. Nelson had strong personal relations with these key people, and they were highly supportive. In addition, the support of Congressman Bob Kastenmeier, newspaper reporters John Chapple and Chick Sheridan, brothers Louis Hanson and Martin Hanson, Culver Prentice, and Patrick Lucey was essential, as was my participation in working on the proposal from 1962 to its enactment in 1970 and beyond. Too numerous to mention were those supporters in the media, in conservation organizations, and in other public and private agencies, as well as citizens. Over the years the same faces appeared and reappeared at critical junctures in the process. Their sustained support and their willingness to write letters, drive long miles to testify at hearings, give talks, and attend meetings was critical to final enactment.

As the Apostle Islands proposal was wending its way through the Congress, activists in the state of Minnesota were following a similar path in enacting Voyageurs National Park during the same time period. Continuity was critical to the Apostle Islands, as it was to Voyageurs—although there had been interest in the northern Minnesota area for a "national park" of some sort from before the turn of the century, and various studies had been conducted in the region.

Governor Elmer L. Anderson, in a 1962 public address to local, state, and federal officials, as well as the public, called for studies on establishing a national park in the Kabetogama area, a large peninsula along the U.S.-Canadian border. This was a clarion call for action, which the governor placed before the people of Minnesota. Long after he had left the governor's office, he continued to use his public reputation to support and work toward a national park. Some forty-two years later, in a preface to Fred Witzig's book on Voyageurs National Park, he wrote, "people never lose when pursuing a worthy cause . . . substantial public improvements take time to accomplish. They do not happen overnight . . . they happen when interested people devote themselves for a long time in tireless effort to achieve a worthy goal."[32] He was a political/public leader akin to Gaylord Nelson, who also pursued a worthy cause. The public can indeed be grateful for Nelson's long, tireless effort to create the Apostle Island National Lakeshore.

Presidential Leadership

John F. Kennedy had set the stage with his message on conservation to Congress in February 1961, the first such message in decades. A second message followed a year later. In addition to the traditional pro-resource development and conservation management programs for the West, he called for new additions to the National Park System to build upon the precedent set in 1961 by the establishment of the Cape Cod National Seashore, which was the first park established for which funding was authorized by the federal government. Congress was quick to respond and introduced numerous bills for additional national seashores and lakeshores. The president's visit to the Apostle Islands, with Martin Hanson as tour guide, put the proposal on the front page of the nation's newspapers and brought it to the attention of people in Wisconsin and elsewhere. It also notified key policy and political decision makers that indeed there was something worthy of national attention in northern Wisconsin. Kennedy's visit and his comments pledging federal assistance to the region were immeasurably important to those who had to wage the long, arduous struggle to get the lakeshore enacted.

Lyndon Johnson continued the Kennedy programs and indeed expanded them greatly. More significant conservation and environmental legislation was enacted in his five years as president than at any other period in our history. The Apostle Islands National Lakeshore was one element in that agenda (although not authorized until Nixon was in office), and although it is possible to secure approval of new parks that are not a part of a president's program, presidential support was (and is) enormously important in cutting through the myriad bureaucracies that exert influence over such proposals. This was especially true for the Apostle Islands, given the complexities of the proposal, especially as it related to tribal matters. In spite of Johnson's support, the nation's increasing involvement in Vietnam put enormous pressure on the federal budget, and in lieu of asking Congress to enact the lakeshore proposal in 1966 (Nelson had introduced the bill in 1965), Johnson called for additional studies. In 1967 he fully endorsed the proposal and called for action by

Congress, a significant step, but the loss of a full year provided additional time for the Red Power movement to gather strength, a factor that dramatically influenced final lakeshore boundaries after having almost killed the proposal.

With the election of Richard Nixon, the future of the lakeshore was uncertain. This became eminently clear early in 1969, when NPS officials, testifying on the Apostle Islands, raised grave concerns regarding the lack of funding for existing projects, let alone new authorizations. Some months later, the Bureau of the Budget, in an effort to slow the growth in the federal budget and ostensibly to control inflation, froze new park spending. Aspinall immediately canceled all hearings on new parks. Had it not been for that, the lakeshore might well have been enacted in 1969. As it turned out, another full year was lost.

Perhaps the Nixon administration recognized the political hazard of stopping all new park proposals; perhaps Walter Hickel needed political support for his new urban parks programs. In any event, the administration made the decision not to stop new parks in rural regions and to push the new Urban Parks Program by requesting substantial funding additions to the Lands and Waters Conservation Fund. That decision in 1970 made enactment of the lakeshore possible, and although some worried that Nixon might veto the legislation because of Native American unrest and a reduced boundary that brought into question national status for the area, he did not do so. Perhaps he also recognized the strong bipartisan support the bill had and that a veto may well have been overridden, an event any president wishes to avoid, especially on a relatively minor issue.

Lakeshore Planning Strategies

The current management plan fits the original congressional intent nicely; 97 percent of the lakeshore was identified as a "natural zone" that in turn qualified these lands as wilderness when in 2004 Congress established the Gaylord Nelson Wilderness Area. In the 1960s, no one envisioned the recreation explosion in snowmobiling, mountain biking, cross-country skiing, scuba diving, and sea kayaking. As outdoor recreation technologies advance, and they will, the islands will be threatened more and more by unpredictable human impacts. Limiting motorized equipment of any kind on the islands and on adjacent water will achieve a long-range goal of ensuring a quiet zone so critical for a wilderness experience. It would have been preferable to protect some of the adjacent water as wilderness, but according to Lakeshore Superintendent Krumenaker, politically this would never have gone through.[33] Exceptions for the occasional commercial fisherman, the excursion boat, and water taxis would be reminders to the transient visitor that indeed solitude in an environment largely void of human noises is an opportunity that is rare and one to be treasured. Eventually limits on use will be required to maintain a quality outdoor experience.

In retrospect, the suggestion for a national monument on Madeline Island should also have been pursued more vigorously with representatives of the State Historical Society of Wisconsin, with recognized historians in the area, and with a cross section of NPS historians. Madeline Island has the greatest historical significance of any site in western Lake Superior. Although many of the sites had been destroyed at the time of the Department of the Interior subcommittee study, a carefully developed, justifiable report on the significance of the island to the region's history and the potential for interpreting that history would have made for a persuasive case with Congress to establish a monument. Moreover, only a modest amount of private land would have been required. Under the circumstances at the time of the USDI subcommittee study, we were too quick to accept the judgment of one historian in the NPS who did not favor the idea.

Also, the third boundary recommended by the NPS in its first preliminary master plan for the lakeshore is the one that the subcommittee should have recommended. The twenty-one islands and the lake bottom were included in their entirety, which would have meant, in the transfer of the state islands, an additional 184,000 acres of lake bottom. This contrasts with the authorized one-quarter mile water boundary, which does not include the lake bottom. The lake bottom would have included the important cultural resources, shipwrecks especially, that rest there. Unfortunately, the importance of lake bottom cultural resources for management by the NPS was not raised either in the congressional debate or at the time of the state land transfer. The subcommittee was too quick to accept the fourth boundary, which reduced the shoreline area to thirty miles on the peninsula and confined the land area to a narrow strip; a reduction from 50,000 to 6,000 acres. The water boundary was also eliminated. At the time, however, the decision seemed reasonable. Some private landowner opposition, and probable opposition from some residents of the village of Cornucopia, was avoided. Moreover, the narrow strip of land was adequate for a scenic highway and for hiking trails, campsites, and other recreational facilities. The highway especially would receive the heaviest use of any portion of the lakeshore, and it did help considerably in meeting federal criteria that required that recreation areas provide opportunities for large numbers of recreationists. More thought should have been given to G. M. Lamb's recommendations in the 1930s that the Bayfield Peninsula strip should be at least twenty miles long and *three or four miles in width*, and also to the 1930s Cape Hatteras precedent stressing that boundaries reach to the hinterlands important for scientific, historical, and scenic purposes. (We were not aware of this history.)

This history brings out nicely the values of interdisciplinary planning. With the planning authorities granted by the secretary of the Interior, specialized knowledge on the many complex issues in the lakeshore could be brought to bear: attorneys, geologists, foresters, landscape architects, recreation planners, mineral and water experts, fish and wildlife biologists, and historians all contributed. The participants not only brought their specialized knowledge to the task at hand, but they also helped to ensure that their agencies would support the proposal. As noted earlier, cultural history was the only subject that could have benefited from a broader base of knowledge and perspective.

Bad River and Red Cliff Tribes

Lakeshore proponents acted in good faith with the two local tribes from the time of the 1962 Bad River Tribal Council Resolution through enactment in 1970. All of the conditions in the original resolution that could be met were met.

One of the problems encountered with the tribes was the frequent and rapid turnover of tribal chairs. During the period the lakeshore was under consideration there were eleven different chairs; five at Bad River and six at Red Cliff. Regardless of political changes on the reservations, we kept the Native Americans informed of every step in the process. The involvement by non-Natives in engendering Native American hostility to the proposal was obviously something over which there was little control.

Would it have been possible to handle tribal issues differently? Ideally, if the tribal councils had had sufficient staff (which they did not), they could have developed the proposal, and the Department of the Interior employees could have served as technical advisors when requested (given the lack of tribal staff resources evident when the Bad River Tribal Council requested Nelson find funds for an attorney to represent their interests in the House hearings, which Nelson did). Had they struggled with the many complex issues raised in the planning process and with the political and bureaucratic forces that had to be dealt with, the final product would have been theirs, and although it might have been similar to the lakeshore legislation it might well have been different. In effect, they would have been bargaining with the federal government for the best possible package they could put together, not the other way around, where it appeared to them that we were bargaining with them.

Had the tribes done the planning, what might have evolved? For example, they might have developed plans for a Native American national park on the peninsula and in the sloughs that would be managed in conjunction with NPS management of the islands. The NPS could act in a technical and advisory role and perhaps as a source of funds for capital developments and management, as was done in a proposal for a Grand Portage Monument in collaboration with the NPS and the Grand Portage Tribal Council (with which I was also involved), but it too was caught in the crossfire of the Red Power movement and was killed.

Another scenario might have been the development of tribally run parks on the two reservations without the technical and financial assistance of the NPS. Funding such a strategy would have been difficult and would have probably required admission fees to offset costs. The complicated problems of fractionated ownership, allotments, and alienated lands would also have to be resolved to make for viable tribal parks. Under these scenarios, or that of the lakeshore as it was proposed, the Native Americans would still have faced the question of permitting the public to use their limited tribal acreage for recreation. The question then was, and is, would they?

Lastly, the lakeshore plan could have been developed solely around the islands, and as Nelson observed in 1970 House hearings, all the arguments could have been avoided if the tribal lands had not been included at all.

Thoughts for the Future

Any number of excellent ideas surfaced during the long debate over the lakeshore that were not implemented. The natural resources of the region are obviously still there and have not been destroyed by irreversible development. Today, new programs and approaches could be tested for their substantive and political acceptability. The Apostle Islands National Lakeshore does not exist in a vacuum; it cannot stand alone. What happens around it is even more important than what happens within it. Thus, the people in the region—the citizens, political leaders, government employees—have a responsibility to care for the maintenance of the Lake Superior ecosystem that in the long run will determine the health and vitality of the lakeshore.

Appendix One

A CHRONOLOGY OF SIGNIFICANT EVENTS REGARDING
THE APOSTLE ISLANDS NATIONAL LAKESHORE

August 1928	President Calvin Coolidge visits the Apostle Islands
January 11, 1930	A bill to authorize a study of the Apostle Islands for a national park (enacted May 9, 1930)
January 20, 1931	Report by Harlan P. Kelsey recommending that a national park not be created in the Apostle Islands
August 1931	Second National Park Service investigation of a proposed national park in the Apostles
1934–35	The National Park Service recommends that Wisconsin create a state park in the Apostle Islands
1935	Joint resolution of the Wisconsin Legislature to investigate a state park in the Apostle Islands and to inquire regarding a national park
1935	Third National Park Service study of a national park in the Apostle Islands
March 19, 1936	Conrad L. Wirth closes the file on a proposed national park in the Apostle Islands
1939	The Wisconsin State Planning Board recommends a state park in the Apostle Islands
1940s	World War II interrupts planning for state or national parks, including the Apostle Islands
March 1950	Milwaukee County Conservation Alliance calls for a study on the feasibility of acquiring all of the Apostle Islands
1955	Joint resolution of the Wisconsin Legislature for the possible acquisition of the Apostle Islands

August 1955	Approval by the Wisconsin Conservation Commission of a "Policy on Acquisition of an Apostle Islands Wilderness Area"
January 1959	Wisconsin Conservation Department buys Stockton Island
January 1959	Wisconsin Conservation Department establishes the Apostle Islands State Forest consisting of Oak, Stockton, Basswood, Hermit, and Manitou Islands
May 10, 1962	Bad River Tribal Council requests a study of the feasibility of the establishment of a "National Shoreline-Recreational Area" in the Bad River Reservation
May 22, 1962	Wisconsin Governor Gaylord A. Nelson presents the Bad River Tribal Council Resolution to Secretary of the Interior Stewart Udall
June 11, 1962	Edward Crafts, director of the Bureau of Outdoor Recreation, inspects the area
1963	President's Recreation Advisory Council establishes criteria for National Recreation Areas
January 26, 1963	Citizens' Committee for an Apostle Islands National Lakeshore established
March 25, 1963	First draft bill prepared on the Apostle Islands National Lakeshore
September 1963	First National Park Service master plan
September 24, 1963	President John F. Kennedy visits the Apostle Islands
October 22, 1963	Decision made not to have the lakeshore be a collaborative federal-state project
April 4, 1964	Secretary Udall establishes the Department of the Interior's North Central Field Committee's Subcommittee
November 11, 1964	Second draft bill prepared
January 7, 1965	Third draft bill prepared
Early 1965	Fourth and fifth draft bills prepared
March 1965	Sixth draft bill prepared
March 15, 1965	North Central Field Committee's Subcommittee Report submitted to Washington
July 1965	Seventh draft bill prepared
August 27, 1965	Eighth draft bill prepared

August 28, 1965	Public release and meeting on the Report of the North Central Field Committee's Subcommittee
September 7, 1965	U.S. Senate bill S. 2498 to establish the lakeshore introduced
September 8, 1965	U.S. House of Representatives bill H.R. 10902 to establish the lakeshore introduced
October 1965	Red Cliff Tribe has float on Apostle Islands in Apple Festival Parade; Tribal Council endorses lakeshore
October 10, 1965	Bad River Tribal Council opposes lakeshore
February 2, 1966	President Lyndon B. Johnson calls for completing studies on the Apostle Islands National Lakeshore
January 30, 1967	President Johnson calls for an Apostle Islands National Lakeshore
February 1967	Bad River Tribal Council endorses the lakeshore
June 1967	Red Cliff Tribal Council neutral regarding lakeshore
June 2, 1967	Wisconsin Governor Warren Knowles and the Wisconsin Conservation Commission endorse the Apostle Islands National Lakeshore
June 1–2, 1967	First U.S. Senate Hearings on the lakeshore
August 21, 1967	Senate passes lakeshore bill
1968	Richard M. Nixon elected president; Walter Hickel appointed Secretary of the Interior
January 1968	National Park Service prepares a new lakeshore master plan
July 29, 1968	Second Senate hearings on the lakeshore
March 13, 1969	Red Cliff Tribal Council in opposition to lakeshore
March 17, 1969	Third Senate hearings on the lakeshore
June 26, 1969	Senate passes lakeshore bill
August 19, 1969	First House hearings on the lakeshore
August 19, 1969	Bad River Tribal Council in opposition to lakeshore
September 1969	The Nixon administration calls for a freeze on new park authorizations; all national recreation and park hearings are canceled
February 2, 1970	President Nixon increases funding for LAWCON
March 23–24 and June 3, 1970	Second House hearings on the lakeshore

March 23–24, 1970	Red Cliff and Bad River Tribal Councils state opposition to lakeshore
July 7, 1970	House passes lakeshore bill
September 26, 1970	President Nixon signs the Apostle Islands National Lakeshore Bill
August 13, 1975	Wisconsin Governor Patrick Lucey signs act transferring state lands to the National Park Service
April 23, 1985	Congressman David Obey introduces legislation to include Long Island in the lakeshore
October 17, 1988	President Ronald Reagan signs bill including Long Island in the lakeshore

Appendix Two

Participants frequently occupied a number of different positions during the lakeshore history. They are identified here in their major roles. Only people who played a significant role are listed.

Anderson, Norman C., chair of the Wisconsin State Assembly Committee on Conservation

Appelbaum, Stuart, staff assistant to Congressman Robert Kastenmeier

Aspinall, Wayne N., chair of the U.S. House of Representatives Committee on Interior and Insular Affairs

Baker, John, "On Wisconsin" editorial writer for the *Milwaukee Journal*

Beale, John, chief state forester, Wisconsin Conservation Department

Bechtel, William, administrative assistant to U.S. Senator Gaylord A. Nelson

Belindo, John, executive director of the National Congress of American Indians

Bender, Bob, chair of the Bad River Tribal Council

Besadny, Carroll D., secretary of the Wisconsin Department of Natural Resources

Brewer, William C., Bayfield Peninsula landowner

Brodie, James, Brodie Engineering Corporation of St. Paul, Minnesota

Bromberg, William, first superintendent of the Apostle Islands National Lakeshore

Caldwell, William, Bayfield Peninsula landowner

Carley, David, director of the Wisconsin Department of Resource Development

Caulfield, Henry P., director of Resources Program Staff, Office of the Secretary, U.S. Department of the Interior

Chapple, John, owner, editor, and reporter, *Ashland Daily Press*

Connors, Chuck, member of the Bad River Tribe and employee of the Wisconsin Department of Natural Resources

Connors, Fred, chair of the Bad River Tribal Council

Crafts, Edward P., director of the Bureau of Outdoor Recreation, U.S. Department of the Interior

DeMain, Paul, member of the Lac Courte Oreilles Tribe and advisor to Wisconsin Governor Anthony Earl

Dexter, Frank, owner and editor, *Bayfield County Press*

Dodge, Steve, member of the Menominee Tribe and employee of the Wisconsin Department of Natural Resources

Dryer, William R., biologist, Bureau of Commercial Fisheries, U.S. Department of the Interior

Edmunds, Allen T., planner, National Park Service, U.S. Department of the Interior

Edwards, Rodney, attorney for the Bad River Tribal Council

Fairfield, William, press secretary to Governor Gaylord A. Nelson

Feil, Andrew, planner, National Park Service, U.S. Department of the Interior

Fleischer, Ruth, staff assistant to U.S. Senator William Proxmire

Gehrmann, Bernard, assemblyman, Wisconsin Legislature

Germain, Cliff, ecologist, Wisconsin Department of Natural Resources

Granum, Benedict, staff assistant, Bureau of Indian Affairs, U.S. Department of the Interior

Granum, Griffith Edward, Wisconsin's first state forester

Gross, Harold, attorney, National Congress of American Indians

Haglund, Brent, executive director of the Wisconsin Chapter of The Nature Conservancy

Hanson, Louis J., Apostle Islands National Lakeshore supporter

Hanson, Martin, Apostle Islands National Lakeshore supporter

Harrington, Cornelius L., superintendent, Division of State Parks and Forests, Wisconsin Conservation Department

Hartzog, George B., Jr., director, National Park Service. U.S. Department of the Interior

Hawkes, Elizabeth, attorney, Red Cliff Tribal Council

Heritage, John, staff assistant to U.S. Senator Gaylord A. Nelson

Hickel, Walter, secretary, U.S. Department of the Interior

Hokensen, Robert, Bayfield Peninsula landowner

Hovind, Ralph B., planner, Wisconsin Department of Resource Development

Hummell, Edward, associate director, National Park Service, U.S. Department of the Interior

Jackson, Candace, attorney, Bad River Tribal Council

Jensch, S. W., Bayfield Peninsula landowner, retired administrative law judge residing in Maryland

Johnson, C. E., superintendent, Isle Royale National Park, U.S. Department of the Interior

Johnson, Sam, Chequamegon Point landowner

Jordahl, Harold C., Jr., held a variety of positions within the Wisconsin Department of Resource Development; regional coordinator for the Resources Program staff of the Office of the Secretary, U.S. Department of the Interior; alternate and acting federal co-chair, Upper Great Lakes Regional Commission

Jurgens, Willard E., Bayfield Peninsula landowner

Kasten, Robert, U.S. senator, Wisconsin

Kastenmeier, Robert, U.S. congressman, Wisconsin

Klein, Thomas, executive director, Sigurd Olson Environmental Institute, Ashland, Wisconsin

Knowles, Warren, governor of the state of Wisconsin

Koenings, Roman, superintendent, Division of State Parks and Forests, Wisconsin Conservation Department, and later regional director, Bureau of Outdoor Recreation, U.S. Department of the Interior

Koons, W. B., reporter, *Ashland Daily Press*

Krumenaker, Robert, third superintendent of the Apostle Islands National Lakeshore

Kuhns, Richard, Bayfield Peninsula landowner

LaFollette, Bronson, attorney general of the state of Wisconsin

Lee, Ronald F., regional director, National Park Service, U.S. Department of the Interior

Lewis, Philip, landscape architect, Wisconsin Department of Resource Development

Lucey, Patrick, governor of the state of Wisconsin

Lynch, R. G., outdoor editor, *Milwaukee Journal*

Mackie, Donald J., superintendent of state parks and forests, Wisconsin Conservation Department

MacQuarrie, Gordon, outdoor reporter, *Milwaukee Journal*

Matteson, Summer, biologist, Wisconsin Department of Natural Resources

McElvain, Lee, staff director for the U.S. House of Representatives Committee on Interior and Insular Affairs

McFadzean, William G., chair of the Apostle Islands Residents Committee

Messinger, Clifford, chair of the Wisconsin Chapter, The Nature Conservancy

Miller, Pat, second superintendent of the Apostle Islands National Lakeshore

Mittness, Lewis T., chair of the Wisconsin State Assembly Committee on Conservation

Moody, James, U.S. congressman, Wisconsin

Mott, William Penn, Jr., director of the National Park Service, U.S. Department of the Interior

Nash, Philleo, commissioner of the Bureau of Indian Affairs, U.S. Department of the Interior

Nelson, Gaylord A., governor of the state of Wisconsin and later U.S. senator for Wisconsin

Neuberger, Neil, staff assistant to U.S. congressman David Obey, Wisconsin

Nicotera, Ron, biologist for the Wisconsin Department of Natural Resources

Obey, David, U.S. congressman, Wisconsin

O'Konski, Alvin, U.S. congressman, Wisconsin

Olson, Sigurd, chair of the Wilderness Society

Peters, Bud, logger and landowner, Sand Island, Wisconsin

Peterson, Mark, executive director of the Sigurd Olson Environmental Institute, Ashland, Wisconsin

Pinchot, Gifford, first U.S. forester

Potter, Howard, staff assistant, Bureau of Indian Affairs, U.S. Department of the Interior

Prentice, Dr. B. C., chair of the Citizens' Committee for an Apostle Islands National Lakeshore

Proxmire, William E., U.S. senator, Wisconsin

Rahr, Guido, chair of the Wisconsin Natural Resources Board

Reuss, Henry, U.S. congressman, Wisconsin

Reynolds, John, governor of the state of Wisconsin

Riley, Emmett, superintendent of the Great Lakes Indian Agency, Bureau of Indian Affairs, U.S. Department of the Interior

Schumacher, Donald F., Bayfield Peninsula landowner

Shanklin, John, assistant director of the Bureau of Outdoor Recreation, U.S. Department of the Interior

Shefchik, Frank, chair of the Ashland County Board, Wisconsin

Sheridan, Charles (Chick), reporter, *Washburn Times*

Sigler, Lewis, attorney, Office of the Solicitor, U.S. Department of the Interior

Smith, Charley F. (Frosty), chair of the Wisconsin Conservation Commission

Sprecher, George E., assistant director of the Wisconsin Conservation Department

Stoddard, Charles H., director of the Bureau of Land Management, U.S. Department of the Interior

Swem, Theodore, assistant director of the National Park Service, U.S. Department of the Interior

Swift, Ernest, director of the Wisconsin Conservation Department

Todd, Kenneth, chair of the Ashland County Board, Wisconsin

Udall, Morris, member of the U.S. House of Representatives Committee on Interior and Insular Affairs

Udall, Stewart, secretary of the U.S. Department of the Interior

Vennum, Dr. Thomas, Jr., ethnomusicologist, Smithsonian Institute

Vento, Bruce F., chair of the U.S. House of Representatives Subcommittee on National Parks and Recreation of the Committee on Interior and Insular Affairs

Voigt, Lester P., director of the Wisconsin Conservation Department

Vrooman, David V., attorney, Field Office of the Solicitor, U.S. Department of the Interior

Vukelich, George, environmental conservation writer

Wallin, Victor, assemblyman, Wisconsin Legislature

Westhagen, Eric P., chair of the Apostle Islands Wilderness Council

Whiffen, Larry, chair of the Milwaukee County Conservation Alliance

Whittpenn, Richard, planner, National Park Service, U.S. Department of the Interior

Wilson, Archie, Long Island landowner

Woerpel, Les, chair of the Wisconsin Federation of Conservation Clubs

Appendix Three

Senate

1.	September 7, 1965	S. 2498 by Senators Nelson, Proxmire, and Douglas
2.	January 31, 1967	S. 778 by Senators Nelson and Proxmire (the same bill as S. 2498)
	February 18, 1967	U.S. Department of the Interior letter report
	August 21, 1967	Senate passes bill
3.	January 24, 1969	S. 621 by Senator Nelson (the same bill as S. 778 as passed by the Senate)
	January 16, 1969	U.S. Department of the Interior letter report
	June 26, 1969	Senate passes bill

House

1.	September 8, 1965	H.R. 10902 by Congressman O'Konski (the same bill as S. 2498)
2.	September 26, 1967	H.R. 13124 by Congressmen Kastenmeier, O'Konski, Anderson, Byrnes, Conyers, Dingell, Ford, Fraser, Griffiths, Karth, Laird, McClory, Quie, Reuss, Steiger, and Mr. Zablocki (Companion bill, H.R. 10427 by Congressman Kastenmeier); H.R. 10427 and H.R. 13124 are the same as S. 778 as passed by the Senate
	July 27, 1968	U.S. Department of the Interior letter report
3.	January 3, 1969	H.R. 555 by Congressman Kastenmeier (the same bill as S. 621 as passed by the Senate; H.R. 9306 and H.R. 555 are the same bills)
	March 19, 1970	U.S. Department of the Interior letter report on S. 621 as passed by the Senate and H.R. 555

4. March 20, 1969   H.R. 9306 by Congressmen Kastenmeier, O'Kinski, Byrnes, Conyers, Dingell, Ford, Fraser, Griffiths, Karth, Reuss, Steiger, and Mr. Zablocki (the same as S. 621 as passed by the Senate); H.R. 9306 was passed by the Congress and signed into law

Notes

Introduction

1. The term *national lakeshore* identifies a specific geographical area on the Great Lakes included within the U.S. National Park system. A lakeshore was classified specifically as a "recreation area" and as separate and distinct within National Park Service policy from national parks. In the text we use lakeshore and park rather interchangeably, and we intend the same meaning.

2. Harold C. Jordahl Jr., with Kathleen Lidfors, Annie Booth, and Carl Liller, *A Unique Collection of Islands: The Influence of History, Politics, and Planning on the Establishment of the Apostle Islands National Lakeshore* (Madison: Department of Urban and Regional Planning, University of Wisconsin–Extension, 1994), www.nps.gov/history/history/online_books/apis/apostle.pdf (accessed January 3, 2011).

Chapter 1. The Apostle Islands in Historical Context

1. This chapter owes significantly to contributions by Kathleen Lidfors, formerly a historian with Apostle Islands National Lakeshore in Bayfield, Wisconsin.

2. Emmet J. Judziewicz and Rudy G. Koch, "Flora and Vegetation of the Apostle Islands National Lakeshore and Madeline Island, Ashland and Bayfield Counties, Wisconsin," *Michigan Botanist* 32, no. 2 (March 1993): 68.

3. Edward B. Nuhfer and Mary P. Dalles, *A Guidebook to the Geology of the Apostle Islands National Lakeshore* (Dubuque, IA: W. C. Brown, 1987), 6–8.

4. George Irving Quimby, *Indian Life in the Upper Great Lakes, 11,000 B.C. to A.D. 1800* (Chicago: University of Chicago Press, 1960), 22–26.

5. Robert B. Brander, *Environmental Assessment: Natural Resources Inventory and Management* (Bayfield, WI: U.S. Department of the Interior, National Park Service, Apostle Islands National Lakeshore, 1981), 43–47.

6. William Green, James B. Stoltman, and Alice B. Kehoe, eds., "Introduction

to Wisconsin Archeology: Background for Cultural Resource Planning," *Wisconsin Archeologist* 67 (September–December 1986): 163–395; and Robert J. Salzer, "Other Late Woodland Developments," *Wisconsin Archeologist* 67 (September–December 1986): 302–13.

7. Nearby, on the mainland, a site located on an extinct beach in the Glacial Lake Duluth stage has yielded a pre-ceramic assemblage of stone tools manufactured from nonlocal stone cherts that probably predate 10,000 BC. See Robert J. Salzer and David F. Overstreet, *Inventory and Evaluation of Cultural Resources within the Apostle Islands National Lakeshore, Wisconsin* (Washington, DC: National Park Service, 1976), 29–30.

8. Robert A. Birmingham and Robert J. Salzer, "Test Evacuations at the P-Flat Site" (unpublished manuscript on file at the Logan Museum of Anthropology, Beloit College, Beloit, WI, 1980); Jeffrey J. Richner, *Archeological Investigations at Apostle Islands National Lakeshore, 1979–1980* (Lincoln, NE: U.S. Department of the Interior, National Park Service, Midwest Archeological Center, 1987); and Beverly A. Smith, and Charles E. Cleland, "Analysis of the Faunal Materials from Test Unit 1 of the P-Flat Site, Manitou Island, Lake Superior" (report to the Midwest Archeological Center, United States National Park Service), (Lincoln, NE: June 2, 1982).

9. Reuben Goldthwaites, ed., *The Jesuit Relations and Allied Documents: Travels and Explorations of the Jesuit Missionaries in New France, 1661–1791*, vol. 51 (Cleveland, OH: Burrows Bros., 1896–1901); Radisson 1885, as cited in Salzer and Birmingham, "Test Evacuations."

10. Salzer and Birmingham, "Test Evacuations," 16.

11. John O. Holzhueter, *Madeline Island and the Chequamegon Region* (Madison: State Historical Society of Wisconsin, 1974), 18–20; and Hamilton N. Ross, *La Pointe: Village Outpost* (Ann Arbor, MI: Edwards Bros., 1960), 46–48.

12. James D. Butler, "Early Shipping on Lake Superior," *Wisconsin Historical Society Proceedings* (1895), 87.

13. For a discussion of the emergence of the Ojibwe Nation, see Harold Hickerson, *Ethnohistory of Chippewa of Lake Superior*, American Indian Ethnohistory: North Central and Northeastern Indians, Chippewa Indians, vol. 3 (New York: Garland, 1974).

14. Ross, *La Pointe*, 61–63.

15. Holzhueter, *Madeline Island*, 27–29.

16. Arnold R. Alanen, "Early Agriculture within the Boundaries of the Apostle Islands National Lakeshore: An Overview" (report prepared for the staff of the Apostle Islands National Lakeshore), (Madison: University of Wisconsin–Madison, Department of Landscape Architecture, June 1985), 15; see also *Bayfield Press*, June 13, 1871.

17. Ross, *La Pointe*, 109.

18. Holzhueter, *Madeline Island*, 48–49.

19. Ibid., 44, 50–51.

20. Ross, *La Pointe*, 119.

21. James W. Feldman, "Rewilding the Islands: Nature, History and Policy at the Apostle Islands National Lakeshore" (PhD diss., University of Wisconsin–Madison, 2004).

22. Charles Twining, "Logging on the Apostle Islands: A 19th Century Overview" (unpublished manuscript on file at the Apostle Islands National Lakeshore, Bayfield, WI, 1981), 11–13, 16.

23. Ernest R. Buckley, *Building and Ornamental Stones of Wisconsin*, Wisconsin Geological and Natural History Survey Bulletin 4 (Madison, 1898), 179.

24. *Bayfield County Press*, May 29, 1958; see also "Boutin" in the files of the Bayfield Heritage Association, Bayfield, WI.

25. See Feldman, "Rewilding the Islands," for a discussion of the peripheral economies of the time.

26. Peter A. Rathbun and Mary Yeater Rathbun, "Special History Study: Historic Tourism and Recreation in the Apostle Islands Archipelago" (draft report to the National Park Service, Midwest Region), (Omaha, NE: August 1987), 27.

27. For a discussion of life as a lighthouse keeper, including as a host for interested tourists, see Jim Feldman, "What Do You Do Up Here? Tales of a Lake Superior Lighthouse Keeper," *Wisconsin Magazine of History* 84, no. 4 (2001): 2–15.

28. William H. Tishler, Arnold R. Alanen, and George Thompson, *Early Agricultural Development on the Apostle Islands (Lake Superior, Wisconsin): A Report Prepared for the Staff of the Apostle Islands National Lakeshore, Bayfield, Wisconsin* (Madison: University of Wisconsin–Madison, Department of Landscape Architecture, 1983), 18–19.

29. Alanen, "Early Agriculture," 20.

30. Ibid., 2–6.

31. Holzhueter, *Madeline Island*, 54.

32. Twining, *Logging on the Apostle Islands*, 7.

33. Alanen, "Early Agriculture," 13–14, 23–24.

34. Ross, *La Pointe*, 158.

35. Holzhueter, *Madeline Island*, 57.

36. "Camp Stella," historical files, Apostle Islands National Lakeshore, Bayfield, WI.

37. Peter A. Rathbun, "Special History Study: Commercial Fishing in the Apostle Islands" (draft report to the National Park Service, Midwest Region), (Omaha, NE: September 1987), 67.

38. Ibid., 70.

39. For a recent report on the human activities and resources that occurred throughout the Apostle Islands prior to its designation as a National Park Service property in 1969, see Jane C. Busch, *People and Places: A Human History of the Apostle Islands* (Omaha, NE: Midwest Regional Office, National Park Service, 2008).

Chapter 2. The Apostle Islands National Lakeshore in Political Context

1. Kathleen Lidfors, former National Park Service historian, and Carl Liller, a graduate student at the University of Wisconsin–Madison, collaborated on this chapter.

2. Ronald A. Foresta, *America's National Parks and Their Keepers* (Washington, DC: Resources for the Future, 1984), 11.

3. For an extensive history of this key debate see the discussion in Roderick Nash, *Wilderness and the American Mind* (New Haven, CT: Yale University Press, 1967).

4. Ronald F. Lee, *Family Tree of the National Park System* (Philadelphia: Eastern National Park and Monument Association, 1972), 9–15; Foresta, *America's National Parks*, 16–20.

5. William C. Everhart, *The National Park Service* (New York: Praeger, 1972); Robert Shankland, *Steve Mather of the National Parks* (New York: Knopf, 1951).

6. John Ise, *Our National Park Policy: A Critical History* (Baltimore: Johns Hopkins University Press for Resources for the Future, 1961), 364.

7. Edwin M. Fitch and John F. Shanklin, *The Bureau of Outdoor Recreation* (New York: Praeger, 1970), 46–49.

8. Carol Ahlgren, "The Civilian Conservation Corps and Wisconsin State Park Development," *Wisconsin Magazine of History* 71, no. 3 (Spring 1988): 184–204.

9. Foresta, *America's National Parks*, 35–37.

10. Ise, *Our National Park Policy*, 367–69; Harlan D. Unrau and G. Frank Willis, *Administrative History: Expansion of the NPS in the 1930s* (Washington, DC: National Park Service, 1983), 129ff; Lee, *Family Tree*, 20, 52–60; Foresta, *America's National Parks*, 43–47.

11. Ise, *Our National Park Policy*, 367; National Park Service, *A Study of the Park and Recreation Problem of the United States* (Washington, DC: U.S. Department of the Interior, 1941), v; National Park Service, *Prospectus of Cape Hatteras National Seashore* (Washington, DC: U.S. Department of the Interior, March 1938), 601–11; Unrau and Willis, *Administrative History*, 122.

12. Wisconsin State Planning Board and Wisconsin Conservation Commission, "A Park, Parkway and Recreational Area Plan," *Bulletin* 8 (Madison, WI: January 1939), 59–62.

13. National Park Service, *Study of the Park and Recreation Problem*, 122.

14. Ibid., 131, 186–92, 266–67.

15. John C. Paige, *The Civilian Conservation Corps and the National Park Service, 1933–1942: An Administrative History* (Washington, DC: National Park Service, U.S. Department of the Interior, 1985).

16. U.S. Department of the Interior, news release, May 19, 1970.

17. Lee, *Family Tree*, 52–53.

18. Conrad Wirth, *Parks, Politics, and the People* (Norman: University of Oklahoma Press, 1980), 192.

19. Ickes, quoted in Ise, *Our National Park Policy*, 426–27.

20. Unrau and Willis, *Administrative History*, 156.

21. Ibid., 158–59.

22. Wirth, *Parks, Politics, and the People*, 192–93.

23. National Park Service, *Prospectus of Cape Hatteras National Lakeshore*, March 1938, quoted in Unrau and Willis, *Administrative History*, 157–58.

24. Shankland, *Steve Mather*, 333–34.

25. Wirth, *Parks, Politics, and the People*, 198.

26. Lee, *Family Tree*, 58–59; Foresta, *America's National Parks*, 238–39.

27. Ibid.

28. The NPS involvement in national recreation planning had dwindled during the postwar years. A weak Federal Interagency Committee on Recreation had functioned from 1946 until the early 1960s but had done little to solve the problem of a growing national demand for outdoor recreational opportunities (see Fitch and Shanklin, *Bureau of Outdoor Recreation*, 57–59).

29. Foresta, *America's National Parks*, 63.

30. Wirth, *Parks, Politics, and the People*, 196–97.

31. National Park Service, *Our Fourth Shore: Great Lakes Shoreline Recreation Area Survey* (Washington, DC: U.S. Department of the Interior, 1959).

32. Wirth, *Parks, Politics, and the People*, 200.

33. National Park Service, *Our Fourth Shore*, 2, 21, 39–41, 45–147.

34. U.S. Senate Select Committee on National Water Resources, *Water Resources Activities in the United States: Water Recreation Needs in the United States, 1960–2000*, 86th Cong., 2nd sess., May 1960, Committee print no. 17, iii, 4.

35. Hartzog, quoted in Lee, *Family Tree*, 61.

36. Lee, *Family Tree*, 62–63; see also George B. Hartzog Jr., *Battling for the National Parks* (Mt. Kisco, NY: Moyer Bell, 1988), 102–3.

37. George Hartzog Jr., interview by Kathleen Lidfors, historian, National Park Service, Bayfield, WI, March 7, 1985.

38. Lee, *Family Tree*, 63.

39. Ibid., 77–84.

40. Foresta, *America's National Parks*, 62.

41. Lee, *Family Tree*, 60.

42. Outdoor Recreation Resources Review Commission, *Outdoor Recreation for America: A Report to the President and to the Congress by the Outdoor Recreation Resources Review Commission* (Washington, DC: Superintendent of Documents, 1962).

43. Outdoor Recreation Resources Review Commission, "Federal Agencies and Outdoor Recreation: A Report to the Outdoor Recreation Resources Review Commission," *ORRRC Study Report 13* (Washington, DC: Superintendent of Documents, 1962), viii–ix, 1.

44. Outdoor Recreation Resources Review Commission, "Outdoor Recreation for America," 1–10, 70.

45. Outdoor Recreation Resources Review Commission, "Shoreline Recreation Resources of the United States: A Report to the Outdoor Recreation Resources Review Commission," *ORRRC Study Report 4* (Washington, DC: Superintendent of Documents, 1962), 142–43.

46. Outdoor Recreation Resources Review Commission, "Trends in American Living and Outdoor Recreation: A Report to the Outdoor Recreation Resources Review Commission," *ORRRC Study Report 22* (Washington, DC: Superintendent of Documents, 1962), 77.

47. Fitch and Shanklin, *Bureau of Outdoor Recreation*, 81.

48. National Park Service, *Parks for America: A Survey of Park and Related Resources in the Fifty States and a Preliminary Plan* (Washington, DC: U.S. Department of the Interior, 1964), viii–ix.

49. Henry Caulfield, "The Conservation and Environmental Movements: An Historical Analysis," in *Environmental Politics and Policy*, ed. James P. Lester (Durham, NC: Duke University Press, 1989), 14–40, quote on 28.

50. Fitch and Shanklin, *Bureau of Outdoor Recreation*, 86–91.

51. National Park Service, *Parks for America*, v–vi.

52. Lee, *Family Tree*, 76–77.

53. Fitch and Shanklin, *Bureau of Outdoor Recreation*, 66.

54. Edward P. Crafts had substantial Washington experience, knew Congress, and would effectively organize a new agency. Eventually he would support an Apostle Islands National Lakeshore and other Gaylord Nelson–led initiatives affecting Wisconsin, such as the St. Croix–Namekagon National Wild and Scenic River.

55. Foresta, *America's National Parks*, 64.

56. Recreation Advisory Council, "Federal Executive Branch Policy Governing the Selection, Establishment and Administration of National Recreation Areas," *Policy Circular No. 1* (Washington, DC: March 26, 1963).

57. Lee, *Family Tree*, 77.

58. Thomas R. Huffman, "Protectors of the Land and Water: The Political Culture of Conservation and the Rise of Environmentalism in Wisconsin, 1858–1970" (PhD diss., University of Wisconsin–Madison, 1989), 36–39; see also Thomas R. Huffman, *Protectors of the Land and Water: Environmentalism in Wisconsin, 1961–1968* (Chapel Hill: University of North Carolina Press, 1994).

59. Huffman, "Protectors of the Land and Water," 36–39.

60. Vernon Carstensen, *Farms or Forests: Evolution of a State Land Policy for Northern Wisconsin, 1850–1932* (Madison: University of Wisconsin, College of Agriculture, 1958), 3–18.

61. Denise Gess and William Lutz, *The Fire Storm at Peshtigo: A Town, Its People, and the Deadliest Fire in American History* (New York: Henry Holtz, 2002); Christine Lynn Thomas. "The Role of the Wisconsin Natural Resources Board in Environmental Decision Making: A Comparison of Perceptions" (PhD diss., University of Wisconsin–Madison, 1989), 58.

62. Frederick Jackson Turner, *The Significance of the Frontier in American History* (1893; New York: Frederick Ungar, 1963).

63. Huffman, "Protectors of the Land and Water," 40–41.

64. Gifford Pinchot, address delivered before the Joint Session of Wisconsin Legislature, *Wisconsin State Journal* (Madison), March 24, 1927, p. 1.

65. Huffman, "Protectors of the Land and Water," 53.

66. See Roderick Nash, *The American Environment: Readings in the History of Conservation* (Reading, PA: Addison-Wesley, 1976); and Nash, *Wilderness and the American Mind*.

67. Huffman, "Protectors of the Land and Water," 54.

68. Ibid., 56–60.

69. Wisconsin Conservation Commission, *Activities Progress Report* (Madison, WI: November 30, 1948), 14–15; Wisconsin Conservation Commission, *Activities Progress Report* (Madison, WI: January 24, 1949), 2.

70. Ibid.

71. Huffman, "Protectors of the Land and Water," 66–69.

72. Ibid., 47–48.

73. Ibid., 61–65.

74. Ibid., 90.

75. Wisconsin Conservation Commission, *Activities Progress Report* (Madison, WI: November 30, 1948), 18.

76. Ernest Swift, "We the People," *Wisconsin Conservation Bulletin* (August–September 1944), 21.

77. Harold C. Jordahl, *County Forests in Transition: An Account of the Wisconsin County Forest Crop Revolt, 1960–1963* (Madison: University of Wisconsin–Extension, 1984).

78. Huffman, "Protectors of the Land and Water," 44–47.

79. F. G. Wilson, *E. M. Griffith and the Early Story of Wisconsin Forestry (1903–1915)* (Madison: Wisconsin Department of Natural Resources, 1982), 54–58.

80. Erling Solberg, *New Laws for New Forests* (Madison: University of Wisconsin Press, 1961), 48.

81. Ibid., 46–47.

82. Jordahl, *County Forests in Transition*, 13.

83. William Aberg, "Conservation Reminiscences" (transcript of taped interview conducted by the State Historical Society of Wisconsin, May 25, 1961), 13.

84. Ashland County, Wisconsin, *Comprehensive, Floodplain, Shoreland, Subdivision, Sanitary and Private Sewage Zoning*, adopted November 12, 1980 (this incorporates the 1934 ordinance for forestry and land reservation).

85. Solberg, *New Laws for New Forests*, 45.

86. Ibid., 67–72.

87. Wisconsin Conservation Commission, *Biennial Report, 1952–1954* (Madison, WI: 1954), 9–10.

88. Charles F. Smith, "The Big Cut," *Wisconsin Conservation Bulletin* (May 1960), 4–5.

89. Wisconsin Conservation Commission, *Biennial Report, 1959–1960* (Madison, WI: 1960), 34.

90. J. Vanderwall, "Some Historical Background of the Wisconsin State Park System" (unpublished manuscript; Madison: Wisconsin Conservation Department, February 9, 1953), 1.

91. John Nolen, *State Parks for Wisconsin* (Madison, WI: State Park Board, 1909).

92. Ibid., 37–42.

93. Vanderwall, "Some Historical Background," 2.

94. Wisconsin Conservation Commission, *Biennial Report, 1937–1938* (Madison, WI: 1938), 33–34 (emphasis added).

95. Vanderwall, "Some Historical Background," 6.

96. Wisconsin State Planning Board and Wisconsin Conservation Commission, "Park, Parkway and Recreational Area Plan," 59 (emphasis added).

97. Ibid., 81 (emphasis added).

98. C. L. Harrington, "The Comprehensive State Park Program," *Wisconsin Conservation Bulletin* (January 1948), 4.

99. C. L. Harrington, "Development of Wisconsin's State Parks," *Wisconsin Conservation Bulletin* (June 1948), 5.

100. Wisconsin Conservation Commission, *Activities Progress Report* (Madison, WI: May 31, 1950), 54.

101. Wisconsin Conservation Department, *Minutes*, January 12, 1951.

102. Wisconsin Legislative Council Conservation Committee, *Minutes*, August 23, 1954, 1–4.

103. Ibid.

104. L. P. Voigt, "Thirty Years of Conservation Growth in Wisconsin," *Wisconsin Conservation Bulletin* (March 1955), 23.

105. Wisconsin Conservation Commission, *Wisconsin State Parks Going Downhill—Why?* (brochure; Madison, WI: December 1956) (emphasis in original).

106. Wisconsin Conservation Commission, *Minutes*, March 15, 1957, 3.

107. Wisconsin Conservation Commission, *Minutes*, July 19, 1957.

108. Ibid.

109. Wisconsin Conservation Commission, *Biennial Report, 1958–1960* (Madison, WI: 1960).

110. R. J. Neugebauer, "Conservation Congress Highlights," *Wisconsin Conservation Bulletin* (June 1958), 30.

111. Wisconsin Conservation Commission, *Minutes*, August 5, 1958; joint meeting with the Illinois Conservation Advisory Board, 2, 6–7.

112. R. C. Espeseth, "Spotlight on State Parks," *Wisconsin Conservation Bulletin* (January 1959).

113. Gaylord A. Nelson, June 24, 1959; statement by Governor Nelson to the Joint Meeting of the Senate and Assembly Conservation Committees on the Proposed Conservation Budget; Executive Office press release, Madison, WI.

114. Smith, "Big Cut," 3.

115. Ibid., 4.

116. Wisconsin Conservation Commission, *Minutes*, June 10, 1960, 3–6.

117. Wisconsin Conservation Commission, *Minutes*, May 17, 1960.

118. Wisconsin Conservation Commission, *Minutes*, June 10, 1960.

119. "Land Resources Planning," *Wisconsin Conservation Bulletin* (November–December 1960), 57.

120. Wisconsin Conservation Commission, *Activities Progress Report* (Madison, WI: November 1949), 3.

Chapter 3. A New Era in Wisconsin

1. Thomas R. Huffman, "Protectors of the Land and Water: The Political Culture of Conservation and the Rise of Environmentalism in Wisconsin, 1858–1970" (PhD diss., University of Wisconsin–Madison, 1989), 150. See also Thomas R. Huffman, *Protectors of the Land and Water: Environmentalism in Wisconsin, 1961–1968* (Chapel Hill: University of North Carolina Press, 1994).

2. H. Russell Austin, *The Wisconsin Story: The Building of a Vanguard State* (Milwaukee: Journal Company, 1969), 343–80.

3. John Reynolds had served as attorney general and was elected to the governorship in 1962, succeeding Nelson. He served one two-year term.

4. Patrick Lucey, a key participant in rebuilding the Democratic Party, would serve as lieutenant governor from 1964 to 1966 and as governor from 1970 to 1976. Although Lucey represented a faction within the Democratic Party that did not always agree with Nelson, his support for the lakeshore was strong and consistent, and as governor he would play the key role in the later transfer of the state-owned lands to the NPS (see chapter 11).

5. Philleo Nash, educated as an anthropologist, would serve as Nelson's lieutenant governor from 1958 to 1960. He was defeated in the 1960 election. President Kennedy appointed him commissioner of the Bureau of Indian Affairs in the U.S. Department of the Interior. In that role, Nash strongly supported the lakeshore and the Red Cliff and Bad River Tribes' interests.

6. Huffman, "Protectors of the Land and Water," 156–60.

7. Ibid., 162.

8. Ibid.

9. Ibid.

10. Ibid., 162, 167.

11. Ibid., 186.

12. Ibid., 166–67.

13. Ibid., 172–94.

14. Ibid., 162.

15. Ibid., 189.

16. Ibid., 210–18, 303–5.

17. Ibid., 199–200.

18. Stephen M. Born and Harold C. Jordahl, "The Wisconsin Idea: Today and Tomorrow," 73–78, and Gaylord Nelson, "The Legend and the Legacy," 17–26, both in *The Wisconsin Idea: A Tribute to Carlisle P. Runge* (Madison: University of Wisconsin–Extension, 1981).

19. I. V. Fine and E. E. Werner, "The Tourist-Vacation Industry in Wisconsin" (Madison: University of Wisconsin, School of Commerce, 1981).

20. Huffman, "Protectors of the Land and Water," 242.

21. Ibid., 338.

22. Cited in Huffman, "Protectors of the Land and Water," 341.

23. Ibid., 264.

24. Ibid., 271–94.

25. Ibid., 291.

26. Ibid., 305–7.

27. Ibid., 345–47.

28. Ibid., 309–10.

29. Forest Crop Advisory Committee, "County Forests in Transition" (report to Governor Gaylord A. Nelson) (Madison, WI: August 1962).

30. Harold C. Jordahl, *County Forests in Transition: An Account of the Wisconsin County Forest Crop Revolt, 1960–1963* (Madison: University of Wisconsin–Extension, 1984), 94–95.

31. *The Recreation Potential of the Lake Superior South Shore Area* (Madison: Wisconsin Department of Resource Development, 1963).

32. Huffman, "Protectors of the Land and Water," 376–78.

33. Martin Hanson, an ardent conservationist who lived in northern Wisconsin, became a strong and continuing voice for the lakeshore, along with his brother J. Louis Hanson. He would effectively use the Peoples' Lobby to support the lakeshore.

34. In the 1960s, Louis Hanson chaired the state Democratic Party. With his statewide network of contacts, he could marshal formidable support for the lakeshore.

35. Huffman, "Protectors of the Land and Water," 381–86.

Chapter 4. The 1960s Road to a Lakeshore

1. Warren Bielenberg, *Annual Report, Apostle Islands National Lakeshore* (Bayfield, WI: National Park Service, 1972), 8.

2. Arno B. Cammerer, letter to Hubert H. Peavey, January 19, 1929. Records

of the National Park Service, Record Group 79 (Proposed Parks, 0-32, Apostle Islands), National Archives, Washington, DC (hereafter NPS Records).

3. Harlan P. Kelsey, "Report on Apostle Islands National Park Project: Memorandum for Mr. Horace M. Albright," NPS Records, January 20, 1931, 7.

4. Arno B. Crammerer, memorandum for Director Albright covering report on inspection of the Apostle Islands (Wisconsin) project, n.d., NPS Records.

5. Arno B. Crammerer, letter to Herbert Evison, November 2, 1931, NPS Records.

6. G. M. Lamb, *Report of Investigation of Proposed National Parks, Apostle Islands National Park* (Washington, DC: National Park Service, n.d.), 2–4.

7. Conrad L. Wirth, memorandum to the file, March 19, 1936, NPS Records.

8. Lamb, *Report of Investigation*, 4.

9. Wisconsin State Planning Board and Wisconsin Conservation Commission, "A Park, Parkway and Recreational Area Plan," *Bulletin* 8 (Madison, WI: January 1939).

10. Jim Cook, "Apaches Run Recreation 'Gold Mine,'" *Arizona Republic*, January 14, 1962.

11. Bud Peters made his living in logging and the forest products industries. He would become a sustaining supporter of a lakeshore proposal, despite the fact that he was a major landowner on Sand Island. Local support was crucial for the eventual success of the lakeshore proposal.

12. Martin Hanson, interview by Harold C. Jordahl, September 4, 1989.

13. J. Louis Hanson, interview by Kathleen Lidfors, historian, National Park Service, Bayfield, WI, March 27, 1985.

14. Donald R. Ames, chair of the Bad River Tribe, letter to U.S. Secretary of the Interior, Governor of Wisconsin, and the Commissioner of Indian Affairs, May 10, 1962.

15. Gaylord A. Nelson, interview by Kathleen Lidfors, historian, National Park Service, Bayfield, WI, March 4, 1985.

16. "Shoreline Park Sought for Bad River: Nelson Requests U.S. to Establish 20,000 Acre Recreation Facility in State," *Milwaukee Journal*, May 23, 1962; "Bad River Proposed as Recreation Site," *Milwaukee Sentinel*, May 23, 1962; "Lake Superior Area Suggested for Recreation," *Stevens Point Daily Journal*, May 22, 1962.

17. "Udall Interested in Superior Park," *Wausau Record Herald*, May 31, 1962.

18. Harvey Breuscher, "Lake Superior Recreation Area Proposed by Nelson," *Eau Claire Telegram*, June 12, 1962.

19. "Chequamegon Area Recreation Study Is Called For," *Milwaukee Journal*, July 7, 1962.

20. Roman Koenings, who had replaced retired Neil Harrington, was a strong parks advocate and brought new ideas and energy to the program. Because I had been a key planner for Nelson's initiatives, many of which impinged upon Koenings's areas of responsibility, a degree of competitiveness existed between the two

of us. However, as regional director he seldom confronted me over the lakeshore or other proposals. Problems with BOR came primarily from the Washington office.

21. R. G. Lynch, "State Recreation Area Planned in Apostles," *Milwaukee Journal*, July 22, 1962.

22. Dan Satran, "View, Fish Spectacular on Bad River Reservation," *Capital Times* (Madison), August 13, 1962

23. Harold C. Jordahl, personal notes, 1962–1963.

24. U.S. Department of Agriculture, *Joint Press Release with the United States Department of the Interior*, USDA 397-633, February 5, 1963.

25. Harold C. Jordahl, *Preliminary Draft: Relationship of the Proposed Apostle Islands Region National Lakeshore* (Madison: Wisconsin Department of Resource Development, 1963). This is the only time in the many iterations of legislation for the lakeshore that an advisory commission was mentioned. Most lakeshore and seashore acts during this era mandated advisory commissions. The subcommittee that developed the lakeshore report determined that the secretary of the Interior could, if he wished, establish an informal advisory committee, but it saw no need for a formal one.

26. Ibid.

27. Robert L. Lee, letter to Harold C. Jordahl, August 22, 1963.

28. National Park Service, *Preliminary Draft Plan for Apostle Islands National Lakeshore* (Washington, DC: U.S. Department of the Interior, October 1963).

29. "'JFK' Hails Upstate Resource: U.S. Help Pledged to Develop Region," *Duluth News Tribune*, September 25, 1963.

30. Cy Rice, "Three Try to Stop DeWitt," *Milwaukee Sentinel*, April 9, 1963; Cy Rice, "Bob Kennedy Still Opposed to Doyle," *Milwaukee Sentinel*, April 10, 1963; Cy Rice, "Five Still in Running for Judgeship," *Milwaukee Sentinel*, April 19, 1963; "Kastenmeier Joins Nelson in Backing Doyle for Judge," *Milwaukee Sentinel*, March 16, 1963; "DeWitt Reported to Be Judgeship Leader," *Milwaukee Sentinel*, March 27, 1963; "Hint Rabinovitz Top Judge Choice," *Milwaukee Sentinel*, June 6, 1963; "Rabinovitz Seems Choice for Judgeship," *Milwaukee Sentinel*, July 12, 1963; "Rabinovitz Nominated as Federal Judge," *Milwaukee Sentinel*, September 6, 1963; "Nelson Says JFK May Visit State," *Milwaukee Sentinel*, September 10, 1963; "JFK Visit Definite: Nelson," *Milwaukee Sentinel*, September 12, 1963.

31. William Bechtel, interview by Kathleen Lidfors, historian, National Park Service, Bayfield, WI, March 4, 1985.

32. "President Will Talk at Ashland Stopover," *Milwaukee Journal*, September 15, 1963; "Visit to State to Be Brief," *Milwaukee Journal*, September 19, 1963.

33. Harold C. Jordahl, memorandum to Ruth Chance, September 9, 1963.

34. William Bechtel, *Nelson Newsletter*, September 1963.

35. Ibid.

36. Nelson, interview by Lidfors; emphasis added.

37. Martin Hanson, interview by Jordahl.

38. *Public Papers of the Presidents of the United States: John F. Kennedy* (Washington, DC: U.S. Government Printing Office, 1964), 707–9.

39. Harvey Breuscher, "JFK Sees State Islands, Backs Park," *Wisconsin State Journal* (Madison), September 25, 1963.

40. "'JFK' Hails Upstate Resource: U.S. Help Pledged to Develop Region," *Duluth News Tribune*, September 25, 1963. The origins of field committees can be traced to the so-called Pick-Sloan Plan for the Missouri River Basin. In the mid-1940s, Colonel Lewis Pick of the U.S. Army and Bureau Engineer W. Glenn Sloan of the U.S. Department of the Interior Bureau of Reclamation got together over a bottle of bourbon in a St. Louis hotel and divided up responsibilities for the Missouri River Basin. Congress concurred with the division. To implement this plan, cooperation from other agencies was required. Thus, the Missouri River Basin Inter-Agency Committee was created with one representative from each federal department and the governors of each of the ten states in the basin. The committee had no administrative authority. Lack of coordination in river basin planning between Department of the Interior's bureaus was also evident elsewhere, and field committees were eventually established in all regions of the country except for the Ohio River–Appalachian region and the Upper Mississippi–Western Great Lakes region. In the 1960s, as part of Udall's strategy to bring the Department of the Interior east of the Mississippi, field committees were established for these regions. Although coordinators of the committees had no direct authority, the imprimatur of the secretary's office made the committees useful devices, especially when dealing with natural resource issues that transcended bureau lines. This was especially true in comprehensive river basin planning, a high priority for the Kennedy administration. It would also become important for the Apostle Islands proposal, which involved multiple administrative units.

41. "Prepared Text of President Kennedy's Address at University of Minnesota–Duluth Tuesday Night," *Duluth News Tribune*, September 25, 1963.

42. Fred T. Witzig, *Voyageurs National Park: The Battle to Create Minnesota's National Park* (Minneapolis: University of Minnesota Press, 2004), 91.

43. Harold C. Jordahl, memorandum to Henry Caulfield, October 1, 1963.

44. Henry P. Caulfield, memorandum to Stewart Udall, October 23, 1963.

45. National Park Service Assistant Regional Director, memorandum to the Acting Area Director of the Bureau of Indian Affairs, October 11, 1963.

46. Harold C. Jordahl, memorandum to the Directors of the Resources Program Staff, the Bureau of Outdoor Recreation and the National Park Service, and the Commissioner of the Bureau of Indian Affairs, December 4, 1963; U.S. Department of the Interior, *Preliminary Draft: Relationship of the Proposed Apostle Islands Region National Lakeshore to Recreation Advisor Council Policy Circular No. 1, Federal Executive Branch Policy Governing Selection, Establishment and Administration of National Recreation Areas* (Washington, DC: U.S. Department of the Interior, March 26, 1963).

47. Gordon Josllyn, memorandum to Henry P. Caulfield, December 10, 1963.

48. Field Coordination Assistant, Bureau of Outdoor Recreation, memorandum to Henry P. Caulfield, December 18, 1963.

49. Henry P. Caulfield, memorandum to the Assistant Director of the Bureau of Outdoor Recreation, January 20, 1964.

50. Gaylord A. Nelson, letter to Stewart Udall, February 11, 1964.

51. Edward Crafts, memorandum to Stewart Udall (through the Assistant Secretary for Public Lands Management), March 6, 1964.

52. Stewart Udall, letter to Gaylord A. Nelson, April 4, 1964.

53. Here I made a strategic error. I should have used the word *preferential* rather than *equitable*. This would have required some substantial effort to clear BOR and the legal staff but would have saved many months of argument and later debate.

54. Stewart Udall, letters to Alex F. Roye (chair, Red Cliff Tribal Council), Fred Connors (chair, Bad River Tribal Council), Governor John W. Reynolds, April 4, 1964; Stewart Udall, memorandum to the Under Secretaries, Assistant Secretaries Solicitor and the Director of the Resources Program, April 4, 1964.

55. Harry R. Anderson, letter report to U.S. Senator Henry M. Jackson (chair of the Senate Committee on Interior and Insular Affairs), February 18, 1967.

56. North Central Field Committee, *Subcommittee Minutes*, June 24–26, 1964.

57. Henry P. Caulfield, letter to Harold C. Jordahl, August 6, 1964.

58. Daniel S. Boos and O. M. Bishop, letter to Harold C. Jordahl, January 26, 1965; R. W. Sharp, letter to Harold C. Jordahl, January 26, 1965; Bernard M. Granum and David V. Vrooman (Bureau of Indian Affairs), letter to Harold C. Jordahl, January 29, 1965; Allen T. Edmunds, letter to Harold C. Jordahl, February 5, 1965; Ronald F. Lee, letter to Harold C. Jordahl, June 3, 1965; E. J. Riley, letter to Harold C. Jordahl, February 5, 1965; and William Dryer, letter to Harold C. Jordahl, January 27, 1965.

59. I. V. Fine, "Apostle Islands: Some of the Economic Implications of the Proposed Apostle Islands National Lakeshore," *Wisconsin Vacation-Recreation Papers* III, no. 1 (Madison: University of Wisconsin, School of Commerce, May 1965).

60. Harold C. Jordahl, letter to Henry P. Caulfield, March 15, 1965; North Central Field Committee Subcommittee, *Draft Report, Proposed Apostle Islands National Lakeshore* (Washington, DC: U.S. Department of the Interior, January 1965).

61. Harold C. Jordahl, memorandum to the Director of the Resources Program Staff, March 19, 1965.

62. William E. Rennebohm, memorandum to John A. Beale, April 26, 1965.

63. Donald J. Mackie, letter to James W. Good, Wisconsin Conservation Department, October 1, 1965.

64. Charles F. Smith, letter to Gaylord A. Nelson, December 30, 1965.

65. Henry P. Caulfield, memorandum to U.S. Department of the Interior bureau directors, February 24, 1965.

66. Roman H. Koenings, letter to Harold C. Jordahl, March 10, 1965.

67. Roger M. Bodin, letter to Harold C. Jordahl, March 3, 1965; Harold C. Jordahl, letter to Roger M. Bodin, March 4, 1965; Harold C. Jordahl, memorandum to Henry P. Caulfield, April 16, 1965.

68. "Proposed Apostle Islands National Park Set for Congress Introduction," *Ashland Daily Press*, August 30, 1965.

69. Harold C. Jordahl, letter to Henry P. Caulfield, March 15, 1965.

70. Henry P. Caulfield, memorandum to U.S. Department of the Interior bureau directors, April 30, 1965.

71. Lewis A. Sigler (assistant legal counsel), memorandum to the Director of Resources Program Staff, May 6, 1965.

72. Caryl Johnson, memorandum to the file, May 20, 1965.

73. Harold C. Jordahl, memorandum to Henry Caulfield, August 9, 1965.

74. Director, Bureau of Outdoor Recreation, memorandum to the Director of Resources Program Staff, August 10, 1965.

75. James N. Smith, note to Henry P. Caulfield, August 10, 1965.

76. Edward Crafts, memorandum to Henry P. Caulfield, August 10, 1965.

77. Bureau of Outdoor Recreation, *Relationship of the Proposed Apostle Islands National Lakeshore to Recreation Advisory Council Policy Circular No. 1, "Federal Executive Policy Governing the Selection, Establishment and Administration of National Recreation Areas, March 26, 1963"* (Washington, DC: U.S. Department of the Interior, January 14, 1966).

78. Fine, "Apostle Islands."

79. National Park Service, *Sleeping Bear Dunes National Lakeshore: A Proposal* (Washington, DC: U.S. Department of the Interior, 1961); National Park Service, *Pictured Rocks National Lakeshore: A Proposal* (Washington, DC: U.S. Department of the Interior, 1966), 23; Donald Blome, "The Proposed Sleeping Bear Dunes National Lakeshore: An Assessment of the Economic Impact" (Lansing: Michigan State University, Institute for Community Development and Services, 1967), 3; Institute for Community Development, "The Proposed Pictured Rocks National Lakeshore: An Economic Study" (Lansing: Michigan State University, 1963), 59; and Richard O. Sielaff, Cecil H. Meyers, and Philip L. Friest, "The Economics of the Proposed Voyageurs National Park" (Duluth: University of Minnesota–Duluth, Division of Social Sciences, 1964), 113.

80. Stewart Udall, letter to Senator Henry Jackson, July 10, 1964.

81. U.S. Department of the Interior, *Proposed Apostle Islands National Lakeshore, Bayfield and Ashland Counties, Wisconsin* (Washington, DC: U.S. Superintendent of Documents, March 1965).

82. Henry P. Caulfield, memorandum to the Under Secretaries and Assistant Secretaries, U.S. Department of the Interior, August 31, 1965; James N. Smith, memorandum to U.S. Department of the Interior bureaus, August 31, 1965.

83. "Nelson's Bill Triggers Debate: Apostle Islands—Their Beauty Prompts Plan," *Duluth News Tribune*, August 29, 1965.

84. Advisory Board on National Parks, Historical Sites, Buildings and Monuments, memorandum to Stewart Udall, October 7, 1965.

85. Stanley P. Cain (assistant secretary, Fish, Wildlife and Parks), memorandum to Henry P. Caulfield, September 24, 1965.

86. Edward Crafts, memorandum to Stewart Udall, December 21, 1965.

87. Dan Ogden, *Relationship of the Proposed Apostle Islands National Lakeshore to the Recreation Advisory Council Policy Circular No. 1* (Washington, DC: Bureau of Outdoor Recreation, January 14, 1966).

88. Lyndon B. Johnson, "Special Message to the Congress Proposing Measures to Preserve America's Natural Heritage, February 2, 1966," *Public Papers of the Presidents of the United States, Book I* (Washington, DC: U.S. Government Printing Office, 1965), 195–203.

89. William Bechtal, letter to Harold C. Jordahl, August 2, 1966.

90. Lyndon B. Johnson, "Protecting Our Natural Heritage, Special Message to the Congress of the United States," January 30, 1967.

91. U.S. Senate, *Subcommittee on Parks and Recreation of the Committee on Interior and Insular Affairs*, hearings, February 19, 1967; May 9, 1967; June 1–2, 1967, 5–9.

92. Ibid.

Chapter 5. The Blowup—Or, Do We Have a Lakeshore?

1. Lyndon B. Johnson, "Protecting Our Natural Heritage, Special Message to the Congress of the United States," January 30, 1967.

2. U.S. Senate, *Subcommittee on Parks and Recreation of the Committee on Interior and Insular Affairs*, 91st Cong., 1st sess., hearings, March 17, 1969 (Washington, DC: Government Printing Office, 1970), 43–44.

3. Ibid., 48.

4. Ibid., 45.

5. Ibid.

6. Ibid.

7. Ibid., 48.

8. Ibid., 21.

9. Ibid., 27.

10. Ibid., 36–37.

11. Ibid., 35–39.

12. Ibid., 37–38.

13. Ibid., 38–40.

14. Ibid., 39–41.

15. Ibid., 41.

16. U.S. Senate, *Subcommittee on Parks and Recreation of the Committee on Interior and Insular Affairs*, 91st Cong., 1st sess., hearings, June 25, 1969 (Washington, DC: Government Printing Office, 1970).

17. U.S. House, *Hearings Before the Subcommittee on National Parks and Recreation of the Committee on Interior and Insular Affairs*, 91st Cong., 1st sess., hearings on H.R. 555, H.R. 9306, and S. 621, Serial Number 99-9, August 19, 1969 (Washington, DC: Government Printing Office, 1970), 13.

18. U.S. House, *Hearings Before the Subcommittee on National Parks and Recreation of the Committee on Interior and Insular Affairs*, 91st Cong., 2nd sess., hearings on H.R. 555, H.R. 9306, and S. 621, Serial Number 99-9, March 23–24 and June 3, 1970 (Washington, DC: Government Printing Office, 1970), 237–39.

19. Ibid., 240–46.

20. Ibid., 246–54.

21. Ibid., 332–59.

22. Ibid., 254–85.

23. Ibid.

24. Ibid.

25. A full discussion of the relationship between the two tribal governments, the larger Native American interests nationally, and the lakeshore is found in chapter 12.

26. Robert Kastenmeier, *Newsletter* 3, no. 13 (March 27, 1970).

27. Harold C. Jordahl, letter to Robert Kastenmeier, April 2, 1970.

28. Gaylord A. Nelson, letter to Robert Kastenmeier, April 20, 1970.

29. John Heritage, telephone call with Harold C. Jordahl, April 22, 1970; Lee McElvain, confidential memorandum to members of the House Subcommittee on National Parks and Recreation, May 1, 1970.

30. Robert Kastenmeier, *Newsletter* 3, no. 19 (May 1970).

31. Stuart Applebaum, telephone call to Harold C. Jordahl, May 8, 1970.

32. Wayne N. Aspinall, letter to George B. Hartzog, May 12, 1970.

33. John Heritage, telephone call with Harold C. Jordahl, May 19, 1970; Stuart Applebaum, telephone call to Harold C. Jordahl, May 27, 1970; Stuart Applebaum, telephone call to Harold C. Jordahl, May 28, 1970.

34. "Apostle Islands Bill Gets Hickel's Backing," *Milwaukee Journal*, June 2, 1970; Richard Bradee, "Hickel to Help Apostle Islands Bill," *Milwaukee Sentinel*, June 2, 1970.

35. Ibid.

36. Stuart Applebaum, telephone call to Harold C. Jordahl, June 1, 1970.

37. U.S. House, *Committee on the Interior and Insular Affairs*, 91st Cong., 2nd sess., hearings on H.R. 555, H.R. 9306, and S. 621, Serial Number 99-9, March 23–24 and June 3, 1970 (Washington, DC: Government Printing Office, 1970), 394.

38. Ibid., 417.

39. Ibid., 413.

40. Ibid., 416.

41. Ibid., 423–24.

42. Ibid.

43. George Hartzog, letter to Wayne Aspinall, June 10, 1970; cited in ibid., 434–35.

44. Stuart Applebaum, telephone call to Harold C. Jordahl, June 8, 1970.

45. Lee McElvain, telephone call to Harold C. Jordahl, June 2, 1970.

46. Lee McElvain, memorandum to members of the House Committee on Interior and Insular Affairs, June 10, 1970; "Indian Land Rights Queried," *Milwaukee Sentinel*, June 11, 1970.

47. Robert Kastenmeier, *Newsletter* 3, no. 24 (June 12, 1970).

48. U.S. House, *Providing for the Establishment of the Apostle Islands National Lakeshore in the State of Wisconsin, and for Other Purposes*, report no. 91-1280 (Washington, DC: July 7, 1970), 7.

49. Ibid., 8.

50. Stuart Applebaum, telephone call to Harold C. Jordahl, July 24, 1970.

51. Alvin O'Konski et al., letter to members of the U.S. House of Representatives, September 9, 1970.

52. Loretta Ellis, letter to members of the U.S. House of Representatives, September 9, 1970.

53. "Indians Fight Apostles Project," *Milwaukee Sentinel*, September 15, 1970; "Indian Urges Opposition to Apostle Plan," *Milwaukee Journal*, September 15, 1970; John Heritage, telephone call with Harold C. Jordahl, July 7, 1970; John Heritage, telephone call with Harold C. Jordahl, September 21, 1970.

54. John Heritage, telephone call with Harold C. Jordahl, September 21, 1970.

55. "House Approves Apostle Isle Bill," *Milwaukee Sentinel*, September 11, 1970.

56. Robert Kastenmeier, letter to Harold C. Jordahl, October 1, 1970.

57. Gaylord A. Nelson, interview by Kathleen Lidfors, historian, National Park Service, Bayfield, WI, March 4, 1985.

58. George Hartzog Jr., interview by Kathleen Lidfors, historian, National Park Service, Bayfield, WI. March 7, 1985.

Chapter 6. Long Island at Last

1. "Plover Is Declared an Endangered Species," *New York Times*, December 13, 1985.

2. David Overstreet, Great Lakes Archaeological Center, quoted in Susan M. Monk, *Cultural Resources of Long Island (Chequamegon Point)* (Washington, DC: National Park Service, 1985), 2–3.

3. Surveyor's certificate, signed by John Ross and Jerod W. Day, August 28, 1912, Register of Deeds Office, Ashland County, WI.

4. "Long Island to Be a Mecca for Tourists," *Ashland Daily Press*, August 16, 1912.

5. William Smith and William Tans, "Long Island" (unpublished report; Madison: Wisconsin Department of Natural Resources, August 29, 1975).

6. Patrick H. Miller, letter to Harold C. Jordahl, July 7, 1985.

7. Patrick H. Miller, telephone call to Harold C. Jordahl, July 17, 1985.

8. "Lawmakers Seek to Add Island to Federal Territory," *Milwaukee Journal*, May 5, 1985.

9. David Obey, statement before the House Subcommittee on National Parks and Recreation of the Committee on Interior and Insular Affairs, 99th Cong., 1st sess., June 11, 1985.

10. Martin Hanson, telephone call to Harold C. Jordahl, May 30, 1985; Martin Hanson, telephone call to Harold C. Jordahl, June 2, 1985.

11. Neil Neuberger, telephone call to Harold C. Jordahl, June 3, 1985.

12. Joseph Greenwood, "Opposition Voices against Takeover," *Ashland Daily Press*, June 4, 1985.

13. Ibid.

14. Martin Hanson, telephone call to Harold C. Jordahl, June 4, 1985.

15. Martin Hanson, telephone call to Harold C. Jordahl, Ron Nicotera, Neil Neuberger, and Pat Miller, June 6, 1985.

16. Hanson, telephone call to Jordahl, June 4, 1985.

17. Ibid.

18. "Island Doesn't Belong in the National Park System," *Milwaukee Sentinel*, June 9, 1985.

19. Neuberger, telephone call to Jordahl, June 3, 1985.

20. Gaylord A. Nelson, statement before the House Subcommittee on National Parks and Recreation, June 11, 1985.

21. Obey, statement before the House Subcommittee.

22. William Bechtel, statement on behalf of Wisconsin governor Anthony S. Earl, before the House Subcommittee on National Parks and Recreation, June 11, 1985.

23. Thomas Klein, letter to David Obey, June 6, 1985; Thomas Klein, statement before the House Subcommittee on National Parks and Recreation, June 11, 1985.

24. Christian Ballantyne, Brock Evans, statements before the House Subcommittee on National Parks and Recreation, June 11, 1985.

25. Mary Lou Grier, statement before the House Subcommittee on National Parks and Recreation, June 11, 1985.

26. Archie Wilson, statement before the House Subcommittee on National Parks and Recreation, June 11, 1985.

27. Neil Neuberger, telephone call to Harold C. Jordahl, June 18, 1985.

28. Neuberger, telephone call to Jordahl, June 3, 1985.

29. Miller, telephone call to Jordahl, July 17, 1985.

30. Bruce F. Vento, letter to William Penn Mott Jr., July 9, 1985; Stanley T. Albright, letter to Bruce F. Vento, August 9, 1985; William Penn Mott, letter to Bruce F. Vento, October 10, 1985; Patrick H. Miller, letter to Martin Hanson, October 18, 1985.

31. Bruce F. Vento, letter to the U.S. Coast Guard, June 13, 1985; U.S. Coast Guard, letter to Bruce F. Vento, July 23, 1985.

32. "Opportunity to Keep a Shoreline Pristine," *Milwaukee Journal*, June 17, 1985.

33. Martin Hanson, telephone call to Harold C. Jordahl, September 13, 1985.

34. Martin Hanson, telephone call to Patrick H. Miller, August 29, 1985; Hanson, telephone call to Jordahl, September 13, 1985; Patrick H. Miller, letter to the Ashland County Board of Supervisors, September 24, 1985.

35. Martin Hanson, telephone call to Harold C. Jordahl, November 13, 1985; David Obey, news release, November 13, 1985

36. "Apostle Islands Expansion Backed," *Milwaukee Sentinel*, December 17, 1985; Martin Hanson, telephone call to Harold C. Jordahl, December 13, 1985.

37. David Obey, news release, December 16, 1985.

38. *Congressional Record*, December 16, 1985, H12007-9.

39. Cliff Germain, telephone call to Harold C. Jordahl, January 31, 1986; Summer Matteson, telephone call to Harold C. Jordahl, January 31, 1986; Paul De Main, letter to Thomas Vennum Jr., January 16, 1986.

40. Appended to Paul De Main, letter to Steve Dodge, February 3, 1986.

41. Thomas Vennum, letter to William Proxmire, February 20, 1986.

42. Matteson, telephone call to Jordahl, January 31, 1986.

43. Martin Hanson, telephone call to Harold C. Jordahl, February 3, 1986.

44. Anthony Earl, letter to Robert Bender, February 7, 1986.

45. Martin Hanson, telephone call to Harold C. Jordahl, March 3, 1986.

46. Harold C. Jordahl, letter to Martin Hanson, February 13, 1986.

47. Martin Hanson, telephone call to Harold C. Jordahl, March 20, 1986.

48. Harold C. Jordahl, personal notes, November 28, 1984.

49. Germain, telephone call to Jordahl, January 31, 1986; Matteson, telephone call to Jordahl, January 31, 1986.

50. Brent Haglund, telephone call to Harold C. Jordahl, February 3, 1986.

51. Robert D. Schaub, letter to David Younkman, June 19, 1985; David Younkman, letter to Brent Haglund, July 2, 1985.

52. Brent Haglund, memorandum to John Humke and David Younkman, November 5, 1985.

53. Vennum, letter to Proxmire, February 20, 1986.

54. Brent Haglund, memorandum to the files, February 25, 1986.

55. Hanson, telephone call to Jordahl, March 3, 1986.

56. Brent Haglund, telephone call to Harold C. Jordahl, March 4, 1986.

57. Martin Hanson, telephone call to Harold C. Jordahl, March 4, 1986.

58. Neil Neuberger, telephone call to Harold C. Jordahl, March 4, 1986.

59. Clifford Messinger, letter to David Obey, March 10, 1986.

60. "Land Bills Create Confusion," *Ashland Daily Press*, November 14, 1985.

61. Martin Hanson, telephone call to Harold C. Jordahl, March 14, 1986.

62. Harold C. Jordahl, telephone call to Clifford Messinger, March 17, 1986.

63. Jon Gilbert, "Protection of Long Island: Update on the Acquisition of Long Island by National Park Service," *Masinaigan* (March 1986); Martin Hanson, telephone call to Harold C. Jordahl, March 20, 1986.

64. Patrick H. Miller, unofficial memorandum, March 15, 1986.

65. Mark Peterson, memorandum to Jon Gilbert, Joe Rose, Bob Bender, Fred Strand, Tim Andryk, Brent Haglund, Tom Syverud, and Ron Nicotera, March 27, 1986.

66. *Congressional Record*, October 8, 1986, S15627.

67. Mark Peterson, telephone call to Harold C. Jordahl, March 31, 1986; Patrick H. Miller, telephone call to Harold C. Jordahl, March 31, 1986.

68. Harold C. Jordahl, telephone call to Clifford Messinger, May 1, 1986.

69. Brent Haglund, telephone calls to Harold C. Jordahl, May 5 and 6, 1986.

70. "Kasten Joins Long Island Movement," *Ashland Daily Press*, May 6, 1986.

71. Neuberger, telephone call to Jordahl, June 18, 1986.

72. Brent Haglund, statement before the Senate Subcommittee on Public Lands, Reserve Water and Resource Conservation of the Committee on Energy and Natural Resources, 99th Cong., 2nd sess., June 20, 1986.

73. Robert W. Kasten, statement before the Senate Subcommittee on Public Lands, Reserve Water and Resource Conservation, June 20, 1986.

74. Robert Bender, statement before the Senate Subcommittee on Public Lands, Reserve Water and Resource Conservation, June 26, 1986.

75. Mark Peterson, telephone call to Harold C. Jordahl, July 2, 1986.

76. "Can Kasten Get Senate to Save Island?" *Milwaukee Journal*, September 7, 1986.

77. Neil Neuberger, telephone call to Harold C. Jordahl, September 9, 1986.

78. U.S. Senate, *Including Certain Lands within the Apostle Island National Lakeshore in the State of Wisconsin, Report 99-499*, U.S. Senate, 99th Cong., 2nd sess., September 27, 1986.

79. Rosemary Marcuss, letter on behalf of Rudolph G. Denner, cited in U.S. Senate Committee on Energy and Natural Resources, 99th Cong., 2nd sess., September 27, 1986.

80. *Congressional Record*, October 8, 1986, S15627.

81. "Johnson Family of Racine Protects Rare Bird Habitat," *Nature Conservancy*, Summer 1989.

82. Brent Haglund, telephone call to Harold C. Jordahl, September 30, 1986.

Chapter 7. Planning the Lakeshore

1. Recreation Advisory Council, "Federal Executive Branch Policy Governing the Selection, Establishment and Administration of National Recreation Areas," *Policy Circular No. 1* (Washington, DC: March 26, 1963).

2. Gordon Josllyn, memorandums to Henry P. Caulfield, December 10 and 18, 1963.

3. Outdoor Recreation Resources Review Commission, *Outdoor Recreation for America: A Report to the Congress by the Outdoor Recreation Resources Review Commission* (Washington, DC: U.S. Superintendent of Documents, 1962), 7.

4. Harold C. Jordahl, memorandum to James Smith, December 17, 1965; Harold C. Jordahl, letter to William Bechtel, December 22, 1965; William Bechtel, letter to Martin Hanson, December 17, 1965.

5. Fred T. Witzig, *Voyageurs National Park: The Battle to Create Minnesota's National Park* (Minneapolis: University of Minnesota Press, 2004), 224–34.

6. Andrew G. Feil Jr., memorandum to Harold C. Jordahl, September 25, 1964.

7. Harold C. Jordahl, memorandum to Robert W. Burwell, October 13, 1964; Robert W. Burwell, memorandum to Harold C. Jordahl, November 20, 1964; North Central Field Committee, *Subcommittee Minutes*, October 23 and November 23–24, 1964.

8. U.S. House, *Committee on Interior and Insular Affairs*, 91st Cong., 2nd sess., hearings, March 23–24, 1970 (Washington, DC: Government Printing Office, 1970), 272.

9. Harold C. Jordahl, notes on the Proposed Apostle Islands National Recreation Area, September 23, 1963.

10. Ibid.

11. National Park Service, *Report on Proposed Apostle Islands National Lakeshore, Bayfield, Ashland, Iron Counties, Wisconsin* (Philadelphia: U.S. Department of the Interior, September 1963).

12. Ibid.

13. U.S. Department of the Interior, *Proposed Apostle Islands National Lakeshore, Bayfield and Ashland Counties, Wisconsin* (Washington, DC: U.S. Superintendent of Documents, March 1965), xviii.

14. Andrew G. Feil Jr. and Harry S. Smith, "Report on Development, Boundaries and Costs, Proposed Apostle Islands National Lakeshore" (Philadelphia: National Park Service, Northeast Regional Office, September 1963).

15. North Central Field Committee's Subcommittee, *Subcommittee Minutes*, October 1, 1964.

16. North Central Field Committee's Subcommittee, *Subcommittee Minutes*, November 23–24, 1964.

17. Harold C. Jordahl, memorandum to Allen T. Edmunds, January 30, 1967.

18. Allen T. Edmunds, memorandum to Harold C. Jordahl, January 16, 1967.

19. Ibid.; Jordahl, memorandum to Edmunds, January 30, 1967.

20. Harry R. Anderson, letter report to U.S. Senator Henry M. Jackson, February 18, 1967; Gaylord A. Nelson, letter to Governor Warren P. Knowles, May 18, 1967; L. P. Voigt, letter to Governor Warren P. Knowles, May 29, 1967; Charles F. Smith, statement before the Senate Subcommittee on Parks and Recreation of

the Committee on Interior and Insular Affairs, 90th Cong., 1st sess., June 21–22, 1967, 128; National Park Service, *Map of the National Lakeshore—Apostle Islands*, Map NL-AI-91000 (Washington, DC: Department of the Interior, June 1970).

21. U.S. Department of the Interior, *Proposed Apostle Islands National Lakeshore*, 75–77.

22. Ibid., 70–71.

23. Ibid., 65–66.

24. I. V. Fine and Philip H. Lewis Jr., *Recreational Potential of the Lake Superior South Shore Area* (Madison: Wisconsin Department of Resource Development, 1964), 20–29.

25. The 1968 NPS plan for the entire lakeshore classified land as follows: 84.8 percent (48,791 acres) as Class V Primitive, 12.1 percent (1,730 acres) as Class III Natural Environment, and 0.1 percent (40 acres) as Class VI Historic and Cultural Sites. No land was assigned as Class I High Density Recreation or Class IV Outstanding Natural Feature. Thus, this plan followed the 1965 North Central Field Committee's Subcommittee's recommendations.

26. B. L. Dahlberg, letter to Harold C. Jordahl, September 18, 1965.

27. Harold C. Jordahl, letter to B. L. Dahlberg, September 20, 1968.

28. Edward Schneberger, letter to Harold C. Jordahl, October 16, 1965; U.S. Senate, *Subcommittee on Parks and Recreation of the Committee on Interior and Insular Affairs*, 90th Cong., 1st sess., hearings, June 1–2, 1967 (Washington, DC: Government Printing Office, 1970), 63, 173, 176, 191, 220.

29. U.S. Senate, subcommittee hearings, June 1, 1967, 93.

30. National Park Service, *A Master Plan for Apostle Islands National Lakeshore* (Washington, DC: U.S. Department of the Interior, 1968), 7.

31. Director, Bureau of Outdoor Recreation, memorandum to the U.S. Secretary of the Interior, March 6, 1964; "Madeline Island Park Is Opposed," *Ashland Daily Press*, September 27, 1966; Gene Divine, "Apostle Backers Urge State Park Elimination," *Milwaukee Sentinel*, May 4, 1967.

32. U.S. Department of the Interior, *Proposed Apostle Islands National Lakeshore*, 25–26.

33. The Wilderness Society, memorandum to lake state members and cooperators, May 19, 1969; U.S. Senate, subcommittee hearings, June 1–2, 1967, 67, 176, 220.

34. U.S. Senate, *Subcommittee on Parks and Recreation of the Committee on Interior and Insular Affairs*, 91st Cong., 1st sess., hearings, March 17, 1969 (Washington, DC: Government Printing Office, 1970), 116–17.

35. U.S. Senate, *Subcommittee on Parks and Recreation of the Committee on Interior and Insular Affairs*, 91st Cong., 1st sess., hearings, August 19, 1969 (Washington, DC: Government Printing Office, 1970), 126.

36. U.S. Senate, *Subcommittee on Parks and Recreation of the Committee on Interior and Insular Affairs*, 90th Cong., 1st sess., hearings, June 1–2, 1967 (Washing-

ton, DC: Government Printing Office, 1970), 179; U.S. House, *Hearings Before the Subcommittee on National Parks and Recreation of the Committee on Interior and Insular Affairs*, 91st Cong., 1st sess., on H.R. 555, H.R. 9306, and S. 621, Serial Number 99-9, hearings, August 19, 1969 (Washington, DC: Government Printing Office, 1970), 171.

37. U.S. Senate, *Subcommittee on Parks and Recreation of the Committee on Interior and Insular Affairs*, 91st Cong., 2nd sess., hearings, March 24, 1970 (Washington, DC: Government Printing Office, 1970), 369.

38. National Park Service, 1968 plan.

39. S. 778 in U.S. Senate, *Subcommittee on Parks and Recreation of the Committee on Interior and Insular Affairs*, 90th Cong., 1st sess., hearings, May 9 and June 1–2, 1967.

40. S. 621 in U.S. Senate, subcommittee hearings, March 17, 1969; U.S. Senate, subcommittee hearings, January 16 and March 17, 1969, 6; U.S. Senate, *Apostle Islands National Lakeshore. Report No. 91-276*, 91st Cong., 1st sess. (Washington, DC: June 25, 1969). To accompany S. 621 in U.S. Senate, subcommittee hearings, June 25, 1969; U.S. House, subcommittee hearings, August 19, 1969; U.S. House, subcommittee hearings, March 23–24, 1970; U.S. House, subcommittee hearings, June 3, 1970; U.S. House, subcommittee hearings, March 19, 1970, 237.

41. U.S. House, *Providing for the Establishment of the Apostle Islands National Lakeshore in the State of Wisconsin, and for Other Purposes. Report No. 91-1280* (Washington, DC: July 7, 1970), 4; Wayne Aspinall, *Congressional Record*, September 10, 1970, H. 8559.

42. U.S. House, *Providing for the Establishment*, 90–91.

43. U.S. Department of the Interior, *Proposed Apostle Islands National Lakeshore*, 34–40.

44. Director, U.S. Bureau of Mines, memorandum to Henry P. Caulfield, May 7, 1965.

45. U.S. Department of the Interior, *Proposed Apostle Islands National Lakeshore*, 40–42.

46. Ibid.

47. Harold C. Jordahl, *Preliminary Draft: Relationship of the Proposed Apostle Islands Region National Lakeshore* (Madison: Wisconsin Department of Resource Development, 1963), 4.

48. U.S. Senate, subcommittee hearings, June 1, 1967, 219.

49. U.S. Department of the Interior, *Proposed Apostle Islands National Lakeshore*, 93–96; Harold C. Jordahl, personal notes, 1963; Harold C. Jordahl, memorandum to Henry P. Caulfield, May 11, 1964.

50. U.S. Department of the Interior, *Proposed Apostle Islands National Lakeshore*, 55–56.

51. J. Louis Hanson, interview by Kathleen Lidfors, historian, National Park Service, Bayfield, WI, March 27, 1985.

52. U.S. Senate, subcommittee hearings, June 1, 1967, 128–29.

53. U.S. Senate, subcommittee hearings, March 17, 1969, 29, 31.

54. U.S. Senate subcommittee hearings, May 9, 1967, 63.

55. Public Law 91-424, 91st Cong, 2nd sess., September 26, 1970.

Chapter 8. The Role of Politics in Establishing the Lakeshore

1. William Bechtel, letter to Martin Hanson, February 9, 1967.

2. Baxter Omohundro, "Sen. Nelson Expects Passage of Apostle Islands Bill," *Duluth News Tribune*, February 26, 1967.

3. "Apostle I. Park Bill in Senate," *Superior Evening Telegram*, August 18, 1967; "Senate OK's Apostle Bill: Lakeshore Project to Cost $13 Million," *Milwaukee Sentinel*, August 22, 1967.

4. Gaylord A. Nelson, interview by Kathleen Lidfors, historian, National Park Service, Bayfield, WI, March 4, 1985.

5. Albert Eisele, "Rep. Aspinall Bottleneck for New National Parks," *Duluth News Tribune*, January 4, 1968; "Wild Rivers Bill Up for Consideration," *Duluth News Tribune*, January 19, 1968; *The Nelson Newsletter* (Washington, DC), August 1967, July 1968; Tim Palmer, *Endangered Rivers and the Conservation Movement* (Berkeley: University of California Press, 1986), 144.

6. Richard F. Fenno Jr., *Congressmen in Committees* (Boston: Little, Brown, 1973).

7. Ibid., 165–71, 270–71.

8. Ibid., 99, 256.

9. Ibid., 119, 122.

10. Ibid., 60, 118.

11. Ibid., 271.

12. U.S. House, *Providing for the Establishment of the Apostle Islands National Lakeshore in the State of Wisconsin, and for Other Purposes. Report No. 91-1280* (Washington, DC: Government Printing Office, July 7, 1970), 7.

13. Fenno, *Congressmen in Committees*, 93.

14. Ibid., 121, 123, 260.

15. "Nelson's Bill Triggers Debate: Apostle Islands—Their Beauty Prompts Plan," *Duluth News Tribune*, August 29, 1965.

16. Alvin O'Konski, letter to Roy Hokenson, May 20, 1966.

17. Alvin O'Konski, letter to Michael C. Brecke, March 17, 1967.

18. Alvin O'Konski, letter to William Bechtel, May 1, 1967.

19. U.S. Senate, *Subcommittee on Parks and Recreation of the Committee on Interior and Insular Affairs*, 90th Cong., 1st sess., hearings, June 1–2, 1967 (Washington, DC: Government Printing Office, 1970), 75.

20. "Across the Editor's Desk," *Bayfield County Press*, March 1968.

21. "Apostle Islands Bill Gets No Opposition in House Hearing," *Ashland Daily Press*, July 30, 1968; "Apostle Park Given Boost," *Milwaukee Journal*, July 30, 1968.

22. U.S. House, *Hearings Before the Subcommittee on National Parks and Recrea-*

tion of the Committee on Interior and Insular Affairs, 91st Cong., 2nd sess., hearings on H.R. 555, H.R. 9306 and S. 621, Serial Number 99-9, March 23–24, 1970 (Washington, DC: Government Printing Office, 1970), 246–49.

23. Alvin O'Konski, letter to Robert Kastenmeier, May 1970.

24. Stuart Applebaum, telephone call to Harold C. Jordahl, June 1, 1970; Richard Bradee, "Hickel to Help Apostle Islands Bill," *Milwaukee Sentinel*, June 2, 1970.

25. "House Approves Apostle Isle Bill," *Milwaukee Sentinel*, September 11, 1970.

26. Ibid.

27. U.S. Senate, *Subcommittee on Parks and Recreation of the Committee on Interior and Insular Affairs*, hearings, May 9, 1967 (Washington, DC: Government Printing Office, 1970), 12–18.

28. "Humphrey Lauds Nelson on Lakeshore Park Bill," *Ashland Daily Press*, October 3, 1967.

29. Robert Kastenmeier, statement before House Subcommittee on National Parks and Recreation, 90th Cong., 2nd sess., July 29, 1968 (no hearing record published).

30. John Brynes, letter to Paul Romig, March 6, 1968; Culver Prentice, letter to Wayne Aspinall, March 15, 1968; Victoria McCormick, letter to Melvin Laird, March 4, 1968.

31. Harold C. Jordahl, statement before House Subcommittee on National Parks and Recreation, July 29, 1968 (no hearing record published).

32. U.S. Senate, *Subcommittee on Parks and Recreation of the Committee on Interior and Insular Affairs*, hearings, February 19, May 9, June 1–2, 1967; January 16, March 17, June 25, August 19, 1969; March 23–24, 1970 (Washington, DC: Government Printing Office 1970), 10.

33. Stuart Applebaum, telephone call to Harold C. Jordahl, May 8, 1970.

34. U.S. House, *Providing for the Establishment.*

35. Alvin O'Konski et al., letter to members of the U.S. House of Representatives, September 9, 1970.

36. *Congressional Record*, September 10, 1970, H8557–8568.

37. Ibid.

38. John W. Kole, "House OK's Apostle Isle Lakeshore," *Milwaukee Journal*, September 11, 1970.

39. Harold C. Jordahl, memorandum to the file, September 17, 1970.

40. *Congressional Record*, September 16, 1970.

41. William Bechtel, letter to Harold C. Jordahl, December 27, 1965.

42. William Bechtel, interview by Kathleen Lidfors, historian, National Park Service, Bayfield, WI, March 4, 1985.

43. William Bechtel, letter to Harold C. Jordahl, August 2, 1966.

44. Nelson, interview by Lidfors.

45. Lyndon B. Johnson, "Protecting Our Natural Heritage, Special Message to the Congress of the United States," January 30, 1967.

46. "Apostle Park Closer," *Milwaukee Journal*, August 23, 1967.

47. Lyndon B. Johnson, message to Congress, "To Renew a Nation," March 8, 1968.

48. Ibid.

49. "Apostle Isle Bill Again Introduced," *Milwaukee Journal*, January 24, 1969.

50. John W. Kole, "Apostle Isle Plans Hit New Obstacles," *Milwaukee Journal*, March 18, 1969.

51. National Wildlife Federation, "Administration Quashes Establishment of New Parks," *Conservation Report*, September 26, 1969.

52. Ibid.

53. U.S. Senate, *Subcommittee on Parks and Recreation of the Committee on Interior and Insular Affairs*, 91st Cong., 1st sess., hearings, August 19, 1969 (Washington, DC: Government Printing Office, 1970; "Senate Passes Apostle Isles Lakeshore Bill," *Milwaukee Sentinel*, June 27, 1969.

54. "Apostle Island Plan Delayed," *Wisconsin State Journal* (Madison), September 21, 1969.

55. National Wildlife Federation, "Administration Quashes Establishment of New Parks"; "Cutback to Delay Apostle Park," *Milwaukee Journal*, September 21, 1969.

56. U.S. Department of the Interior, "Secretary Hickel Announces Gateway National Recreation Areas," news release, September 26, 1969; National Wildlife Federation, "Administration Quashes Establishment of New Parks."

57. Ibid.

58. Wildlife Management Institute, "Budget Bureau Says 'Nyet' to Parks and Recreation Areas," *Outdoor News Bulletin*, September 26, 1969; Robert Kastenmeier, "The Apostle Islands," *Washington Perspective*, September 26, 1969.

59. "Conservation Claim U.S. Reneged on Park Promise," *Milwaukee Journal*, September 28, 1969.

60. *Weekly Compilation of Presidential Documents*, 6(7) (February 16, 1970): 169–70.

61. Robert Kastenmeier, letter to Harold C. Jordahl, February 11, 1970.

62. Loren H. Osman, "Udall Plans Survey of Apostles Park Site," *Milwaukee Journal*, April 2, 1964; William Stokes, "Conservation Cause Given Boost: Udall, Nelson Call for Action Now," *Wisconsin State Journal* (Madison), April 3, 1964; John Patrick Hunter, "Udall Hails State's Resource Program," *Capital Times* (Madison), April 2, 1964; John Patrick Hunter, "Film on Apostles Steals Show from Nelson, Udall," *Capital Times* (Madison), April 3, 1964; Gene Divine. "Udall for Midwest Sites: Areas Studied for National Parks," *Milwaukee Sentinel*, April 4, 1964; "Welcome to Cabinet Member: Udall Fights for Tomorrow," *Wisconsin State Journal* (Madison), April 2, 1964.

63. U.S. House, *Hearings Before the Subcommittee on National Parks and Recreation of the Committee on Interior and Insular Affairs*, 91st Cong., 2nd sess., hearings on H.R. 555, H.R. 9306, and S. 621, Serial Number 99-9, May 9, 1967 (Washington, DC: Government Printing Office, 1970), 18–19.

64. Quoted in Thomas R. Huffman, "Protectors of the Land and Water: The Political Culture of Conservation and the Rise of Environmentalism in Wisconsin, 1858–1970" (PhD diss., University of Wisconsin–Madison, 1989), 376–78. See also Thomas R. Huffman, *Protectors of the Land and Water: Environmentalism in Wisconsin, 1961–1968* (Chapel Hill: University of North Carolina Press, 1994).

65. Huffman, "Protectors of the Land," 393–94.

66. Ibid.

67. U.S. House, subcommittee hearings, August 19, 1969, 38.

68. Martin Hanson, interview by Harold C. Jordahl, September 4, 1989.

69. Nelson, interview by Lidfors, March 4, 1985.

70. George Hartzog Jr., interview by Kathleen Lidfors, historian, National Park Service, Bayfield, WI, March 7, 1985.

71. U.S. Senate, *Subcommittee on Parks and Recreation of the Committee on Interior and Insular Affairs*, 90th Cong., 1st sess., hearings, June 1–2, 1967 (Washington, DC: Government Printing Office, 1970), 81–83.

72. Russ Tall, "Apostle Islands Plan Debated," *Midland Cooperator* (Minneapolis), October 14, 1963.

73. Culver Prentice, letters to Harold C. Jordahl, December 19, 1964, December 19, 1965.

74. U.S. House, subcommittee hearings, August 19, 1969, 78–81.

75. Culver Prentice, telephone call to Harold C. Jordahl, January 9, 1970.

76. J. Louis Hanson, interview by Kathleen Lidfors, historian, National Park Service, Bayfield, WI, March 27, 1985.

77. M. Hanson, interview by Jordahl, September 4, 1989.

Chapter 9. The Sellers of Dreams

1. John B. Chapple, "The Wisconsin Islands: The Famous Apostle Islands at the Top of Wisconsin," *Ashland Daily Press*, 1945.

2. Charles Sheridan, "Legends and History of the Apostle Islands," a series of articles originally published in the *Superior Telegram* in 1930 and reprinted in the *Washburn Times* in 1930 and 1931.

3. John Chapple, interview by Harold C. Jordahl, April 5, 1989.

4. Gordon MacQuarrie, "Purchase of Apostle Islands Gets Backing," *Milwaukee Journal*, April 9, 1950.

5. Ibid.

6. Mel Ellis, "Apostle Islands Offer Taste of the Primeval," *Milwaukee Journal*, November 21, 1950.

7. Mel Ellis, "Apostle Islands Offer Excellent Deer Hunting," *Milwaukee Journal*, December 12, 1954.

8. "Apostle Chain Is Being Eyed for Recreation," *Green Bay Press-Gazette*, March 18, 1952.

9. "State's Apostle Islands Have 300 Years of History," *Milwaukee Journal*, November 15, 1953.

10. Arthur Fellows, "Scenery, Fish, Climate, History Are Apostle Island Attractions," *Milwaukee Journal*, October 3, 1954.

11. Gordon MacQuarrie, "Haven from Heat—State Studying Idea of Buying Apostle Chain," *Milwaukee Journal*, August 7, 1955.

12. Gordon MacQuarrie, "Game Men Cast Covetous Eyes on Apostle Island Group for State," *Milwaukee Journal*, August 20, 1955.

13. Gordon MacQuarrie, "The Islands Wisconsin Forgot," *Milwaukee Journal*, March 25, 1956.

14. "Dream Coming True with Island Purchase," *Milwaukee Sentinel*, January 18, 1959.

15. "Shoreline Park Sought for Bad River: Nelson Requests U.S. to Establish 20,000 Acre Recreation Facility in State," *Milwaukee Journal*, May 23, 1962; "Bad River Proposed as Recreation Site," *Milwaukee Sentinel*, May 23, 1962; "Lake Superior Area Suggested for Recreation," *Stevens Point Daily Journal*, May 22, 1962.

16. "Udall Interested in Superior Park," *Wausau Record Herald*, May 31, 1962.

17. Harvey Breuscher, "Lake Superior Recreation Area Proposed by Nelson," *Eau Claire Telegram*, June 12, 1962. More than twenty-six years later, I ran into Breuscher on the University of Wisconsin–Madison campus and asked him if he remembered the trip. He said he certainly did and "thought I had written a good story until I saw George Armour's piece in the *Milwaukee Journal*. It was a classic and Huckleberry Finn would have loved to walk barefoot on that sand." In fact, both Breuscher and Armour, veteran and incisive reporters, were so entranced with the beauty of the sand spit that they had walked a considerable distance down the spit. I waited for them in the last boat to leave, which then broke its motor. If Crafts, in a boat far ahead, had not looked back and observed the situation, the rest of the tour would have been considerably delayed.

18. Don Johnson, "Apostles? 'No Place Like It,'" *Milwaukee Sentinel*, July 19, 1964.

19. "Lucey Commends Nelson Plan for Apostle Islands: Cites Value to North," *Capital Times* (Madison), September 30, 1965; "Island Park Endorsed by Pat Lucey," *Ashland Daily Press*, September 30, 1965.

20. Gaylord A. Nelson, *Legislative Memo* (Washington, DC), September 14, 1965.

21. Gaylord A. Nelson, *Legislative Memo*, November 10, 1965.

22. Gaylord A. Nelson, *Legislative Memo*, April 10, May 15, May 26, June 1967.

23. "National Lakeshore: Ready and Waiting," *Milwaukee Journal*, October 24, 1965.

24. "A Wisconsin Park Proposed by U.S.: National Lakeshore Urged in Apostle Islands Area," *New York Times*, August 29, 1965.

25. "New York Times Full Page on Islands," *Ashland Daily Press*, September 26, 1967.

26. Ron Way, "The Apostle Islands: Scenic Wonderland," *Minneapolis Tribune*, August 17, 1969.

27. William Bechtel, interview by Kathleen Lidfors, historian, National Park Service, Bayfield, WI, March 4, 1985.

28. "Assemblyman Gehrmann Gives Views on National Park," *Ashland Daily Press*, September 23, 1965.

29. "Lakeshore Plan Is a Good One," *Superior Evening Telegram*, September 29, 1965.

30. "Apostle Islands Park," *Mining Journal* (Marquette, MI), October 12, 1965.

31. "Help Wanted for Apostle Islands," *Badger Sportsman* (Chilton, WI), November 2, 1965.

32. Gaylord A. Nelson, *Legislative Memo*, September 14, November 10, 1965.

33. Harold C. Jordahl, letter to Molly Sulewsky, September 15, 1965.

34. I. V. Fine, Ralph B. Hovind, and Philip H. Lewis Jr., *The Lake Superior Region Recreational Potential: A Preliminary Report* (Madison: Wisconsin Department of Resource Development, 1962).

35. "Proposed Apostle Islands National Lakeshore and Plans for Its Development," *National Parks Magazine*, December 1965.

36. "Hearings to Open on Apostle Islands National Park," *Minneapolis Tribune*, May 31, 1965.

37. Miles McMillin, "Will People or Promoters Get Apostle Islands?" *Capital Times* (Madison), May 29, 1967.

38. Gene Divine, "Apostles Hearing Draws Long Line of Supporters," *Milwaukee Sentinel*, June 2, 1967.

39. Wallace W. Morgan, "Apostle Islands Plan Supported," *Duluth News Tribune*, June 2, 1967; Ralph Thornton, "Lakeshore Issue Stirs Village: Some Favor It, Some Don't," *Minneapolis Star*, June 3, 1967.

40. "Nelson Hopes for Approval of Park," *Ashland Daily Press*, June 3, 1967.

41. Merlo J. Pusey, "Proposed Present Great Lakes' Parks Deserve National Status," *Milwaukee Sentinel*, August 21, 1967; Donald Jansen, "A National Lakeshore Is Proposed for Wisconsin," *Ashland Daily Press*, September 26, 1967; Donald Jansen, "National Park Nears Reality," *Wisconsin State Journal* (Madison), September 3, 1967; "The Apostle Islands," *Ashland Daily Press*, September 9, 1967; "Senate OK's Apostle Bill: Lakeshore Project to Cost $13 Million," *Milwaukee Sentinel*, August 22, 1967; "Priceless Shore," *Milwaukee Sentinel*, August 23, 1967.

42. National Park Service, *Proposed Apostle Islands National Lakeshore*, brochure, n.d.

43. Harold C. Jordahl, personal notes, 1967.

44. *Nelson Newsletter* (Washington, DC), July 1968.

45. Gaylord A. Nelson, interview by Kathleen Lidfors, historian, National Park Service, Bayfield, WI, March 4, 1985.

46. Charles Stoddard, letter to Harold C. Jordahl, September 9, 1964; Martin

Hanson, letter to Harold C. Jordahl, April 1, 1964; Culver Prentice, letter to Harold C. Jordahl, December 19, 1965.

47. *Apostle Islands Region*, movie (Wisconsin Department of Resource Development, Ashland and Bayfield Counties, Bureau of Indian Affairs, and National Park Service, 1964).

48. Wisconsin Department of Resource Development, "The Unfinished Task" Conference, Madison, October 10, 1962.

49. George Allez, letter to William Bechtel, August 13, 1963; William Bechtel, letter to Stuart Hanish, August 20, 1963.

50. Martin Hanson, letter to Gaylord A. Nelson, October 11, 1963; Gaylord A. Nelson, letter to Martin Hanson, October 22, 1963.

51. Martin Hanson, letter to Ralph Hovind, November 18, 1963; Stuart Hanish, letter to Regional Directors of the National Park Service and the Bureau of Indian Affairs, November 14, 1963, transmitted by Harold C. Jordahl, November 27, 1963.

52. John Patrick Hunter, "Film on Apostles Steals Show from Nelson, Udall," *Capital Times* (Madison), April 3, 1964.

53. Martin Hanson, letter to Harold C. Jordahl, April 1, 1964.

54. Ray Sale, letter to Bert Minwegen, June 17, 1964.

55. Stuart Hanish, letters to Harold C. Jordahl, September 16, 1964, March 2, 1965; Martin Hanson, letter to William Bechtel, January 29, 1965.

56. J. Louis Hanson, interview by Kathleen Lidfors, historian, National Park Service, Bayfield, WI, March 27, 1985.

57. Fine, Hovind, and Lewis, *Lake Superior Region Recreational Potential*.

58. I. V. Fine, "Apostle Islands: Some of the Economic Implications of the Proposed Apostle Islands National Lakeshore," *Wisconsin Vacation-Recreation Papers* III, no. 1. (Madison: University of Wisconsin, School of Commerce, May 1965); Harold C. Jordahl, memorandum to Henry Caulfield, August 19, 1965; U.S. Department of the Interior, *Proposed Apostle Islands National Lakeshore, Bayfield and Ashland Counties, Wisconsin* (Washington, DC: Superintendent of Documents, March 1965).

59. "Proposed Apostle Islands National Park Set for Congress Introduction," *Ashland Daily Press*, August 30, 1965.

60. John W. Kole, "$11 Million Plan Urged for Apostle Islands," *Milwaukee Journal*, August 29, 1965.

61. "Nelson's Bill Triggers Debate: Apostle Islands—Their Beauty Prompts Plan," *Duluth News Tribune*, August 29, 1965.

62. James J. Tills, "Apostle Islands—Their Beauty Prompts Plan," *Duluth News Tribune*. August 29, 1965.

63. Ray Moucha, "Nelson Details Apostle Islands Park Proposal," *Wisconsin State Journal* (Madison), August 29, 1965; "Nelson Proposal Merits Support: Apostle Islands Recreation Plan," *Wisconsin State Journal* (Madison), September 1, 1965.

64. Jasper Landry, "A 'Must' for Northern Wisconsin Economy," *Mellen Weekly Record*, September 2, 1965.

65. "Sen. G. Nelson Reveals Plans for Fed. Recreation Area," *Bayfield County Press*, September 2, 1965.

66. "Apostle Islands Park," *Milwaukee Journal*, September 5, 1965.

67. "Editorial—Economic Boost for Area," *Iron River Pioneer* (Bayfield County), September 9, 1965.

68. "Apostle Island Plan Deserves Our Support," *Vilas County News-Review*, September 9, 1965.

69. "Growing Late," *Milwaukee Sentinel*, September 7, 1965.

70. "Editorial," WTMJ-TV, Milwaukee, aired September 20, 1965.

71. "National Lakeshore: Ready and Waiting," *Milwaukee Journal*, October 24, 1965.

72. "Bayfield CC Votes for Island Park," *Ashland Daily Press*, September 16, 1965.

73. "Apostle Islands Plan Merits Support," *Sawyer County Record*, September 16, 1965.

74. "Plan for Bad River Public Area Has Pros and Cons," *Milwaukee Journal*, May 24, 1962.

75. "Chequamegon Area Recreation Study Is Called For," *Milwaukee Journal*, July 7, 1962.

76. R. G. Lynch. "State Recreation Area Planned in Apostles," *Milwaukee Journal*, July 22, 1962.

77. Ibid.

78. "Idea of National Park on Superior's South Shore Needs Much Study," *Milwaukee Journal*, April 7, 1964.

79. Thomas R. Huffman, "Protectors of the Land and Water: The Political Culture of Conservation and the Rise of Environmentalism in Wisconsin, 1858–1970" (PhD diss., University of Wisconsin–Madison, 1989), 90–91.

80. Ernest Swift, *Conservation News* (Washington, DC: National Wildlife Federation), November 1, 1964.

81. Ernest Swift, letters to Ralph Hovind, November 27, December 2, 1964; Ralph Hovind, letter to Louis S. Clapper, November 20, 1964; Ralph Hovind, letter to Ernest Swift, November 30, 1964; Louis S. Clapper, letter to Ralph Hovind, November 23, 1964.

82. "Apostle Islands Park," *Milwaukee Journal*, September 5, 1965.

83. "National Park Status Will Save Apostles Area for Future," *Milwaukee Journal*, April 19, 1967; "Apostle Park Closer," *Milwaukee Journal*, August 23, 1967; "Johnson Calls Again for National Park in Apostle Area," *Milwaukee Journal*, January 31, 1968; "Citizens Must Speak for Preservation of Apostle Islands," *Milwaukee Journal*, August 12, 1969; "Lake Superior Gem, Apostle Islands Tract Saved," *Milwaukee Journal*, September 13, 1970.

84. *Congressional Record*, proceedings and debates of the 91st Cong., 2nd sess., no. 181, pt. 2, October 14, 1970.

85. "Think before You Leap," *Bayfield County Press*, October 10, 1963.

86. Eleanor Knight, "Editorial: Bayfield to Fit into $15 Million Tourist and Recreation Program," *Bayfield County Press*, February 4, 1965; Eleanor Knight, "Gamble While You Gambol," *Bayfield County Press*, March 11, 1965; "Sen. G. Nelson Reveals Plans for Fed. Recreation Area," *Bayfield County Press*, September 2, 1965.

87. "Bayfield Assoc. Not for Park," *Ashland Daily Press*, October 20, 1965.

88. "Letters to the Editor," *Chicago Daily News*, March 28, 1968; "Letters to the Editor," *Duluth News Tribune*, June 3, 1967.

89. "Across the Editor's Desk," *Bayfield County Press*, March 1968.

90. Culver Prentice, letter to Wayne Aspinall, March 15, 1968.

91. Wayne N. Aspinall, letter to Culver Prentice, March 22, 1968.

92. U.S. House, *Hearings Before the Subcommittee on National Parks and Recreation of the Committee on Interior and Insular Affairs*, 91st Cong., 2nd sess., hearings on H.R. 555, H.R. 9306, and S. 621, Serial Number 99-9, March 23–24, June 3, 1970 (Washington, DC: Government Printing Office, 1970), 334–38.

Chapter 10. The Local Citizens and the Lakeshore

1. Wisconsin Conservation Commission, *Minutes*, September 21, 1962; L. P. Voigt in Wisconsin Conservation Commission, *Minutes*, November 2, 1962.

2. Russ Tall, "Apostle Islands Plan Debated," *Midland Cooperator* (Minneapolis), October 14, 1963.

3. "Island Sale to State Is Favored," *Milwaukee Sentinel*, June 24, 1969; "Ashland Board Votes to Sell Islands," *Milwaukee Sentinel*, June 25, 1969.

4. Tall, "Apostle Islands Plan Debated."

5. Ashland County Board of Supervisors, resolution, March 1, 1966.

6. "Island Park Sizzles: Meeting Called," *Ashland Daily Press*, April 19, 1967.

7. "Island Park Group Pushes for Coordination in the Creating of Federal Park," *Ashland Daily Press*, May 27, 1967.

8. U.S. Senate, *Subcommittee on Parks and Recreation of the Committee on Interior and Insular Affairs*, 90th Cong., 1st sess., hearings, June 1–2, 1967 (Washington, DC: Government Printing Office, 1970), 131–33.

9. Ibid.

10. Martin Hanson, letter to William Bechtel, April 21, 1967.

11. U.S. Senate, subcommittee hearings, June 1–2, 1967, 286; U.S. Senate, *Subcommittee on Parks and Recreation of the Committee on Interior and Insular Affairs*, 91st Cong., 1st sess., hearings, June 25, 1969 (Washington, DC: Government Printing Office, 1970), 16.

12. U.S. House, *Hearings Before the Subcommittee on National Parks and Recreation of the Committee on Interior and Insular Affairs*, 90th Cong., 1st sess., hearings

on H.R. 555, H.R. 9306, and S. 621, Serial Number 99-9, June 1, 1967 (Washington, DC: Government Printing Office, 1970), 157.

13. U.S. House, *Hearings Before the Subcommittee on National Parks and Recreation of the Committee on Interior and Insular Affairs*, 91st Cong., 1st sess., hearings on H.R. 555, H.R. 9306, and S. 621, Serial Number 99-9 August 19, 1969 (Washington, DC: Government Printing Office, 1970), 97.

14. U.S. House, *Committee on Interior and Insular Affairs*, 91st Cong., 2nd sess., hearings, June 6, 1970 (Washington, DC: Government Printing Office, 1970), 158, 386.

15. Tall, "Apostle Islands Plan Debated."

16. U.S. Senate, subcommittee hearings, May 9, June 1–2, 1967, 310.

17. Fred Huybrecht, letter to Stewart Udall, William Proxmire, Gaylord Nelson, and Alvin E. O'Konski, March 25, 1965.

18. U.S. Senate, subcommittee hearings, May 9, June 1–2, 1969, 146.

19. Ibid., 144–46.

20. U.S. Senate, subcommittee hearings, March 17, 1969, 96–97.

21. U.S. Senate, subcommittee hearings, May 9, June 1–2, 1969, 86.

22. U.S. House, subcommittee hearings, August 19, 1969, 83.

23. U.S. House, committee hearings, June 3, 1970, 303.

24. U.S. Senate, subcommittee hearings, May 9, June 1–2, 1969, 86.

25. "Advocates, Pickets Appear at Islands Hearing," *Ashland Daily Press*, August 19, 1969.

26. U.S. House, subcommittee hearings, August 19, 1969.

27. U.S. Senate, subcommittee hearings, June 1–2, 1967, 116.

28. U.S. House, committee hearings, March 23–24, 1970, 326–32, 360–67, 375–80.

29. In earlier testimony, William Sivertson of Ashland, owner of a portion of Long Island, had warned the House subcommittee of the dangers of Lake Superior: "The main thing that concerns me about this national park is the safety involved. I do not know if men understand or have ever been out on a rough sea in your life but this Lake Superior, its waves are over 25 feet high and I have seen many people, a lot of casualties around Long Island and you get novice and layman people out in the lake in 16 or 20 foot boats and they are nothing but trouble. . . . Do you want to see lives taken? No, you do not and I do not, because when you get laymen in here, I think, gentlemen, you are in for a shock" (U.S. House, subcommittee hearings, August 19, 1969, 59–160). Tragically, Sivertson drowned in a storm twenty years later while attempting to reach his property on Long Island from the mainland.

30. J. H. Bruce, letter to Wayne N. Aspinall, May 20, 1970. Placed into House subcommittee hearings, March 23–24, 1970, 330.

31. U.S. House, committee hearings, March 23–24, 1970, 375–79.

32. U.S. House, committee hearings, July 7, 1970, 11–15.

33. U.S. Senate, subcommittee hearings, May 9, 1967, 37.

34. Ibid., 33–41, 58.

35. U.S. Senate, subcommittee hearings, March 17, 1969, 81–95.

36. "Sen. G. Nelson Reveals Plans for Fed. Recreation Area," *Bayfield County Press*, September 2, 1965.

37. U.S. Senate, subcommittee hearings, March 23–24, June 3, 1967, 114–15.

38. Ibid., 273–74.

39. Ibid., 132.

Chapter 11. The State and the Apostle Islands

1. Gifford Pinchot, address delivered before the Joint Session of Wisconsin Legislature, *Wisconsin State Journal* (Madison), March 24, 1927, 1 (emphasis added).

2. Wisconsin Department of Administration, *Wisconsin Blue Book* (Madison: 1954), 306.

3. Wisconsin State Planning Board and Wisconsin Conservation Commission, "A Park, Parkway and Recreational Area Plan," *Bulletin* 8 (Madison: January 1939).

4. Wisconsin Department of Administration, *Wisconsin Blue Book*, 293.

5. Ibid., 294.

6. Wisconsin Legislative Council Conservation Committee, *Minutes*, September 26, 1955, 2–3.

7. Wisconsin Conservation Commission, *Activities Progress Report* (Madison: August 31, 1949), 3.

8. Wisconsin Conservation Commission, *Minutes*, May 12, 1950, Wisconsin Department of Natural Resources, Central Files, Madison, 17.

9. Ibid.

10. Wisconsin Conservation Commission, *Minutes*, November 10, 1950, Wisconsin Department of Natural Resources, Central Files, Madison, 25–26.

11. Ashland County Board of Supervisors, *Proceedings*, 1951–1952, 26.

12. Ibid., 26–27.

13. Wisconsin Conservation Commission, *Minutes*, February 20, 1952, Wisconsin Department of Natural Resources, Central Files, Madison, 1.

14. Wisconsin Legislative Council Conservation Committee, *Progress Report*, July 28, 1952, 8.

15. Mel Ellis, "Apostle Islands Offer Taste of the Primeval," *Milwaukee Journal*, November 21, 1950; "Apostle Chain Is Being Eyed for Recreation," *Green Bay Press-Gazette*, March 18, 1952.

16. *Green Bay Press-Gazette*, March 18, 1952.

17. Wisconsin Conservation Commission, *Minutes*, July 12, 1952, Wisconsin Department of Natural Resources, Central Files, Madison, 2–4.

18. Wisconsin Conservation Commission, *Minutes*, November 10, 1950, Wisconsin Department of Natural Resources, Central Files, Madison, 25–26.

19. Ashland County Board of Supervisors, *Proceedings*, 1952–1953, 97.

20. G. E. Sprecher, memorandum to L. P. Voigt, July 6, 1954.

21. "Ask State to Buy Apostle Islands," *Capital Times* (Madison), August 27, 1954 (emphasis added).

22. Ludwig Trammel, letter to Victor Wallin, January 6, 1955.

23. Wisconsin State Legislature, *Joint Resolution 103A*, 1955.

24. "Ask State to Buy Apostle Islands."

25. Earl Sachse, letter to Guido Rahr, February 2, 1955 (emphasis added).

26. Wisconsin Conservation Commission, *Minutes*, February 9, 1955, Wisconsin Department of Natural Resources, Central Files, Madison, 7–8; L. P. Voigt, letter to Earl Sachse, February 24, 1955.

27. A. W. Schorger, letter to L. P. Voigt, March 14, 1955.

28. Earl Sachse, letter to L. P. Voigt, March 22, 1955.

29. University of Wisconsin, *Report of the Committee Investigating Stockton Island, Ashland County, Wisconsin*, 1955.

30. Ray M. Stroud, letter to L. P. Voigt, May 5, 1955.

31. Wisconsin Land Committee, *Minutes*, April 1, 1955.

32. Wisconsin Legislative Conservation Commission, *Minutes*, May 6, 1955, Wisconsin Department of Natural Resources, Central Files, Madison.

33. L. P. Voigt, letter to the Wisconsin Conservation Commission, May 23, 1955.

34. Stroud, letter to Voigt, May 5, 1955.

35. B. L. Dahlberg, memorandum to L. P. Voigt, May 17, 1955.

36. Wisconsin Conservation Commission, *Minutes*, August 11–12, 1955, Wisconsin Department of Natural Resources, Central Files, Madison.

37. John Beale, memorandums to L. P. Voigt and Edward Schneberger, June 3, July 22, 1955.

38. Ashland County Board of Supervisors, *Proceedings*, August 19, 1955, 133.

39. Wisconsin Legislative Council Conservation Committee, *Minutes*, September 26, 1955, 3–4.

40. Wisconsin Legislative Council Conservation Committee, *Minutes*, January 9, 1956, 2–3.

41. Wisconsin Legislative Council Conservation Committee, *Minutes*, March 16, 1956, 1–2.

42. W. E. Scott, memorandum to L. P. Voigt, April 2, 1956.

43. Wisconsin Legislative Council Conservation Committee, *Minutes*, August 24, 1956, 5–6.

44. John Beale, memorandum to Edward Erdlitz, November 24, 1956.

45. John Borkenhagen, memorandum to Edward Erdlitz, November 24, 1956.

46. Wisconsin Legislative Council Conservation Committee, *Final Report to the Governor and the 1957 Legislature*, vol. 2 (Madison: 1957), 33–34.

47. Wisconsin Conservation Commission, *Minutes*, January 9, 1959, Wisconsin Department of Natural Resources, Central Files, Madison, 8–10.

48. John Beale, memorandum to L. P. Voigt, December 24, 1958.

49. Wisconsin Conservation Commission, *Minutes*, January 9, 1959, Wisconsin Department of Natural Resources, Central Files, Madison, 8–10.

50. "Apostle Isle Sold to State," *Milwaukee Journal*, January 10, 1959; "State Buys Island in Lake Superior," *Green Bay Press-Gazette*, January 12, 1959; "Dream Coming True with Island Purchase," *Milwaukee Sentinel*, January 18, 1959.

51. John Beale, memorandum to L. P. Voigt, March 3, 1959.

52. Wisconsin Conservation Commission, *Minutes*, March 12, 1959, Wisconsin Department of Natural Resources, Central Files, Madison, 25; John Beale, memorandum to L. P. Voigt, March 3, 1959.

53. Wisconsin State Senate, *Joint Resolution 39*, March 17, 1959.

54. Ashland County Board of Supervisors, *Proceedings*, 1959–1960, 59.

55. Ernest Swift, "Politics in Conservation" (lecture delivered at Stevens Point, Wisconsin, May 14, 1960).

56. Wisconsin Legislative Council Conservation Committee, *Minutes*, October 31, 1960, 8–10.

57. Ashland County Board of Supervisors, *Proceedings*, April 19, 1960, 50–51.

58. Wisconsin Legislative Council Conservation Committee, *Minutes*, October 31, 1960, 6–10.

59. Wisconsin Legislative Council Conservation Committee, *Minutes*, October 3–4, 1960, 4.

60. I. V. Fine, "Apostle Islands: Some of the Economic Implications of the Proposed Apostle Islands National Lakeshore," *Wisconsin Vacation-Recreation Papers* III, no. 1 (Madison: University of Wisconsin, School of Commerce, May 1965).

61. I. V. Fine, and E. E. Werner, "The Tourist-Vacation Industry in Wisconsin" (Madison: University of Wisconsin, School of Commerce, 1981).

62. Wisconsin Conservation Commission, *Policy on Acquisition of an Apostle Islands Wilderness Area* (Madison: August 12, 1955).

63. Wisconsin Department of Resource Development, *The Biennial Report to the Legislature of 1963 on the Activities of the Natural Resources Committee of State Agencies* (Madison: February 26, 1963), 83; Wisconsin Department of Resource Development, *A Plan for Wisconsin* (Madison: 1963).

64. Harold C. Jordahl, personal notes, 1963; Wisconsin Department of Resource Development, *Biennial Report to the Legislature of 1963*, 58–59; Wisconsin Department of Resource Development, *Plan for Wisconsin*, 71.

65. Wisconsin Department of Resource Development, *Plan for Wisconsin*.

66. Jordahl, personal notes, 1963.

67. John Beale, memorandum to George E. Sprecher, Donald J. Mackie, and Edward Schneberger, December 1, 1964; Edward D. MacDonald, memorandum to Donald J. Mackie, July 15, 1964.

68. U.S. Department of Agriculture, *Resources and Recreation in the Northern Great Lakes Region* (Washington, DC: 1963); U.S. Department of the Interior, *Preliminary Draft: Preliminary OEDP for Northwestern Wisconsin* (Madison: 1963).

69. U.S. Department of the Interior, *Preliminary Draft*.

70. Wisconsin Department of Resource Development, *The Outdoor Recreation Plan* (Madison: 1966), 138.

71. Ibid., 55–56.

72. Fine, "Apostle Islands," 8, 14.

73. North Central Field Committee, *Subcommittee Minutes*, October 1, 1964.

74. Northwest Wisconsin Regional Planning Commission, *Northwestern Wisconsin Comprehensive Planning Program* (Madison: January 31, 1965), 145.

75. "Speakers Stress Islands Potential," *Duluth News Tribune*, March 26, 1965.

76. Harold C. Jordahl, memorandum to Henry P. Caulfield, July 7, 1965; Harold C. Jordahl, letter to Governor Warren P. Knowles, July 7, 1965.

77. "Knowles to Be Named to Committee," *Milwaukee Sentinel*, September 11, 1965.

78. "'Think Big' Says Gov. Knowles in Speech Here," *Ashland Daily Press*, October 11, 1965.

79. Gaylord A. Nelson, "Apostle Islands Project," *Ashland Daily Press*, May 15, 1967; Gaylord A. Nelson, letter to Governor Warren P. Knowles, May 18, 1967.

80. U.S. Senate, *Subcommittee on Parks and Recreation of the Committee on Interior and Insular Affairs*, hearings, June 1–2, 1967 (Washington, DC: Government Printing Office, 1970).

81. Warren P. Knowles, letter to Leon Lewandowski, November 13, 1968.

82. Ibid.

83. U.S. House, *Hearings Before the Subcommittee on National Parks and Recreation of the Committee on Interior and Insular Affairs*, 91st Cong., 2nd sess., hearings on H.R. 555, H.R. 9306, and S. 621, Serial Number 99-9, hearings, March 24–25, 1970 (Washington, DC: Government Printing Office, 1970), 242.

84. Harold C. Jordahl, telephone call to Stuart Applebaum, June 1, 1970.

85. Bronson LaFollette, letter to Stewart Udall, September 15, 1965; Stewart Udall, letter to Bronson LaFollette, October 5, 1965.

86. U.S. Senate, subcommittee hearings, June 1–2, 1967, 75–77.

87. "Island Park Endorsed by Pat Lucey," *Ashland Daily Press*, September 30, 1965; "Lucey Commends Nelson Plan for Apostle Islands: Cites Value to North," *Capital Times* (Madison), September 30, 1965.

88. "Carley Asks Bold Action on Parks," *Duluth News Tribune*, April 17, 1966.

89. U.S. Senate, subcommittee hearings, June 1–2, 1967, 77–78.

90. U.S. House, subcommittee hearings, August 19, 1969, 25–26.

91. Victor Wallin, letter to Alvin O'Konski, March 29, 1967.

92. U.S. Senate, subcommittee hearings, June 1–2, 1967, 108–9.

93. Jordahl, personal notes, 1963.

94. L. P. Voigt, letter to Governor Warren P. Knowles, May 29, 1967.

95. U.S. Senate, subcommittee hearings, June 1–2, 1967, 126–31.

96. U.S. House, subcommittee hearings, June 23–24, 1970, 243.

97. Summarized in Harold C. Jordahl, memorandum to Pat Miller, July 28, 1980.

98. Gaylord A. Nelson, interview by Kathleen Lidfors, historian, National Park Service, Bayfield, WI, March 4, 1985.

99. Wisconsin Natural Resources Board, *Minutes*, October 6, 1970.

100. L. P. Voigt, letter to Patrick Lucey, June 14, 1971.

101. Harold C. Jordahl, letter to Blake Kellogg, August 3, 1971.

102. William Bromberg, letter to Chester L. Brooks, December 8, 1971; Chester L. Brooks, letter to William Bromberg, December 17, 1971.

103. William Bromberg, telephone call to Harold C. Jordahl, July 1971.

104. Wisconsin Natural Resources Board, *Minutes*, July 15, 1971.

105. William Bromberg, letter to Harold C. Jordahl, August 8, 1972.

106. Patrick Lucey, letter to Chester Brooks, January 11, 1973.

107. Patrick Lucey, letter to L. P. Voigt, March 20, 1973; Milton E. Reinke, letter to Farnum Alston, March 1, 1973.

108. Wisconsin Natural Resources Board, *Minutes*, April 11, 1973.

109. L. P. Voigt, letter to Farnum Alston, April 17, 1973.

110. Chief, Office of Land Acquisition, Northeast Regional Office, National Park Service, memorandum to Chief, Land Acquisition, National Park Service, Duluth, July 25, 1973.

111. Chief, Office of Land Acquisition, National Park Service, Duluth, letter to Farnum Alston, July 30, 1973.

112. Harold C. Jordahl, letter to Farnum Alston, August 1, 1973.

113. L. P. Voigt, letter to Farnum Alston, September 18, 1973; Farnum Alston, letter to L. P. Voigt, January 30, 1974, October 8, 1973.

114. Elmer T. Nitzschke, letter to Farnum Alston, January 15, 1974.

115. Milton E. Reinke, note to Harold C. Jordahl, January 25, 1974.

116. Farnum Alston, letter to L. P. Voigt, January 30, 1974; L. P. Voigt, letter to Farnum Alston, February 20, 1974.

117. James A. Kurtz, memorandum to L. P. Voigt, January 30, 1974.

118. Governor of Wisconsin, joint news release with U.S. Department of the Interior, March 4, 1974.

119. L. P. Voigt, letter to Farnum Alston, June 18, 1974.

120. Wisconsin Department of Administration, *Wisconsin Blue Book* (Madison: 1975).

121. Wisconsin Natural Resources Board, *Minutes*, January 10, 1975.

122. Elmer T. Nitzschke, letter to James A. Kurtz, February 12, 1975.

123. Regional Director, National Park Service, letter to the Field Solicitor, U.S. Department of the Interior, March 19, 1975.

124. Lewis T. Mittness, telephone call to Milton E. Reinke, March 1975; Milton E. Reinke, letter to Lewis T. Mittness, March 24, 1975.

125. L. P. Voigt, letter to Richard A. Sterns, April 7, 1975.

126. Governor of Wisconsin, Press Release, August 13, 1975.

127. Ibid.

128. U.S. Public Law 91-424 (S. 621); Chapter 1.026(2), Wisconsin Statutes, 91st Cong., 2nd sess., September 26, 1970.

129. Patrick H. Miller, letter to Harold C. Jordahl, December 9, 1975.

130. Wisconsin Natural Resources Board, *Minutes*, January 21–22, 1976.

131. Ibid.

Chapter 12. The Apostle Islands National Lakeshore and the Native Americans

1. Nancy Lurie, *Wisconsin Indians* (Madison: State Historical Society of Wisconsin, 1980).

2. Ibid.; Donald J. Fixico, ed., *An Anthology of Western Great Lakes Indian History* (Milwaukee: American Indian Studies, University of Wisconsin–Milwaukee, 1985).

3. Joe Rose (Bad River Chippewa), interview by Annie L. Booth, August 14, 1989.

4. Lurie, *Wisconsin Indians*.

5. Fixico, *Anthology of Western Great Lakes Indian History*; Lurie, *Wisconsin Indians*.

6. This section is based upon the following sources: Fixico, *Anthology of Western Great Lakes Indian History*; Lurie, *Wisconsin Indians*; Basil Johnston, *Ojibwa Heritage* (Toronto: McClelland and Stewart, 1976); Carol Mason, *Introduction to Wisconsin Indians: Prehistory to Statehood* (Salem, NC: Sheffield, 1988).

7. C. W. Loomer, "Land Tenure Problems in the Bad River Indian Reservation of Wisconsin," *Research Bulletin* 188 (Madison: Agricultural Experiment Station, University of Wisconsin, December 1955).

8. Charles E. Aguar, *Tourist and Recreational Resources: Bad River Indian Reservation—Wisconsin* (Washington, DC: U.S. Department of the Interior, April 1965), 18.

9. Ibid., 68.

10. Stewart Udall, letters to Alex F. Roye, Fred Connors, and John W. Reynolds, April 4, 1964.

11. U.S. Department of the Interior, *Proposed Apostle Islands National Lakeshore, Bayfield and Ashland Counties, Wisconsin* (Washington, DC: Superintendent of Documents, March 1965), 2.

12. Ibid., xvii.

13. Alex Roye, letter to Stewart Udall, May 22, 1964.

14. North Central Field Committee, *Subcommittee Minutes*, June 24–26, September 30, 1964; Harold C. Jordahl, memorandum to Henry P. Caulfield, July 30, 1964.

15. Harold C. Jordahl, memorandum to Henry P. Caulfield, May 18, 1965.

16. U.S. Senate, *Subcommittee on Parks and Recreation of the Committee on Interior and Insular Affairs*, 90th Cong., 1st sess., hearings, May 9, 1967 (Washington, DC: Government Printing Office, 1970), 21.

17. Ibid., 13.

18. U.S. House, *Hearings Before the Subcommittee on National Parks and Recreation of the Committee on Interior and Insular Affairs*, 91st Cong., 2nd sess., hearings on H.R. 555, H.R. 9306, and S. 621, Serial Number 99-9, March 23–24, June 3, 1970 (Washington, DC: Government Printing Office, 1970), 348–49.

19. U.S. Department of the Interior, *Proposed Apostle Islands National Lakeshore*, 109.

20. U.S. Senate, subcommittee hearings, May 9, 1967, 2.

21. U.S. Department of the Interior, *Proposed Apostle Islands National Lakeshore*, 109.

22. Ibid., 110.

23. Letter from the Assistant Secretary of the Interior to the Chair of the Senate Committee on Interior and Insular Affairs, February 18, 1967, cited in U.S. Senate, subcommittee hearings, May 9, 1967, 5–8.

24. U.S. Senate, *Subcommittee on Parks and Recreation of the Committee on Interior and Insular Affairs*, 90th Cong., 1st sess., hearings, August 17, 1967 (Washington, DC: Government Printing Office, 1970), 2–3.

25. Assistant Secretary of the Interior, letter to the Chair of the House Committee on Interior and Insular Affairs, July 27, 1968; Assistant Secretary of the Interior, letter to the President of Senate, January 16, 1969.

26. U.S. House, subcommittee hearings, March 23–24, 1970, 279–83.

27. Max N. Edwards, letter to Gaylord A. Nelson, October 1, 1963.

28. Harold C. Jordahl, notes from a meeting with Emil Kaminiski, October 11, 1963.

29. Commissioner, Bureau of Indian Affairs, letter to Gaylord A. Nelson, October 2, 1963.

30. Field Solicitor, U.S. Department of the Interior, memorandum to Harold C. Jordahl, November 23, 1964.

31. George Thompson, letter to L. P. Voigt, December 30, 1964.

32. Gaylord A. Nelson, *Legislative Memo* (Washington, DC), November 10, 1965.

33. "Apostle Islands Park," *Milwaukee Journal*, September 15, 1965.

34. Harold C. Jordahl, memorandum to William Bechtel, December 31, 1965.

35. Bronson LaFollette, letter to Harold C. Jordahl, March 28, 1966; Bronson LaFollette, letter to Joseph Preloznik and Phillip S. Habermann, January 3, 1968.

36. E. J. Riley, letter to Harold C. Jordahl, April 6, 1966.

37. George Ackley and Albert Whitebird, letter to Senators Gaylord Nelson and William Proxmire and Congressman Alvin O'Konski, April 12, 1965.

38. Bronson LaFollette and Rodney Edwards, statements recorded in U.S. Senate, *Subcommittee on Parks and Recreation of the Committee on Interior and Insular Affairs*, hearings, 90th Cong., 1st sess., June 1, 1967 (Washington, DC: Government Printing Office, 1970), 77, 101.

39. U.S. Department of the Interior, *Proposed Apostle Islands National Lakeshore*, 106–7.

40. Harold C. Jordahl, notes from a meeting with Emil Kaminiski, October 11, 1963.

41. Commissioner of the Bureau of Indian Affairs, letter to Gaylord A. Nelson, October 2, 1963.

42. Harold C. Jordahl, letter to Emmett Riley, October 13, 1966.

43. Harold C. Jordahl, statement before U.S. House Subcommittee, *Hearings Before the Subcommittee on National Parks and Recreation of the Committee on Interior and Insular Affairs*, 90th Cong., 2nd sess., hearings on H.R. 555, H.R. 9306, and S. 621, Serial Number 99-9, July 29, 1968 (Washington, DC: Government Printing Office, 1970).

44. L. P. Voigt, letter to Gaylord A. Nelson, September 30, 1964; Harold C. Jordahl, memorandum to the Director of the Resources Program staff, August 9, 1964.

45. U.S. House, subcommittee hearings, August 19, 1969, 57.

46. Fred Connors, letter to Martin Hanson, May 9, 1969.

47. S. 778 in U.S. Senate, subcommittee hearings, May 9, June 1–2, 1967, 4.

48. Victoria Gokee, quoted in Sandra Cote, "Apostle Islands Law Arouses Anger, Hope," *Milwaukee Journal*, November 15, 1970.

49. U.S. Department of the Interior, *Proposed Apostle Islands National Lakeshore*, 71–77.

50. Howard Potter, interview by Harold C. Jordahl, April 5, 1989.

51. "Nelson's Bill Triggers Debate: Apostle Islands—Their Beauty Prompts Plan," *Duluth News Tribune*, August 29, 1965.

52. Gaylord A. Nelson, *Legislative Memo* (Washington, DC), November 10, 1965; Bernard M. Granum, telephone call to Harold C. Jordahl, October 1965.

53. Elizabeth Hawkes, letter to William Bechtel, April 17, 1967.

54. U.S. Senate, subcommittee hearings, May 9, June 1–2, 1967, 183, 225, 246, 248, 261, 266.

55. U.S. Senate, *Subcommittee on Parks and Recreation of the Committee on Interior and Insular Affairs*, 91st Cong., 1st sess., hearings, March 17, 1969 (Washington, DC: Government Printing Office, 1970), 46–56, 123–26.

56. Ibid., 46–56, 123–26.

57. U.S. Senate, subcommittee hearings, March 17, 1969, 46–56, 123–26.

58. Ibid.

59. "Bad River Tribe Has Mixed Feelings on Recreation Plan," *Ashland Daily Press*, October 12, 1965; Bad River Tribal Council, *Resolution*, October 7, 1965.

60. "Bad River Tribe Has Mixed Feelings"; E. J. Riley, letter to Harold C. Jordahl, October 18, 1965.

61. Harold C. Jordahl, memorandum to the file, April 6, 1966.

62. E. J. Riley, letter to Harold C. Jordahl, February 17, 1967.

63. U.S. Senate, subcommittee hearings, May 9, June 1–2, 1967, 101–5.

64. Ibid., 107–8.

65. Connors, letter to Martin Hanson, May 9, 1969.

66. Fred Connors, letter to Howard Potter, September 1969.

67. Gilbert A. Larson, letter to Edward A. Hummel, April 11, 1969.

68. "Letters to the Editor," *Chicago Daily News*, March 28, 1968 (emphasis added).

69. "Views Conflict on Isle Project," *Duluth News Tribune*, May 24, 1967.

70. Hawkes, letter to William Bechtel, April 17, 1967.

71. Harold C. Jordahl, memorandum to Fred Madison, July 31, 1967.

72. Albert Whitebird, letter to Gaylord A. Nelson, March 17, 1967.

73. Robert L. Bennett, letter to the Assistant Legislative Counsel, Bureau of Indian Affairs.

74. Harold M. Gross, letter to Gaylord A. Nelson, April 1, 1969.

75. Precedents existed for the amendment that provided for tribal council approval. For example, in the congressional act of 1966 providing for the establishment of the Bighorn Canyon National Recreation Area, a specific provision stated that "No part of the tribal mountain lands or any other lands of the Crow Indian Tribe of Montana shall be included within the recreation area unless requested by the Council of the tribe" (Public Law 89-664, October 15, 1966). Similar procedures were included in the act establishing the Grand Portage National Monument in Minnesota (U.S. Senate, *Apostle Islands National Lakeshore: Report No. 91-276*, U.S. Senate, 91st Cong., 1st sess. [Washington, DC: June 25, 1969], 5–6). Also, the congressional review provision was similar to that provided in the National Wild and Scenic Rivers Act of 1968 (U.S. Senate, June 25, 1969, 6). A year after the passage of the Bighorn Canyon National Recreation Area, Secretary of the Interior Udall signed a fifty-year agreement with the Crow Tribe to include its lands in the recreation area. The agreement had been requested by the tribe. Udall said, "This arrangement will permit a splendid Indian-owned resource to be put to use for the recreational advantage of the public while the Indians themselves derive substantial economic benefits from the influx of tourists." Edison Red Bird, the tribal chair, pointed out, "Under this agreement certain rights or privileges including the sale of fishing or hunting permits, native handicrafts, overnight accommodations and boat, camper and auto supplies will be extended to the tribe." The tribe was to become the principle concessioner for the recreation area. Udall felt that this collaboration with the NPS established a new feature in government–Native American relations that could serve as a model for the United States (U.S. Department of the Interior, news release, December 1, 1967). The

hunting and fishing question on the Bighorn had been resolved with language similar to that which was incorporated into the Apostle Islands National Lakeshore bill: "Nothing in this section shall impair the rights under other law of the Crow Tribe and its members to hunt and fish on lands of the Crow Tribe that are included in the recreation area" (Public Law 89-664, October 15, 1966). By 1970 NPS Director George Hartzog was able to report to the House Subcommittee on National Parks and Recreation that concession agreements had been signed, and one of the NPS's largest concessioners had pledged his skilled hotel and restaurant operations to train members of the Crow Tribe (U.S. House, subcommittee hearings, June 6, 1970, 414).

76. John Belindo, Statement to U.S. House, subcommittee hearings, June 25, 1969, 6.

77. Harold M. Gross, letter to Gaylord A. Nelson, May 29, 1969.

78. E. J. Riley, letter to Howard Potter, June 13, 1969.

79. Harold M. Gross, letter to Gaylord A. Nelson, June 17, 1969 (emphasis added).

80. U.S. House, subcommittee hearings, August 19, 1969, 57–58.

81. Ibid.

82. Ibid., 56–57.

83. Ibid., 49–56.

84. Ibid., 136–38.

85. U.S. House, subcommittee hearings, March 23–24, June 3, 1970, 305–6.

86. Ibid., 303–14.

87. Ibid., 305–6.

88. Ibid., 305–6.

89. Martin Hanson, interview by Harold C. Jordahl, September 4, 1989.

90. J. Louis Hanson, interview by Kathleen Lidfors, historian, National Park Service, Bayfield, WI, March 27, 1985.

91. For specific discussion of the Red Power movement of the 1960s and 1970s, see Sandra L. Cadwallader and Vine Deloria Jr., *The Aggressions of Civilization: Federal Indian Policy since the 1880s* (Philadelphia: Temple University Press, 1984); Rex Weyler, *Blood of the Land: The Government and Corporate War against the American Indian Movement* (New York: Everest House, 1982); and Peter Matthiessen, *In the Spirit of Crazy Horse* (New York: Viking Press, 1991). For texts written from the Native American perspective, including contemporary writings, see Vine Deloria Jr., *Behind the Trail of Broken Treaties: An Indian Declaration of Independence* (New York: Delacorte Press, 1974); Vine Deloria Jr., *Custer Died for Your Sins: An Indian Manifesto* (New York: Macmillan, 1969); Vine Deloria Jr. and Clifford M. Lytle, *American Indians, American Justice* (Austin: University of Texas Press, 1983); and Vine Deloria Jr. and Clifford M. Lytle, *The Nations Within: The Past and Future of American Indian Sovereignty* (New York: Pantheon Books, 1976). For the U.S. government's reaction to the Red Power movement, see U.S.

Senate Committee on the Judiciary, *Revolutionary Activities within the DC—The American Indian Movement, Hearing Before the Subcommittee to Investigate the Administration of the Internal Security Act and Other Internal Security Laws*, 94th Cong., 2nd sess., April 6, 1976.

92. Alvin M. Josephy Jr., *Red Power: The American Indian's Fight for Freedom* (New York: McGraw-Hill, 1971), 43.

93. The term *American Indian* or *Native American* is roughly as accurate as the term *European*. All cover somewhat arbitrarily joined-together sets of cultures and political activities that indeed are deeply different. Treating all tribes as the same is roughly like treating France and Germany as indistinguishable from each other. Approximately four hundred cultural-linguistic groups are thought to have inhabited the North American continent prior to the European invasion. Tribes formed alliances, but they were equally as likely to war against each other and indeed often formed alliances with Europeans against other tribes. These cultural differences and lack of "Indian" allegiances persist in the present.

94. Jennings C. Wise, *The Red Man in the New World Drama: A Political-Legal Study with a Pageantry of American Indian History* (New York: Macmillan, 1971), 372–77.

95. Deloria and Lytle, *American Indians, American Justice*, 235.

96. Josephy, *Red Power*, 198.

97. Ibid., 226–29.

98. Gaylord A. Nelson, interview by Kathleen Lidfors, historian, National Park Service, Bayfield, WI, March 4, 1985.

99. Shirley J. Hatchett, "Indian Uprising," *Milwaukee Journal*, May 28, 1970.

100. "New Apostles Plan Frees Indian Land," *Milwaukee Sentinel*, April 24, 1970; Lee McElvain, confidential memorandum to members of the House Subcommittee on National Parks and Recreation, May 1, 1970.

101. Stuart Applebaum, telephone call to Harold C. Jordahl, May 28, 1970.

102. U.S. House, subcommittee hearings, June 3, 1970, 421–22, 425, 429, 431.

103. Ibid.

104. Nez Perce Tribal Chair, telegram to James A. Haley, House Committee on Interior and Insular Affairs, June 2, 1970.

105. U.S. Department of the Interior, news release, May 19, 1970.

106. Mutual Radio Network News, broadcast date July 3, 1970.

107. Harold C. Jordahl, telephone call to the Bureau of Indian Affairs, Ashland Office, July 1970; Richard Bradee, "Leases Offered on Apostles Site," *Milwaukee Sentinel*, August 4, 1970; "New Controversy over Apostles," *Ironwood (MI) Daily Globe*, August 4, 1970.

108. Bradee, "Leases Offered on Apostles Site"; "New Controversy over Apostles."

109. *Congressional Record*, September 9, 1970, H8557–8568.

110. Ibid.

111. Ibid.

Chapter 13. Reflections

1. Margaret A. Littlejohn and Steven J. Hollenhorst, *Apostle Islands National Lakeshore Visitor Study*, Social Science Program, National Park Service, Visitor Services Project, Report 157 (April 2005).

2. I. V. Fine, "Apostle Islands: Some of the Economic Implications of the Proposed Apostle Islands National Lakeshore," *Wisconsin Vacation-Recreation Papers* III, no. 1 (Madison: University of Wisconsin, School of Commerce, May 1965).

3. Daniel J. Stynes, *Impacts of Visitor Spending on the Local Economy: Apostle Islands National Lakeshore 2004* (Washington, DC: Social Science Program, National Park Service, 2006), i.

4. Ibid., ii.

5. Fine, "Apostle Islands."

6. U.S. Public Law 91-424, cited in National Park Service, *Statement for Management, Apostle Islands National Lakeshore* (Bayfield, WI: 1977).

7. Warren Bielenberg, *Annual Report, Apostle Islands National Lakeshore* (Bayfield, WI: National Park Service, 1972).

8. Linda Witkowski, interview by Annie L. Booth, August 19, 1991; Robert Krumenaker, interview by Annie L. Booth, August 28, 2008.

9. Robert Krumenaker, briefing note, "Facilities Management Needs Have Increased Significantly," Apostle Islands National Lakeshore, August 1, 2008; Apostle Islands National Lakeshore, *Newsletter* 2 (July 2006).

10. Krumenaker, interview by Booth.

11. William Bromberg, memorandum to the Director of the Northwest Region, National Park Service, August 15, 1972.

12. Lonni Pelto, chief, business services, Apostle Islands National Lakeshore, email to Robert Krumenaker, superintendent, Apostle Islands National Lakeshore, August 27, 2008.

13. Thomas A. Heberlein, Trudy McKinnel, and Laurie Ervin, "Recreational Boating across Time and Place" (presented at the Apostle Islands Boating Research Report to the Public, Ashland, WI: November 8, 1986).

14. Patrick Miller, letter to Harold C. Jordahl, July 7, 1985.

15. Tom Bredow and Jeff Hepner, Apostle Islands National Lakeshore park rangers, interview by Annie L. Booth, August 19, 1991.

16. Krumenaker, interview by Booth.

17. "Apostle Islands: Gaylord Nelson Wilderness," http://www.nps.gov/apis/parkmgmt/wilderness.htm (accessed August 3, 2008).

18. Krumenaker, interview by Booth.

19. Alford J. Banta, interview by Annie L. Booth, August 17, 1991; Krumenaker, interview by Booth.

20. James W. Feldman, "Rewilding the Islands: Nature, History and Policy at the Apostle Islands National Lakeshore" (PhD diss., University of Wisconsin–Madison, 2004).

21. Krumenaker, interview by Booth.

22. William Cronon, "The Riddle of the Apostle Islands," *Orion*, May/June 2003.

23. Jay Austin, "Rapid Warming of Lake Superior," February 2007, http://www .d.umn.edu/~jaustin/ICE.html (accessed January 8, 2009).

24. B. M. Lofgren, F. H. Quinn, A. H. Cliles, R. A. Assel, A. J. Eberhardt, and C. L. Luukkonen, "Evaluation of Potential Impacts of Great Lakes Water Resources Based on Climate Scenarios of Global Circulation Models," *Journal of Great Lakes Research* 28, no. 4 (2002): 537–54.

25. "Red Cliff Band of Lake Superior Chippewa Indians," http://witribes.wi .gov/docview.asp?docid=9253&locid=57 (accessed August 3, 2008).

26. William Bromberg, telephone call to Harold C. Jordahl, July 1971.

27. Krumenaker, interview by Booth.

28. Richard Gurnoe, interview by Annie L. Booth, August 20, 1991.

29. "Red Cliff Band of Lake Superior Chippewa Indians."

30. Robert Krumenaker, briefing note, "Native American Treaty-related Rights," Apostle Islands National Lakeshore, August 1, 2008; Krumenaker, interview by Booth.

31. Gaylord A. Nelson, interview by Kathleen Lidfors, historian, National Park Service, Bayfield, WI, March 4, 1985.

32. Fred T. Witzig, *Voyageurs National Park: The Battle to Create Minnesota's National Park* (Minneapolis: University of Minnesota Press, 2004), vii.

33. Krumenaker, interview by Booth.

Index